Changes and Innovations in the Education Institutions

China's Path to Education Modernization

Zhenguo Yuan
General Editor

Vol. 2

Changes and Innovations in the Education Institutions

From Regulation to Empowerment

Edited by
Guorui Fan

PETER LANG
Lausanne • Berlin • Bruxelles • Chennai • New York • Oxford

Library of Congress Cataloging-in-Publication Data

Names: Fan, Guorui, editor.
Title: Changes and innovations in the education institutions: from regulation to empowerment / Edited by Guorui Fan.
Description: New York: Peter Lang, 2023.
Series: China's path to education modernization; Vol. 2
Includes bibliographical references.
Identifiers: LCCN 2021061329 (print) | LCCN 2021061330 (ebook)
ISBN 978-1-4331-6908-3 (hardback)
ISBN 978-1-4331-9448-1 (ebook pdf) | ISBN 978-1-4331-9449-8 (epub)
Subjects: LCSH: Educational change—China. | Educational innovations—China. | Education and state—China.
Classification: LCC LA1131.82 .C43 2023 (print) | LCC LA1131.82 (ebook) |
DDC 379.51—dc23/eng/20211006
LC record available at https://lccn.loc.gov/2021061329
LC ebook record available at https://lccn.loc.gov/2021061330
DOI 10.3726/b19271

Bibliographic information published by the **Deutsche Nationalbibliothek.**
The German National Library lists this publication in the German National Bibliography; detailed bibliographic data is available on the Internet at http://dnb.d-nb.de.

Cover design by Peter Lang Group AG

ISBN 978-1-4331-6908-3 (hardback)
ISBN 978-1-4331-9448-1 (ebook)
ISBN 978-1-4331-9449-8 (epub)
DOI 10.3726/ b19271

Original title: 从规制到赋能:教育制度变迁创新之路
Guoroi Fan.

Published by Peter Lang Publishing Inc., New York, USA
info@peterlang.com - www.peterlang.com

Table of Contents

List of Figures

List of Tables

General Preface to "China's Path to Education Modernization" Book Series

DEEPENING REFORM IN AN ALL-ROUND WAY AND ACCELERATING THE REALIZATION OF EDUCATION MODERNIZATION

In December 1978, the Third Plenary Session of the Eleventh Central Committee of the Communist Party of China established the ideological line of emancipating minds and seeking truth from facts, and made major decisions with regard to Reform and Opening Up. Since Reform and Opening Up began, China's economy has had 40 years of continuous growth. Per capita GDP has jumped from 171st in the world to 70th[1], total GDP has jumped from 9th to 2nd[2], and China's contribution rate to the global economy has increased from 3.05% in 1978 to 31.53% in 2016[3]. This is a miracle in Chinese history and a miracle in world history.

China's education has been an important component of this miracle and an important driving force for creating it. The gross enrollment rate for preschool education in China increased from 12.62% in 1981 to 77.4% in 2016, surpassing the average level of middle- and high-income countries by 5 percentage points; the consolidation rate of nine-year compulsory education reached 93.4% in 2016, surpassing the average level of high-income countries; and the gross enrollment rate for high-school education increased from 39.56% in 1981 to 87.5% in

2016, which is 5 percentage points higher than the average of middle-and-high-income countries. The gross enrollment rate for higher education increased from 1.6% in 1981 to 42.7% in 2016, surpassing the average level of middle-and-high-income countries by 6 percentage points. At the same time, China has performed outstandingly well in terms of PISA scores and the development of universities, showing a significant increase in the quality of education.

The development of education has brought about major changes in China's human resources structure. The average number of years of education received by those aged 16–59 rose from less than 5 years in 1981 to 10.35 years in 2016, and the proportion of people with a college education or above rose from 0.58% in 1982 to 12.44% in 2015.[4] The expected years of schooling in China in 1990 was 8.8 years, ranking 119th in the world; in 2015, expected years of schooling increased to 13.5 years, and China's world ranking rose to 83rd.[5] China has transformed from a populous country into a human resources country and is increasingly moving towards becoming a human resources power.

Revealing the successful experiences and reasons for China's Reform and Opening Up is becoming an increasingly strong interest in the academic world, and also the responsibility of Chinese scholars. The famous American Sinologist John King Fairbank (1907–1991) published the book *The United States and China* 70 years ago. This was the first time a Western scholar had created a monograph with a comparison between China and the United States. In this work, Fairbank said that China was undergoing a modernization movement. The most fundamental feature of this movement was China's decision to abandon all the traditions and institutions of its own country, and then to use all Western civilization and institutions, including language, as a counterpart. Therefore, China's modernization was a process in which the West continued to impact China and China continued to respond. For a long time, this "impact-response model" was a consensus among Western scholars on the nature of China's upcoming modernization path (Fairbank, 2000: 132–134, 451). However, in the book *China: A New History* published two days before his death, Fairbank (2001: 492–493) wrote: "After 50 years of experience and observation, I have found that China's modernization is probably not a result of the impact-response model, but a result of its own internal genetic changes and internal development impulses."

Ronald H. Coase (1910–2013), a Nobel Prize Winner in Economics, published a book called *How China Became Capitalist* when he was 102 years old with his assistant Ning Wang. In this book, he wrote: "China is very successful, and her development will continue. However, China's economic development cannot be explained using traditional Western economics. China's successful reform is an unexpected result of human behavior" (Ronald & Wang: 1, 206–210).

This world is a pluralistic one. There is not only one path to modernization, and most certainly, there is not only one standard path. The successful practice of China and its education modernization proves that there are multiple channels and forms for realizing modernization, and fully demonstrates the global significance of China's modernization success.

Education Modernization Is a Consistent Theme in China's Reform and Opening Up of Education

Practice has shown that the history of reform and development in Chinese education since Reform and Opening Up began is a history of exploration and struggle for the modernization of education, and it is a history of leaping forward in the modernization of socialist education with Chinese characteristics.

In 1983, Xiaoping Deng wrote an inscription for Beijing Jingshan School, "Education should be oriented towards modernization, facing the world, and facing the future." This reflected the Chinese people's yearning and determination for the development of education in a focused way and established the ideological foundation and strategic direction for the reform and development of China's education.

In 1985, *The Decision of the Central Committee of the Communist Party of China on the Reform of the Education institution* clarified the grand mission of the modernization of socialist education: "Not only must we make full use of and make efforts to improve existing talents, but we must also greatly enhance the Party's understanding of education work. Facing modernization, facing the world, and facing the future, for the development of China's economy and society in the 1990s and the beginning of the next century, we will prepare new and qualified talents at all levels that can adhere to the socialist direction on a large scale."

In 1993, the Central Committee of the Communist Party of China and the State Council issued *The Outline of China's Education Reform and Development*, which further clarified the goal of China's education reform and development: "After several decades of efforts, establish a relatively mature and perfected socialist education institution and realize the modernization of education."

In July 2010, *The National Medium-and-Long-Term Education Reform and Development Plan Outline (2010–2020)* clearly stated: "By 2020, education modernization will have been basically realized, a learning-based society will have been basically formed and China will have entered the ranks of powerful countries when it comes to human resources." This outline required the preparation of human resources in advance to realize the country's basic modernization.

In 2017, at the 19th Congress of the Chinese Communist Party, it was once again stressed: "Becoming a strong country in terms of education is a basic project of the great rejuvenation of the Chinese nation. Education must be prioritized, the modernization of education must be accelerated, and education must be carried out in a way that satisfies the people." The report further emphasized the sense of urgency needed to achieve education modernization.

In summary, education modernization has always been a consistent theme and distinctive banner in China's reform and development of education. It has become the ideal pursuit and the spiritual motivation for concentrating the powers of all aspects of the country on education development. It not only provides talent security and intellectual support for the modernization of industry, agriculture, national defense and science and technology, it also is of decisive significance for building a prosperous, strong, democratic, civilized, harmonious, and beautiful modern socialist country.

The Deepening of Reform and Opening Up Is a Powerful Driving Force in Education Modernization

The modernization of Chinese education has always been accompanied by Reform and Opening Up. Education modernization has established an overall direction for the reform and development of education. Reform and Opening Up has not only provided a powerful impetus for the realization of education modernization but also pointed out the basic path for the rapid advancement of China's education modernization.

In 1977, the college entrance examination (gaokao) institution was reinstated and students were sent abroad to study, announcing the arrival of China's Reform and Opening Up. Since then, education reform has gradually developed and constantly deepened in the context of Reform and Opening Up across the whole country. After the period 1977–1985 of bringing about order from chaos, the general launching of Reform and Opening Up from 1985 to 1993, the comprehensive deepening of Reform and Opening Up from 1993 to 2010, and the deepening of comprehensive education reform since 2010, a completely new situation in the modernization of socialist education with Chinese characteristics has been created.

1977 to 1985: Liberating thought and bringing about order from chaos. From the late 1950s onwards, since the focus of the work of the whole party was never transferred to economic construction, and because of the influence of "leftist" thinking with "class struggle as the key link," not only had education not been given the important status it deserved for a long time, it was also frequently attacked in previous political movements. "The Cultural Revolution" even went to the extreme of using this mistaken "leftist" thinking to reject knowledge and abolish education. As a result, the cause of education was seriously damaged, and a vast number of educators were severely devastated, not only delaying the growth of a whole generation of young people but also rewidening the gap between China's education industry and those of developed countries throughout the world, which had been narrowing in many respects. After the Third Plenary Session of the Eleventh Central Committee of the Communist Party of China, following the guiding ideology of restoring order, the Party Central Committee made a series of new judgments and decisions on education, and China's education cause was restored and reemerged on the road of vigorous development.

1985–1993: Education reform is fully initiated. Three feet of ice and snow are not formed overnight. In the early days of Reform and Opening Up, the mistaken idea of holding education, knowledge, and talented people in contempt was still widespread; the influence of the "Left" of the education front had not been completely overcome; and the situation of education work not meeting the needs of socialist modernization had not yet been fundamentally reversed in the short term. Faced with China's opening up to the outside world, invigoration of internal affairs, the full-scale development of economic institution reform, and the emergence of a new global technological revolution, the backwardness of China's education industry and the drawbacks of the education institution were even more prominent. In particular, in the division of administrative authority for education, the relevant government departments overregulated and overcontrolled schools, especially colleges and universities, resulting in a lack of vitality in schools at all levels; and the situations that the government should have been managing more closely were not managed properly. In terms of education structure, basic education was weak, the number of schools was insufficient, quality was not high, and there was a serious lack of qualified teachers and necessary equipment; vocational and technical education, which was urgently needed for economic construction, was not properly developed; the proportion of the curriculum, professional structure, and school-running levels was out of balance within higher education. At the same time, schools of all levels and types had outdated curriculums, uninspired teaching methods, monotonous teaching methods, and serious neglect of practical stages, each separating from the needs of economic and social development to different extents and falling behind in the development of contemporary scientific culture. To this end, *The Decision of the Central Committee of the Communist Party of China on the Reform of the Education institution* clearly stated: "To fundamentally change this situation, we must start with the education institution and systematically carry out reforms." The decision also established the fundamental guiding principle of "education serves the building of socialism and the building of socialism depends on education," which was the need to start with the reform of the education institution, and, correspondingly, reform the labor and personnel institution by means of streamlining administration and decentralization and expanding schools' autonomy in running themselves, allowing a significant increase in awareness and abilities needed for education institutions of all kinds at all levels to actively adapt to the needs of economic and social development.

1993 to 2010: Education Reform Is Comprehensively Deepened. During this period, after the return to order and the gradual development of various educational reforms, nine-year compulsory education began to be implemented in a planned and phased manner; vocational and technical education was developed to a considerable extent; higher education developed rapidly, a system with various levels, various forms, and subjects was basically completed; adult education and ethnic education of various forms was greatly developed; and the institution of rural basic education enacting local responsibility and hierarchical management achieved remarkable results. However, China's education was still relatively backward in general, and still was not suited to the needs of accelerating Reform and Opening Up and modernization. The strategic position of education had not yet been fully implemented in practice; education investment was insufficient, teachers were underpaid, and school conditions were poor; educational ideology, teaching content, and teaching methods were different from reality to different extents; there were obvious weak links in school ideological and political work; and the education management institution and operational mechanisms appeared to be relatively rigid. To this end, the 14th National Congress of the Communist Party of China clearly stated that "education must be placed in a strategic position of priority development and we must strive to raise the ideological, moral, and scientific and cultural level of the entire nation. This is the fundamental plan for realizing China's modernization." In order to implement this major strategy, the Central Committee of the Communist Party of China and the State Council issued *The Outline of China's Education Reform and Development*, which proposed "national fiscal education expenditures" (including: financial allocations for education at all levels, urban and rural education surcharges, funds for corporations to run primary and secondary schools, and tax reductions and exemptions for school-run industries) for the first time, accounting for 4% of the gross national product at the end of the century. At the same time, it was decided that a comprehensive and step-by-step approach should be adopted for the reform of the education institution; the pace should be accelerated; the overly managed and overly controlled institution should be reformed; and a new education institution compatible with the reform of the socialist market economic institution, political institution, and scientific and technological institution should be initially established. The issuance of this programmatic document promoted China's education to a new level of internationalized, long-lasting, and diversified schooling.

Since 2010: Education Enters a New Phase of Comprehensive Reform. After more than 30 years of hard work, the Chinese education institution is gradually improving and the level of schooling is continuously improving. In the first decade of the 21st century, urban and rural free compulsory education was fully realized, vocational education developed rapidly, higher education entered the stage of popularization, and education fairness took a major step forward. However, in the face of the deepening of economic globalization, the rapid advancement of science and technology, the increasingly fierce competition for talents, and the new demands on education in the face of economic upgrading and social transformation, China's education still faces a series of major challenges. There are many deep contradictions. These are mainly manifested in the following ways: Concepts of education are relatively backward, content methods are relatively old, primary and secondary school students are overburdened with school work, and quality of education is difficult to advance; students are not adaptable to society and employment, and innovative, practical, and compound talents are extremely scarce; the education institution mechanism is imperfect, teaching in schools is uninspired, the education structure and layout are not reasonable, education development in urban and rural areas and regions is not balanced, and the education development in poverty-stricken areas and ethnic areas is relatively lagging; and there is a lack of investment in education and the strategic status of education as a priority for development has not yet been fully implemented. To this end, it is necessary to deepen the comprehensive reform of education, especially the reform of key areas and key stages, with the fundamental mission of developing the moral character of young people, with reform and innovation as a powerful driving force, and promoting fairness and quality as a strategic focus to promote reform of the examination enrollment institution and deepening the separation of management and evaluation as an important starting point, and making efforts to cultivate innovative, compound, practical, and international talents. In this regard, *The National Medium-and-Long-Term Education Reform and Development Plan Outline (2010–2020)* promulgated by the Central Committee of the Communist Party of China and the State Council in 2010 made a comprehensive deployment, from which a new journey of transitioning from a big education country to a strong education country and realizing profound development began.

The New Era Has Opened Up Even Broader Prospects for Education Modernization

In 2017, the 19th National Congress of the Communist Party of China was successfully held, heralding a new era of socialism with Chinese characteristics. The General Assembly made the historical judgment that the main contradiction in Chinese society had been transformed into a contradiction between the growing needs of the people for leading good lives and unbalanced and insufficient development. A two-stage goal was proposed: From 2020 to 2035, on the basis of building a well-off society in an all-round way, the state was to fight for another

15 years to basically realize socialist modernization. From 2035 to the middle of this century, on the basis of basically realizing modernization, the state will fight for another 15 years to build China into a prosperous, strong, democratic, civilized, harmonious, and beautiful modernized socialist power.

The future development of China and the great rejuvenation of the Chinese nation depend on talents, with a strong foundation in education. A strong country must first have a strong education institution. The report of the 19th National Congress of the Communist Party of China clearly stated that building a country with a strong education institution is a basic project for the great rejuvenation of the Chinese nation. It emphasizes that education should be given priority in development, education modernization should be accelerated, and an education institution that the people are satisfied with should be properly run. This has established a new orientation for China's education reform and development in the new era, where new goals have been put forward, and new paths pointed out. For 2035 and even 2050, education must adhere to comprehensive and deep reforms, resolutely breaking all ill-conceived ideological concepts and institutional mechanisms unfit for the times, breaking through the barrier of solidification of interests, absorbing the beneficial results of human civilization, respecting the laws of education and the laws of talent growth, making greater efforts in the optimization of the structure and layout of education, taking greater steps in education fairness and quality improvement, taking more effective measures in stimulating educational vitality, systematically innovating talent training models, comprehensively improving the ability to supply individualized, diversified, and high-quality education services, adhering to the path of socialist education with Chinese characteristics, and continuously promoting the modernization of the education governance system and governance capacity.

Summarizing Experiences, Facing the Future, and Heading Out into the World

The tremendous changes in China's education in the past 40 years of Reform and Opening Up have improved the character of everyone in the country, enhanced overall national strength, and benefited hundreds of millions of people. Reviewing the historical process of China's educational reform and opening up, analyzing the solutions to various complex problems in various important historical stages, summarizing the successful experiences of the advancement of education, and deeply understanding regular characteristics after phenomena have occurred: these have had an irreplaceably important significance in enriching and developing the theoretical system of socialist education with Chinese characteristics and determining the confidence in strengthening the road to socialist education with Chinese characteristics. To this end, we have organized the compiling of this series "China's Path to Education Modernization – Commemorating 40 Years of Reform and Opening Up in Education," and listed it as a key topic in the Shanghai Academy of Social Sciences' "40 Years of Reform and Opening Up" research series. This series is guided by the value of modernization of socialist education with Chinese characteristics, based on the progression of history and major events, and is divided into 10 volumes. Systematic attempts have been made to summarize the experiences and achievements of education theory innovation, institutional innovation, policy innovation, and leap-frog education development at all levels and of all kinds, and due efforts have been made to build a theoretical education system and discourse system with Chinese characteristics.

The mission of theoretical research is not only to understand the world but also to transform the world. The ultimate goal of understanding the rules is leading practice. China's education has completed the transition from a weak education country to a big education country. Answering the question of how to move from a big education country to a strong education country is a much more arduous task and a greater cause. Facing a future that is more orientated towards information, the internet and data and facing a future filled with uncertainty, we must deepen our understanding of the laws of education, and strengthen our understanding of the laws of talent growth and the creation of talents so that we can continue to advance and accelerate the pace of education modernization. A fairer, higher quality, and more dynamic education institution will continue to advance along the correct path of socialism with Chinese characteristics.

The achievements of China's education have not only benefitted the Chinese people but also made their own contributions to educational innovation around the world. There is no path or model for achieving education modernization by copying others. In the past 40 years of China's reform and opening up of education, we have actively studied and learned from the world's advanced concepts and successful experiences, adhered to respecting the laws of education, and insisted on getting a foothold in China's territory to run education, successfully opening up a path towards education modernization with leap-frog development in a country with a large population, uneven development, and low overall development level. Summarizing these 40 years of reform and opening up of education, we can provide the Chinese experience and Chinese wisdom for the realization of education modernization around the world. We can also make efforts towards accelerating the modernization of China's education, gradually bringing it closer to the center of the world stage and continuing to make even greater contributions to humanity.

Series editor-in-chief Zhenguo Yuan
May 2018

NOTES

1 Source: United Nations Statistics Office (https://unstats.un.org) The statistical caliber is per capita GDP (current US$), of which 187 countries were counted in 1978 and 212 were counted in 2016. The data in this article for China does not include data for the Hong Kong Special Administrative Region of China, the Macao Special Administrative Region of China and the Taiwan region of China, unless otherwise stated.
2 Source: United Nations Statistics Office (https://unstats.un.org). The statistical caliber is GDP (current US$), of which 187 countries were counted in 1978 and 212 were counted in 2016.
3 Source: World Bank database (https://data.worldbank.org.cn/indicator). The statistical caliber is GDP (dollar constant price in 2010), calculated according to the formula "China's contribution rate to world economic growth = China's GDP growth / world GDP growth increment × 100%".
4 Source: Report from the National Bureau of Statistics of the People's Republic of China on the main figures of the 1982 census (http://www.stats.gov.cn/tjsj/tjgb/rkpcgb/qgrkpcgb/200204/t20020404_30318.html), main data report of the 2015 National 1% Population Sample Survey (http://www.stats.gov.cn/tjsj/zxfb/201604/t20160420_1346151.html).
5 Source: United Nations Development Programme Regarding Expected Years of Schooling (Years) http://hdr.undp.org/en/data#. There were statistics for 172 countries in 1990 and for 191 countries in 2015.

REFERENCES

Fairbank, J. K. (2000). *The United States and China* (4th ed.). Beijing: World Affairs Press.

Fairbank, J. K. (2001). *John King Fairbank on China: A new history* (Y. Xue, Trans.). Taiwan, China: Zhengzhong Book Company (in Chinese).

Ronald, H. C., & Wang, N. (2013). *How China became capitalist* (Y. Xu & L. Zhemin, Trans.). Beijing: CITIC Press Group (in Chinese).

Introduction: Education Institutions and Education Reforms

GUORUI FAN

I. INSTITUTIONS, EDUCATION INSTITUTIONS, AND EDUCATION INSTITUTION RESEARCH

The term "institutions" is an important concept in sociology, political science, economics, and educational research. Harvard University philosophy professor John Bordley Rawls (1921–2002) stated in his classic book *A Theory of Justice* (1971): "I would like to take an institution as a public regulated system, which determines positions and statuses and the rights, obligations, powers, and exemptions of both. These regulations specify certain types of conduct as permitted, others as prohibited, and when violations occur, certain punishments and retaliatory measures are given" (1971: 47). Economist Douglass C. North (1920–2015) believed that "institutions are a set of rules of ethical norms, law-abiding procedures, and behaviors that are designed to constrain individual behavior that seeks to maximize the benefits or utility of a subject" (1981: 201–202). Theodore W. Schultz defines institutions as rules of conduct involving social, political, and economic behavior (Schultz, 1968). In fact, institutions include rules of conduct, but also refer to a variety of economic, social, political, and other organizations or institutions formed by people.

In a nutshell, an institution refers to the regulations or norms that members are required to abide by, and in a broader sense, a societal structure that regulates individual actions and regulates social relations between people in a rule or mode of operation that implies certain social values. This includes a specific social scope; a series of habits; ethics; laws (including constitutions, laws, regulations); precepts; regulations (including regulations formulated by the government) within a specific stage of development, etc.; informal restraints involving social recognition; and formal constraints and their implementation mechanisms regulated by the state that shape the order and ecology of a society.

The establishment and improvement of an institution is always connected to factors such as the polity and the culture of the country and the region. As Rawls stated, "An institution exists at a certain time and place when the actions specified by it are regularly carried out in accordance with a public understanding that the system of rules defining the institution is to be followed" (1999: 48). With the construction and development of modern countries and the establishment and improvement of modern public education systems, the role of education in national development is becoming increasingly crucial. Different countries and regions have formed different education institutions due to their differences in polity and culture. The reform and development of education in various countries is increasingly dependent on social changes promoted by the state. In the process of promoting education reforms, the state constructs education institutions with a variety of educational policies and laws, and thereby shapes the educational ecology.

In the development process of educational research, the research on "institutions" and their changes has been drawing rising attention and focus. A couple of scholars are exploring the diversity of educational institutions from the perspective of international comparative education. As early as the first decade of the 1900s, Sir Michael Ernest Sadler (1861–1943), a pioneer in comparative education research and a supporter of the British public school system, proposed to study foreign education systems with the correct spirit and a rigorous academic attitude (1900; Bereday, 1964). Issac Leon Kandel's (1881–1965) monograph *Studies in Comparative Education* was a systematic evaluation of national education systems in six countries (Kandel, 1933). In 1956, John Francis Cramer and George Stephenson Browne published the book *Contemporary Education: A Comparative Study of National Systems* (1956). In the 1960s, Arthur Henry Moehlman examined the educational systems of four different cultural regions in Europe, Asia, Africa, and the Americas (Moehlman, 1963). At the same time, in France, Fernand Oury (1920–1997) and others created institutional pedagogy, which was aimed at exploring the dialectical relationship between educational institutions, educational processes, and educational behavior (Oury and Vasquez, 1968). Since the 1980s, research on educational institutions has become increasingly rich, such as Edward Ignas and Raymond J. Crosini's *Comparative Educational Systems* (1981); Brian Holmes and John Cameron et al.'s three volume

International Handbook of Educational Systems (Holmes, 1983; Cameron, 1983; Cameron and Hurst, 1983; Cowen and McLean, 1984); *The Encyclopedia of Comparative Education and National Systems of Education* edited by Neville T. Postlethwaite (1988); H.J. Steyn and C.C. Wolhuter's *Education Systems of Emerging Countries, Challenges of The 21st Century* (2000); and Rebecca Marlow-Ferguson et al.'s comprehensive and systematic survey of educational institutions worldwide (Marlow-Ferguson, 2002).

China is an ancient country with a traditional culture that stretches back thousands of years (Shaughnessy, 2005). It has always adhered to the tradition of respecting teachers and revering education (Lee, 2000). Since the implementation of the reform and opening-up policy in 1978, China has begun to explore the gradual development of the market economy and the economy has developed rapidly. At the same time, it has been constantly exploring the establishment of an education institution that is compatible with the market economy (Guo and Guo, 2016).

After forty years of reform, opening up, and modernization, Chinese society has entered a new stage in the development of socialism with Chinese characteristics in the new era (Xi, 2017).

Since the introduction of the reform and opening-up policy, with the deepening of education reform and development, China's education development has achieved great progress. The achievement of these developments and progress can largely be attributed to the country's top-down promotion. As an important medium for fulfilling the strategic visions of the national education reforms, education institutions and policies are the institutional arrangements and textual presentations of educational decision-making on particular educational issues and hence play vital roles in the process of education reform and development. At this special moment of the 40th anniversary of the beginning of China's reform and opening-up policy, the Faculty of Education of East China Normal University planned the book series "China's Path to Education Modernization," the series to which this book belongs. Shouldering the mission of forming the thought and institutional system on socialism with Chinese characteristics for a new era, we investigate, with the assistance of literature, China's education reforms and development in the grand setting of China's social, political, and economic changes over the past forty years, examine the major landmark education policies and events in China's education reforms, review, summarize, and reflect on the changes of China's education institutions and comprehensively analyze the successes and failures of China's education institutions construction with a view to improving the socialist education institutions system with Chinese characteristics, and providing lessons and intellectual wisdom we can draw on from history to guarantee and promote the new development of China's education in the future.

II. THE METHODOLOGY OF EDUCATION INSTITUTIONS RESEARCH

Factors affecting the changes and innovations of the education institutions include not only sociopolitical and economic factors outside the education system but also factors such as the contradictions and tasks of the internal development of the education system, as well as the logical factors of the education institutions system itself. Therefore, a study of the course of the changes of China's education institutions over a forty-year period is a complex project. During the course of the study, we adhered to the following methods, with an aim to simplifying the complexity and making a clear and detailed analysis:

(1) **The Uniformity of History and Logic.** The changes and shaping of the education institutions are the result of historical development. Engels (1859: 43) stated: "The process of thought should begin from wherever history begins, and the further development of the process of thought is merely a reflection of the historical process in an abstract, theoretically consistent form." The process of change in the education institution over the past forty years of Reform and Opening Up has been advancing but has been full of twists and turns. Inquiry into the logic of the reforms in the education institutions are naturally in accordance with the historical processes of education reform. Thus, the major events and the logic of education reform and institution building need to be put into the historical process of Reform and Opening Up for extra investigation so that the historical truth of education reform can be restored.

(2) **Education Institutions Analysis in the Context of Social Institutions Analysis.** Changes in the education institution are the results of educational policies and educational reforms, and are closely linked to changes in society, politics, and economics, all of which affect each other. An education institution is in reality a national education institution managed by the government. It "aims for formal education, implements overall control and supervision, is at least partly under the responsibility of the government and is the sum of varied education institutions nationwide with interrelated components and processes" (Archer, 1979: 54). The development and changes of the socialist education institutions with Chinese characteristics are particularly closely connected to party and politics and state system reform, and are affected by a national development strategy centered around economic construction. Therefore, an examination of the changes in the education institutions calls for a systematic study that puts the education institutions and education reforms into a dynamically

developing social system, in the structural transformation and development of education, social politics, and economic factors, and in the context of the speeches of party and state leaders, relevant policy documents of the Central Committee of the Communist Party of China and the State Council, relevant national laws and regulations, education laws, regulations, rules, and policy texts of the Ministry of Education, local governments, and educational administration departments.

(3) **Changes in the Education Institutions in the Context of the Development of Education.** The establishment and improvement of the education institutions aim to straighten out the relationship between diverse educational elements. The fundamental purpose is to promote the healthy development of education. During the process of education development, the main contradictions in the development of education at different historical stages and the differences in main tasks require protection from different education institutions. Therefore, in the process of straightening out the changes in the education institutions, it is necessary to undertake the study in the context of education development.

(4) **The Analysis of Major Education Reform Events in the Context of Institutions System Construction and …** The education institutions is a complex system consisting of a series of institutional elements, including the school running institution, the education system, the school leadership and management institutions, the education personnel institutions, the education finance institutions, and the examination and enrollment institutions. At different stages of education development, differences between the main contradictions and main tasks in the development of education have led to different iconic education reform events in different historical periods. These major educational reform events are highly relevant to a certain education institutional element and to the improvement of the entire educational system. Therefore, in the course of the research, it is necessary to connect all the dots and conduct an even more thorough study by putting major educational reform events in the context of the systematic construction of the entire education institutions system.

(5) **Coherence of the Top-Level Design and Practice Process of the Education Institutions.** Faced with the prominent contradictions and tasks in the development of education, the state and local governments, as well as education administration departments, seek institutionalized measures to solve problems in education through a series of decision-making behaviors. In the course of practice, due to the development and changes of society and education itself, it is necessary to adapt this institutionalized top-level design to the actual situation so as to innovate and improve the institutions design. Therefore, during the research process, it is necessary

to systematically examine the top-level design of the education institutions and practices such as the implementation, revision, adjustment, and improvement of educational reforms.

III. THE STRUCTURE OF THIS BOOK

Based on the historical facts of China's educational institutions changes during the forty years of reform and opening-up, this book employs the dynamic changes of education laws, policies, and institutions as clues, the facts and experiences of international education reform and development as references, with historical retrospect and institutional review and evaluation as the focus, and the analysis of the key elements of the education system as the path, comprehensively and systematically analyzing the evolution of the education institutions. This book focuses on the macro-education institution level which includes changes in the relations between the government, schools and society, school leadership and management, curriculum and teaching materials, teacher training, management and development, education evaluation, examination and enrollment, education supervision, education financing, international education exchanges and cooperation, and other education institutions issues, thereby describing the development process of constructing a positive educational ecology and releasing educational vitality through education institutions innovation, and deeply exploring the institutional innovation factors reflected in significant, transformative education reform events. By presenting and analyzing these institutional factors and the laws, policies, systems, mechanisms, and cultural factors behind them, this book profoundly reveals the inherent contradictions of the changes in the educational institutions, conducts a thorough analysis of the internal mechanism of the changes in the educational institutions, and looks forward to the future trends of modernization in China's educational governance system and governance capacity.

REFERENCES

Archer, M. S. (1979). *Social origins of educational systems.* Abingdon, OX: Sage.

Bereday, G. Z. F. (1964). Sir Michael Sadler's "Study of Foreign Systems of Education". *Comparative Education Review*, 7(3), 307–314.

Cameron, J. (1983). *International handbook of educational systems. Vol. 2: Sub-Saharan Africa.* Chichester, England: John Wiley.

Cowen, R., & McLean, M. (1984). *International handbook of educational systems. Vol.3: Asia, Australia and Latin America.* Chichester, England: John Wiley.

Cramer, J. F., & Browne, G. S. (1956). *Contemporary education: A comparative study of national systems* (2nd ed.). New York: Harcourt, Brace and World, Inc.

Engels, F. (1859). Karl Marx: "A Contribution to the Critique of the Political Economy" (Review). In The Central Committee of the Communist Party of China's Compilation Bureau of Marx, Engels Lenin and Stalin (1995). *Selected works of Marx and Engels (Volume II).* Beijing: People's Publishing House.

Guo, S., & Guo, Y. (Eds.). (2016). *Spotlight on China: Changes in education under China's market economy.* Rotterdam, Netherlands: Sense Publishers.

Holmes, B. (1983). *International handbook of educational systems. Vol. 1: Europe and Canada.* Chichester, England: John Wiley.

Ignas, E., & Corsini, R. J. (Eds.). (1981). *Comparative education systems.* Itasca, IL: F.E. Peacock.

Kandel, I. L. (1933). *Studies in comparative education.* Boston: Hought Mifflin.

Lee, T. G. C. (2000). *Education in traditional China: A history.* Leiden, Netherlands, Koninklijke, Brill.

Marlow-Ferguson, R. (2002). *World education encyclopedia: A survey of educational systems worldwide* (2nd ed.). Farmington Hills, MI: Gale Group.

Moehlman, A. H. (1963). *Comparative educational system.* Washington: Center for Applied Research in Education.

North, D. C. (1981). *Structure and changes in economic history.* New York: W.W. Norton & Company, Inc.

Oury, F., & Vasquez, A. (1968). *Vers une pédagogie institutionnelle.* Paris: Maspero.

Postlethwaite, T. N. (Ed.). (1988). *The encyclopedia of comparative education and national systems of education.* Oxford: Pergamon Press.

Rawls, J. B. (1971/1999). *A theory of justice* (Rev. ed.). Cambridge, MA: Harvard University Press.

Sadler, M. E. (1900). How far can we learn anything of practical value from the study of foreign systems of education? Printed at the Surrey Advertiser Office.

Schultz, T. W. (1968). Institutions and the rising economic value of man. *American Journal of Agricultural Economics, 50*(5), 21–35.

Shaughnessy, E. L. (Ed.). (2005). *China: Empire and civilization.* New York: Duncan Baird Publishers/Oxford University Press.

Steyn, H. J., & Wolhuter, C. C. (Eds.). (2000). *Education systems of emerging countries, challenges of the 21st century.* Keurkopie: Noordbrug.

Xi, J. (2017). Decisive victory in building a well-off society in an all-round way: Winning a great victory for socialism with Chinese characteristics in the new era: Report from the 19th National Congress of the Communist Party of China. October 18. Retrieved from http://www.gov.cn/zhuanti/2017-10/27/content_5234876.htm (in Chinese).

CHAPTER ONE

Government, Society, and Schools

GUORUI FAN

When investigating the process of China's reform and development of education over the past forty years, it is not difficult to find that the main problem encountered in the reform of the education institutions has been the constant management of the relationship between the government, schools, and society. Through forty years of development, China's education institutions institution has gradually been restored, improved, and optimized. The structural relationships between different fields, levels, and elements of the education institutions have gone from the state of disorder to order, from centralization to decentralization, from regulation to empowerment, and from management to governance, forming a school-running institution with government-run as the main body, the active participation from the whole society, and public and private schools developing together. A hierarchically administered education management institution and school institutions have gradually been formed, and the capacity of education to serve the public and the capacity of education governance have been constantly improving, which is now forming a foundational education institutions that is dynamic, efficient, open, and conducive to scientific development.

SECTION 1 THE HISTORY OF EDUCATION INSTITUTIONS REFORM IN CHINA

The reforms in education and the changes in the education institutions over the past forty years of reform and opening-up have experienced a return to order from chaos, and restoration and reconstruction of the education institutions, with the comprehensive initiation of education reforms, the exploration of institutional reforms that follow market mechanisms to promote the development of education, the adjustment of education policy from the pursuit of efficiency to a focus on equity, as well as the promotion of the comprehensive reform of the education field, the acceleration of the construction of the education governance institution, the modernization of governance capacity, among other development stages.

I. Gaining Order from Chaos: The Restoration and Reconstruction of the Education Institutions (1978–1984)

Looking at the historical process of China's social and educational reforms, the founding of PRC in 1949 enabled the Chinese society to leap from a feudal autocratic society, which had persisted for millennia, to a people's democratic society. Chinese society has undergone a socialist transformation, a comprehensive and large-scale construction of socialism on the basis of completing the transformation from new democracy to socialism. The Chinese education institutions were continuously optimized in the process of exploring the establishment of a national, scientific, and mass cultural education institution[1]. However, the exploration and development were never smooth sailing. During the "Cultural Revolution," which lasted for a decade, there was a prevalence of incorrect "leftist" thinking, "causing the Party, the country and the people to suffer their most serious setbacks and losses since the founding of the People's Republic" (The Central Committee of CPC, 1981). The function of serving proletarian politics in education was strengthened, and schools became the tools of the dictatorship of the proletarian[2]. The education institutions, education order, and education ecology suffered severe damage. After the "Cultural Revolution," the correction of "leftist" errors and the complete reversal of the serious situation caused by the "ten years of internal chaos" resulted in increasingly strong social appeals for the Party and the country to reemerge from the crisis, but because of the confinements of the "Two Whatevers" policy[3], this desire to conform to the trend of the times was severely hampered, and all social undertakings "progressed hesitantly" (The Central Committee of CPC, 2009). In December 1978, the Third Plenary Session of the 11th Central Committee of CPC was held to bring order out of chaos. The session "marked a great turning point in the history of our Party since the founding of PRC, opening a new era of China's reform and opening-up" (Hu, 2008).

Emancipating Minds and Establishing the Strategic Focus of Economic Construction.

The Third Plenary Session of the Eleventh Central Committee of CPC fully affirmed that the scientific institutions of Mao Zedong Thought must be fully and accurately grasped. At the same time, it corrected the "leftist" mistakes that were made in the "Cultural Revolution" and broke through the thought constraints of dogmatism and personal worship, criticized and negated the incorrect "Two Whatevers" policy, evaluated discussions on the standard of truth, established "practice is the sole criterion for testing truth" as the fundamental principle of the Party's ideological guideline, and decided on setting the guidelines of emancipating minds, opening up ways of thinking, seeking truth from facts, and being unified to look forward and thus reestablish the Marxist ideological guideline of seeking truth from facts. The Third Plenary Session of the 11th Central Committee decisively stopped using the slogan "Taking class struggle as the key link" and made the historic decision to transfer the focus of the Party and the state work to economic construction and implementation of reform and opening-up. "The purpose is to promote the liberation and development of social productive forces, realizing the modernization of the country, enriching the Chinese people, and revitalizing the great Chinese nation, to promote the self-improvement and development of the Chinese socialist institution, to give new vitality to socialism, and to build and develop socialism with Chinese characteristics" (Hu, 2007).

The Establishment of the Belief that "Knowledge and Talents Should Be Respected."

During the "Cultural Revolution," influenced by the "leftist" thinking, faulty ideas such as "the more knowledge one possesses, the more reactionary one is" and "intellectuals are the Stinking Old Ninths"[4] prevailed. Even after the "Cultural Revolution" ended, the concept of the "two estimates" from the "National Education Conference Minutes"[5] of 1971 was still a spiritual shackle that plagued teachers and intellectuals at that time. Xiaoping Deng clearly pointed out that the "two estimates" were not in line with reality and fully recognized the seventeen years of education and the contributions of the teaching teams before the "Cultural Revolution" (Deng, 1977a). Out of the strategic thinking on the demand for modernization talents, he pointed out: "We must achieve modernization. The key is to develop science and technology. The development of science and technology cannot be realized without education. It is impossible to achieve modernization only with empty talk. We must have knowledge and we must have talents." "A kind of culture must be created within the Party: respect for knowledge and respect for talent" (Deng, 1977b). The "two respects" proposal played an important role in implementing policies on intellectuals and building a culture of respecting teachers and education throughout the whole society. In December 1978, the Third Plenary Session of the 11th Central Committee of CPC proposed to "vigorously strengthen the scientific and educational work necessary for realizing modernization" (The 11th Central Committee of CPC, 1978). In March 1979, the Central Committee of CPC abolished the *National Education Conference Minutes* of 1971 and completely overthrew the "two estimates," clearing away the obstacles faced by education and science field at the time on their path of returning to order from a state of chaos.

The Restoration and Reconstruction of Order in Education. After the "Cultural Revolution," the urgent task placed before educators was to restore and reconstruct order in education. At the National Education Conference of 1978, Xiaoping Deng required "schools to vigorously strengthen revolutionary order," "improve the quality of education and improve the teaching quality of science and culture" (Deng, 1978: 103, 105). Following this, the twelve-year academic institution of primary and secondary schools (which had been reduced to ten years during the "Cultural Revolution") was revived, the professional grade institution was restored, and the degree institution was implemented, thereby restoring and reconstructing institutional order in education. From September to October of 1978, the Ministry of Education (MOE) referred to the relevant documents of the seventeen years before the "Cultural Revolution,"[6] revising and issuing *The Provisional Work Regulations for Full-time Secondary Schools (Draft), The Provisional Work Regulations for Full-time Primary Schools (Draft),* and *The Provisional Work Regulations for National Key Higher Education Institutions (Draft),* rectifying and restoring the working institutions for higher, secondary, and primary education institutions, respectively. Even though some scholars believe that choosing the education institution of the seventeen years before the "Cultural Revolution" as a model for restoring and rebuilding order in education and developing education in the new era was an "unfinished cause of restoring order from chaos" (Yang, 2008: 711), however, in the absence of an international perspective that could only emerge after reform and opening-up, and without local experience that could be used for reference, this was a reasonable option given the emergent circumstances. The restoration and reconstruction of educational order laid a good institutional foundation for future education reforms.

Establishing the "Three-Orientations" Education Guiding Principle. On the National Day of 1983, Xiaoping Deng wrote an inscription for Beijing Jingshan School: "Education should be oriented towards modernization, towards the world, and towards the future" (1993). This new method, referred to as the "three orientations," coupled with Xiaoping Deng's "new generation with four qualifications" (1980: 123) cultivation objectives which was raised from the perspective of socialist spiritual civilization, produced an extensive and profound impact on China's education reforms and development in the 1980s and 1990s. The "three orientations" accurately revealed a historical turning point in China's education development history, from "class conflicts as the key guideline" and isolationism in education to reform and opening-up and education for "economic construction as the center." "The three orientations" depicted the future direction of Chinese education development from three different dimensions: taking roots in tradition while moving towards modernization, focusing on China with a global perspective, and focusing on the present with a future perspective.

Resuming the College Entrance Examination (Gaokao) Institution. During the "Cultural Revolution" period, college entrance examinations were stopped, affecting the development of a whole generation and also causing a shortage of talents for national construction.[7] In 1977, Xiaoping Deng, who had just returned to work, stuck to his beliefs and proposed the resumption of the examination admission institution for higher education institutions. "This year, we must be resolute and resume the recruitment of university students directly from high school graduates by examinations instead of recommendations," and believed that this "may be a good way of letting talents emerge early and make achievements early" (Deng, 1977b). In October of that year, the State Council officially approved the MOE's *Opinions on the Enrolment of Colleges and Universities in 1977*, stipulating that from 1977 the enrollment institution for higher education institutions was to undergo reform, unified enrollment examinations were to be resumed, and the college entrance examination institution was to be formally restored. The restoration of the college entrance examination institution was a major achievement in restoring order from chaos. It was also the beginning of the restoration and reconstruction of the education institutions and of bringing China's education into a new order. It was a new beginning for China's education modernization.

Restoring the Key School Institution. As early as the 1950s, facing the country's construction and a serious shortage of educational resources because of the need for specialized talents, China implemented the key school institution. During the "Cultural Revolution" period, which witnessed the spreading of the concepts including "the uselessness of knowledge" and "anti-intellectualism," the key school institution was abolished. In May of 1977, Xiaoping Deng pointed out: "Education requires two legs to walk, we must not only pay attention to the scaling up of the education, and also need to pay attention to the improvement of education. Hence, it is necessary to set up key primary schools, key secondary schools, and key universities. It is necessary to have people go through rigorous examinations and have the best talents gathered in key secondary schools and universities" (1977b). In January 1978, the MOE issued *The Trial Program for Running a Number of Key Primary and Secondary Schools*, proposing the formation of a "small pyramid" structure for key primary and secondary schools nationwide, and the focus of funding, school-running conditions, faculty staff, student quality, and other aspects was to be favorably directed towards the key schools. The key school institution has played a historic role in effectively concentrating the use of existing educational resources, improving school-running conditions for some key schools, improving the quality of education, and "producing more talents at a faster rate," thus meeting the needs of the state and society for high-quality talents. In view of the intrinsic relationship between the characteristics of key schools and the arising phenomena of "the craze for choosing top schools" and "test-oriented education" due to the limited educational resources, China began exploring the reforms of the key school institution in the mid-1980s.

II. Reforming the Education Institution: The Deployment and Development of Education Institutions Reform (1985–1991)

In May 1985, in the first National Education Conference, after the introduction of the reform and opening-up, *The Decision of the Central Committee of CPC on the Reform of the Education Institution* (hereinafter referred to as *The Decision*) was discussed and adopted. *The Decision* and the *two Decisions* (The Central Committee of CPC, 1984; The Central Committee of CPC, 1985b) successively issued by the CPC Central Committee on economic institution reform and science and technology institution reform, at around the same time, constituted the general framework of social reform and development characterized by institutional reforms during that period, and greatly promoted the modernization of the Chinese society.

The Change in the Direction of the Functions of Education. *The Decision* sought to find a solution for "how to bring about an upswing in education with limited financial and material resources to meet the urgent needs of socialist modernization" and "to better drive the motivation, and enhance the unification of all the levels of government, teachers, students, staff, and all the other stakeholders through reforms to achieve a shared vision and promote the emergence of plenty solutions by tapping the potential of all, with an aim to improve education year after year." In the concept of the function of education, *The Decision* puts forward that "education must serve socialist construction and socialist construction must rely on education." Obviously, this expression went beyond *The Instructions Regarding Education Work* issued by the Central Committee of CPC and the State Council in September 1958 that put forward the education policy of "political service of education for the proletariat, and the combination of education and productive labour," and influenced Chinese education for as long as 20 years. The new education policy has been consistent with the development strategy of "taking economic construction as the centre" since the Third Plenary Session of the 11th Central Committee. *The Decision* pointed out that "the fundamental purpose of education institution reform is to improve the character of the nation, enlarge the pool of talents, and develop extraordinary talents." From emphasizing education as a political service to focusing on the function of education in promoting economic and social development, affirming the value of education was a tremendous improvement in ideological concepts. This reorientation of values was implemented in the subsequent education reforms. For example, in February 1993, the Central Committee of CPC and the State Council's *Outline of China's Education Reform and Development* put forward the "Three Benefits" principle of education institution reform, that is, "conducive to persisting in the socialist direction of education and cultivate participants of and successors to the socialist cause who develop morally, intellectually, physically and aesthetically; conducive to motivate the government, the whole of society and teachers, students and staff at all levels to improve the quality of education, scientific research and school-running efficiency; conducive to promoting education to better serve socialist modernization."

Streamlining Administration, Delegating Power, and Increasing School Autonomy. After the "Cultural Revolution," following the return to order from chaos in the field of education, the issue of school autonomy was put on the agenda. As early as the end of 1979, the presidents of four universities in Shanghai published an article in the *People's Daily* calling for a reform of the higher education institution and for granting higher education institutions the autonomy to run by themselves, which elicited strong reactions from the society (Su et al., 1979). *The Decision* sought to reflect the urgent needs and experiences of increasing school autonomy in various areas across the nation at that time. In terms of the relationship between central and local education management powers and responsibilities, "reform the management institution, and resolutely implement the principle of streamlining administration and decentralizing and increasing school autonomy while strengthening macro management." In the field of basic education, "the responsibility for the development of basic education is given to the local governments" and "the principle of basic education that the responsibility of basic education belongs to the local governments and implement management by levels is to be enacted." The central government decided on "major policies and macro-planning," that "the basic education management authority is granted to the local governments," and that "the formulation and implementation of specific policies, institutions and plans, the leadership, management and inspection of the school, as well as responsibilities and powers are all handed over to the local governments." This institution was later confirmed by *The Compulsory Education Law of PRC* promulgated in April 1986. In order to promote the development of compulsory education, *The Decision* first proposed the "Two Growths" principle of the education expenditure institution, which was "the growth rate in fiscal expenditure on education from the central and local governments should be higher than that of regular treasury revenue, and gradually increasing the average education spending per student." In order to guarantee the commitment of the local government to the development of education, *the Decision* also required that, in addition to state funding, "an appropriate proportion of local standby financial resources should be used for education, and township fiscal revenue should be primarily used for education." It also permits local "expropriation of education surcharges" for "purchasing teaching facilities to improve basic education." These institutional requirements were also included in the *Compulsory Education Law*[8], thereby establishing that the responsibility for rural compulsory education was mainly in the hands of county and township (town) governments, and the funds for rural basic education were mainly provided by the county and township governments. In 1987, the National Education Commission and other institutions pointed out that after giving local government the responsibility for basic education, "full use should be made of the important role of the county in managing basic education in rural areas" and "expanding the responsibility and authority of rural school management at the township level" and also emphasized that "this is an important feature of this reform." In the reform of the rural basic education management institution, the village plays a role in taking care of decrepit buildings, improving school conditions, improving the payment for teachers, raising funds for the salary of private teachers, managing school property, safeguarding school rights, encouraging children at school age to enter school, participating in the supervision of school work, and other roles (The State Education Commission and the Ministry of Finance of PRC, 1987). Delegating the power of basic education management to the local governments, the establishment of provincial, county, and township hierarchical management and creating the compulsory education financial management institution with the township as the main contributor, motivated the local government and played a positive role in promoting the development of basic education. However, in the compulsory education institution with the township as the main contributor, there was insufficient focus on education management. Objectively speaking, the dependence of education on the level of local economic development was one of the key reasons for the unbalanced development of education in China.

The Principal Accountability Institutions. With regard to the relationship between the government and schools and the Party-government relations within schools, after the founding of PRC, the state implemented two models of the principal accountability institution: one is under the leadership of the school Party branch and the local Party committee and the other is the principal accountability institution under the leadership of the education administrative department. *The Decision* proposed that "schools gradually implement the principal accountability institution", and then clarified the relationships of rights and responsibilities between the school Party branch, the principal, the school council, and the faculty representatives. "The Party organizations in the school should be freed from the past state of all-inclusive responsibilities and concentrate on strengthening Party building and strengthening theoretical and political work." "Schools with the right conditions should set up an authoritative school committee made up from a limited number of people and presided over by the principal to serve as a deliberative body. It is necessary to establish and improve a faculty congress institution with teachers as the main body so as to strengthen democratic management and democratic supervision." Thus, in view of the separation of rights and responsibilities, it was required that guaranteed that the school's internal management mechanism operates effectively. In spite of the fact that in subsequent reforms and developments there was still some controversy regarding the principal accountability institution of primary and secondary schools, this institution played a positive role in promoting independent school running and independent development of primary and secondary schools (Xiao, 1989, 1990, 1993, 2000).

After the political turmoil of 1989, the reform of the education institution fell into a state of stagnation. After Xiaoping Deng gave a speech during his southern tour of 1992, a new round of reform and development was launched.

III. Exploring Market Mechanisms and Promoting the Development of Education with Institutional Reforms (1992–2002)

The transition from a traditional planned economy to a market economy, and from a concept to the strategic planning, experienced a complex understanding and transformation process from "a planned economy in the main, with market regulations assisting" (Hu, 1982) and a "planned commodity economy" (The Central Committee of CPC, 1984) to a "socialist market economy" (Jiang, 1992). In the spring of 1992, Xiaoping Deng made a series of important speeches during his visits to Wuchang, Shenzhen, Zhuhai, and Shanghai (Chen, 1992; Deng, 1992), which launched a new round of emancipation of minds, reform and opening-up, and a new development path centered around economic growth. In June 1994, the second national education conference since the introduction of reform and opening-up was held, where a proposal was made to establish an education institution that was compatible with a socialist market the economy (The State Council of PRC, 1994a). In order to respond to the grand goals and tasks of the cross-century socialist modernization construction put forward by the 15th CPC National Congress in 1997 of "implementing the strategy of rejuvenating the country through science and education and sustainable development, deepening the reform of science and technology and the education institution, and promoting the integration of science, technology, education with the economy" (Jiang, 1997), the MOE formulated a cross-century construction blueprint for the reform and development of education: *The Action Plan for Education Revitalization in the 21st Century*. In June 1999, the Third National Education Conference since the launching of reform and opening-up was held. Setting off from the strategic heights of meeting the challenges of the 21st century, reform of the education institution and structure was deepened, quality education was comprehensively promoted, the strategy of rejuvenating the country through science and education was implemented, and an education institution that was compatible with a socialist market economic institution and the needs of political and technological institution reforms was deployed (The Central Committee of CPC and the State Council of PRC, 1999).

The Establishment of an Education Institution That Is Compatible with the Socialist Market Economic Institution. In 1993, the Central Committee of CPC and the State Council's *China's Education Reform and Development Program* proposed that education reform should adhere to the "Three Benefits" principle, "reforming this institution which is insufficiently open and over-regulated" and "establishing a new education institution that is compatible with the socialist market economic institution and the reforms of the political institution and science and technology institutions." The 1990s witnessed the implementation of this mission. In terms of the reform of the schooling institution, on the one hand, "further establish the central and provincial (autonomous regions, municipalities directly under the central government) education management institutions in which management and accountability are established by levels," and on the other hand, "change the status quo that schools are all run by governments, and gradually establish an institution in which schools are mainly run by the government with the engagement of the society as well." For the secondary education and below, "optimize the institution of school running and management by levels," in which basic education is mainly run by local governments. Higher education "is to implement the institution in which government implements macro management, colleges and universities run by themselves with the participation of the society." In other words, the policy emphasized that universities and colleges were mainly run by central and provincial governments with the participation of all sectors of the society. In terms of the relationship between the government and schools, the government's functions were to be transformed "from the direct administrative management of schools, to macro management by legislation, grants, planning, information services, policy guidance and other necessary administrative means." "According to the principle of the separation of government institutions and public-sector institutions, the rights and obligations of higher education institutions are clarified by legislation, so that higher education institutions can truly become legal entities that are self-running with the participation of society." "Schools should be good at exercising their powers, shouldering their responsibilities, and establishing a self-developing and self-restraining operational mechanism that actively adapts to the needs of economic construction and social development." Thoughts and strategies including streamlining administration and delegating power, implementing management by levels, and granting school with autonomy have continued the education reforms of *The Decision* in the mid-1980s, and have been strengthened and improved in relevant national education policy documents since then. For example, in May 1995, the National Education Commission proposed: "The goal of the reform of the higher education management institution is to basically form an organically integrated institutional framework before the year 2000 or shortly after in which the respective responsibilities of organizers, managers and school runners are clarified, education investments are made through multiple channels with financial appropriations as the main one, the central and provincial, autonomous regions, and municipalities directly under the Central Government are responsible for two-level management and division of labour, with planning mainly done by the People's governments of provinces, autonomous regions, and municipalities directly under the Central Government" (The General Office of the State Council of PRC, 1995). However, the multichannel funding of education, the development of private education, the transformation of public schools, the expansion of universities, and other policies and institutions for developing education industry with an economic focus also generated a series of new issues.

Localization of Education Management. For the compulsory education management institution, the "school-running and management by levels" institution stipulated in the *Compulsory Education Law of the 1980s* was implemented in the 1990s. The reform of China's urban and rural economic institution had just started, and the overall financial resources of the government were still relatively limited. Under these circumstances, moving the responsibility of rural compulsory education down to townships and towns helped motivate local schools and energize the development of basic education. In fact, township Party committees, governments, and villagers' committees played an active role in raising education funds, collecting rural education surcharges, accelerating school construction, renovating dilapidated school buildings, improving teachers' incomes, and encouraging school-age children to enter schools. School-running conditions received different levels of improvement, with major contributions made towards accelerating the development of basic education, especially the nine-year compulsory education. However, this kind of education management institution, which is called "localization" (Chen, 1996), unintentionally created the dependence of compulsory education on township finance, and as a result the regional gaps in rural basic education continuously enlarged. A serious situation appeared whereby the salaries of rural primary and secondary school teachers across the whole country were in arrears. After the reform of the fiscal and taxation that we carried out in 1994[9], the financial expenditure of rural basic education was basically borne by the townships and by farmers, and because of the large differences in the level of economic development in different places, the imbalance in the area of compulsory education development (in counties) was intensified. Since 2000, the implementation of "tax and fee reform" in rural areas has eliminated rural education surcharges and rural donations, and the financing channels for rural education became even more simplified. There was a shortage of funds for rural education, which made the development of rural basic education and the operation of rural schools difficult. In 2001, the state changed the management institution of rural compulsory education, which was dominated by townships for 15 years, clarifying "the enactment of an institution under the leadership of the State Council where local governments are responsible, managed by level, and county government as the main stakeholder"[10] (The State Council of PRC, 2001a). Even so, some places still emphasized that "the county is the mainstay, but the township government's responsibilities must not be lessened," requiring "on the one hand, it is necessary to implement the county-based management institution and increase the responsibility and authority of the county-level government to manage basic education; on the other hand, we must continue to motivate the township to participate in school running" (Zhu, 2001). The "county-centered" education management institution has centralized the basic education management authority to the county level. To a certain extent, it tackled the problem of over-decentralization of education management and insufficient education funding, which was only provided for townships and towns. It played a positive role in guaranteeing the basic needs of rural basic education, particularly in the guarantee of teachers' salaries; but for many counties with weak financial resources, county-level finances still could not shoulder the responsibility of financing rural compulsory education.

Raising Funds for Education through Multiple Channels. In 1993, the CPC Central Committee and the State Council proposed to "reform and improve the education investment institution and increase education funding," emphasizing that "increasing investment in education is a fundamental measure in realizing the strategic position of education. Governments at all levels, all sectors of society and individuals must work hard to increase the investment in education and ensure that education development is prioritized." "It is necessary to gradually establish a institution where funds mainly come from state financial appropriations, and are supplemented by taxes and fees for education, miscellaneous fees for non-compulsory education students, incomes from school-run industries, social donations and education funds" (The Central Committee of CPC, 1993). At that time, the so-called multichannel education investment institution included the following paths: national financial appropriations, education tax, tuition and miscellaneous fees, school-running industry income, social donation fund-raising, education funds, research funding, education loans, interest, and so on. With regard to school fees, in 1996, *The Interim Measures for the Administration of Charges for Compulsory Education Schools* issued by the National Education Commission and another two departments permitted the collection of miscellaneous fees and borrowing fees during the compulsory education phase, "all used to supplement the shortage of public funds for schools"; *The Interim Measures for the Administration of Charges for General Senior Secondary Schools*, released at the same time, stipulated that "high school education is a non-compulsory education, and therefore schools charge tuition fees according to relevant state regulations." "Tuition fees are one of the necessary sources of school funding." In situations where government financial resources were insufficient, some local governments actively explored and put forward slogans such as "Education for the People by the People," established the "People's Education Funds Institutions," and relied on the masses to run education and contribute to the popularization of nine-year compulsory education[11]. However, the so-called Education for the People by the People basically meant that farmers used their own money to carry out "compulsory education," which added a serious financial burden to the farmers. "For many countries, decentralization implies that the responsibilities that government departments are unwilling to take on will be passed down to the decentralized institutions who will not be provided with appropriate funding" (Whitacre, 1997). Multichannel financing for education as a result of the shortage of institutional education funds, along with the development of private schools and school institution transformation and reforms, inevitably led to arbitrary charges in education. For instance, the "school choice fee" brought about serious concern from the public. Although a report by the United Nations Economic and Social Council that criticized China's school fees as being "too high to allow the poor to go to school" was widely received as being exaggerated, however, there was some partial truth behind the argument that "decentralization may make it even more difficult for the right to education to be enjoyed equally, because education funding inevitably become the responsibility of the local poor communities and families," and "making families and communities undertake education funding will widen the gap between the rich and the poor" (Economic and Social Council & United Nations, 2004), which directly led to the regulating of arbitrary charges in education for more than ten years at the beginning of the new century.

Developing Private Education. In 1985, *The Decision* proposed that "local governments should encourage and guide state enterprises, social groups and individuals in school running." In July 1989, Shanghai promulgated *The Measures for the Administration of School Running by Social Forces*, and set basic education as one of the types of school running by social forces in a legislative sense. Private education was first developed in the fields of nonacademic education and non-formal education. In 1992, the 14th National Congress of CPC stated "encouraging school running through social funding with diverse channels and forms and having the people run schools, changing the methods of school running only by government" (Jiang, 1992). In February 1993, the Central Committee of CPC and the State Council promulgated the regulation: "Change the format of government-run schools, and gradually establish a institution in which government-run schools are the mainstay and a variety of stakeholders in society jointly run schools." "The state actively encourages social groups and individual citizens to run schools according to the law and adopts the guiding principle of actively encouraging, strongly supporting, correctly guiding and strengthening management" (The Central Committee of CPC, 1993). Consequently, private education was promoted to secondary and higher vocational education and vocational training. In 1997, *The Regulations for the Administration of Social Forces in Running Schools*, the first administrative regulations of PRC for regulating private education, were issued, marking the beginning of a new stage in the lawful running, management, and administration of Chinese private schools. In June 1999, the CPC Central Committee and the State Council stated: "Actively encourage and support social forces to run schools in a variety of forms, meet the growing needs of the people for education, and encourage the joint development of government-run schools, public schools and private schools, with government-run schools as the mainstay. Any form of school running that conforms to relevant national laws and regulations can be experimented boldly." "A small number of private primary schools and junior high schools are allowed to be established, with an aim to provide opportunities for school choice within this scope." "Actively develop pre-school education that is based at community including both public and private kindergartens." "It is necessary to formulate preferential policies according to local conditions (such as preferential land use, exemption of infrastructure supporting fees, etc.) and support social forces in running schools" (The Central Committee of CPC, 1999). In practice, in the process of gradually establishing a socialist market economic institution in the 1990s, the transformation of the state-owned economy and the development of the non-state economy provided appropriate external conditions for the rise and development of private education. Although the government's financial investment into public education increased year by year, the increase of fiscal public education funds could not keep up with the rapid development of demand for education. The unbalance between supply and demand of educational resources was still a basic problem that challenged China's education development, as quality education was a scarce resource. Some parents who made their way out of poverty and became rich and had relatively high expectations for their children's education had a strong desire to choose a good school for their children to receive education, which exacerbated the unbalance between supply and demand in quality education. The implementation of the education localization policy created the initial institutional conditions for the rise of private education. After more than ten years of development, Chinese private schools formed a pattern of the joint development of schools in diverse forms, which include, from the perspective of the main school-running body, schools run by private enterprises, enterprise groups (including joint-stock enterprises), social institutions and education groups, and schools which received donations from domestic and foreign bodies, and individuals. Jiaojiang District Education Bureau of Taizhou City in Zhejiang Province tried out the "education shareholding institution" and set up a joint-stock school[12]. These experiments have enriched the connotations of private education from different aspects.

Developing the Education Industry and Converting Public Schools. In 1992, *The Decision of the Central Committee of CPC and the State Council on Accelerating the Development of the Tertiary Industry* pointed out that the attribute of education was to be redefined from "superstructures" to being a part of "social productivity," clearly defining education as a tertiary industry and a fundamental industry in the tertiary industry that has a global and leading impact on the development of the national economy. The concept of educational industry theory gradually became a new perspective for the development of education (Zhang, 1993). In June 1999, the Central Committee of CPC and the State Council clearly proposed to "develop the education industry" (The Central Committee of CPC, 1999). If it can be said that Peking University's method of "tearing down the wall and opening for business"[13] was purely a kind of economic behavior, and a simple mechanical response to the concept of developing the education industry, then the impact of converting schools in basic education was an exploration of the introduction of market mechanisms into the field of education[14]. Since 1993, some provinces and regions in China have started pilot projects in different forms for public primary and secondary schools. In terms of policy, school conversion reforms were mainly based on the relevant documents of the State Council and the National Education Commission. For example, the State Council issued a document in 1994 that stated: "Encourage enterprises and institutions and other social forces to run schools through multiple channels and in multiple forms according to national laws and policies. Areas with the right conditions can also implement forms such as 'private schools with public support' and 'public schools with private support' (The State Council, 1994a)". In April 1996, *The National Education Project "Ninth Five-Year Plan" and the 2010 Development Plan* stated: "Existing public schools may also be converted to 'private schools with public support' or 'public schools with private support' when conditions permit." By 2010, the school-running institution, which is mainly government-run with the participation of all sectors of society, has been established in general and the joint development of public schools and private schools have been realized to a large extent. In January 1997, the State Education Commission proposed: "All places in the compulsory education phase in the reform of the school-running institution, can implement a variety of school-running forms including 'private schools with public support', 'public schools with private support', schools with social participation, private schools and so on, according to their actual circumstances." (The State Education Commission, 1997) In June 1998, the MOE recognized and supported "the Study of the Reform of the School-Running Institution in Primary and Secondary Schools" as a "new topic of current basic education reform," and believed different forms of school-running, including "private schools with public support" and "public schools with private support" forms, to be appropriate supplements to government-run schools during the compulsory education period, and that this was "still in the stage of exploration and experimentation" (The General Office of the State Council of PRC, 1998). Each of the experimental explorations in reforms of public schools in different places had their own characteristics. A series of educational reforms with market-oriented exploration emerged. Among them, the impacts of the reforms in Changxing in Zhejiang[15], Suqian in Jiangsu[16], and Lanli[17] in Hubei have been far reaching. Through pilot reforms of the public primary and secondary school institutions, a number of schools were converted which played an active role in raising funds for education through multiple channels in particular historical periods, improving school running conditions, promoting the faster development of basic education, expanding quality education resources, and meeting the diverse educational needs of the local people. However, due to the imperfect laws and regulations and the imperfect policy institution, the reform process saw challenges such as the unclear nature of school-running, substandard converting actions, high charges in the name of converting, and serious loss of state-owned educational assets, which affected the benefits of education to the public and its balanced development.

Expanding University Recruitment to Drive Economic Growth. The concept that education is an industry has directly affected the student enrollment policies of Chinese universities for more than a decade. The first half of the 1990s witnessed the emergence of the trend of higher education from elite education to popularization. In April 1996, the National Education Commission proposed that by 2010, the number of students enrolled in higher education institutions would increase to about 9.5 million, the number of students per 100,000 population would reach 700, and the gross enrollment rate would reach the higher education development target of around 11% (MOE, 1996). In the following two years, the call for expanding the enrollment scale of colleges and universities continued to rise, and a consensus on enrollment expansion was reached. The MOE and other relevant departments also held a variety of forms of discussion on enrollment expansion and began to accelerate the pace of enlarging enrollment plans. In December 1998, the MOE proposed *The Action Plan for Education Revitalization in the 21st Century* to actively and steadily develop higher education. By the year 2000, "the higher education enrolment rate reached about 11%." By 2010, "there was a large expansion in the scale of higher education, with an enrolment rate close to 15%." At the same time, Tang Min, the chief economist at the Asian Development Bank at the time, proposed to the Central Committee of the CPC that the number of university enrollments should be doubled in three years[18]. At the beginning of 1999, the National Planning and Development Committee put forward twelve proposals to the central government to further expand domestic demand and promote economic growth, explicitly proposing to expand the enrollment of higher education institutions. In June 1999, the National Planning and Development Commission and the MOE adjusted the expansion plan for general colleges and universities, from 1.08 million in the previous year to 1.54 million, an increase of 43%. In 1999, actual enrollment reached 1.597 million. In 2002, the number of students enrolled for colleges and universities nationwide was 3.205 million, the number of students in colleges and universities was 16 million, and the gross rate of enrollment in higher education reached 15%, entering the stage of popularization of higher education and realizing *The Action Plan for Education Revitalization for the 21st Century* eight years ahead of the original schedule. In 2006, Chen Zhili, State Councillor at the time, pointed out on a range of occasions that China had entered the stage of popularization of higher education[19]. In May 2006, it was decided at a State Council executive meeting, where the achievements in university enrollments were acknowledged, that "according to the current situation of colleges and universities, it is necessary to appropriately control the growth rate of enrollments and keep the enrollment scale relatively stable" (General Office of the State Council, 2006). In March 2012, the MOE pointed out that higher education was adhering to a "focus on quality improvement and bring out the full potential for the development of education by its intrinsic momentum" and "maintaining relatively stable enrollments of undergraduate students in public colleges and universities" and that the more-than-decade-long expansion of university enrollments was paused (MOE, 2012). In basic education sector, in the conversion of public schools, the market mechanism was introduced partially for exploring the reform of the education institutions. However, the direct purpose of university enrollments expansion came out of the need to stimulate domestic economic demands due to the impact of the Asian financial crisis and the sluggish export-oriented economy (foreign trade). In the reform of university enrollment, the original plan of the MOE was to better satisfy the "Three Needs," respectively, the needs of China's economic and social development in the 21st century, the needs of improving the qualities of the people, and the needs of people for receiving higher education.

However, in the face of the urgent need for national economic construction and by the requirements of the State Council, the completed enrollment plan was readjusted in just over ten days (Ji, 2009). Due to the introduction of a policy of college fees and charges during the previous higher education reform process,[20] Tang Min's suggestion was, in essence, to have more families bearing the costs of higher education (Bai, 2006). In fact, household spending on university education for children increased from 18% in 1999 to 31.5% in 2005 (Zhao & Sheng, 2008). The economic purpose of university enrollment expansion was also proved by the effects of enrollment expansion. In 2003, Zhang Baoqing, then vice minister of the MOE, said: "In 1998, the total amount of tuition fees collected by colleges and universities nationwide was more than 7 billion yuan. In 1999, this fee income exceeded 10 billion yuan" (2000). The expansion of enrollment for universities done for the purpose of economic growth objectively satisfied the public's eagerness to receive higher education, and adapted to the strong demands for high-level and high-quality professionals in a context of sustained and rapid economic and social development, and effectively alleviated the stresses brought about by the College Entrance Examination, pushing China to move from a populous country to a country with large human resources. However, the expansion of enrollment inevitably led to problems such as excessive burdens on families of students, disorderly teaching in universities, declining quality of education, and high employment competition on graduates.

The concept and practice of developing the education industry by market mechanisms invited the attention of the international community. In 1999, the World Bank pointed out in its *21st Century China Education Strategic Objectives* report that China was transforming into a socialist market economy. It suggested that the government should establish a more effective education management institution and identify key strategic issues that need to be prioritized in the near, medium, and long term. Short-term goals included increasing special education funding for less developed areas, improving the effectiveness of financial education grants at all levels of government, and improving towards a more effective evaluation institution for educational effectiveness. The medium-term goal was to build a funding institution that ensured the effective operation of the entire education institution, while the long-term goal was to narrow the imbalances in development between regions and improve the quality of education in an all-round way, as opposed to promoting education industrialization (Beemer et al., 1999).

IV. From Efficiency to Equity, Adjustment, and Sustainability of Educational Institutions Reform (2003–2009)

Since the reform and opening-up, China's economic and social development has made great progress, but the development model centered on economic construction and simply pursuing GDP growth not only led to resource waste, environmental pollution, and other problems but also caused deep-seated problems such as gaps between the rich and the poor, urban and rural differences, and differences in regional development, as well as uncoordinated economic and social development. The "scientific outlook on development" (Hu, 2004) with the connotations of "people-oriented," "all-round development," "coordinated development," and "sustainable development" came into being at an opportune time. Against this background, industrialization of education was questioned. From 2003 to 2004, MOE clearly expressed its opposition to the industrialization of education. At that time, Minister of Education Zhou Ji believed that "the concepts of 'education industrialization' and 'school corporatization' and running public schools by new mechanism and selling public schools, are not in line with the requirements of perfecting the socialist market economic institution. We must resolutely stop all of these practices." "We must adhere to the principle of public welfare of education, emphasize that education development should focus on government investment, strengthen the government's responsibility in developing education, and make education the most important task of the government" (MOE, 2004). In June 2006, the revised Compulsory Education Law for the first time comprehensively expounded the characteristics and nature of compulsory education in the form of law, which defined that "compulsory education is the education uniformly implemented by the state that all school-age children and adolescents must receive. It is a public welfare undertaking that the state must be committed." It further emphasizes the public welfare, the uniformity, and the mandatory nature of compulsory education. In October 2006, the Sixth Plenary Session of the 16th CPC Central Committee put forward the policy that "we should be committed to prioritizing the development of education and promoting education equity" (The Central Committee of CPC, 2006). Jintao Hu, the General Secretary of the CPC Central Committee at the time, pointed out in the report of the 17th National Congress of CPC that "educational equity is an important foundation for social equity" and "[we must] persist with the public welfare nature of education." Therefore, in the education institution reform and policy orientation, the concern for education equity replaced the previous pursuit of quantity, scale, and speed and began to focus on the regulation of arbitrary charges, conversion of schools, rural education, and the promotion of the balanced development of compulsory education.

Managing Arbitrary Education Fees. The multichannel financing of education based on market mechanisms has led to an increasingly serious phenomenon that arbitrary education fees were levied, and the phenomenon of regulating arbitrary fees thus became a due obligation. As early as 1996, *The Interim Measures for the Administration of Charges for Ordinary High Schools* issued by the National Education Commission and three other departments, while allowing high schools to charge tuition fees from students, required: "improving the rules and regulations for fee charges management, and seriously investigating and punishing arbitrary concoctions of pretexts to collect new fees, expansion of the scope of fees and the raising of fee standards … according to relevant state regulations." In April 2001, the state demanded "intensifying efforts to control unreasonable charges made by schools, particularly focusing on dismissing arbitrary charges in rural primary and secondary schools" (The General Office of the State Council, 2001). Besides, it was required that the standards for the provision of miscellaneous fees and accommodation fees for rural compulsory education schools should be uniformly formulated by the pricing and financial department of the province (including autonomous region, municipality directly under the Central Government) in conjunction with the education department, and both the standards established by the government or departments below the local (city) level and the fees and charges designated by the local governments should be canceled. Schools were not permitted to charge tuition materials fees, school construction fees, education funding fees, uniform fees, or various apportionments or "ride-along" fees. However, arbitrary fees in education were not controlled, becoming increasingly fierce. As a result, between 2009 and 2016, the MOE and other ministries and commissions jointly issued an annual document concerning the regulation of education fees the arbitrary education fees. In May 2002, the state began to require all types of schools to implement the education fee notification institution (The State Planning Commission of PRC et al., 2002). In 2004, full implementation of the "one-fee institution" charging method was required in compulsory education schools. Except for miscellaneous fee collection, teaching material fees, and exercise book fees levied according to the prescribed standards, it was made forbidden to charge other fees (MOE et al., 2004) in the hope of curbing the trend of arbitrary charges. However, during this period, arbitrary charges in a range of forms still existed, either by schools themselves or in conjunction with social training institutions or by entrusting various training courses ("occupation classes") for the purpose of selecting students, as well as cross-region student enrollment and fee collection, admissions and fees through any examination method, collecting fees through the recruitment of talented students, collecting donations by enrollment, and public schools collecting fees by recruiting students under the pretense of being private schools (MOE et al., 2012). Apart from reasons such as the shortage of education funds and the economic benefits of collecting fees, it was also a result of the unclear boundaries of the policy between "reasonable" charges and "arbitrary" charges when the policy allowed "reasonable" charges while putting a stop to "arbitrary" charges[21]. As for the phenomenon of arbitrary charges at the high school education stage, this was exacerbated by a policy of "three limitations" which aimed at regulating arbitrary charges but actually made the schools charge extra fees[22]. The "three limitations" policy which allowed public high schools to select students under some conditions was conducive to curbing the differentiated treatments and arbitrary charges, but the policy itself lacked a legal basis and legalized the purchasing of school placements with money, transforming orderly educational competition based on academic achievements into a competition between parents' economic capital and social capital instead of students' performance, contributing to a culture of high and arbitrary fees in education. By 2014, relevant provinces and cities had clearly banned the enrollment of school selection students according to the "three limitations" policy.

Cleaning Up and Regulating State-Run Converted Schools. It was apparent that the pilot reform of the school-running institution in public primary and secondary schools since the 1990s has to a certain extent broadened the channels for financing education and promoted the development of education using social funds. However, during this process, some problems emerged, such as non-standard local reform practice and fees being too high, especially the phenomenon of simply selling and converting public schools, which seriously deviated from educational objectives and the reform direction of the school-running institution. Conversion of schools justified education fees to a certain degree. Therefore, when regulating arbitrary education fees, it was necessary to clean up and standardize converted schools. Since 2004, all districts and counties of Shanghai began sorting out and adjusting state-run converted schools; six converted schools were either converted into public schools or merged into other public schools or converted schools (Zhang & Zhuang, 2005). In May 2005, the MOE required "strengthening the management of schools in accordance with the rule of law, further standardizing school-running practice, and effectively curbing the rising momentum of school-selection at the compulsory education stage. Public schools at the compulsory education stage may not hold or organize key schools in disguise. Public schools with good resources should not be converted to private schools nor impose high fees in the name of conversion" (MOE, 2005). On this basis, the state adjusted the relevant policies for the reform of the school-running institution of primary and secondary public schools in December 2005, requiring "first closing and then cleaning up" in order to get prepared for the clean-up and overhaul of arbitrary charges of converted schools. From January 2006, "completely halt the approval of new converted schools and new fee standards of converted schools", and at the same time, comprehensively investigated, cleaned up, and standardized the existing converted schools (The National Development and Reform Commission et al., 2005). In April 2006, the MOE and six other departments requested the "strengthening of the leadership of the reform of the school-running institution, comprehensively stopping the examination and approval of new converted schools and new fee standards of converted schools," "carrying out a comprehensive clean-up of schools that call themselves converted schools yet have arbitrary charges." Any public school that was converted into a private school must comply with the "four independences" principle. "It is strictly forbidden to have practices such as 'school within a school', 'one school, two institutions' and collecting arbitrary fees under the name of reform."[23] *The Compulsory Education Law*, revised in June 2006, became the legal basis for managing, regulating, and converting schools through the regulation that compulsory education "is a public welfare undertaking that must be guaranteed by the state." Accordingly, in August 2006, MOE stated: "From the date of the implementation of the newly revised 'Compulsory Education Law', no department or individual may change or disguise the nature of a public school in the compulsory education stage, and public schools must not be sold or transferred." "According to the law, local administrative departments of education at all levels must stop the examination and approval of the converting of public schools at the compulsory education stage. The provincial administrative departments of education shall, in conjunction with departments such as finance and state-owned assets management departments, must carry out a comprehensive clean-up of schools that have been converted at the local compulsory education stage" (MOE, 2006). In August of 2008, the MOE further requested the clarification of the "direction of converted schools," either converted to public schools or private schools. During the process of cleaning up and standardizing converted public schools, it was necessary to adopt a strategy of "progression and regression" under the premise of clarifying the property attributes of schools, the nature of school-running, and ensuring that public education resources were not lost. "Progression" here referred to operating in accordance with the private school mechanism and must be divested from public schools. According to Article 6 of *The Regulations for the Implementation of the Law on the Promotion of Private Education*, the "five independences" must be fully implemented[24], the problem of teacher placement must be properly solved, the legitimate rights and interests of teachers must be guaranteed, and the loss of state-owned assets must be prevented. "Regression" here referred to restoring the public nature of schools, and in strict accordance with relevant laws and regulations, properly resolving the withdrawal of non-state capital and the various creditor's rights and debts formed by the school in the course of running schools. Compulsory education schools enroll students according to the proximity of their homes to the schools, no longer charging high tuition fees according to the standard of converted schools, and require the government to assume corresponding school-running responsibilities to ensure that the school funds needed for school-running are put in place. Public school privately run, public schools with private support, or private schools with public support and other forms of charging standards were all abolished. During this process, some provinces and districts also stipulated that if the original status of a converted school was a quality education resource (such as a key middle school), then it must restore its properties as a public school, and it could be converted into a private school running mechanism (Zhang & Zhuang, 2005). In accordance with this principle, some converted schools directly restored their attributes as public schools, and some subtly restored the public nature of converted schools through flexible measures such as school mergers and school relocations. As of then, cleaning up and standardization of converted schools were being carried out all over the country. For example, Tianjin completely stopped the enrollment of converted primary schools in 2006; by 2008, it had completely finished the cleaning-up and standardization work for converted junior high schools (Sun, 2006). The cleaning-up rules for converted schools enabled a number of quality education schools to return to their nature of public schools, guaranteeing and promoting equity in education.

Actively Promoting the Balanced Development of Compulsory Education. While regulating arbitrary charges in education and the overhaul and conversion of schools, the state has actively promoted the balanced development of compulsory education. Since *The Decision* in 1985, which put forward the popularization of nine-year compulsory education and the *Compulsory Education Law*, revised in 1986, which put forward the enactment of a nine-year compulsory education institution in China, compulsory education in China has undergone the three stages of unbalanced development, the transition from unbalanced development to balanced development, and balanced development (Ruan, 2013). In June 2002, the MOE proposed that "the development of basic education is a responsibility that all levels of government should meet to the full" as well as "the active promotion of the balanced development of schools in the compulsory education stage," and from this, compulsory education gradually began to shift towards balanced development (MOE, 2002). In September 2003, the first National Rural Education Work Conference was held since the founding of PRC. At the same time, the State Council proposed the following development targets: "By 2007, the popularization of nine-year compulsory education in western regions (hereinafter referred to as 'Pujiu') will reach a population coverage rate of more than 85%; the illiteracy rate of young and middle-aged adults will fall below 5%" (The State Council of PRC, 2003). In May 2005, the MOE made the request of "further shifting the focus of compulsory education on to the success of every school and paying attention to the healthy growth of every child; effectively curbing the trend of a widening gap in education between urban and rural areas, between regions and between schools; actively improving the conditions for running rural schools and weak urban schools, and gradually realizing the balanced development of compulsory education" (MOE, 2005). *The Compulsory Education Law* revised in 2006 stipulates that "the State Council and local People's governments at or above the county level should rationally allocate educational resources and promote the balanced development of compulsory education." In January 2010, the MOE issued a document requesting that local education administrative departments at all levels consider compulsory education as the top priority of education reform and development, and promote balanced development as an important task of compulsory education reform and development (MOE, 2010b). In the same year, *The National Medium-and-Long-Term Education Reform and Development Plan Outline (2010–2020)* (hereinafter referred to as *The Plan Outline*) regarded "balanced development" as a "strategic task of compulsory education." In 2011, all provinces (including autonomous regions and municipalities) passed the national "Pujiu" inspection, and have comprehensively popularized urban and rural free compulsory education within 25 years, which fundamentally reached the target of "having a school to go to" for school-age children and adolescents, laying a solid foundation for improving the qualities of all citizens. However, there are still significant gaps in school running and education quality between different regions, between urban and rural areas, and between schools; and the contradiction of the growing demands for high-quality education and the insufficient supply still exists. In this context, further promoting the balanced development of compulsory education, focusing on improving the level of school running in rural schools and weak schools, and comprehensively improving the quality of compulsory education have more practical significance (The State Council of PRC, 2012). In November 2012, the 18th National Congress of CPC put forward the development strategy of "making efforts to deliver education that is satisfactory to the people" and "achieving equal development of the nine-year compulsory education" (Hu, 2012). Facing the new requirements of the building of a moderately prosperous society in all respects, and the deepening development of new urbanization on "comprehensively improving school running conditions and the quality of education in compulsory education," as well as the reform of the household registration institution, the adjustment of family planning policies, and the huge challenges for the planning and layout of urban and rural compulsory education schools brought about by population and student mobility, in 2016, the state brought the balanced development of compulsory education to a new stage of "coordinating the promotion of unified reform and development of urban and rural compulsory education in the county," and called for "accelerating the uniformity of standards for the establishment of urban and rural compulsory education schools in the county, unified standards for teacher authorization, unified quotas for public funds per student, unified standards for basic equipment allocation, and the 'two exemptions and one subsidy' policies covering urban and rural areas" (The State Council of PRC, 2016a).

Reforming the Guarantee Mechanism for Rural Compulsory Education Funding. Looking back on the progress of the balanced development of compulsory education, in terms of institutional reform and policy adjustment, it was first manifested in a fundamental change in the understanding of the nature and role of compulsory education, recognizing that "compulsory education is the top priority in education work, a public welfare undertaking that the state must guarantee, a fundamental public undertaking that must be prioritized for development, and a fundamental undertaking for poverty alleviation" (The State Council of PRC, 2016b). This guaranteed the public welfare status of compulsory education and incorporates compulsory education into the national fundamental undertakings' development strategy. Secondly, it also established and optimized a rural compulsory education funding guarantee mechanism, and increased investment in education. In 2003, the National Conference on Rural Education established the rural compulsory education management institution, which was to be "under the leadership of the State Council, with local governments in charge, implementing management by level, and with the county as the main body." It further clarified the responsibility of governments at all levels to ensure financial input for rural compulsory education. Governments at all levels were required to further increase investment, and new education funds were to be used mainly in rural areas. "In the reform of taxes and fees[25], the investment in rural compulsory education after reform is guaranteed to be not lower than pre-reform levels and efforts must be made to improve the investment" (The State Council of PRC, 2003). In May 2005, the MOE requested "the establishment and optimization of a public finance institution that guarantees the balanced development of compulsory education" and "prioritizing the funds needed to promote the balanced development of compulsory education. It asked for effective implementation of the 'three growths' of education funds[26] and newly added education funds were to be mainly used for rural areas. In terms of funding, it established a policy leaning towards reforming weak schools, and required that additional urban education fees should primarily be used for the transformation of weak schools" (MOE, 2005). The State Council further requested that the reform of the rural compulsory education funding guarantee mechanism be further deepened. "In accordance with the basic principles of 'clarifying responsibility at all levels, central and local governments sharing responsibility, increasing financial input, improving the level of protection, and step-by-step implementation,' gradually rural compulsory education should be comprehensively incorporated into the scope of public financial security, and a rural compulsory education funding guarantee mechanism where central and local governments shoulder different types of spending and proportionally share responsibilities will be established" (The State Council of PRC, 2005). *The Compulsory Education Law*, revised in 2006, further clarified that "the state fully includes compulsory education into the scope of financial security" and incorporated "the three growths" of education funding into the scope of the rule of law. Thirdly, the "Two Exemptions and One Supplement"[27] policy was gradually enacted to expand policy coverage. The "Two Exemptions and One Supplement" policy began in 2001 when the state proposed to gradually implement the government's free textbook institution for rural primary and middle school students in poverty-stricken areas (The General Office of the State Council of PRC, 2001).

In 2003, the State Council proposed that "by 2007, all students in the national rural compulsory education stage with economic difficulties in the family will be able to benefit from the 'Two Exemptions and One Supplement' policy" (The State Council of PRC, 2003). In December 2005, the State Council requested that "all tuition and miscellaneous fees for rural compulsory education students should be exempted, textbooks should be provided free of charge for students whose families are living in poverty and boarding students' living expenses should be subsidized" (The State Council of PRC, 2005). Tuition and miscellaneous fee exemption covered all rural compulsory education students. In October 2006, the Central Committee of CPC requested: "Implementing of the rural compulsory education funding guarantee mechanism, and eliminating compulsory education teaching and miscellaneous fees in rural areas and gradually in urban areas, and fully implementing of the policies of free provision of textbooks for students with financial difficulties in the family and subsidized living expenses for boarding students, guaranteeing that the children of migrant workers would be able to receive compulsory education" (The Central Committee of CPC, 2006). On the basis of the full implementation of the reform of the rural compulsory education funding guarantee mechanism, the "Two Exemptions and One Supplement" policy was expanded from rural areas to cities. From the fall semester of 2008, all tuition and miscellaneous fees for students in public compulsory education schools in urban areas were exempted (The State Council of PRC, 2008). At the Fifth Session of the 12th National People's Congress in 2017, Premier Li Keqiang put forward: "Unify the policy of 'Two Exemptions and One Supplement' for urban and rural compulsory education students" (Li, 2017a). So far, the "Two Exemptions and One Supplement" policy has achieved "three uniformity." First, the policy of "Two Exemptions and One Supplement" for urban and rural compulsory education are uniform, changing from the original policy where rural students benefitted from the "Two Exemptions and One Supplement" policy while urban students were only exempt from tuition and miscellaneous fees. Free textbooks are provided for students with low-income families, and living expenses are subsidized for boarding students whose families face economic difficulties to the implementation of the "Two Exemptions and One Supplement" policy for all urban and rural compulsory education students. Second, quotas for public funds for urban and rural compulsory education schools are uniform and based on average student numbers. Third, central and local funding sharing mechanisms are uniform, changing the original policy whereby the central government implemented different funding mechanisms for urban and rural areas, that is, the central government was only responsible for the funding of compulsory education in rural areas and funding for compulsory education in cities was the responsibility of local governments and the central government awarded appropriate subsidies, which now have been adjusted to a uniform proportional responsibility mechanism for urban and rural compulsory education where the central and local government shoulder different types of spending.

V. Deepening the Comprehensive Reform in the Field of Education and Moving towards the Participation of Multiple Parties in Education Management (2010–Present)

With the leap-forward development of the economy, China exceeded Japan in terms of GDP in 2010 and became the second largest economy in the world. Although China's per capita GDP figures are still not desirable, China has been enlisted in the ranks of world powers with strong development momentum, a fact that cannot be disputed. In November 2012, the 18th National Congress of CPC proposed the goal of building a moderately prosperous society in all respects and deepening reform and opening-up in an all-round way, establishing the general strategy of "The Overall Plan for Development in Five Areas"[28] to construct socialism with Chinese characteristics and the realization of socialist modernization and the great rejuvenation of the Chinese nation. In November 2013, the Third Plenary Session of the 18th CPC Central Committee called for comprehensive deepening of reforms, improvement and development of the socialist institution with Chinese characteristics, and promotion of the modernization of the national governance institution and governance capacity (Hu, 2012). In October 2014, the Fourth Plenary Session of the 18th CPC Central Committee put forward the general goal of comprehensively promoting the rule of law by "establishing a legal institution for Chinese socialism and building a law-based socialist country." In December 2014, Jinping Xi put forward the strategic vision of "completely building a moderately prosperous society in all respects, comprehensively deepening reforms, comprehensively promoting law-based governance, and comprehensively enforcing strict Party self-governance" (2014, 2015, 2016). In October 2015, the Fifth Plenary Session of the 18th CPC Central Committee established the new concept of pursuing innovative, coordinated, green, and open development and having its fruits shared by everyone (The Central Committee of CPC, 2015). In October 2017, the statement "socialism with Chinese characteristics has entered a new era" was made at the 19th National Congress of CPC, expounding the thoughts and theories of socialism with Chinese characteristics in the new era, and clearly describing the "two one-hundred year" timetable and road map for comprehensively building a modernized, powerful socialist country (Xi, 2017b).

New Problems, New Goals, and New Missions in the Reform and Development of Education in the New Era. After forty years of reform and development, the main challenge in Chinese society has been transformed from the "contradiction between the ever-growing material and cultural needs of the people and the backwardness of social production" (The Central Committee of CPC, 1981) at the beginning of reform and opening-up to "contradiction between unbalanced and inadequate development on the one side and the people's ever-growing desire for a better life on the other" in the new era of socialism with Chinese characteristics (Xi, 2017b), manifesting that the people's needs for better lives are becoming increasingly widespread, where not only are there higher demands in terms of material goods and cultural lifestyles, but also for concepts such as democracy, the rule of law, fairness, justice, security, and the environment. In the field of education, this new contradiction is manifested in the contradiction between the people's demand for quality education and the unbalanced, inadequate development of education. Hence, we witnessed the changes from the beginning of reform and opening-up when *The Decision* proposed "enacting nine-year compulsory education in a step-by-step manner" and the whole country focused on promoting the popularization of nine-year compulsory education to the focus on promoting the balanced development of compulsory education. The public's expectation of every child "having a school to attend" has been realized in general. However, with the development of society, the public's demand for education has evolved into "attend a good school," which includes both the desire for quality education and the desire for education selection that can meet their individualized development. There is also a yearning for a fair and equitable education order and modernized education. The modernization of education is part of a gradual development process. *The Planning Outline* proposed that the phased goal of "basically achieving education modernization by 2020" is "basically realizing the modernization of education, basically forming a learning society, and turning China into a powerhouse in terms of human resources." To this end, we must "adhere to the priority of education development," "work hard to satisfy the people's expectations for education," guarantee "the access to childcare and education" (Xi, 2017b), and develop modern education with Chinese characteristics at a world-class level, "granting every child the opportunity to become a talent" (Hu, 2012).

Reform of the Examination Admissions Institution. Clearly, the reform of the examination enrollment institution is considered to be an important issue in "deepening the comprehensive reform of the field of education." The examination enrollment institution since reform and opening-up has been considered to be "in general accordance with the national conditions, and recognized by society as authoritative and fair," but at the same time, it has also produced phenomena and problems that aroused strong public reaction, including the belief that only scores matter which affects the overall development of students, the heavy burden as a result of strong impacts of the College Entrance Examination on the rest of a student's life, gaps between urban and rural areas in terms of enrollment opportunities, increasing school selection in primary and secondary schools, as well as cheating and violation of enrollment rules (The State Council of PRC, 2014). In 2010, *The Planning Outline* proposed "promoting the reform of the examination enrollment institution," "exploring ways to separate enrollment and examinations so that government implement macro management, professional institutions implement examinations, schools enroll students according to law, provide several opportunities for students to make selections and hence gradually establish an examination admission institution with classified examinations, comprehensive evaluations, and enrollment by multiple dimensions." This reform proposal was included in the scope of *Deepening Comprehensive Reform in the Field of Education* by the Central Committee of CPC, requiring "the exploration of an operation mechanism that promotes the relative separation of enrollment and examinations, provides multiple chances for student to sit examinations, implement independent enrollment by schools according to law, implement examinations by professional examination institutions, guarantee government's macroeconomic management, and society takes part in inspection" (The Central Committee of CPC, 2013). In 2014, the State Council issued a document requesting pilot reforms of the enrollment institution, and the reforms of the enrollment institution were comprehensively promoted in 2017. "By 2020, we will have basically established a modern education examination enrollment institution with Chinese characteristics, built an examination enrollment model with classification examination, comprehensive evaluation, and multiple-dimension admission to improve institutional mechanisms that promote equity, scientific selection of talents and effective supervision" (The State Council of PRC, 2014).

In the new round of the college entrance examination reform experiments, according to the national unified deployment, the 2014 new College Entrance Examination enrollment reform was piloted in Shanghai and Zhejiang. During this piloting process, Shanghai and Zhejiang improved high school–level examinations and standardized the comprehensive quality evaluation of high school students. In 2017, in order to respond to the first phase of the new comprehensive reform of the college entrance examination, the two local governments deepened the reform of college entrance examination content, focusing on the candidates' abilities to think independently and apply the knowledge they had learned to analyze and solve problems. Both actively experimented a multidimensional admission mechanism based on College Entrance Examination scores and performances in the Academic Test for the Senior High School Students with reference to comprehensive quality evaluation, increasing two-way selection opportunities of colleges and universities and students. As a result, the pilot work of the new college entrance examination reform has been smoothly implemented. According to the relevant requirements of MOE, the four provinces and municipalities of Beijing, Tianjin, Shandong, and Hainan were the second batch of comprehensive reform pilot areas for the College Entrance Examination, which entered the comprehensive college entrance examination reform implementation phase in the fall semester of 2017 (MOE, 2017b).

Modernization of the Education Governance Institution. It requires strong institutions to guarantee the development of modern education with Chinese characteristics to a world-leading level. In order to implement the task of "deepening comprehensive reforms in the field of education" put forward by the 18th National Congress of CPC (Hu, 2012), in 2013, the CPC Central Committee requested "in-depth promotion of the separation of management and evaluation, expansion of provincial government education coordinating powers and school running autonomy for schools, improvement of the internal governance structure of schools; strengthening of national education supervision, entrusting social institutions to carry out education evaluation and monitoring; improving government subsidies, government purchase services, student loans, fund incentives, donation incentives institutions, etc., and encouraging the engagement of social forces in the establishment of education institutions" (The Central Committee of CPC, 2013).

In May 2015, the MOE required that: "The new model of public education governance should be established by 2020, in which education run by the government by the rule of law, schools are governed by themselves according to the law, and all sectors of society participate in and supervise education according to law, providing an important institutional guarantee for the general realization of education modernization" (MOE, 2015b). In September 2017, *The Opinions on Deepening the Reform of Education Institutions and Mechanisms* proposed that the main goal of deepening the reform of the education institutions and mechanisms was: "By 2020, the fundamental institutional institution of education will have been generally established, with education institutions and mechanisms are full of vitality, efficiency and openness which is conducive to scientific development. The issues and difficulties in education that people are concerned about will have had some solutions, and the model of education governance, in which government implements macro-management by the rule of law, schools run themselves in accordance with the law, society get engaged in an orderly way and all the forces work collaboratively to develop education, has be optimized with an aim to provide institutional support for the development of world-class modern education with Chinese characteristics."

Compared with the traditional education management institution characterized by regulation, the modernization of the education governance institution, which is characterized by the separation of management; operation and evaluation; and the combination of delegating power, improving regulation, and upgrading services, possesses a strict institutional logic (Fan, 2017a). The core of the modernization of the education governance institution is rationalizing the relationship of the elements of the education institution, energizing every element, and thus energizing the entire education institution. Specifically, it is to straighten out the relationships of the government, schools, and society, and the various relationships within each of the three.

As for the relationships between the government and society, and the government and schools, we should streamline administration and delegate power, transform government functions, and promote the combination of delegating power, improving regulation, and upgrading services.

In 2015, relevant documents of the State Council put forward the governance principles of "streamlining administration and delegating power, supervising according to law, and promoting justice and transparency, consistency of rights and responsibilities, and co-governance with society" to transform government functions (The State Council of PRC, 2015a). In the same year, the Fifth Plenary Session of the 18th CPC Central Committee proposed to deepen the reform of the administrative management institution, further transformed government functions, continued to streamline administration and delegate power, promoted the combination of delegating power and improving regulation, and upgraded services, improved government efficiency, and energized market and social creativity with an aim to build and develop a new governance institution (The Central Committee of CPC, 2015). "The transformation of government functions is a profound change from concept to institution, and it is a self-reform with a sharp knife cutting inwards."

"By promoting the separation of government and enterprises, the separation of government and capital, the separation of government and public sector, and the separation of government and market agencies, matters that should not be managed by the government have been handed over to the market or society, and matters that should be managed by the government are managed more effectively. The focus of government has been turned towards strengthening macro-regulation, strict market supervision, social management and public services to achieve standardized and orderly, open and transparent, convenient and efficient government management, to become a government that the people are satisfied with" (Li, 2017b).

During the process of advancing the modernization of the national governance institution and governance capacity, the reform of Party and state institutions is deepened on the basis of transforming local government functions and institutional reforms (The Central Committee of CPC, 2018). In the field of education, in 2017 *The Opinions on Deepening the Reform of Institutional Mechanisms in Education* put forward "persisting with the combination of delegating power, improving regulation, and upgrading services," "deepening the streamlining of administration and delegating of power, and promoting the decentralization and regulation, upgrading the service reform, and resolutely delegate the powers that should be delegated, properly managing matters that should be managed, and strengthening oversight over delegated matters when they are being handled and after they have been handled to build new relationships of the government, schools, and society."

In the process of education management, through the method of list management, the government manages matters that it should manage and schools are granted the educational powers that they should be entitled to. By the construction of the education standards institution, the government leads the development of education, promotes schools in running themselves according to law, and strengthens oversight over delegated matters when they are being handled and after they have been handled in the development of education. The powers in education that should be delegated to society must be delegated to society. Social institutions are guided and cultivated to participate in education, and professional education services provided by social organizations are purchased, which serves the development of schools, teachers, and students. As for schools, they run themselves according to law (Fan, 2017b), and the operation of school power is ensured through scientific and rational institutions and mechanisms. It is necessary to regulate the internal power relations of schools through school charters, and at the same time improve the internal governance structure of schools, including all teachers, students, parents, and society (community) resources in schooling, serve the independent development of schools, and at the same time form a combination of effective supervision forces.

In the field of higher education, through the construction of a modern university institution, the reforms of university charters and the internal governance structure are promoted so that universities have greater autonomy in running themselves, academic powers of academic organizations such as academic committees are exerted, evaluation mechanisms of teachers' professional titles are improved, salary distribution institutions are improved, the modern university institutions are optimized, and the enthusiasm and initiative of a vast number of teaching and research staff to teach and educate people are promoted and their enterprising spirit are stimulated (MOE et al., 2017b). At the same time, the construction of a number of world-class universities and first-class disciplines are speeded up, "deepening the comprehensive reform of colleges and universities, accelerating the construction of a modernized university institution with Chinese characteristics, focusing on breaking down institution and mechanism barriers and accelerating the establishment of institutions and mechanisms that are dynamic, efficient, open, and conducive to the scientific development of universities" (The State Council of PRC, 2015b). Social organizations participate in education, both in the running of schools and in educational services and evaluation. As for the former, *The Promotion of the Private Education Law of PRC*, which was revised in November 2016, established a classified management institution for private education (The Standing Committee of the National People's Congress of PRC, 2016; The State Council of PRC, 2016a). Relevant policies that followed have further established and improved the classified management and classified registration mechanisms of private schools as well as supervision and management mechanisms, providing legal protection and policy support for the respective development of for-profit and nonprofit private schools. As for the latter, the "separation of management, operation and evaluation" is not limited to social institutions participating in the "evaluation" of education. The activities and actions of social organizations "participating in education" also include participation in school establishment, participation in school management, participation in school education activities, and participation in school evaluation (Du & Fan, 2017). At present, educational social organizations cannot meet the needs of educational development in terms of quantity or qualifications. Hence, on the one hand, it is necessary to vigorously cultivate social organizations and enhance their qualifications and capabilities for participating in education, and on the other hand, through the establishment of rules and regulations, the mechanisms and procedures for social organizations participating in education should be standardized.

SECTION 2 THE VALUES AND STRATEGIES OF EDUCATION INSTITUTIONS REFORM

After forty years of reform and development, both the scale and quality of China's education have been greatly improved. The net enrollment rate of primary schools, the gross enrollment rate of middle schools, and the gross enrollment rate of higher education institutions have increased steadily. In terms of the average years of schooling and the completion rate of tertiary education, the gaps between that of China and that of developed countries have been narrowed. Preschool education is becoming more standardized and its scale is developing continuously, compulsory education is gradually moving towards quality and balanced development, general high school education is displaying a diversified and characteristic development trend, the modern vocational education institution is constantly improving, and the speed of bringing out the full potential for the development of higher education is accelerating with the development of first-class universities and disciplines of the world. The amount of public education spending as a proportion of GDP has always remained above 4%, and it has gradually approached the average level of G20 countries. In other words, "the overall level of education development has entered the upper and middle ranks of the world" (The State Council of PRC, 2017). Looking back on forty years of development of reform and opening-up in education, it is important to summarize and refine the valuable experiences and points of wisdom gained in the process.

I. Persisting with Education Serving the People

"Institutional ethics" are the ethical pursuits, moral principles, and value judgments inherent in institutions. In the process of education modernization, answering the question of whom education serves in the perspective of institutional ethics is unavoidable. The first National Education Conference, held shortly after the founding of PRC in 1949, established the education construction policy of "education serves workers and peasants, and serves production and construction." At the beginning of reform and opening-up, the education policy of "serving proletarian politics" was changed to "serving socialist construction." In February 1993, *The China Education Reform and Development Outline* proposed "promoting equity as the basic education policy of the country" and believed that "educational equity is an important foundation for social equity," "Government should take the primary responsibility for educational equity, and the whole of society must jointly promote educational equity." In June 1999, the Third National Education Conference put forward the following: "We must fully implement the Party's education policy, adhere to the principle of education serving socialist modernization, serving the people, with the fundamental purpose of adhering to the integration of education and social practice in order to improve the quality of the people, with a focus on cultivating students' innovative spirit and practical abilities, and striving to nurture capable young people well-prepared to join the socialist cause with lofty ideals, integrity, knowledge, a strong sense of discipline, and all-round moral, intellectual, physical and aesthetic grounding with a hard-working spirit" (Jiang, 1999). For the first time, the principle of "serving the people" was included in education policy. In 2002, the report of the 16th National Congress of CPC and *The Planning Outline* in July 2010 defined the education guideline as "we should fully implement the Party's education policy, insisting that education serves socialist modernization construction, serves the people, and should be integrated with production and social practice, take promoting the rounded development of people as the fundamental task of education, and train participants of and successors to the socialist cause who develop morally, intellectually, physically and aesthetically," which once again reaffirmed the requirement of "education serving the people." In November 2012, the report of the 18th National Congress of CPC put forward the following: "Putting people first as the core requirement for thoroughly applying the Scientific Outlook on Development, we must always make realizing, safeguarding and developing the fundamental interests of the overwhelming majority of the people the starting point and goal of all the work of the Party and country. We must respect the people's creativity, protect their rights and interests, and make continued progress in enabling the people to share in the fruits of development and in promoting well-rounded development of the person," "ensure that education serves socialist modernization and the people," and "work hard to run education to the satisfaction of the people."

In 2017, the report of the 19th National Congress of CPC put forward: "Being committed to a people-centered approach," observe "the Party's fundamental purpose of wholeheartedly serving the people," "regard as our goal the people's aspirations to live a better life," "always put the people's interests above all else, see that the gains of reform and development benefit all our people in a fair way, and strive to achieve shared prosperity for everyone," and "accelerate the modernization of education and providing education that the people are satisfied with." At the first meeting of the 13th National People's Congress held in 2018, Premier Li Keqiang said: "We must accelerate the modernization of education, and provide education to the people's satisfaction so that everyone has equal opportunities to change their own destiny through education and make their own dreams come true." In forty years of reform and development, from the universal coverage of nine-year compulsory education to the implementation of *The Guideline for Popularizing High School Education* (MOE et al., 2017a), from focusing on solving kindergarten admission difficulties to compulsory education admission according to the proximity of students' residency to the schools, from the balanced development of compulsory education to promoting the integrated development of urban and rural compulsory education, from the implementation of free compulsory education to improving the student financial aid institution, from protecting the safety, health, and education rights of left-behind children in rural areas (The State Council of PRC, 2016c) to "safeguarding the rights of persons with disabilities to have equal access to education" (The State Council of PRC, 1994b), focusing on formulating targeted policies for the development of education with emphasis on registered impoverished populations in areas such as counties that are key targets in the state poverty alleviation development program and counties in contiguous poor areas (hereinafter referred to as poverty-stricken counties) (MOE et al., 2016a), the aim of "striving to make every child have access to equal and quality education" is gradually realized.

II. Continuing to Deepen Education Reform

Looking back over the forty-year development process, Chinese society has advanced in twists and turns. The policy of reform and opening-up established by the Third Plenary Session of the 11th Central Committee of CPC has become the main theme of an era. At the beginning of reform and opening-up, Xiaoping Deng proposed that "development is of paramount importance" (Deng,

1992), China "must achieve development, and must adhere to openness and reform" (Deng, 1987), "reform is a road China must take to develop productive forces" (Deng, 1985), and adhering to reform and opening-up is the hope for solving China's problems (Deng, 1989). As of now, reform and opening-up has entered a stage of comprehensively deepening reform, and the pattern of interests has solidified. "The overall goal of comprehensively deepening reform is improving and developing the institution of socialism with Chinese characteristics and promoting the modernization of the national governance institution and governance capacity." The aim of comprehensively deepening reform is "to further free our minds, further release and develop productive forces, and further unleash and boost the vigor of our society, and to work with resolve to remove institutional barriers in all areas"; in terms of reform methods and strategies, "there is more emphasis on implementing systematic, integrated and coordinated reform" (The Central Committee of CPC, 2013). As for education reform, it experienced different stages from *The Decision* issued in 1985, which focused on straightening out the relationships between the central government and the local government, and the government and schools, to the restoration of the college entrance examination institution, reform of the basic education curriculum, establishment of a modern university institution, a series of individual or regional reforms, and continuous promotion of the development of education.

Since 2012, education reform has entered the deep-water area and tackling period, and entered a new stage of "deepening the comprehensive reform of the education field" (Hu, 2012). Education reform involves a wider scope and a higher degree of relevance, and it is more difficult to solve deep-seated problems. A range of problems involves multiple departmental responsibilities, multiple policy packages, and interests of multiple parties. It is difficult to improve the effectiveness of the institution by relying on original single reforms or partial breakthroughs. On the basis of continuing to deeply implement national education institution pilot reforms, it is necessary to understand reforms and strengthen the top-level design of reforms using the perspectives of systematic thinking, overall awareness, and universal connection. We need to adhere to being problem-oriented and goal-oriented; undertake integrated planning; take a holistic approach; reform the institutional mechanisms, laws, and regulations that do not meet the requirements of the reality; shift from traditional education management to education governance; promote the separation of management, operation, and evaluation; build new relationships between the government, schools, and society; coordinate the promotion of the reform of education methods, school-running methods, management institutions, and guarantee mechanisms; and continuously promote the modernization of the education governance institution and governance capacity.

III. Continuing to Open Up Education

Reform and opening-up are the twin engines of China's modernization development. Reform means continuously releasing internal momentum with guidance from the government. Opening-up means being continuously engaged in globalization and gaining momentum from the outside. The fundamental reason for the long-term stagnation and backwardness of old China was that it was closed-off to the outside world. The modernization process has resulted in an "open world." Only when it interacts with other countries and integrates into the globalization process can any country enter the fast lane of modernization.

China's opening-up to the outside world began in the early 1980s with the urgent needs of the four modernizations of introducing and using foreign talents and capital (Deng, 1983); gradually opening-up coastal port cities, cities along the Yangtze River, provincial capitals bordering coastal areas, and provincial capitals of inland areas by opening the Shenzhen, Zhuhai, Shantou, and Xiamen Special Economic Zones; forming a comprehensive, multilevel, wide-ranging opening-up institution which includes special economic zones, coastal open cities, coastal open areas, open port cities along the Yangtze River, open towns along the bordering regions, and open cities of the provincial capitals inland. Upon entering the new era, as Jinping Xi said in September 2015 when he met with former US President Barack Obama, "reform and opening-up is China's fundamental national policy and the fundamental driving force of China's development in the future." "The door of China's opening-up will never be closed" (Huo et al., 2018). In the field of education, young and middle-aged scholars have been sent to study abroad, foreign experts have been invited to come to China to give lectures, publicly funded students have been going to study abroad, individuals have been allowed to study abroad at their own expenses, international students have been allowed to come to study in China, Sino-foreign cooperative education institutions and programs have been developed, and international exchanges have been continuously enriched. In 2002, China joined the World Trade Organization, adjusted its foreign education service trade strategy in a timely manner, further optimized the institutions of the education opening-up, and increased its openness in education. In 2003, *The Regulations on Sino-foreign Cooperation in School Running* was promulgated to promote the healthy development of Sino-foreign cooperative education. Since 2006, *The Program for Discipline Innovation and Introduction of Talents in Higher Education Institutions* (*Plan 111*[29]) has been implemented to speed up the construction of world-class universities among China's higher education institutions. Since 2007, "National Post-graduate scholarship for studying abroad for the Construction of High-Level Universities" has been implemented, and first-class graduate students have been selected to study under the supervision of world first-class professors, to study at world first-class disciplines, or top world first-class universities. In 2008, "The Thousand Talents Program" (The General Office of the Central Committee of CPC, 2008) was implemented to introduce a number of strategic scientists, leading talents in technological innovation and entrepreneurship and young talents who could make breakthroughs in key technologies, develop high-tech industries, and lead the development of emerging disciplines. In 2010, the "Study in China Program" was initiated to establish an institution for managing the service and work for onshore international students in China that is compatible with China's international status and scale and level of education, with a view to "making China the largest destination country in Asia for international students by 2020" (MOE, 2010a). Since then, the internationalization of education in China began to shift from an input type to an output type, and education opening-up entered a new era of accelerating the pace of "going out." In April 2016, the General Office of the CPC Central Committee and the General Office of the State Council issued *The Several Opinions on Properly Carrying Out the Opening-up of Education in the New Era*, to improve the working mechanism of "the selection, dispatch, management, return, and use of Chinese students having overseas studies"; to accelerate the development of international education to improve its quality; to reform and improve relevant institutions and mechanisms such as those for access, review, evaluation and certification, and exit, and improve school-running for international education; to introduce world-class universities and disciplines with their own character with an aim to enhance China's educational strength and innovation abilities; to enrich personal and cultural exchanges with other countries, properly telling the Chinese story, and properly spreading the voice of China; and to improve the openness of China's education to the outside world. "China will strengthen educational exchanges with countries around the world, expand opening-up in education, and actively support the development of education in developing countries" (Xinhua News Agency, 2013); strengthen practical cooperation with major countries, neighboring countries, developing countries, and multilateral institutions; promote the "Belt and Road" Education Action Plan (MOE, 2016b); actively participate in global education governance; improve the level of education openness and management; and promote educational win-win cooperation. Chinese education is contributing to "the collaboratively building of a community with a shared future for mankind" (Xi, 2017a) in its own unique way.

IV. Persisting with Education as a Priority of Development

Since the introduction of reform and opening-up, the Party and the state have always insisted on placing education in the strategic position of the priority for development, but its connotations and expressions in different historical periods were different. As early as the beginning of reform and opening-up, Xiaoping

Deng proposed that the fundamental task of socialism was developing productive forces, science and technology were the primary productive forces, the key to modernization was science and technology, and the development of science and technology relied on education, which made it the national strategy to develop the economy based upon the development of science, technology, and education[30]. In 1992, at the 12th National Congress of CPC, it was proposed that "education must be placed in the strategic position of priority development, and efforts should be made to improve the intellectual, moral, and scientific and cultural standards of the whole nation," "which is vital for realizing China's modernization" (Jiang, 1992). In May 1995, the Central Committee of CPC issued *the Decision on Accelerating the Progress of Science and Technology*, and for the first time put forward the "Implementation of the Strategy of Rejuvenating the Country through Science and Education" and "insisting on education as the foundation, putting science, technology and education in an important position in economic and social development, increasing the country's strength in science and technology as well as its ability to transform science and technology into real productive forces, improving the scientific and technological cultural quality of the whole nation, and moving economic construction on to the track of building on the base of scientific and technological progress and the quality of workforce in order to accelerate the realization of the country's prosperity." In October 2006, the *Decision of the Central Committee of CPC on Several Major Issues Concerning the Construction of a Harmonious Socialist Society* stated: "We must be committed to prioritizing the development of education and promoting education equity. We must fully implement the Party's principles on education, vigorously implement the strategy for invigorating China through science and education and the strategy on developing a quality workforce. We must fully implement quality education, deepen education reform, improve education quality, build a modern national education institution and lifelong education institution, and ensure that people have opportunities to access good education." Thus, the strategic role of prioritizing the development of education was transformed from promoting economic development into promoting education equity. The 18th National Congress of CPC put education at the forefront of improving people's lives and strengthening social construction. "Education is the cornerstone of national rejuvenation and social progress. We must persist in giving priority to education development, fully implement the Party's principles on education, and persist in education serving socialist modernization and serving the people" (Hu, 2012), integrating education serving socialist modernization and serving the people. In September 2013, at an event commemorating the first anniversary of the UN's Global Education First Initiative, Jinping Xi pointed out that: "China will firmly implement the strategy of for invigorating China through science and education, always put education in a strategic position of priority development, continually expand investment, and strive to develop education for all and lifelong education, building a learning society, striving to give every child the access to education, and striving to make 1.3 billion people enjoy a better and more equal education and acquire the ability to develop themselves, contribute to society, and benefit the people" (Xinhua News Agency, 2013). At the Ninth National Congress of the CPC, the goal of building a strong education country was established and used as a "foundational project for the great rejuvenation of the Chinese nation." To this end, it was stated: "We must give priority to education, deepen education reform, accelerate education modernization, and provide education that satisfies the people" (Xi, 2017b). With the aim to build a strong education country and realize the great rejuvenation of the Chinese nation, it included new connotations to the concept of "prioritizing the development of education." The fundamental measure for prioritizing the development of education was to increase investment in education. In 1993, *The China Education Reform and Development Plan* proposed the strategic goal of "raising government budgetary spending on education to 4% of GDP by 2012." In 1995, the *People's Republic of China Education Law* proposed the "Three Growths" of government spending on education (the growth of financial appropriations to education by People's governments at all levels should be higher than the growth of fiscal recurrent income, and average spending on education per student should be gradually increased to ensure the gradual increase in salaries of teachers and per capita public expenditure of students, justifying the increase in government spending on education investment with a legal basis). From 1998, the proportion of the central government's budgetary spending on education increased by one percentage point every year for three consecutive years, and central level government recurrent expenditure on education increased by 48.9 billion yuan in five years, highlighting the central government's determination, will, and wisdom in giving priority to the development of education. In 2006, the *Decision of the Central Committee of CPC on Several Major Issues Concerning the Construction of a Harmonious Socialist Society* proposed "ensuring that the growth of government budgetary spending on education is significantly higher than the growth rate of fiscal recurrent income, and gradually making government budgetary spending on education to 4% of GDP," 4% being the only numerical indicator in *The Decision*. In 2010, the Central Committee of CPC and the State Council printed and distributed the *National Medium-and Long-Term Education Reform and Development Plan Outline (2010–2020)*, which once again emphasized "raising government budgetary spending on education to 4% of GDP by 2012." In 2011, the State Council required people's governments at all levels to further optimize the structure of fiscal expenditures, reduce general expenditures, increase financial resources to focus on education, increase the proportion of government budgetary spending on education in the total public fiscal expenditure, increase the budget for education funding, ensure that the growth rate of government budgetary spending on education is significantly higher than the growth rate of fiscal recurrent income, and strictly implement the statutory growth requirements for education funding (The State Council of PRC, 2011). In 2012, the state's fiscal education funds exceeded 2 trillion yuan, which took 20 years for this figure to account for 4% of GDP. The road of reform and development is not smooth. In 2013, *The Decision of the Central Committee of CPC on Comprehensively Deepening the Reform of Some Major Issues* required deepening the reform of the fiscal and taxation institution, improving the budget management institution, and "clearing and standardizing major expenditures connected with the increases in fiscal revenue expenditure or linked to the increases of GDP." As a result, *the Decision* disconnected the links and connections in general. Despite the requirement, the State Council's *13th Five-Year Plan for National Education Development* in 2017 still proposed "insisting on ensuring that the priority of fiscal expenditure at all levels of the People's government's is in the field of education, and ensuring that the requirement of national government budgetary spending on education generally accounting for no less than 4% of GDP are met." The change from "generally not linked" to "generally not lower than" reflects the country's determination in implementing the strategy of prioritizing the development of education. From 2012 to 2016, national fiscal education expenditures accounted for 4.28%, 4.30%, 4.15%, 4.26%, and 4.22%, respectively, of GDP (The MOE, 2013, 2014, 2015a, 2016a, 2017a). The strategy of prioritizing education development has been guaranteed, and public education funding has been on a sustainable and stable growth path.

SECTION 3 THE ADJUSTMENTS AND INNOVATIONS OF THE EDUCATION INSTITUTIONS

Reforms are to adjust the relations of production and the rebalancing of interests. If we say that the first 30 years of reform and opening-up was focusing on promoting economic construction and accumulating large amounts of social wealth in accordance with the principle of "efficiency first," then the challenge facing further reform is to reach the rebalancing of interests, which is redistribution of social wealth based on the principle of "equity" as a means of further promoting the harmonious and sustainable development of the whole of society. Therefore, comprehensively deepening reforms is the need to "resolutely break all outdated thoughts, concepts, institutions and mechanisms, and break through the fence of vested interests" (Xi, 2017b).

For the Chinese society, the forty years of reform and opening-up has been the process of moving from restoring and rebuilding social order to breaking through institutional barriers to stimulate social vitality, from planned economy to market economy, and from uniform, and centralized management to the construction of a governance institution with the participation of multiple stakeholders. The conflicts, games, and compromises among a range of stakeholders ran through these processes. Changes and innovations in the education institutions inevitably involved a series of complex relationships between centralization and decentralization, the planned economy and market economy, government and society, government and schools, schools and society, and so on. The process of educational reform was to seek balance and harmony in the relations of all parties so that their passion and vitality were stimulated while a rational order was maintained.

I. Adjusting the Relationship between Governments at the Central Level and Local Level

Since the beginning of reform and opening-up, the core of the reform of the education institution has been "motivating all levels of government, teachers, students and workers, and all walks of society in a better way." In the process of government education management, the core has been "motivating all levels of government to run schools." One of the actions of the reform has been "handing over the responsibility of developing basic education to the local governments" (The Central Committee of CPC, 1985a). However, when the responsibility of education management was placed in towns and villages, it caused serious imbalances in the development of education in different regions. In 2001, the State Council issued the *Decision on the Reform and Development of Basic Education*, and changed the rural compulsory education management institution of 15 years which had the township as the core, clarifying "the implementation of a institution under the leadership of the State Council, and the responsibility of the local government, with management by level that is centered at the county level." The establishment and improvement of an education management institution "planned at the provincial level and centered at the county level" has become a beneficial exploration for deepening the reform of the education institution and promoting the balanced development of education in different regions.

Taking curriculum reform as an example, for forty years, an appropriate balance between the authority of the national curriculum and the flexibility of the local school curriculum has been sought after, and the balance of educational authority relationship among schools, local governments, and central governments has never been broken. Since the founding of PRC, in the curriculum and teaching materials institutions of primary and secondary schools, the institution of uniform teaching plans, uniform syllabus, and uniform teaching materials and textbooks used throughout the country was in general implemented. At the beginning of reform and opening-up, against the background of the *Decision of the*

CPC Central Committee on the Reform of the Education Institution on the "streamlining of administration and delegating power" education reform, the National Education Commission gave Shanghai a special policy to carry out experiments on reform of the primary and secondary school curriculum in 1988. Shanghai initiated "first round curriculum reform," trying to change the "test-oriented education" textbook institution centered on gaining entrance to universities, change the curriculum model with compulsory courses as the main body, and achieve the "three major breakthroughs" of "learning burden reduction and education quality improvement," "strengthening foundations and cultivating abilities," and "personal quality improvement and personality development." After five years of commitment, Shanghai developed a curriculum plan, a curriculum standard teaching materials and teaching aids software which were suitable for primary and secondary schools in economically developed areas, and conducted relevant experiments (Sun et al., 2016: 25) to provide useful implications for the reform of the basic education curriculum throughout the country. In the 1990s, the National Board of Education proposed that the general high school curriculum should be collectively managed by the central, local, and school levels and stipulated respective management authority at all levels; "a three-level management model for curriculum textbooks was established to protect and promote the applicability of the curriculum for different regions, schools, and students, and the implementation of guided, gradual decentralization" (The Secretariat of the National Curriculum Professional Committee, 2001: 90).The reform of the basic education curriculum initiated at the beginning of the new century required "changing the situation of over-centralized management of curriculum, implementing three-level curriculum management at the national, local, and school levels, and enhancing the adaptability of the curriculum for local governments, schools, and students." The implementation of the three-level curriculum management institution involves decentralizing the power of curriculum management, which was originally over-concentrated at the state level, to local governments and schools, and enabling local governments and schools to participate in curriculum development, thereby forming the coexistence of the national curriculum, local curriculum, and school curriculum, making the curriculum more adapted to the particular education and teaching contexts of local governments and schools, and reflecting the trend of decentralization of the curriculum management institutions from centralization to limited decentralization. Curriculum involves not only the classic question of "what knowledge is most valuable" (Spencer, 1884) but also the key question of "whose knowledge is the most valuable" (Apple, 2004). In order to fully implement the Party's educational policy and integrate the cultivation and implementation of the socialist core values into the whole process of national education, from 2012 onwards, the MOE organized the edition of the textbooks for the three courses of Ethics and the Rule of Law, Chinese and History for compulsory education. In the fall semester of September 2017, it was put into use at the initial grades of compulsory education across the whole country. In the textbook review institutions, "the four rounds" review institution comprising a subject review, comprehensive review, special review, and final review was implemented for the first time to ensure the overall quality of the textbooks. In March 2017, the MOE set up a textbook bureau to be responsible for the planning, construction, and management of curriculum textbooks. In July of the same year, the State Council established the National Textbook Committee to guide and coordinate the textbook development for the whole country.

In the process of advancing the modernization of the education management institution, "promoting regional phased reform and opening-up should be carried out under the premise of strengthening top-level design, and strengthening top-level design should be planned with an aim to promote the regional phased reform and opening-up" (Xi, 2014: 68). As stated in the *Opinions on Deepening the Reform of Educational Institutions and Mechanisms*, adhering to the integration of top-level design and grassroots exploration not only strengthens institution planning but also respects the spirit of innovation at the grassroots level. We should fully motivate the initiative and creativity of local governments and schools to implement reforms, and turn successful experiences into institutions and policies in time. The distinctive feature of the reform of the education institutions in the new era is strengthening top-level design, including deepening the reform of the examination and enrollment institutions, the construction of a modern vocational education institution, the construction of first-class universities and disciplines, comprehensive revise of education law, and other major education reforms, which have all been reviewed at State Council executive meetings and reported to the Central Government Comprehensive Reform Deepening Leadership Group meetings and Political Bureau of the Central Committee of the CPC meetings for review, and finally fully promoted and concretely implemented by the State Council and relevant ministries and commissions. In March 2018, in order to strengthen the centralized and unified leadership of the Party Central Committee on education work, according to the Third Party Plenary Session of the 19th CPC Central Committee entitled *The Plan for Continuing the Reform of Party and Government Institutions*, the Central Education Work Leadership Group was established as the Party Central Committee's decision-making and coordination body. Its main responsibilities include researching, organizing, and implementing principles and policies that uphold Party leadership and strengthen the Party's construction in the field of education, researching and deploying theoretical and political work and ideological work in the field of education, reviewing the national education development strategy, medium- and long-term planning, and major education policies and institution reform plans to coordinate and solve major problems in education work. This is of great significance for strengthening the top-level design of education reform, effectively tackling the relationships between the central and local governments, the nationwide and local situations, and enhancing systematic, integrated, and coordinated reform to create an overall positive effect. On the other hand, China's education reform enters the "deep water zone" in which we must tackle a range of difficult challenges. Many regions and schools have set off from reality, focus on identifying and resolving problems, summarizing and refining many new experiences of reform and exploration, and some reform experiences that have been proven to be effective in practice have provided important practical support for macro decision-making at the national level. From 2014, Qingdao City began making efforts to promote reform experiments of managing schools according to law and constructing modern school institutions, sorting out the list of self-governing powers, and fully implementing the list to delegate the powers to public schools. On this basis, in February 2017, the Qingdao Municipal Government promulgated the *Qingdao Regulations for the Management of Primary and Secondary Schools* in the form of local laws and regulations, standardizing school-running autonomy such as "the principal may nominate and appoint a vice-principle in accordance with the regulations," the school "may recruit professional and high-level talents in short supply," and "establish internal institutions, and select the person to serve as the head of the institution according to regulations." In recent years, Shanghai, as a pilot region, has taken the country's lead in launching comprehensive reforms of education. Under the guidance of the top-level design of national macro education reforms, Shanghai has actively explored and put forward many new ideas and new measures. In December 2017, the Shanghai Municipal People's Congress formulated and passed the country's first local higher education regulations, *The Shanghai Higher Education Promotion Regulations*, which included new achievements and new experiences into educational regulations and solidified them in the form of law. This new regulation provides strong guarantees of the rule of law for the modernization of Shanghai's higher education governance institution and the healthy and sustainable development of higher education in Shanghai (Fan, 2018).

In future education reforms, overall reforms and innovations including national education laws, education institutions, education standards, and educational strategic planning should be planned and implemented uniformly at the national level. Besides, education reforms involving key issues and difficult problems should be gradually expanded and dynamically adjusted on the basis of experiments in some regions. Regional- and school-level reforms should give full play to the enthusiasm and initiative of grassroots education reform, encouraging local governments and schools to be bold and innovative, and courageous in exploration, thereby forming a mechanism of promoting reform and innovation of education institutions combining top-level design and grassroots exploration, comprehensive advancement and focused breakthroughs, and the construction of rule of law and reform and innovation.

II. Straightening out Intergovernmental Relations

Intergovernmental relations refer to the vertical and horizontal complex relationships within the government and the relations between governments in different regions. For governments of the same region, it mainly involves horizontal intergovernmental relations between departments of the same government level. Within the government's education governance institution, in addition to the education administration department directly in charge of education affairs, other departments including the Development and Reform Commission, Organization Department, Finance Department, Department of Human Resources and Social Security, Departments for Staffing, Department of Housing and Urban and Rural Development, Department of Science and Technology, the State-Owned Assets Supervision and Administration Commission, Department of Industry and Information Technology, and Taxation Bureau all have their own governance logic and corresponding educational management responsibilities. However, the long-standing phenomena of not taking the overall interest into account and multi-headed administrative situations, frequently hampered communication, prevarication, and buck-passing between education administrative departments and other government functional departments have had a serious impact on the order of school running.

During the process of putting reform into practice, some regions have attempted to coordinate the educational management activities of relevant government functional departments by education administration departments. *The Regulations on the Promotion of Higher Education in Shanghai* proposed the establishment of a consultation and coordination mechanism for the reform and development of higher education at the municipal level, which takes the responsibilities of reviewing the major policies of the reform and development of higher education, and coordinating and resolving major issues in the development of higher education. Besides, the Higher Education Investment and Evaluation Advisory Committee was established to provide consultation and evaluation on major investment policies for higher education, and supervise and inspect the use of funds. *The Measures for the Administration of Primary and Secondary Schools in Qingdao* stipulate that "relevant departments shall conduct evaluations, appraisals, evaluations, competitions, inspections and other activities related to primary and secondary schools, and report the plan for the following year to the education administrative department before the end of November each year. The education administrative department compiles a staffing catalogue and announces it to the school at the beginning of the following year." These practical explorations have accumulated useful experience for deepening the reform of the government's education management institution, establishing and improving the educational governance mechanism of government coordination and intergovernmental consultation.

III. Restructuring Government-School Relations

In 1985, *The Decision* proposed "reforming the management institution, resolutely streamlining administration and delegating power, and expanding schools' autonomy in running schools while strengthening government macro-management," thereby reallocating authority in education which greatly changed the traditional educational administrative legal relationship. Since then, expanding school autonomy has always been the main theme of education reform. In 2017, the General Office of the CPC Central Committee and the General Office of the State Council's *Opinions on Deepening the Reform of the Institution and Mechanism of the Education* made "granting schools autonomy according to law" an important part of the educational governance structure which is "energetic, efficient, open and conducive to scientific development." Autonomy of schools in school running stems from the delegating of power from the government. For the government, it is necessary to scientifically plan the type, scale, and speed of the development of national and regional education so that each school has their own development vision which is scientific and rational; it is necessary to establish and optimize an institution of education standards so that schools have standards to go by during the process of becoming autonomous in the running of the school; it is necessary to delegate powers that schools should have through list management so that schools have powers to use; it is necessary to strengthen operational and post-operational oversight, supervising and guaranteeing that the school uses school running powers according to law; it is necessary to provide a reasonable allocation of educational resources for schools, and provide professional services to enable schools to continue to develop healthily.

IV. Giving Play to the Role of Social Organizations and Market Participation in Education

Due to public dissatisfaction with the quality of education, the 1990s witnessed the emergence of a wave of education reforms across the world, which aimed at the marketization of the education supply, improvement of the quality of education through market mechanisms, and focus on the accountability of educational performance (Goertz & Duffy, 2001; Headington, 2000; Heller, 2001; Mahony & Hextall, 2000). During this process, trends towards quality education or competitive schooling appeared, emphasizing education quality management and quality assurance, school monitoring and evaluation, school choice, education vouchers, marketization, the participation of parents and community in governance, as well as performance-based funding mechanisms (Cheng, 2015; Cheng & Townsend, 2000; Mukhopadhyay, 2001; Pang et al., 2003).

In October 1992, the 14th National Congress of CPC proposed the establishment of a socialist market economy institution so that the market plays a basic role in resource allocation under the state's macro regulation. Against this background, in February 1993, *The Outline of China's Reform and Development of Education* stated: "The reform of the education institution should adopt a comprehensive and step-by-step approach, accelerate its pace, reform the institution that is overly managed and overly controlled, basically establish a new educational institution that is compatible with the socialist market economic institution reform, political institution reform, and science and technology institution reform." Originally, the relationship between the government and schools was the core of the traditional educational governance relationship. The statement in *The Decision* in 1985 of "resolutely streamlining administration and delegating power and expanding school autonomy in running schools" showed that the relationship between the government and schools was the most important target in the reform of the education institution then. However, ever since China began establishing a market economy, this relationship has undergone profound changes, and the government-school relationship has evolved into a relationship between the government, schools, and markets. In the case of a serious shortage in government education spending, the initial exploration of introducing market mechanisms into the field of education was done firstly to "encourage running schools by multiple channels and multiple forms of fund raising and participation of the society" (Jiang, 1992). The state adopted the policy of "actively encouraging, vigorously supporting, correctly guiding, and strengthening management" for social groups and private citizens to run schools according to law, "gradually establishing a institution in which the government runs schools for the main part and various stakeholders in society from all walks of life jointly run schools" (The Central Committee of CPC, 1993). Secondly, it was done to explore the reform of the conversion of public schools. In practice, schools of different forms emerged, including private schools with public support, public schools with private support, and public schools.

In the subsequent development process, private education in the legal framework of the *People's Republic of China Private Education Promotion Law* developed from "investors can obtain reasonable returns from the surpluses in school running" (The Standing Committee of the National People's Congress of PRC, 2016) to the classified management methods of profit-making private schools or nonprofit schools, which realized the goal of classified management and development (The Standing Committee of the National People's Congress of PRC,

2016). In contrast, the conversion of public schools to private schools was stopped, cleaned up, and standardized owing to the muddle-up of official duties with private affairs in the process of development, the loss of state-owned educational assets, and damage to the nature of education as public welfare.

With the development of China's market economy, in the process of deepening economic institution reform, the role of the market in resource allocation has transformed from having a "basic role" to a "decisive role" (Xi, 2017b). In the process of advancing the modernization of the governance institution with the separation of management, operation and evaluation, and the combination of decentralization, regulation and service, in addition to participating in running schools, social organizations are participating in public affairs including education with their own professional advantages and market mechanisms. As pointed out in the *CPC Central Committee's Decision on Comprehensively Deepening the Reform of Certain Major Issues*, "We will promote government purchases of public services by means of contract and entrustment, and introduce a competition mechanism into general-affairs management services." "We need to innovate the ways of delivering public education services, improves the mechanisms of government procurement of education service, and promotes government procurement services in areas including decision-making consultation, school management, provision of compulsory education and pre-school education degrees, teacher training, special population services, education quality, and school performance evaluation, thus improving the quality and efficiency of public education services." (MOE, 2015b) Various professional organizations including online education resources, relevant sports and art groups, education management companies, educational evaluation services, and health care and security institutions participate in education services, support, supervision, and evaluation with their rich educational resources and professional services.

V. Promoting School Running Autonomy for Schools

As mentioned above, "expanding school running autonomy for schools" is an aspect of education reform proposed in the 1985 *Decision* that endures to this day. *The Decision* proposed that "schools gradually implement the principal accountability institution" and constructed a school organization framework made up of the school Party branch, the principal, the school council, and the faculty representative assembly. Within this, "Party organizations in schools must free themselves from the past state of taking charge of everything and concentrate their efforts on strengthening Party building and strengthening theoretical and political work." Schools with the right conditions should set up a prestigious school council made up of a small number of people and chaired by the principal to serve as a review and appraisal organization. At the same time, they should establish and improve the school faculty congress institution with teachers as the main body to strengthen democratic management and democratic supervision. With the continuous deepening of education reform, the leadership institution of Chinese schools has been constantly changing, further strengthening and improving the Party's leadership over schools. Public higher education institutions adhere to and improve the president accountability institution under the leadership of the Party committee, while in primary and secondary schools and private schools the core political role of grassroots Party organizations is given full play to (The General Office of the Central Committee of CPC, 2014).

In the process of advancing the modernization of education governance institution and governance capacity, although there is currently no *School Law* that clearly defines and regulates the responsibilities and rights of the school-running process, still, with a view to implement the legally defined autonomy of schools of all types and at all levels, schools' legal-based autonomy can be transformed into concrete charter-based autonomy through the formulation and improvement of school charters (university charters) so that schools can run themselves with autonomy based on those rules. Through school institutional institution construction, management institutions for teaching, scientific research, students, personnel, assets and finance, logistics, security, external cooperation, student organizations, student associations, and other aspects can be formulated and improved, and various procedures, internal organization rules, and procedural rules can be established and improved. Party leadership of schools should be further strengthened and improved; the principal accountability institution for ordinary primary and secondary schools and secondary vocational schools and the president accountability institution under the leadership of Party committees of higher education institutions should be improved. We must improve the principal accountability institution of ordinary primary and secondary schools and secondary vocational schools, and establish school councils which include the heads of schools, teachers, students parent representatives, community representatives, etc. Focus should be put on giving play to the decision-making role of school councils on school charters, development plans and annual work reports, major education and teaching reforms of schools, and important issues involving students, parents, and community work with the optimization of democratic decision-making procedures (MOE, 2015b). We must strengthen the establishment of school boards, councils and academic committees of colleges and universities, faculty and workers' congresses, student representative assemblies, parent committees, and other organizations, improving the internal governance structure of schools, improving democratic decision-making procedures, and legally ensuring the participation of faculty, staff, and students in the democratic management and supervision of schools. We should set up institutions of promoting school transparency to guarantee the rights of faculty staff, students, and the public so that they know the major issues and important institutions of the school. Schools should be encouraged to actively carry out self-evaluation, and schools' internal quality assurance institution and mechanism should be improved. In addition, professional evaluation by third-party social organizations should be introduced. Hence, a scientific, standardized, and fair education supervision, monitoring and evaluation institution can be established. We should improve the school legal relief institution to safeguard the legitimate rights and interests of schools, teachers, and students. A series of reforms for the construction of education institutions is now gradually promoting the formation of a benign mechanism to ensure the independent development, characteristic development, and sustainable development of schools. In recent years, all parts of the country have gradually pushed forward reform experiments to expand the autonomy of primary and secondary schools in a number of aspects, which include the principal accountability institution, school-running modes, resource allocation, personnel management, and collaborative school running. For example, Shandong Province issued *The Opinions on Promoting Comprehensive Reform of Basic Education* in 2014, piloting the abolition of administrative ranks of schools and principals, gradually pushing the reform of principal grading institution in the primary and secondary schools, actively exploring grading management methods that are compatible with the principal grading institution, and establishing management institutions that promote the professional development of principals and guarantee that educators run schools.

A school is an ecosystem. As part of the environment of the ecosystem, education management institutions and management mechanisms impact and restrict the vitality of a school while the vitality of a school also depends on the establishment and improvement of its internal organization mechanisms. The vitality of the school is manifested in the pursuit of educational values, education ideals, responsibilities, and missions shared by the school leaders and the faculty. It is manifested in the way that the school institutions and operational mechanism can stimulate, promote, and guarantee the internal organization and individuals of the school to give full play to its initiative and creativity. It is manifested in the active learning, independent learning, and independent development of students with the guidance and help of teachers in school and in various studies and activities designed together by students and teachers.

When looking at China's education in the grand history of reform and opening-up over the past forty years, it is not difficult to find that the development history of China's educational undertakings is the history of China's education reform and the history of changes and innovations in China's education institutions. The development of modern public education has been closely related to the transformation and development of the country and society. The construction, innovation, and development of scientific and rational education institutions is not only an important part of education reform and development but also the institutions guarantee for the development of education. In this process, the environment of educational reform development at different historical stages was different, the major educational issues were different, and the specific strategies for education reform were different, but the educational purpose, value, and guideline as the basis of the education institution remain unchanged. The institutional ethics of education serving the people has not changed. The overall strategy of continuously deepening education reform and continuously expanding opening-up has not changed, and the strategy of giving priority to education development has not changed.

In this development process, the reform of the education institution is manifested in the reasonable adjustment and game of powers and interests among various education stakeholders and in education such as those among government at different levels and their departments, among government, schools, social organizations, and markets, as well as among school leaders, teachers and parents. The process of China's education reform since reform and opening-up has been a process of continuous deepening of the reform of education institutions and mechanisms. It has also been a process of continuous improvement of the socialist education institution with Chinese characteristics. It has been a process of pushing scattered reforms with education policies and regulations to legally regulate education order and promote the construction and improvement of the education institutions. It has also been a process of rebuilding education order and breaking through restrictions, delegating powers by the rule of law, and promoting negotiations and co-governance. It has been a process of seeking appropriate tension between different educational stakeholders and stimulating their vitality. It has been a process from regulation to empowerment. This has accumulated valuable ethical foundations for change and rational resources for educational decision-making in current and future educational reforms. The main task of the reform of the education institutions and mechanisms in the new era is to construct and improve an institution of "government macro-management according to law, autonomy of schools in school running according to law, the orderly participation of the society, and the joint efforts of all parties" so that education is "vibrant, efficient, more open, and conducive to scientific development." As Minister of Education Chen Baosheng stated, the reform plan for the main frame of education with "multiple pillars" has basically been established, and education reform has entered the stage of "comprehensive construction and interior decoration." The task of future education development is further promoting the balanced development of education and solving the problems of inadequacies and imbalances and meeting the growing needs of the people in enjoying more equal and higher quality education (Cai, 2017).

Looking to the future, we are entering an era of universal access to new internet-based technologies. The internet, internet-based big data, and artificial intelligence are affecting the lives, work, learning, and thinking of every one in a comprehensive and in-depth manner. In this way, web-based learning resources have made school education no longer the only source of knowledge, and immersed learning makes learning and education happen in any situation any time. Education institutions reform in the past forty years has been based on institutionalized school education. When the institutionalized, systematic, and standardized school education institution and its functions undergo revolutionary changes, and the new educational model based on online and offline blended learning becomes the "new normal," it is inevitable to hear the call for new education institutions and educational governance mechanism that can serve, guarantee, and promote this "new normal" education.

NOTES

1 September 29, 1949, the first session of the Chinese People's Political Consultative Conference adopted the provisional constitutional role of the Common Program of the Chinese People's Political Consultative Conference, which stipulates that: "The cultural education of PRC is that of new democracy, that is, national, scientific, and mass cultural education."

2 The idea that "Schools should become tools of the dictatorship of the proletarian" was proposed by Lenin: "In terms of national education, the task that the Russian Communist Party has given itself is: Finish the revolution that began in October of 1917, that is, transform schools from being tools of class rule of the bourgeoisie into tools that destroy this rule and completely eliminate social class divisions. Schools should become tools of the dictatorship of the proletarian" (Lenin, 2012). Lenin's idea that "schools should become tools of the dictatorship of the proletarian" refers to schools "disseminating general communist principles" and "spreading the influence of the proletariat in terms of ideology, organization and educational aspects to the semi-proletarian and non-proletarian classes among the working masses" (functions of education) and this is strictly different from "dictatorship" (a function of repression) in the sense of violent suppression of the exploiting class (Chen, 1993: 255–260).

3 February 7, 1977 joint editorial from *The People's Daily*, *Red Flag* Magazine, and the *PLA Daily*, "Study the Documents Well and Grasp the Key Link", which stated: "We will resolutely uphold whatever policy decisions Chairman Mao made, and unswervingly follow whatever instructions Chairman Mao gave." This had the aim of raising the flag of Chairman Mao. After the concept of the "Two Whatevers" was proposed, it met with resolute opposition from Xiaoping Deng, Yun Chen and others, and triggered a big discussion on the issue of the standards of truth (Deng, 1977c); Yun Chen put forward the idea that one should "not blindly follow the instructions of superiors or books; consider only information which has been ascertained" (Chen, 1995: 371).

4 "The Stinking Old Ninth" is a Chinese dysphemism for intellectuals.

5 From April 15 to July 31, 1971, the National Education Conference was held in Beijing. In the "National Education Conference Minutes" adopted by the meeting and approved by Mao Zedong, the so-called "two estimates" were put forward, namely: "17 years after liberation, 'Chairman Mao's proletarian education line has basically not been implemented', 'the

bourgeoisie have become dictators over the proletariat'; 'the worldview of most teachers and a large number of students trained after liberation is basically bourgeois'". Starting from these "two estimates", the meeting confirmed and reaffirmed policies such as the long-term school leadership of "worker propaganda teams", the re-education of intellectuals into workers, peasants and soldiers, the selection of workers, peasants and soldiers to go to universities, and shortening the university institution. The "two estimates" caused the majority of intellectuals to be severely suppressed for a long time. On November 18, 1977, the People's Daily published the article "A Great Dispute on the Education Front" by MOE's Great Criticism Group, criticizing the "two estimates".

6 In 1961, the Central Committee of CPC promulgated *The Provisional Work Regulations for Higher Education Institutions Directly Under MOE (Draft)* (Higher Education 60 Articles); in 1963, it issued *The Provisional Work Regulations for Full-time Secondary Schools (Draft)* (Secondary Education 50 Articles) and *The Provisional Work Regulations for Full-time Primary Schools (Draft)*. These three regulations played an important role in regulating education order, improving the quality of education, and promoting the development of education at the time.

7 At the beginning of the "Cultural Revolution", in order to thoroughly penetrate the "Cultural Revolutionary Movement" at colleges and high schools, the Ministry of Higher Education issued a series of notices in 1966, first delaying the admission of students at higher education institutions, and then proposing the enrollment methods of "cancellation of examinations", and "adopting the combination of recommendation and selection". In 1971, the Central Committee of CPC approved the "National Education Conference Minutes", requiring colleges and universities to adhere to a "voluntary registration, mass recommendation, leadership approval, and school review" approach, recruiting excellent workers, peasants and soldiers with more than two to three years of practical experience and a history of attending junior high school or above. In June of 1977, MOE's Higher Education Institution Student Enrollment Work Conference still proposed the adoption of recommending for workers, peasants and soldiers to go to college, as was done in the "Cultural Revolution". This opinion was opposed by Xiaoping Deng, who had just returned to work that year. Xiaoping Deng believed that "it is necessary to go through rigorous examinations and gather the best talents in key middle schools and universities" (Deng, 1977b).

8 *The Compulsory Education Law of PRC* stipulates that: "The proportion of the state's growth in financial allocation for compulsory education should be higher than the proportional growth of fiscal recurrent income, and the average educational cost per student should be gradually increased." "Local people's governments at all levels levy additional education fees in urban and rural areas, mainly for the implementation of compulsory education in accordance with the regulations of the State Council."

9 The fiscal and taxation reforms that we carried out in 1994 saw the introduction of an institution for the sharing of fiscal revenue between the central government and local governments. The essence of the institution was to effectively deal with the relationship between the responsibility and financial powers of the central government and the local government. The institution is a fiscal institution generally implemented by market economy countries that uses fiscal means to implement macroeconomic regulations of the economy. After the reform, fiscal revenue continued to be concentrated upwards while township finance was the weakest. Under the principle that the financial burden of education expenditures at a certain level was to be undertaken by the government department at that same level, local governments tended to focus on

higher education and urban basic education for fund allocation. Rural basic education received even less financial input from the provincial and municipal governments. Rural basic education investment was basically financed by the township finance and by farmers.

10 Lanqing Li, the Vice Premier of the State Council at the time pointed out at a video conference on improving the rural compulsory education management institution held by the General Office of the State Council in April 2002: "The key to adjusting and improving the rural compulsory education management institution is realizing two major changes: shifting the main responsibility for rural compulsory education from the farmers to the government, and shifting the government's main responsibility for rural compulsory education from the township to the county."

11 In the 1980s, Pingdu County of Shandong Province took the lead in creating the "People's Education Fund Institution", implementing the "three-education co-ordination" of basic education, vocational education and adult education, and "the combination of science and education through agriculture". It was named as a National Basic Education Advanced County (City), Advanced County (City) for Literacy Work, Advanced County (City) for Early Childhood Education, Advanced County (City) for Special Education, and Advanced County (City) for "The Two Basics" work. In 1987 and 1988, the whole country and Shandong Province held a rural education exchange experience and on-site meetings for local economic construction in Pingdu County, Shandong Province. The experience of Pingdu has been affirmed and promoted by the central and local governments (Ding, 1989a, 1989b; Han, 1990).

12 In October 1996, the Jiaojiang District Education Bureau of Taizhou City, Zhejiang Province proposed the concept of an "education shareholding institution", introduced the Weishusheng Education brand from Panjin in Liaoning Province, and established "Shusheng Education Co., Ltd." in December of that year to prepare for the establishment of "Sunson Middle School"; In September 1997, "Sunson Middle School" began to enroll students. Shusheng Wei was made the honorary president of Sunson Middle School in 2007 (The Research Group of "Study of the Jiaojiang Education Joint Shareholding Institutions School Running Model", 1999; Wu and Ning, 2004).

13 In March 1993, Peking University made a decision that caused widespread controversy at that time: The 600-meter-long South Wall was torn down and converted into a roughly 25,000 square meter commercial street. Suddenly, "Peking University had torn down the wall and opened for business", and this became one of the symbols of the industrialization and marketization of education in China.

14 Regarding the relationship between education and the market, there were three different views in the academic world at that time: Education is an industry and can be fully market-oriented; education is a special industry, some parts of which can be operated by the market; although education has certain industrial attributes, in terms of its basic nature, it should be classified as a public good and cannot and should not be marketed (Fan, 1995, 2005; Lao, 2003).

15 In July 2001, the Changxing County Education Bureau issued "The Notice on the Use of Education Vouchers", stipulating that from 2001, all freshmen attending private schools could obtain an education voucher worth 50 yuan RMB, and new students who had been enrolled for vocational schools could obtain an education voucher worth 30 yuan, and this was where China's "education voucher" practice started off. In December 2002, the Zhejiang Provincial Department of Education held an on-site meeting in Changxing to discuss the theory, policy and operation of education vouchers, encouraging experiments in other counties of the province, and being the first in the country to promote the "education vouchers" institution

throughout the province. By the end of 2003, many counties and cities across the province had carried out a range of forms of "education voucher" experiments (Wu, *et al.*, 2005).

16 On the evening of September 21, 2003, China Central Television's "Focus Interview" program broadcast the two cases of the key middle school of Jiangsu Province, Suqian Middle School, acting as a pilot school for the reform of the state-owned private school-running institution, whose students that were originally enrolled in the school, had to pay high tuition fees to attend the school and the case of the Sucheng District Government of Suqian Municipal Government auctioning off Maling Middle School (Lu and Wang, 2004).

17 On October 9, 2003, the County Party Committee and County Government of Jianli, Hubei Province, jointly issued "The Implementation Opinions on the Comprehensive Reform of Basic Education in Jianli County" (Jianli County [2003] No. 17), which stated: "Encourage social organizations and individuals outside governmental institutions to utilize non-state finances to invest in education in our county. Under the premise that the school is determined to make a profit in running the school, investors can take a return within 10% of the total amount of the capital, encouraging social organizations and individuals to buy or lease current national education assets to carry out private education. The specific measures for acquisition and leasing are separately stipulated. Encourage investment of social funds in education in various forms such as debt-to-equity swaps and new investment shares. Under the premise that schools make profits, dividends are distributed according to shares, and social forces are encouraged to undertake school logistics and services such as hosting the school's new modern education technology and other individual project services." Since then, Jianli County has pushed 700 primary and secondary schools on to the market. break the tenure status of teachers whose salaries are determined according to their post. County finances are to be allocated directly to the number of students, students can choose their own schools; the school's decision-making body, a democratic managing committee, is to be made up of the funders, school principal, teacher representatives, and parent and guardian representatives. School investors can obtain a return of less than 10% of the total investment each year. In August 2005, the Jianli County Government and Xiangyu Education Group signed an agreement. Xiangyu Education Group invested in Jianli to build a new high school campus, a junior high school and a modern gymnasium; Jianli County will restructure the former Jianli Middle School. Xiangyu Education Group owns 15 years of entrusted management of Jianli Number One Junior High School, and uniformly allocates the people, property and materials of the school (Ding, 2004; Li and He, 2006; Huang, 2010).

18 In November 1998, at the time of the Asian Financial Crisis, Tang Min, then chief economist of the Asian Development Bank, and his wife Xiaolei Zuo proposed to the Central Committee of the CPC that the number of college enrollments should be expanded. This proposal was quickly adopted by the State Council's premier Rongji Zhu and the deputy premier Lanqing Li, who was in charge of education. Min Tang's suggestion was based on the following background: At that time, the number of Chinese university students was much smaller than that of countries with similar development levels; the general public was eager to have their children to receive higher education, and the government had a responsibility to satisfy their wishes as much as possible; in 1998, state-owned enterprise reforms brought a large number of laid-off workers into the employment market; expanded enrolment can delay student employment, avoid large numbers of young people participating in fierce competition for employment, increase spending on education, stimulate domestic demands, and drive the development of related industries; the state proposed to maintain a target economic growth rate of 8%, when

at that time the economic growth rate was 7.8%. There was an urgent need to expand domestic demands. Education was considered to be the greatest demand of the public. The ratio of teachers to students was low in colleges and universities, so schools would be capable of handling the increased enrolment. The popularization of higher education was related to the great cause of Chinese national rejuvenation. Min Tang's suggestions included: expanding the scale of the enrollment of higher education, doubling it in three years; establishing corresponding student aid policies, improving student loans, bursaries, and scholarship institutions; further deepening education reforms and cultivating talents needed by society; enrolment should be expanded more for schools that are doing well than schools that are not doing so well. Min Tang's suggestion at the time attracted criticism from all walks of life, especially the higher education sector, and the opposition lingered for quite a long time (Tang, 2006a, 2006b; Gao, 2007).

19 In February 2006, Chen Zhili, the State Councilor at the time, pointed out at the opening ceremony of the Fifth International Conference on Higher Education in Havana that: "The number of students enrolled in higher education in China has reached 21 million, ranking first in the world, and the gross enrollment rate has reached 21%, entering the internationally recognized stage of popularization of higher education, and achieving an unprecedented progress" (Chen, 2006a, 2006b).

20 *The Outline of China's Education Reform and Development* believes that "higher education is non-compulsory education, and students should pay to go to college in general." Therefore, it is necessary to "reform the practice of students going to college being covered by the state and gradually implementing the charging institution."

21 For Instance, the 2006 *Decision of the Central Committee of CPC Regarding Some Important Issues in the Building of a Harmonious Socialist Society*, where it is said: "Standardize school fees and standards, and resolutely stop the arbitrary charges in education."

22 The so-called "three-limits" policy meant that government-run public high schools could enroll a certain number of school choice students on the premise of having completed the year's enrollment plan, but students' scores for enrollment could not be below a certain score (going against the regulation by admitting new students with a score below the minimum admission score was not allowed), the number of students must be limited (class numbers prescribed by the state were not allowed to be exceeded, the number of school selection students must not exceed the proportion prescribed by the local government), the amount of fee must be limited (school selection student fee standards was proposed by the education administrative department, approved by the provincial people's government and then announced to the public. Schools may not raise the standard without authorization).

23 The principle of 'the four independences' of private schools means that private schools must have independent legal persons, independent campus and buildings, independent implementation of fund accounting and personnel management, and independent education and teaching (MOE, 2006).

24 "Private schools that have public schools participating in school running shall have independent legal personality, have campuses and basic education and teaching facilities separate from public schools, shall implement independent financial accounting institutions, independently enroll students, and independently issue academic certificates" (The State Council of PRC, 2004).

25 In 2000, China began to carry out pilot work on rural tax and fee reforms in order to alleviate the burden on farmers. One of the reform measures was to "eliminate education fundraising in rural areas" (The Central Committee of CPC, and the State Council of PRC, 2000). In 2001,

after the reform of rural taxation and fees by the State Council, the reform of the management institution for rural compulsory education was deployed accordingly: "Ensuring the funding of rural compulsory education. In the process of rural tax and fee reform, we must attach great importance to the stability and development of rural compulsory education. Rural tax and fee reform must reform the rural compulsory education management institution correspondingly, changing from the previous institution in which the rural government and local farmers raised funds to run schools, to county-level governments organizing and managing rural compulsory education. The education funds are included in county-level finance, and the rural compulsory education funding guarantee mechanism are established and improved, strengthening the county-level government's function of coordinating teacher management and teachers' salary payment. The responsibility of managing the salary of rural primary and secondary school teachers is moved up to the county level, and the county-level finance departments will pay teachers salaries in full and on time according to the standards set by the state. Provincial governments should refer to the actual public funds of the rural primary and secondary schools before the reform and verify the local standards and quotas accordingly, deducting the appropriate fees collected by the school. The remaining part is arranged by the county-level local financial budgets. The central and provincial governments should increase their support for rural compulsory education, support compulsory education in poverty-stricken counties through transfer payments, and arrange special funds for the renovation of dilapidated buildings and school building construction in rural primary and middle schools in poverty-stricken areas to ensure the healthy development of compulsory education in rural areas" (The State Council of PRC, 2001).

26 Compulsory education funds are invested in the "three growths", those being, "the growth rate of the financial appropriations of the State Council and local people's governments for implementing compulsory education should be higher than the growth rate of fiscal recurrent income, the growth in funding of compulsory education based on the average number of students in school should be guaranteed and the gradual growth of salaries of education workers and average public fees for students should be guaranteed" (The Standing Committee of the National People's Congress of PRC, 2006).

27 "Two exemptions and one supplement" includes exemptions from tuition and miscellaneous fees during compulsory education, free textbooks for students with financial difficulties in the family and subsidized living expenses for boarding students.

28 "The Overall Plan for Development in Five Areas" refers to economic construction, political construction, cultural construction, social construction, and ecological civilization construction.

29 "The Program for Introducing Discipline Innovation and Introduction of Talents to Higher Education Institutions", also known as "Plan 111", jointly implemented by MOE and the State Administration of Foreign Experts Affairs, aims to promote the construction of world-class universities in China's higher education institutions and aims at the forefront of international discipline development. Based on national key disciplines, more than 1,000 outstanding talents from the top 100 leading universities and research institutions in the world are introduced and gathered, forming a high-level research team and building about 100 world-class discipline talent bases. In September 2005, MOE and the State Administration of Foreign Experts Affairs released the *Eleventh Five-Year Plan for the Program of Introducing Discipline Innovation and Introduction of Talents to Higher Education Institutions (2006–2010)* (Ministry of Education [2005] No. 6), which initiated the Program of Introducing Discipline Innovation and

Introduction of Talents to Higher Education Institutions; In 2006, *The Regulations for the Bases of Discipline Innovation and Talent Introduction in Higher Education Institutions* was released (Ministry of Education [2006] No. 4); In November 2016, in order to adapt to the new era of opening up and the "double first-class" construction needs of higher education institutions, MOE and the State Administration of Foreign Experts Affairs issued a new *The Regulations for the Implementation and Management of The Program for Introducing Discipline Innovation and Introduction of Talents to Higher Education Institutions* (See, MOE, *et al.*, 2016b)

30 Xiaoping Deng pointed out that: "For us to realize modernization, the key is that science and technology must be strengthened. Developing science and technology cannot happen without education" (Deng, 1977c). "The opinions I have mentioned about education, science and technology, and intellectuals are to be taken as strategic guidelines and strategic measures. In the long run, it is the time to solve this issue" (Deng, 1988). "For faster development of the economy, we must rely on science & technology and education" (Deng, 1992).

REFERENCES

Apple, W. M. (2004). *Ideology and curriculum* (3rd ed.). New York and London: Routledge.

Bai, L. (2006). Graduate unemployment: Dilemmas and challenges in China's move to mass higher education. *The China Quarterly*, *185*(1), 128—144 (in Chinese).

Beemer, H., et al. (1999). *Strategic goals for Chinese education in the 21st century (Report No.1 8969-CHA). Human Development Sector Unit, East Asia and Pacific Region.* World Bank, November 30. Retrieved from http://documents.worldbank.org/curated/en/203951468768863829/pdf/multi-page.pdf.

Cai, J. (2017). Education reform enters 'Comprehensive Construction Interior Decoration' stage. *China Education Daily*, October 20 (in Chinese).

Chen, B. (1996). Localization of education: Achievements, problems and prospects. *Education and Economy*, (1), 42—45 (in Chinese).

Chen, G. (1993). *Marxist education research.* East China Normal University Press (in Chinese).

Chen, X. (1992). Spring greets the eyes as the east wind comes – Comrade Xiaoping Deng in Shenzhen. *People's Daily*, March 31 (in Chinese).

Chen, Y. (1995). *Selected works of Yun Chen* (Volume III). Beijing: People's Publishing House (in Chinese).

Chen, Z. (2006a). Zhili Chen speaks at the opening ceremony of the fifth international conference on higher education. Retrieved from http://www.ce.cn/xwzx/ Gnsz/gdxw/200602/14/t20060214_6083059.shtml (in Chinese).

Chen, Z. (2006b). Strengthen leadership and implement work, and strive to properly carry out employment of college graduates – The State Councilor Zhili Chen's speech at a meeting on college graduate employment work coordination. Retrieved from http://www.gov.cn/ldhd/2006-06/09/content_305329.htm (in Chinese).

Cheng, Y. C. (2015). Paradigm shift in education: Towards the third wave research. In L. Hill & F. Levine (Eds.), *World education research yearbook 2014* (Selected Papers from pp. 5—29). New York: Routledge.

Cheng, Y. C., & Townsend, T. (2000). Educational change and development in the Asia-Pacific region: Trends and issues. In T. Townsend, & Y. C. Cheng (Eds.), *Educational change and development in the Asia-Pacific region: Challenges for the future* (Selected Paper from pp. 317—344). The Netherlands: Swets & Zeitlinger.

Deng, X. (1977a). Several opinions on science and education work (August 8). In X. Deng (1983). *Selected works of Xiaoping Deng* (Volume II) (Selected Paper from pp. 48—49). Beijing: People's Publishing House (in Chinese).

Deng, X. (1977b). Respect for knowledge, respect for talents (May 24). In X. Deng (1983). *Selected works of Deng Xiaoping* (Volume II) (Selected Paper from pp. 40). Beijing: People's Publishing House (in Chinese).

Deng, X. (1978). Speech at the national education work conference (April 22). In X. Deng (1983). *Selected works of Xiaoping Deng* (Volume II). Beijing: People's Publishing House (in Chinese).

Deng, X. (1980). The inscriptions for *The China Youth Daily* and *The Counselor* Magazine (May 26, 1980). The Literature Research Office of the Central Committee of CPC (Eds.) (1995). *Xiaoping Deng on education*. Beijing: People's Education Press (in Chinese).

Deng, X. (1983). Using foreign intelligence and expanding opening to the outside world (July 8). In X. Deng (1993). *Selected works of Xiaoping Deng* (Volume III) (Selected Paper from pp. 32). Beijing: People's Publishing House (in Chinese).

Deng, X. (1985). Reform is a road China must take to develop productive forces (August 28). In X. Deng (1993). *Selected works of Xiaoping Deng* (Volume III) (Selected Paper from pp. 136). Beijing: People's Publishing House (in Chinese).

Deng, X. (1987). Strengthening education with four basic principles and adhering to the policy of reform and opening up (January 20). In X. Deng (1993). *Selected Works of Xiaoping Deng* (Volume III) (Selected Paper from pp. 202). Beijing: People's Publishing House (in Chinese).

Deng, X. (1988). Science and technology are the primary productive forces (September 5, 12). In X. Deng (1993), *Selected works of Xiaoping Deng* (Volume III) (Selected Paper from pp. 275—276). Beijing: People's Publishing House (in Chinese).

Deng, X. (1989). What overwhelms everything is stability (February 26, 1989). In X. Deng (1993). *Selected works of Xiaoping Deng* (Volume III) (Selected Paper from pp. 284). Beijing: People's Publishing House (in Chinese).

Deng, X. (1992). Main points of speeches given in Wuchang, Shenzhen, Zhuhai, Shanghai and other places (January 18-February 21, 1992). In X. Deng (1993). *Selected Works of Xiaoping Deng* (Volume III) (Selected Paper from pp. 373—377). Beijing: People's Publishing House (in Chinese).

Deng, X. (1993). Inscription for Jingshan School (October 1, 1983). In X. Deng (1993). *Selected works of Xiaoping Deng* (Volume III) (Selected Paper from pp. 35). Beijing: People's Publishing House (in Chinese).

Ding, P. (2004). Jianli education reform: Selling 700 schools. Retrieved from http://finance.sina.com.cn/roll/20040109/1123596885.shtml (in Chinese).

Ding, R. (1989a). Talking about the People's Education Fund Institutions in Pingdu County. *China Education Journal*, (1), 12—16 (in Chinese).

Ding, R. (1989b). The problem with establishing a People's Education Fund Institutions in Rural Areas. *Education Research*, (2), 20—24 (in Chinese).

Du, M., & Fan, G. (2017). Social organization participation in education: Mechanisms and strategies. *Educational Research*, (4), 60—64 (in Chinese).

Economic and Social Council & United Nations. (2004). *The right to education*. Report submitted by the Special Rapporteur, Katarina Tomasevski (E/CN.4/2004/45), 15 Jan. New York: United Nations.

Fan, G. (1995). A commentary on the theory that "Education Adapts to the Market Economy". *Education Research*, (8), 56—61+66 (in Chinese).
Fan, G. (2005). Government, society, and schools—Design of the modern school institutions based on the school-based management concept. *Education Development Research*, (1), 12—17 (in Chinese).
Fan, G. (2017a). Reform of separation of management and evaluation in education: Theoretical hypothesis and practice path. *Educational Science Research*, (5), 5—12 (in Chinese).
Fan, G. (2017b). Exploration of the reform of the institutions and mechanisms of primary and secondary schools running themselves according to law based on the separation of educational management and evaluation. *Education Research*, (4), 12—17 (in Chinese).
Fan, G. (2018). Providing legal protection for the modernization of Shanghai's higher education governance. *Wenhui Daily*, March 16 (in Chinese).
Gao, H. (2007). Economist Min Tang never regrets calling for university enrolment expansion. *Guangzhou Daily*, August 27 (in Chinese).
Goertz, M. E., & Duffy, M. C. (2001). *Assessment and accountability institutions in the 50 States, 1999—2000*. CPRE Research Report Series (in Chinese).
Han, W. (1990). The Stone of Other Hills Can Attack Jade – The Enlightenment of the People's Education Fund Institutions of Pingdu County, Shandong Province. *Jiangxi Education*, (2), 30—34 (in Chinese).
Headington, R. (2000). *Monitoring, assessment, recording, reporting and accountability: Meeting the standards*. London: David Fulton.
Heller, D. E. (Ed.). (2001). *The states and public higher education policy: Affordable, access, and accountability*. Baltimore: John Hopkins University Press.
Hu, Y. (1982). Create a New Era of Socialist Modernization in an All-round Way——Report at the Twelfth National Congress of the Communist Party of China. Retrieved from http://cpc.people.com.cn/GB/64162/64168/64565/65448/4526430.html (in Chinese)
Hu, J. (2004). Establish and Implement the Scientific Concept of Development. In The Document Editing Committee of the Central Committee of CPC (Eds.), (2016). *Selected works of Jintao Hu* (Volume II). Beijing: People's Publishing House (in Chinese).
Hu, J. (2007). Waving High the Great Banner of Socialism with Chinese Characteristics, Fighting for a New Victory in Building a Well-off Society in an All-round Way – Report from the 17th National Congress of CPC, October 15. Retrieved from http://www.most.gov.cn/yw/200710/t20071026_56736.htm (in Chinese).
Hu, J. (2008). Speech at the 30th Anniversary of the Third Plenary Session of the Eleventh Central Committee of the Communist Party, December 18. Retrieved from http://www.gov.cn/test/2009-10/13/content_1437699.htm (in Chinese).
Hu, J. (2012). Unswervingly Advancing Along the Road of Socialism with Chinese Characteristics, Struggling to Build a Well-off Society in an All-round Way – Report from the 18th National Congress of CPC, November 8. Retrieved from http://theory.people.com.cn/n/2012/1109/c40531-19530534-3.html (in Chinese).
Huang, X. (2010). Public school entrusted management reform: Problems and trends. *China Education Journal*, (11), 30—34 (in Chinese).
Huo, X., Meng, N., & Tian, F. (2018). Jinping Xi Meets with US President Barack Obama. Retrieved from http://www.xinhuanet.com/world/2015-09/25/c_1116681366.htm (in Chinese).

Ilyich Lenin, V. (1919). Russian Communist Party (Bolshevik) Program Draft. In Central Compilation and Translation Bureau of Marx, Engels, Lenin and Stalin of the Central Committee of CPC (ed.) (2012). *Collected works of Lenin* (Vol. 3, pp. 744). Beijing: People's Publishing House.

Ji, B. (2009). Enlargement of Enrollment to Promote the Development of Higher Education into the Fast Lane. *China Education News*, September 21 (in Chinese).

Jiang, Z. (1992). Accelerating the Pace of Reform, Opening Up, and Modernization, and Winning a Greater Victory in the Cause of Socialism with Chinese Characteristics — Report from the 14th National Congress of CPC, October 12. Retrieved from http://www.gov.cn/test/2007-08/29/content_730511.htm (in Chinese).

Jiang, Z. (1997). Holding High the Great Banner of Xiaoping Deng Theory and Pushing the Construction of Socialism with Chinese Characteristics into the 21st Century – Report from the 15th National Congress of CPC, September 12. Retrieved from http://www.most.gov.cn/jgdj/xxyd/zlzx/200905/t20090518_69740.htm (in Chinese).

Jiang, Z. (1999). The Fundamental Purpose of Education Must be Improving the Moral Quality of the People (June 15). In Z. Jiang (2006). *Selected works of Zemin Jiang* (Volume II) (Selected Papers from pp. 157). Beijing: People's Publishing House (in Chinese).

Lao, K. (2003). The trend of China's educational reform at the turn of the century: The relationship between education and the market. *Peking University Education Review*, (3), 10—16 (in Chinese).

Lenin (2012). The Draft Programme of the R.C.P. (B.). In Central Compilation and Translation Bureau of Marx, Engels, Lenin and Stalin of the Central Committee of the CPC. *Collected works of Lenin* (Volume 3) (Selected Papers from pp. 744). Beijing: People's Publishing House.

Li, K. (2017a). Government Work Report – On March 5, 2017 at the Fifth Session of the Twelfth National People's Congress. *People's Daily*, March 17 (in Chinese).

Li, K. (2017b). Speech at the National Television and Telephone Conference on Deepening Optimized Service Reform of Combining Streamlining Administration and Decentralization and Laissez-Faire Management, June 13. Retrieved from http://www.xinhuanet.com/politics/2017-06/29/c_1121236906.htm (in Chinese).

Li, S., & He, H. (2006). Inspection of Jianli Public High-Quality High School Reform. *Southern Review* (Biweekly), May 1 (in Chinese).

Lu, Y., & Wang, X. (2004). Thinking from the Case of 'Transformation' in Public Schools: On the Equality and Efficiency of Education. *Basic Education Research*, (4), 20—25 (in Chinese).

Mahony, P., & Hextall, I. (2000). *Reconstructing teaching: Standards, performance and accountability.* London: Routledge.

MOE. (2002). *Notice of MOE on Several Problems Regarding the Strengthening of the Management of Basic Education in School Running* ([2002] No. 1), February 26. Retrieved from http://old.moe.gov.cn/publicfiles/business/htmlfiles/moe/moe_441/201006/88981.html (in Chinese).

MOE. (2004). Opposing "Education Welfare" and "Education Industrialization". Retrieved from http://news.sina.com.cn/e/2004-03-01/16491934828s.shtml (in Chinese).

MOE. (2005). *Several Opinions of MOE on Further Promoting the Balanced Development of Compulsory Education* (MOE [2005] No. 9), May 25. Retrieved from http://www.moe.gov.cn/srcsite/A06/s3321/200505/t20050525_81809.html (in Chinese).

MOE. (2006). *Several Opinions of MOE on Implementing "The Compulsory Education Law" to Further Regulate School Running Behavior in Compulsory Education* ([2006] No. 19), August 24. Retrieved from http://old.moe.gov.cn//publicfiles/business/htmlfiles/moe/s3321/201001/xxgk_81811.html (in Chinese).

MOE. (2010a). *Notice of MOE on the Printing and Distributing of "Study in China Program"* ([2010] No. 68), September 21. Retrieved from http://www.moe.gov.cn/srcsite/A20/moe_850/201009/t20100921_108815.html (in Chinese).

MOE. (2010b). *Opinions of MOE on Implementing a Scientific Outlook on Development and Further Promoting the Balanced Development of Compulsory Education* ([2010] No. 1), January 4. Retrieved from http://www.moe.gov.cn/srcsite/A06/s3321/201001/t20100119_87759.html (in Chinese).

MOE. (2012). *Opinions of MOE on Comprehensively Improving the Quality of Higher Education* ([2012] No. 4), March 16. Retrieved from http://www.moe.gov.cn/srcsite/A08/s7056/201203/t20120316_146673.html (in Chinese).

MOE. (2013). Announcement on Statistics of the Implementation of National Education Funding in 2012 ([2013] No. 7), December 18. Retrieved from http://www.moe.gov.cn/srcsite/A05/s3040/201312/t20131227_161346.html (in Chinese).

MOE. (2014). Announcement on Statistics of the Implementation of National Education Funding in 2013 ([2014] No. 4), October 31. Retrieved from http://www.moe.gov.cn/srcsite/A05/s3040/201410/t20141031_178035.html (in Chinese).

MOE. (2015a). Announcement on Statistics of the Implementation of National Education Funding in 2014 ([2015] No. 9), October 9. Retrieved from http://www.moe.gov.cn/srcsite/A05/s3040/201510/t20151013_213129.html (in Chinese).

MOE. (2015b). *MOE's Opinions on Deeply Advancing the Separation of Education, Management and Evaluation and Promoting the Transformation of Government Functions* ([2015] No. 5), May 4. Retrieved from http://www.moe.gov.cn/srcsite/A02/s7049/201505/t20150506_189460.html (in Chinese).

MOE. (2016a). Announcement on Statistics of the Implementation of National Education Funding in 2015 ([2016] No. 9), October 30. Retrieved from http://www.moe.gov.cn/srcsite/A05/s3040/201611/t20161110_288422.html (in Chinese).

MOE. (2016b). *Notice of MOE on the Printing and Distribution of "The Educational Initiative of Promoting the Construction of the Belt and Road Initiative"* ([2016] No. 46), July 13. Retrieved from http://www.moe.gov.cn/srcsite/A20/s7068/201608/t20160811_274679.html (in Chinese).

MOE. (2017a). Announcement on Statistics of the Implementation of National Education Funding in 2016 ([2017] No. 6), October 10. Retrieved from http://www.moe.gov.cn/srcsite/A05/s3040/201710/t20171025_317429.html (in Chinese).

MOE. (2017b). *Notice of MOE on Properly Carrying Out Work in the Enrollment of Ordinary Colleges and Universities in 2017* ([2017] No. 1), February 13. Retrieved from http://www.moe.gov.cn/srcsite/A15/moe_776/s3258/201702/t20170224_297252.html (in Chinese).

MOE (The Ministry of Education of PRC). (1996). *The National Education Project "Ninth Five-Year Plan" and 2010 Development Plan* (Teaching Plan [1996] No. 45). Retrieved from http://www.moe.gov.cn/jyb_sjzl/moe_177/tnull_2485.html (in Chinese).

MOE, et al. (2004). *Opinions of MOE, National Development and Reform Commission, and Ministry of Finance on Implementation of the "One-fee Institutions" Charging Method at the National Compulsory Education Stage* (Education Finance [2004] No. 7). Retrieved from http://www.moe.gov.cn/srcsite/A05/s7052/200403/t20040317_181246.html (in Chinese).

MOE, et al. (2012). *Notice of MOE, National Development and Reform Commission and Auditing Office on Printing and Distributing The Eight Measures for Managing Unreasonable Charges in School Selection at the Compulsory Education Stage* (MOE [2012] No. 1), January 20. Retrieved from http://old.moe.gov.cn//publicfiles/business/htmlfiles/moe/moe_1793/201202/130873.html (in Chinese).

MOE, et al. (2016a). *Notice of MOE and Five Other Departments on the Printing and Distribution of the "13th Five-Year Plan for Education Poverty Alleviation"* ([2016] No. 18), December 16. Retrieved from http://www.moe.gov.cn/srcsite/A03/moe_1892/moe_630/201612/t20161229_293351.html (in Chinese).

MOE, et al. (2016b). *Notice of MOE and the State Administration of Foreign Experts Affairs on the Printing and Distribution of "Measures for the Implementation and Management of the Program of Introducing Talents of Discipline to Universities"* ([2016] No. 4), November 3. Retrieved from http://www.moe.gov.cn/srcsite/A16/s3340/201611/t20161129_290299.html (in Chinese).

MOE, et al. (2017a). *Notice of MOE and Three Other Departments on the Printing and Distribution of the "High School Stage Education Popularization Plan (2017—2020)"* ([2017] No. 1), March 24. Retrieved from http://www.moe.gov.cn/srcsite/A06/s7053/201704/t20170406_301981.html (in Chinese).

MOE, et al. (2017b). *Several Opinions of MOE, the Central Organizing Committee, the Development and Reform Commission, the Ministry of Finance, and the Ministry of Human Resources and Social Security on Deepening the Reform of the Streamlining of Administration and Decentralization and Laissez-Faire Management and the Optimization of Services in the Field of Higher Education* ([2017] No. 7), March 31. Retrieved from http://www.moe.gov.cn/srcsite/A02/s7049/201704/t20170405_301912.html (in Chinese).

Mukhopadhyay, M. (2001). *Total quality management in education.* New Delhi: National Institute of Educational Planning and Administration.

Pang, I., Isawa, E., Kim, A. Knipprath, H., Mel, M. A., & Palmer, T. (2003). Family and community participation in education. In J. P. Keeves & R. Watanabe (Eds.), *International handbook of educational research in the Asia-Pacific region* (Selected Papers from pp. 1063—1080). The Netherlands: Kluwer Academic Publishers.

Ruan, C. (2013). The evolutionary logic and future trends of China's compulsory education balanced development policy. *Educational Research*, (7), 37—45 (in Chinese).

Secretariat of the National Curriculum Professional Committee. (2001). *China curriculum research and reform in the 21st century.* Beijing: People's Education Press (in Chinese).

Spencer, H. (1884). *What knowledge is of most worth.* Michigan: The University of Michigan Library.

Su, B., Li, G., Liu, F., & Deng, X. (1979). Give Higher Education Institutions a Little Autonomy. *People's Daily*, December 6 (in Chinese).

Sun, G. (2006). Student Enrollment for Restructured Primary Schools Stops This Year. *Tianjin Daily*, May 22 (in Chinese).

Sun, Y., et al. (2016). *25 Years of Curriculum Reform in Shanghai (1988—2013).* Shanghai: Shanghai Education Press (in Chinese).

Tang, M. (2006a). Is Enrolment Expansion Wrong? RetrDieved from http://finance.sina.com.cn/economist/jingjixueren/20060206/09432318575.shtml (in Chinese).

Tang, M. (2006b). Talking Again About Whether Enrolment Expansion is Wrong. *South Reviews*, March 1 (in Chinese).

The 11th Central Committee of CPC. (1978). Communiqué of the Third Plenary Session of the 11th Central Committee of CPC (Passed December 22, 1978). Retrieved from http://cpc.people.com.cn/GB/64162/64168/64563/65371/4441902.html (in Chinese).

The Central Committee of CPC. (1981). *Resolutions on Certain Historical Issues of the Party since the Founding of PRC* (adopted at the Sixth Plenary Session of the 11th Central Committee of

CPC on June 27). Retrieved from http://www.people.com.cn/item/20years/newfiles/b1040.html (in Chinese).

The Central Committee of CPC. (1984). *The Decision of the Central Committee of CPC on Economic Institutions Reform* (adopted at the third plenary meeting of the 12th Central Committee of CPC on October 20). *People's Daily*, October 21 (in Chinese).

The Central Committee of CPC. (1985a). *The Decision of the Central Committee of CPC on the Reform of the Education Institutions* ([1985] No. 12), May 27. Retrieved from http://www.moe.gov.cn/jyb_sjzl/moe_177/tnull_2482.html (in Chinese).

The Central Committee of CPC. (1985b). *The Decision of the Central Committee of CPC on the Reform of the Science and Technology Institutions* (March 13). *People's Daily*, March 20 (in Chinese).

The Central Committee of CPC. (1993). *Notice of the Central Committee of CPC on Printing and Distributing "The Outline of China's Education Reform and Development"* ([1993] No. 3), February 13. Retrieved from http://www.moe.gov.cn/jyb_sjzl/moe_177/tnull_2484.html (in Chinese).

The Central Committee of CPC. (1999). *The Decision of the Central Committee of CPC on Deepening Education Reform and Comprehensively Promoting Quality Education*, June 13. Retrieved from http://old.moe.gov.cn/publicfiles/business/htmlfiles/moe/moe_177/200407/2478.html (in Chinese).

The Central Committee of CPC. (2006). *Decision of the Central Committee of CPC on Several Major Issues Concerning the Construction of a Harmonious Socialist Society* (adopted at the Sixth Plenary Session of the 16th Central Committee of CPC on October 11). Retrieved from http://www.gov.cn/govweb/gongbao/content/2006/content_453176.htm (in Chinese).

The Central Committee of CPC. (2009). *Resolution of the Central Committee of CPC on Certain Questions in the History of the Party since the Founding of the People's Republic of China*. Beijing: People's Publishing House (in Chinese).

The Central Committee of CPC. (2013). *Decision of the Central Committee of CPC on Several Major Issues Concerning Comprehensively Deepening Reform* (adopted at the Third Plenary Session of the 18th Central Committee of CPC on November 12). Retrieved from http://www.scio.gov.cn/zxbd/nd/2013/document/1374228/1374228.htm (in Chinese).

The Central Committee of CPC. (2015). *Proposal of the Central Committee of CPC on Formulating the Thirteenth Five-Year Plan for National Economic and Social Development* (adopted at the Fifth Plenary Session of the 18th Central Committee of CPC on October 29). Retrieved from http://cpc.people.com.cn/n/2015/1103/c399243-27772351.html (in Chinese).

The Central Committee of CPC. (2018). *The Decision of the Central Committee of CPC on Deepening the Reform of Party and State Institutions* (Adopted at the Third Plenary Session of the 19th Central Committee of CPC on February 28). Retrieved from http://www.gov.cn/zhengce/2018-03/04/content_5270704.htm (in Chinese).

The Central Committee of CPC & the State Council of PRC. (1999). *The Decision of the Central Committee of CPC and the State Council on Deepening Education Reform and Promoting Quality Education in an All-round Way* (June 13). Retrieved from http://old.moe.gov.cn/publicfiles/business/htmlfiles/moe/moe_177/200407/2478.html (in Chinese).

The Central Committee of CPC, the State Council of PRC. (2000). *Notice of the Central Committee of CPC and the State Council on Carrying Out Pilot Work on the Reform of Rural Taxes and Fees* ([2000] No. 7), March 2. Retrieved from http://zgb.mof.gov.cn/zhengwuxinxi/zhengceguiding/200806/t20080618_46331.html (in Chinese).

The General Office of the Central Committee of CPC. (2008). *Notice of the General Office of the Central Committee of CPC on Forwarding "The Opinions of the Central Talent Work Coordination*

Group on Implementing the Thousand Talents Program" ([2008] No. 25), December 23. Retrieved from http://old.moe.gov.cn//publicfiles/business/htmlfiles/moe/s3321/201001/81828.html (in Chinese).

The General Office of the Central Committee of CPC. (2014). *The Implementation Opinions of the General Office of the Central Committee of CPC on Adhering to and Improving the Principal Responsibility Institutions under the Leadership of Party Committees of General Higher Education Institutions* ([2014] No. 55), October 15. Retrieved from http://www.gov.cn/zhengce/2014-10/15/content_2766861.htm (in Chinese).

The General Office of the State Council of PRC. (1995). *The General Office of the State Council's Forwarded Notice to the State Education Commission "Several Opinions on Deepening the Reform of the Higher Education Institutions"* ([1995] No. 43), May 29. Retrieved from http://www.people.com.cn/item/flfgk/gwyfg/1995/gwyfg1995.html (in Chinese).

The General Office of the State Council of PRC. (1998). *The Notice of the General Office of the State Council, Forwarded to MOE "Several Opinions on the Experimental Work in the Reform of the School Institutions in the Compulsory Education Phase"* ([1998] No. 96), June 25. Retrieved from http://old.moe.gov.cn//publicfiles/business/htmlfiles/moe/s3321/201001/81828.html (in Chinese).

The General Office of the State Council of PRC. (2001). *Notice of the General Office of the State Council Forwarded to the Reform Office and Other Departments Regarding Opinions on Lowering the Prices of Textbooks for Primary and Secondary Schools and Deepening Reform of the Textbook Management Institutions* ([2001] No. 34), June 4. Retrieved from http://www.gov.cn/zhengce/content/2016-09/30/content_5114294.htm (in Chinese).

The General Office of the State Council of PRC. (2006). Jiabao Wen Presides Over State Council Executive Meeting to Listen to Higher Education Work Reports, etc. Retrieved from http://www.gov.cn /ldhd/2006-05/10/content_277511.htm (in Chinese).

The National Development and Reform Commission, et al. (2005). *Notice of the National Development and Reform Commission and MOE on Preparing for the Work of Clearing, Reorganizing and Restructuring Schools* ([2005] No. 2827), December 30. Retrieved from http://www.moe.gov.cn/jyb_xxgk/gk_gbgg/moe_0/moe_1133/moe_1147/tnull_14529.html (in Chinese).

The Research Group of "Study of the Jiaojiang Education Joint Shareholding Institutions School Running Model". (1999). A new exploration of developing the investment potential of folk education—A research report on the 'Joint Shareholding Education Institutions' of Jiaojiang. *Education Research*, (3— 12–16 (in Chinese).

. (2006). *Compulsory Education Law of PRC* (revised on June 29, 2006). Retrieved from http://www.gov.cn/ziliao/flfg/2006-06/30/content_323302.htm (in Chinese).

The Standing Committee of the National People's Congress of PRC. (2016). *Decision of the Standing Committee of the National People's Congress on Amending "The Promotion of Private Education Law of PRC"* (adopted at the 24th meeting of the Standing Committee of the 12th National People's Congress on November 7). Retrieved from http://www.moe.gov.cn/s78/A02/zfs__left/s5911/moe_619/201612/t20161213_291732.html (in Chinese).

The State Council of PRC. (1994a). *Opinions on Implementation of the State Council's "Outline Plan for China's Education Reform and Development"* (Promulgated by the State Council [1994] No. 39), July 3. Retrieved from http://www.moe.gov.cn/jyb_sjzl/moe_177/tnull_2483.html (in Chinese).

The State Council of PRC. (1994b). *Regulations on Education for Persons with Disabilities* ([1994],No. 161), August, 23. Retrieved from http://www.gov.cn/zhengce/content/2017-02/23/content_5170264.htm (in Chinese).

The State Council of PRC. (2001a). Decision of the State Council on the Reform and Development of Basic Education ([2001] No. 21), May 29. Retrieved from http://www.gov.cn/gongbao/content/2001/content_60920.htm (in Chinese).

The State Council of PRC. (2001b). *Notice of the State Council on Further Improving the Pilot Work of Rural Tax and Fee Reform* ([2001] No. 5), March 24. Retrieved from http://www.gov.cn/zhengce/content/2016-09/18/content_5109014.htm (in Chinese).

The State Council of PRC. (2003). *Decision of the State Council on Further Strengthening Rural Education Work* ([2003] No. 19), September 17. Retrieved from http://www.moe.gov.cn/jyb_xxgk/moe_1777/moe_1778/tnull_27725.html (in Chinese).

The State Council of PRC. (2004). *Regulations for the Implementation of the Law on the Promotion of Private Education* (The Order of the State Council, No. 399), March 5. Retrieved from http://www.gov.cn/zwgk/2005-05/23/content_200.htm (in Chinese).

The State Council of PRC. (2005). *Notice of the State Council on Deepening the Reform of the Guarantee Mechanism for Rural Compulsory Education Funds* ([2005] No. 43), December 24. Retrieved from http://www.gov.cn/gongbao/content/2006/content_185157.htm (in Chinese).

The State Council of PRC. (2008). *Notice of the State Council on Properly Carrying Out Work on Exempting Tuition and Miscellaneous Fees for Students in Urban Compulsory Education* ([2008] No. 25), August 12. Retrieved from http://www.gov.cn/zwgk/2008-08/15/content_1072915.htm (in Chinese).

The State Council of PRC. (2011). *Opinions of the State Council on Further Increasing Financial Investment in Education* ([2011] No. 22), June 29. Retrieved from http://www.gov.cn/zwgk/2011-07/01/content_1897763.htm (in Chinese).

The State Council of PRC. (2012). *Opinions of the State Council on Deeply Promoting the Balanced Development of Compulsory Education* ([2012] No. 48), September 5. Retrieved from http://www.gov.cn/zhuanti/2015-06/13/content_2878998.htm (in Chinese).

The State Council of PRC. (2014). *Implementation Opinions of the State Council on Deepening the Reform of the Examination Admission Institutions* ([2014] No. 35), September 3. Retrieved from http://www.gov.cn/zhengce/content/2014-09/04/content_9065.htm (in Chinese).

The State Council of PRC. (2015a). *Notice of the State Council on Printing and Distribution of the Work Plan for Promoting the Transformation of Government Functions in the Combination of Decentralization and Delegation in 2015* ([2015] No. 29), May 12. Retrieved from http://www.gov.cn/zhengce/content/2015-05/15/content_9764.htm (in Chinese).

The State Council of PRC. (2015b). *Notice of the State Council on Printing and Distributing an Overall Plan for Coordinating the Promotion of Construction of World-Class Universities and First-Class Disciplines* ([2015] No. 64), October 24. Retrieved from http://www.moe.gov.cn/jyb_xxgk/moe_1777/moe_1778/201511/t20151105_217823.html (in Chinese).

The State Council of PRC. (2016a). *Several Opinions of the State Council on Encouraging Social Forces to Establish Education and Promoting the Healthy Development of Private Education* ([2016] No. 81), December 29. Retrieved from http://www.gov.cn/zhengce/content/2017-01/18/content_5160828.htm (in Chinese).

The State Council of PRC. (2016b). *Several Opinions of the State Council on Coordinating the Promotion of Reform and Development of Urban and Rural Compulsory Education Integration in County Areas* ([2016] No. 40), July 2. Retrieved from http://www.gov.cn/zhengce/content/2016-07/11/content_5090298.htm (in Chinese).

The State Council of PRC. (2016c). *Opinions of the State Council on Strengthening Care and Protection Work for Left-behind Children in Rural Areas* ([2016] No. 13), February 4. Retrieved from http://www.moe.gov.cn/jyb_xxgk/moe_1777/moe_1778/201602/t20160215_229575.html (in Chinese).

The State Council of PRC. (2017). *Notice of the State Council on Printing and Distributing the 13th Five-Year Plan for the Development of National Education* ([2017] No. 4), January 10. Retrieved from http://www.moe.gov.cn/jyb_xxgk/moe_1777/moe_1778/201701/t20170119_295319.html (in Chinese).

The State Education Commission. (1997). *Several Principled Opinions on Regulating School-running Behavior at the Current Compulsory Education Stage* ([1997] No. 1), January 14. Retrieved from http://www.moe.gov.cn/jyb_sjzl/moe_177/tnull_2483.html (in Chinese).

The State Education Commission & the Ministry of Finance of PRC. (1987). *The Opinions of the State Education Commission and the Ministry of Finance on Several Issues Concerning the Reform of the Management Institutions of Rural Basic Education* (Education Policy Research [87] No. 002), June 15 (in Chinese).

The State Planning Commission of PRC, et al. (2002). *Notice of the State Planning Commission, the Ministry of Finance, and MOE on Printing and Distributing "The Public Notification Institutions for Education Fees"* (State Planning Commission [2002] No. 792), May 27. Retrieved from http://www.moe.gov.cn/jyb_xxgk/moe_1777/moe_1779/tnull_27743.html (in Chinese).

Whitacre, P. (1997). *Education decentralization in Africa as viewed through the literature and USAID projects.* Washington DC, Academy for Education Development and USAID, January.

Wu, H., & Ning, D. (2004). From a Modern Enterprise Institutions to a Modern School Institutions—A Rational Reflection on the Practice of Jiaojiang's "Modern School Institutions". *Journal of Zhejiang University (Humanities and Social Sciences)*, (—, 2–8 (in Chinese).

Wu, H., et al. (2005). The status quo, problems and prospects of China's education voucher practice. *Education Development Research*, (6B— 15–19 (in Chinese).

Xi, J. (2014). *The governance of China*. Beijing: Foreign Languages Press (in Chinese).

Xi, J. —014–2016). Coordinating and promoting the "Four Comprehensives" strategic layout (December 13, 2014 – January 29, 2016). In Xi, J. (2017). *The governance of China* (Volume 2) (Selected Papers from pp. 22). Beijing: Foreign Languages Press (in Chinese).

Xi, J. (2017a). Building a community of common human destiny (January 18, 2017). In Xi, J. (2017). *The governance of* China (Volume II) (Selected Papers from pp—537–548). Beijing: Foreign Language Press (in Chinese).

Xi, J. (2017b). Decisive Victory in Building a Well-Off Society in an All-round Way: Winning a Great Victory with Socialism with Chinese Characteristics in the New Era – Report from the 19th National Congress of CPC, October 18. Retrieved from http://www.gov.cn/zhuanti/2017-10/27/content_5234876.htm (in Chinese).

Xiao, Z. (1989). Primary and Secondary Schools Should Continue to Implement the Principal Responsibility Institutions – Review and Thoughts on the Management Institutions Reform of Primary and Secondary Schools after the Founding of PRC. *China Education Daily*, October 17 (in Chinese).

Xiao, Z. (1990). Thoughts on the principal responsibility institutions. *Primary and Secondary School Management*, (—, 2–5 (in Chinese).

Xiao, Z. (1993). Primary and Secondary Schools Should Promote the Enactment of the Principal Responsibility Institutions. *China Education Daily*, March 30 (in Chinese).

Xiao, Z. (2000). Proposals and connotations of the principal responsibility institutions. *Primary and Secondary School Management*, (1—, 2–5 (in Chinese).

Xinhua News Agency. (2013). President Jinping Xi Delivers a Video Message at the First Anniversary of the United Nations " Global Education First Initiative". *People's Daily*, September 27 (in Chinese).

Yang, D. (2008). 30 Years of Reform and Development in China's Education Institutions. In Zou, D. (ed.) (2008). *China Economic Development and Institutions Reform Report No. 1: China's 30 Years of Reform and Opening-up* —978–2008) (Selected Papers from pp. 711). Beijing: Social Science Literature Publishing House (in Chinese).

Zhang, B. (2000). College Fees: Strictly Standardizing Management and Implementation of Supporting Measures, *People's Daily*, June 9 (in Chinese).

Zhang, D., & Zhuang, Y. (2005). Allow Students to Study at High-Quality Schools: A Group of Transformed Schools in Shanghai Return to State-Run Schools. *Jiefang Daily*, May 13 (in Chinese).

Zhang, T. (1993). A brand new view of scientific research of education: Theory of the education industry. *Guangzhou Education*, (5— 12–16 (in Chinese).

Zhao, L., & Sheng, S. (2008). Financing China's higher education expansion. In Hall, S. T., & Lewis, M. W. (eds.) (2008). *Education in China 21st century issues and challenges*. New York: Nova Science Publishers.

Zhu, Z. (2001). Zhejiang Provincial Governor Chai Songyue Emphasizes Importance of Having the County as the Mainstay but not Reducing the Responsibility of Township Governments when Discussing Improvement of the Province's Basic Education Management Institutions. *China Education News*, November 17 (in Chinese).

CHAPTER TWO

The School Leadership and Administration Institutions

YEMEI WEI

Since Reform and Opening Up began, the greatest advantage of the development of Chinese school education has been the upholding of the Party's leadership, from bringing about order from chaos, building the constitution and establishing institutions to the current changes towards openness, democracy, and pluralism. These changes were all completed under the leadership of the Party. School leadership and management institutions are also stabilizing and improving in a process of continuous change. This chapter mainly reviews and analyzes the evolution and changes of the school leadership institution, the principal ranking institution, and the modern school institution since Reform and Opening Up began as a way of optimizing the internal governance structures of schools and enhancing their self-governance levels.

SECTION 1 DEVELOPMENT HISTORY OF THE SCHOOL LEADERSHIP AND MANAGEMENT INSTITUTIONS

Since Reform and Opening Up began, China's school leadership and management institution has undergone many reforms and has come through four stages: the reform and gestation stage, the policy interpretation stage, the volatility and practice adjustment stage, and finally the gradual continuation and the gradual improvement stage.

Shortly after the Third Plenary Session of the Eleventh Central Committee of the Communist Party of China closed, educational theorists represented by Zongliu Xiao discussed the reform of the leadership institution of primary and secondary schools, pointing out the shortcomings of the *School Principal Division of Responsibility Institution Under the Leadership of the Party Branch* for primary and secondary schools mentioned in the *Provisional Work Regulations for Full-time Primary Schools* (*Trial Draft)* and the *Provisional Work Regulations for Full-time Secondary Schools (Trial Draft)* promulgated by the former Ministry of Education in September 1978. In the field of higher education, the School Principal Division of Responsibility Institution under the Leadership of the Party Committee was specified in the newly revised "*Higher Education Article 60*" in 1978 to be unable to meet the needs of social development after Reform and Opening Up. In August 1980, Xiaoping Deng made the report "On the Reform of the Party and State Leadership Institution" at an enlarged meeting of the Political Bureau of the Central Committee, demanding that "the principals, deans, directors and so on under the leadership of the Party should also consider further reform in a prepared and step-by-step manner" (Deng, 1994).

In 1985, *The Decision of the Central Committee of the Communist Party of China on the Reform of the Education Institution* proposed that the Chinese school administration institution "gradually implements the principal responsibility institution." However, facing a lack of understanding of the institution by grassroots people, it was mainly only those who were on the front line of educational theory and practice who could parse the policy. Meanwhile, basic education and higher education circles carried out trial and promotion of the principal responsibility institution from point to point. By the end of 1988, the principal responsibility institution was basically recognized and initially implemented in most parts of the country.

In 1989, Chinese education faced new, urgent circumstances. The school leadership and management institution centered on the principal responsibility institution was questioned and the determination to implement the principal responsibility institution in some areas began to waver. In the end, the principal responsibility institution for primary and secondary schools was preserved, but the principal responsibility institution of higher education institutions failed to continue to be implemented, and the principal responsibility institution under the leadership of the Party committee gradually began to step out on to the stage of history. In the following few years, the leadership and management institution lingered in the adjustment stage for higher education institutions, but primary and secondary schools were deep in the implementation stages.

After the promulgation of *The Outline for Chinese Education Reform and Development* in 1993, the principal responsibility institution was implemented in all types of schools at the middle and lower levels, and the implementation of the principal responsibility institution under the leadership of the Party committee was further determined at higher education institutions. The policy documents that followed mainly continued to emphasize the existing leadership and management institution, and the reform of institutional mechanisms entered a phase of gradual continuation and gradual improvement. For example, after the implementation of the principal responsibility institution, methods for strengthening the construction of principal teams were put on the agenda, and calls for the professionalization of principals led to the reform of the principal ranking institution. Since the beginning of the new century, an education institution innovation objective centered on a modern school institution was established. *The National Medium-and-Long-Term Education Reform and Development Plan Outline (2010–2020)*, promulgated in 2010, further promoted the modern university institution with Chinese characteristics and primary and secondary school management institutions. The establishment of school regulations charters and the construction of the democratic participation institution have been continuously improved in this development. The internal governance structure of schools, with governance in accordance with the law, scientific decision-making, and democratic participation in schools, has been gradually established.

SECTION 2 THE GRADUALLY STABILIZING SCHOOL LEADERSHIP INSTITUTIONS

The school leadership institution is a fundamental institution for managing and leading schools, and is related to whether the school is well run or not (Xiao, 2002). It must be adjusted in accordance with the changes in a country's situation and objectives, otherwise the institution will find it difficult to meet the demands that the developments of the times have on schools. Since Reform and Opening Up began, the Chinese school leadership institution has undergone a series of evolutions that have closely followed changes in the times. It can be said that the evolutionary history of the school leadership institution is a perfect history of the primary and secondary school principal responsibility institution as well as the principal responsibility institution of higher education institutions under the leadership of the Party committee. This section will mainly be an analysis of the changes to China's basic education and higher education leadership institutions since Reform and Opening Up.

I. Basic Education: From the School Principal Responsibility Institution under the Leadership of the Party Branch to the Principal Responsibility Institution

Since the founding of the People's Republic of China, Chinese primary and secondary schools have implemented a variety of school leadership institutions. Soon after liberation, the school board institution was implemented; during the first five-year plan, the principal responsibility institution was implemented; after the rectification movement in 1957, the principal responsibility institution under the leadership of the Party branch was implemented; in the 1960s, *The Provisional Work Regulations (Draft)* for full-time primary and secondary schools stipulated the implementation of the principal responsibility institution under the leadership of the local Party committee and the supervisory education administration department; after the National Education Work Conference in 1978, MOE reissued the *Provisional Work Regulations for Full-time Primary Schools* (Draft) and the *Provisional Work Regulations for Full-time Secondary Schools* (Draft), stipulating the implementation of the principal work division responsibility institution under the leadership of the Party branch. It can be seen that school power has been constantly switching between the masses, the executives, and the Party committee, with an attempt to find a balance between democracy and regulation, and also seeking a good way to overcome the problem of there being no differentiation between the Party and the government and the Party taking the place of the government. In short, before the principal responsibility institution was implemented, the leadership institutions of Chinese primary and secondary schools were constantly seeking a way out of this instability and uncertainty.

(1) Proposals and Developments of the Principal Responsibility Institution

Before *The Decision of the Central Committee of the Communist Party of China on the Reform of the Education Institution* (hereinafter referred to as *The Decision*) required the implementation of the principal responsibility institution in 1985, the principal work division responsibility institution under the leadership of the Party branch was the leadership institution implemented in primary and secondary schools for the longest time. For that time, this institution was beneficial in overcoming the chaos brought about by the "10 years of turmoil" and helped bring China's education cause on to the right track. However, with the shift in the Party's work focus after the Third Plenary Session of the 11th Central Committee, its drawbacks became increasingly apparent. The main manifestations of this were: the separation of "leadership" and "responsibility," whereby the principal possesses responsibilities but no power, resulting in conflicts between primary and secondary school secretaries and principals; all major issues of the school had to be decided after discussion by the Party branch, whereby the Party and government are inseparable and the Party acts as the government (Xiao, 1985). In summary, it seems that this leadership institution became increasingly unfavorable in terms of its inability to stimulate enthusiasm for various subjects in various aspects, and thus, this was not conducive to a progression towards a more scientific and democratic way of managing schools (Beijing Municipal Education Commission et al., 1987). To address this, the 1985 *Decision* required that "schools gradually implement the principal responsibility institution, and they must establish a prestigious school committee with a small number of members chaired by the principal to serve as a deliberative body." This provision not only provided requirements for the implementation of the principal responsibility institution but also further guidance for its further improvement. The school committee can also supplement the personal wisdom of the principal to a certain extent.

After the *Decision* came out, the reform of the leadership institution of primary and secondary schools in various regions gradually began to advance from point to point. However, at the time, there were still many educators who did not have a completely clear understanding of the principal responsibility institution and the relationship between the Party and the government. In 1987, the Beijing Municipal Education Commission, the Education Bureau, and the Education Union published "*The Need for 'The Principal Responsibility Institution' — Answering the Queries of Principals*," which gave detailed explanations on various issues including the reasons for the implementation of the principal responsibility institution, whether or not it weakens or undermines the Party's leadership and whether or not it affects the master status of teaching staff (Beijing Municipal Education Commission et al., 1987). However, this did not have a substantial effect. After the political turmoil of 1989, doubt was cast on the principal responsibility institution. Some education administration departments even ordered primary and secondary schools to resume their original leadership institutions. In 1989, Zongliu Xiao wrote the essay "Primary and Secondary Schools Should Continue to Implement the Principal Responsibility Institution — Reviews and Reflections of Management Institution Reform of Primary and Secondary Schools after the Founding of the People's Republic of China" (Xiao, 1989). In this essay, he pointed out that "the Rectification and Anti-Rightist Movement of 1957 negated the principal responsibility institution, the Cultural Revolution negated the principal responsibility institution … We cannot stop the reform of the internal management institution of a school because of a 50-day political storm, and further, we cannot negate the principal responsibility institution for a third time." The author takes a dialectical view of the principal responsibility institution and carries out a pertinent analysis of its rationality and limitations. On October 24, the MOE at the time He Dongchang delivered a speech pointing out that primary and secondary schools can continue to implement the principal responsibility institution, which implied that the institution had emerged from its predicament (Xiao, 2000).

In 1993, the Central Committee of the Communist Party of China and the State Council issued the *Outline of China's Education Reform and Development* (hereinafter referred to as the *Outline*), which required "the implementation of the school principal responsibility institution for all types of schools at and below the junior high level." In contrast to the *Decision*, the *Outline* did not use the term "gradually," which also implies that the principal responsibility institution was to be implemented nationwide. At the end of 1993, a "School Leadership Institution Reform" research group from Huazhong Normal University conducted a questionnaire survey on 189 rural primary and secondary schools in the provinces of Hubei, Hunan, Henan, Jiangxi, and Guangdong. The results showed that 59.8% of the schools had implemented the principal responsibility institution, and it was in widespread use in large- and medium-sized cities. The research team believed that the implementation of the principal responsibility institution improved the efficiency of school management, promoted the legalization of school management, promoted the reform of the management institution within schools, and also brought attention to education management research. However, on the whole, reform of the school leadership institution was too slow; the principal's school-running authority was not in place, especially with regard to personnel and financial power (financial resources of principals were limited due to lack of funding); the schools' relationships to the Party and the government were not fully straightened out; democratic management and democratic supervisory power of education workers had not been generally implemented; the relationship between schools and the higher education authorities had not been straightened out; and theoretical research and theoretical publicity of school leadership institution reform were relatively lagging (Central China Normal University "Study on the Reform of the School Leadership System" Research Group, 1996). Despite these limitations, the country's determination to implement the principal responsibility institution has not wavered since then.

(2) The Development Trend of the Principal Responsibility Institution

Since entering the 21st century, the MOE has always emphasized persistence with and improvement of the principal responsibility institution. Article 26 of the *Compulsory Education Law of the People's Republic of China* from 2006 stipulates that schools should implement the principal responsibility institution, and *The National Medium-and-Long-Term Education Reform and Development Plan Outline (2010–2020)* requires the improvement of the principal responsibility institution for primary and secondary schools and secondary vocational schools. In 2011, the MOE issued the *National Medium-to-Long-term Plan for the Development of Educational Talents (2010–2020)*, which requires "the formulation and implementation of detailed implementation rules for the principal responsibility institution of ordinary primary and secondary schools and secondary vocational schools, the formulation of basic professional standards for principals of primary and secondary schools and secondary vocational schools, setting up a healthy entry standard qualification institution for primary and secondary school principals, promoting the professionalization and improving the management level of principals." In 2013, *The Professional Standards for Principals of Compulsory Education Schools* set the standards for principals from six aspects: planning school development, building a culture of education, leading the curriculum, leading the growth of teachers, optimizing internal management, and adapting to the external environment. In 2015, *MOE's Opinions on Deeply Advancing the Separation of Education, Management and Evaluation and Promoting the Transformation of Government Functions* required adhering to and improving the principal responsibility institution of ordinary primary and secondary schools and secondary vocational schools. But so far, the operational procedures of the principal responsibility institution have not been perfected. At the same time, with the continuous deepening of education reform, its drawbacks have gradually become more apparent. For example, it is the case that "whatever the principal says goes" when it comes to management decision-making within schools, but when it comes to the relationship between the government and the school, the education administration department directly interferes with the school's management affairs and intercepts the personnel and financial authority of the principal. In short, the principal is subject to too many external controls, but is less constrained within the school, and the school's democratic management mechanism is not yet sound. Therefore, in 2012, *The Comprehensive Promotion of the Implementation of the Outline of Governing Schools in Accordance with the Law* required that "primary and secondary schools should improve the principal responsibility institution, establish a school committee with representatives of teachers, students and parents, and improve the democratic decision-making process." In 2015, *MOE's Opinions on Deeply Advancing the Separation of Education, Management and Evaluation and Promoting the Transformation of Government Functions* provided environmental support for the adjustment of the relationship between the government and schools, as well as regulations on the construction of school committees for the implementation of the principal responsibility institution. In December 2017, the MOE issued *The Compulsory Education School Management Standards*, requesting "the establishment of a problem consultation mechanism, listening to relevant opinions and suggestions from students, educators and parents, effectively solving corresponding contradictions; adhering to democratic centralism and regularly holding school meetings, improving the school faculty congress institution and so on." It can be said that the separation of management and evaluation and the reform of the internal governance structure of schools has paved the way for better implementation of the principal responsibility institution.

II. Higher Education: From the Principal Responsibility Institution to the Principal Responsibility Institution under the Leadership of the Party Committee

Since the founding of the People's Republic of China, the leadership institution of China's higher education institutions has been the principal responsibility institution (see *Provisional Regulations for Higher Education Institutions* issued in 1950), the school committee responsibility institution under the leadership of the school Party committee (see *Instructions Regarding Education Work* issued by the Central Committee of the Communist Party of China and the State Council in 1958), the school committee responsibility institution headed by the principal under the leadership of the Party committee (see *Provisional Work Regulations for Higher Education Institutions Directly Under MOE (Draft)* in 1961, or *Higher Education Article 60*), and the work division responsibility institution for principals under the leadership of the Party committee (see the revised *Higher Education Article 60* from 1978) (Li, 2000). In the 1980s, explorations began into the principal responsibility institution (Gong & Wang, 2011).

(1) Exploration and Termination of the Principal Responsibility Institution

In 1984, the Central Publicity Department and the MOE held a symposium in Chengdu on the pilot work of the principal responsibility institution in nine provinces and cities, and determined that fifteen colleges and universities including Beijing Normal University, Tongji University, Liaoning University, and Northwestern Polytechnic University had piloted the institution (Feng, 1985). In 1985, *The Decision of the Central Committee of the Communist Party of China on the Reform of the Education Institution* proposed that "schools gradually implement the principal responsibility institution." "Party organizations in schools should be freed from the past state of all-inclusiveness and concentrate their energies on strengthening the establishment of the Party as well as strengthening ideological and political work." In October 1987, the report of the 13th National Party Congress required that "Party organizations in institutions should also gradually switch to a role of guaranteeing and supervision along with the implementation of the executive head responsibility institution" (Zhao, 1987). In 1988, the State Education Commission promulgated *The Opinions on Gradually Implementing the Principal Responsibility Institution in Higher Education Institutions*, proposing that "higher education institutions must gradually implement the principal responsibility institution in accordance with the principle of separation of the Party and the government," requiring that experiences of implementation be earnestly summed up, for further work to be done on straightening out relationships between the Party and the government, and to switch over to the principal responsibility institution when conditions are ripe. Some higher education institutions across the country had begun to pilot the principal responsibility institution, and 103 of them were determined to have implemented it (Li & Wang, 2000).

In 1989, the State Education Commission convened a national conference on higher education work, which specifically called for strengthening the Party's leadership role in higher education institutions. On August 28 of the same year, the Political Bureau of the CPC Central Committee discussed and approved the *Notice of the Central Committee of the Communist Party of China on Strengthening Party Building*, clearly stating that "higher education institutions implement the principal responsibility institution under the leadership of the Party committee. The scope of the trials for the principal responsibility institution was to be no longer expanded. Experiments could continue for trials that had gone well. Regardless of the type of leadership institution implemented, the Party committee is the political core of the school, comprehensively leading ideological and political work, managing cadres, and at the same time, supporting the executive leadership to work independently and responsibly, and to refrain from taking on administrative affairs." In this regard, progress of the principal responsibility institution halted in the field of higher education and could even be said to have retreated.

(2) Development of the Principal Responsibility Institution under the Leadership of the Party Committee

In 1990, in order to strengthen the Party's role in higher education institutions, the Central Committee of the Communist Party of China's *Notice on Strengthening Party Building in Higher Education Institutions* required that the leadership institution of higher education institutions be clarified and that the leadership position of the Party committee be adhered to. In 1993, the Central Committee of the Communist Party of China and the State Council issued the *Outline of China's Education Reform and Development*, requiring "higher education institutions that have implemented the principal responsibility institution under the leadership of the Party committee to have discussions and make decisions on major issues with the Party committee, while also ensuring that the executive leadership fully exercise its authority."

The Higher Education Law of the People's Republic of China, which came into effect on January 1, 1999, clearly stipulates in the form of law that "state-run higher education institutions implement the principal responsibility institution under the leadership of higher education institution grassroots committees of the Communist Party of China." At the same time, legal requirements were also made regarding the duties of Party committees and principals. Article 39 stipulates that "higher education institution grassroots committees of the Communist Party of China shall, in accordance with the relevant regulations of the Constitution of the Communist Party of China, uniformly lead the work of schools and support principals in using their power independently and responsibly. The main responsibilities of the leadership are: implementing the political line, guiding the principles and policies of the Communist Party of China, adhering to the direction of socialist education, leading the ideological and political work and moral education of schools, discussing and making decisions on the establishment of internal organizations within schools and on which candidates should head the internal organizations, discussing major issues such as the reform, development, and basic management institution of schools, and ensuring the completion of various tasks centered on cultivating talents." Article 41 stipulates that the principals of higher education institutions be fully responsible for the teaching, scientific research, and other administrative management work of schools and exercise the following functions and powers: formulate development plans, formulate specific rules and regulations and annual work plans, and organize for their implementation; organize teaching activities, scientific research, and ideological and moral education; formulate internal organization plans, recommend vice principal candidates, appoint and dismiss the heads of internal organizations; appoint and dismiss teachers and other internal staff, manage student statuses, and implement rewards or punishments for students; plan and implement annual budgets, protect and manage school production, and safeguard the legitimate rights and interests of the school; and any other functions or powers as stipulated in the regulations charter. It can be seen from the above that the Party committee is mainly responsible for major ideological, political, personnel, and school development affairs, while the principal is mainly responsible for the administrative affairs of the school.

Following on from this, many policy documents have played a role in consolidating and improving the principal responsibility institution under the leadership of Party committees of higher education institutions. In 2007, *The Opinions of the Party Group of MOE of the CPC on Strengthening the Construction of Grassroots Party Organizations in Ordinary Higher Education Institutions* called for "fully understanding the importance and urgency of strengthening the construction of grassroots Party organizations in higher education institutions in the new situation," and the general requirements for the construction of grassroots Party organizations in higher education institutions. The main principles and mission objectives were described in detail, and the working institutions and operational mechanisms of grassroots Party organizations in higher education institutions were required to be improved. *The National Medium-and-Long-Term Education Reform and Development Plan Outline (2010–2020)* stated: "Public schools must adhere to and improve the principal responsibility institution under the leadership of Party committees. They must improve the rules of procedure and decision-making procedures, implement the powers of Party committees and principals according to law, and improve the school's principal selection and appointment method. They must give full play to the important role of academic committees in curriculum building, academic evaluation, and academic development." In 2011, the MOE issued the *National Medium-to-Long-term Plan for the Development of Educational Talents (2010–2020)*, which stated the need to: "formulate and implement opinions of implementation of the principal responsibility institution under the leadership of Party committees of higher education institutions, adhere to and improve the principal responsibility institution under the leadership of Party committees of public higher education institutions, and explore the establishment of a mechanism that plays an active role in higher education councils, boards of directors, or academic committees." In 2014, *The Implementation Opinions of the General Office of the Central Committee of the Communist Party of China on Adhering to and Improving the Principal Responsibility Institution under the Leadership of Party Committees of General Higher Education Institutions* was issued, requiring Party committees to lead the work of schools in a unified manner, for principals to preside over the administration work of schools and for the administrative deliberation and decision-making institution of the Party committee to be perfected. In short, democratization, decentralization, and rule of law are the main trends in the development of China's university leadership institution.

SECTION 3 COMPREHENSIVE ADVANCEMENT OF THE REFORM OF THE PRINCIPAL RANKING INSTITUTION

The principal ranking institution refers to the abolition of the administration ranking of the school and the principal, the establishment of an independent principal ranking sequence, channels of promotion, a salary institution and ranking evaluation criteria, as well as a principal management institution that engages in ranked appointment making (Li, 2016). It breaks the institution of lifetime appointments for principals and replaces it with an appointment institution. Its essence is promoting the professionalization of principals. Its changes have experienced the previous local exploration, and the process of piloting and advancing the country in the later period reflects the determination of the government in doing away with school administration.

I. From the Administration Ranking Institution to the Principal Ranking Institution

Before the implementation of the principal ranking institution, most school principals in the country took office by way of appointment, and the principal had an administration ranking. This institution was formed by linking the ranks and salaries of primary and secondary school principals to the administration rankings of schools during wage reform in the 1980s. Its purpose was to improve the statuses of primary and secondary schools. The principals of key middle schools in cities, districts, and counties as well as junior high schools and central primary schools were attached to leading roles of departments, assisting roles of departments, leading roles of sections, and assisting roles of sections. With the development of society, the following problems of this institution have gradually shown themselves: First, it is difficult to appoint the appropriate person. In order to solve individual-level or salary problems, the organization department or personnel department appoints cadres who do not understand teaching to serve as the principal of the school; second, the principal's professional development is restricted. Under the management of the administration institution, the principal is busy with various meetings, inspections, and other duties. "Government affairs" and "external affairs" are all given to one person, and many principals abandon professional promotion in the face of rank promotion. Third is that there is no way to achieve rational flow between principals. The administration level of the principal is linked to the school and so principals are not willing to serve in schools that have a lower administration level. To a certain extent, this affected the rise in management levels of weak and rural schools, and thus the gap in the allocation of educational resources and in school-running standards grew larger and larger. Fourth is the disunity of human rights and powers. The rights of the principal are in the personnel department, while his powers are in education administration. Some principals have an even higher administration rank than supervisors and leaders of education administration departments, making it difficult for these departments to guide and manage the realities of the school (Basic Education Curriculum and Textbook Development Center, MOE, 2015: 4–5). It is precisely in this context that in the face of some of the above problems many regions have begun to explore the reform of the principal ranking institution.

II. The Principal Ranking Institution: From "Trial" to "Complete Advancement"

In 1993, Shanghai took the lead in proposing the idea of implementing the primary and secondary school-level principal ranking institution. In the following year, this was piloted in Jing'an and Luwan districts. In 1997, Shanghai continued to expand the pilot, and integration work for the establishment of the principal ranking institution was completed in Jing'an District, Luwan District, and expanded pilot areas. Beijing's Xicheng District, Guangzhou's Tianhe District, Liwan District and Haizhu District, Zhongshan City (Guangdong Province), Weifang City (Shandong Province), and other places also followed the pilot (Hao, 2016). At the national level, in 1999 *The Decision of the Central Committee of the Communist Party of China on Deepening Education Reform and Comprehensively Promoting Quality Education* proposed "the need to continue consolidating and improving the job training and certification institution for primary and secondary school principals, as well as the need to pilot the principal ranking institution, and gradually improve the principal selection and appointment institution." In 2000, *The Decision of the State Council on the Reform and Development of Basic Education* (hereinafter referred to as *The Decision*) required "the reform of the selection and appointment of primary and secondary school principals and the management institution … the implementation of an appointment institution for primary and secondary school principals, clarification of the job qualifications for principals, gradual establishment of an institution for principals to be openly recruited and compete for posts, implementing a fixed term of office for principals that may be extended or renewed, and actively promoting the principal ranking institution." From "trial" to "active advancement," the principal ranking institution has been affirmed at the national level and will be greatly developed.

Under the impetus of national policy, the Shanghai Municipal Committee Organization Department, the Shanghai Education Work Committee, and the Shanghai Municipal Education Commission issued *The Notice on Printing and Distribution of "The Opinions on Implementation of the Principal Ranking Institution in Primary and Secondary Schools in Shanghai"* in 2000 and promoted the principal ranking institution for primary and secondary schools throughout the city. It was stipulated that primary and secondary school principals were to be divided into five ranks and twelve classes, namely: special principals; rank one first-class and rank one second-class principals; rank two first-class, rank two second-class, rank two third-class, and rank two fourth-class principals; rank three first-class, rank three second-class, rank three third-class, rank three fourth-class principals; and rank four first-class and rank four second-class principals. The evaluation index institution of each rank includes three primary indicators (including personal accomplishment, professional accomplishment, and school-running effectiveness) and eight secondary indicators (including mental disposition, moral quality, thoughts on school-running, school management, education and teaching, teacher building, school performance, and social impact), and each secondary indicator has clear evaluation criteria (Hao, 2016). The ranking and evaluation index institution of the principals and secretaries of Shanghai secondary vocational schools is more complicated than ordinary primary and secondary schools as it includes six primary indicators, twelve secondary indicators, and twenty-four tertiary indicators. Jury committees at all levels are composed of eleven to seventeen people, Party and government leaders, and principals of prestigious schools and experts each account for one third. The salary of the principal is composed of three parts: ranking salary, basic salary, and performance salary. The differences in the first, second, third, and fourth ranks are 60 yuan, 40 yuan, 30 yuan, and 20 yuan, respectively. The appointment authority of Shanghai primary and secondary school principals is still assigned to the organization department, personnel department, and education department according to the original school level. However, once the reserve talents are appointed as principals, the management authority is the responsibility of the education department.

The exploration of the principal ranking institution started in Shanghai. While practicing the ranking institution, it retained the principal administration level and is characterized by a "dual track" institution; Weifang City even abolished the principal administration level at one time, and to a certain extent this can be said to have been even more pioneering (Basic Education Curriculum and Textbook Development Center, MOE, 2015: 23–58). Since 1999, Weifang City has been piloting the principal ranking institution in Gaomi (a county-level city). In 2001, it was piloted in the municipal schools of Weifang City. In September of 2004, the Weifang Municipal Party Committee and the Municipal Government issued *The Opinions on the Implementation of the Principal Ranking Institution in Primary and Secondary Schools*, and in August of 2011, issued *The Opinions on Deepening and Perfecting Reform of the Implementation of the Principal Ranking Institution of Primary and Secondary Schools*, and a management institution promoting the professional development of principals and ensuring the school-running ability of educators was established from the institutional level (National Research Centre for Educational Development, MOE, 2013). Weifang's principal rankings are divided into three series: elementary schools, junior high schools, and high/junior high vocational schools. Each series is divided into four ranks and eight grades, namely, special principals, senior principals (grades one, two, and three), intermediate principals (grades one, two, and three) and junior principals (grades one and two); and the number of special principals is controlled to within 2% of the total number of primary and secondary school principals in the city. A grade promotion and dynamic management institution has been implemented. The grade of the principal is based on satisfaction levels of school-running, school-running performance, professional school-running ability, and so on and evaluations are made by a team of education experts. The evaluation indicators are shown in Table 2.1.

Table 2.1 Weifang City Principal Ranking Evaluation Index Institution (Liu et al., 2014)

Primary indicator	Weight	Secondary indicator	Weight	Tertiary indicator	Weight
Personal quality	30	Importance assessment ability	20		
		Personal ability	10		
Job performance		School education quality	50	Training of excellent students	20
				Large area improvement	10
				Art student training	10
				Personality features	10
		School management level	20		

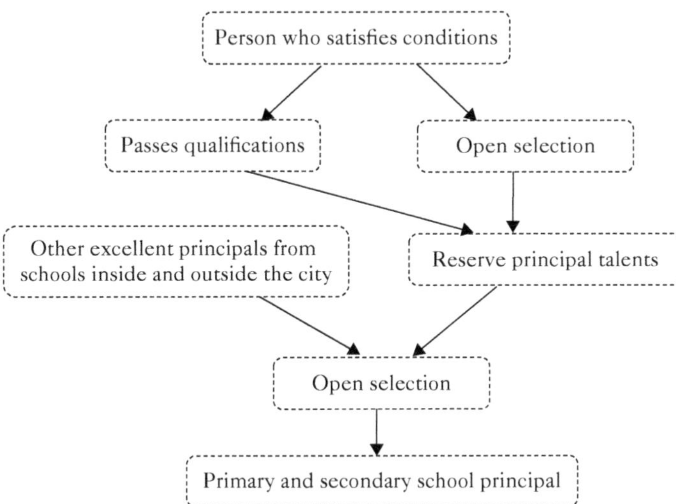

Figure 2.1 Weifang City Primary and Secondary School Principal Selection Stages.

Source: Basic Education Curriculum and Textbook Development Center, MOE (2015), *On the Road to Expert School Running—Interpretation of Principal Ranking Institution Reform*, Beijing: Educational Science Press, pp. 23–58.

Weifang City's team of education experts come from a unified resource pool of expert judges in the city. The team is composed of well-known principals, education experts, and outstanding teachers and is updated every two years. The experts of the team who evaluate the principal are randomly selected from a database of experts and the team is usually composed of seven to eleven people. At the same time, teacher and parent representatives of the schools that require the appointment of a principal are required to be present and participate in the evaluation through questionnaire evaluation, acknowledgment survey, and other methods (Basic Education Curriculum and Textbook Development Center, MOE, 2015: 23–58). During the selection of specific principals, suitable talents are mainly selected through the stages shown in Table 2.1.

Along with the implementation of the principal ranking institution, Weifang has also set up a series of supporting measures to ensure the effective implementation of the institution. For example, upgrades in the rankings of principals require exchanges between principals of quality schools and urban schools with rural schools and weak schools, and so the ranking institution has thus eliminated concerns about principal exchanges. The performance salary of principals is made up of four parts: basic salary, post salary, allowance, and ranking salary. It is determined according to the ranking of the principal, the size of the school, and the conditions of running the school. The finance department determines the salary of the principal according to the rank of the principal. At the same time, the education administration department delegates powers to the principal by firstly expanding the principal's personnel rights, allowing the principal to form a trial cabinet, and independently and openly electing the middle-level administrative cadres; secondly, by delegating the power to make academic appointments for the school; thirdly, by carrying out entrance examination and curriculum reform; and fourthly, by delegating the power to evaluate and commend teachers. At the same time, the performance appraisal institution, democratic management institution, mass satisfaction evaluation institution, with the assistance of the Party's leadership, and supervision institution are used to supervise the principal. In addition, the principal training institution, the professionalization institution of the leadership of the education administration department, the qualification institution of the head of the education administration department, the supervision implementation mechanism, the third-party evaluation institution, the personnel reform and management institution, and other relevant institutions were established one after another to ensure the smooth implementation of the principal ranking institution in Weifang. By the end of 2004, Weifang City had fully implemented the principal ranking institution.

When viewed from the national level, although the *Decision* of 2000 required the active promotion of the principal ranking institution, no clear stipulations were made for the pilot implementation areas. In 2003, the Ministry of Personnel and the MOE jointly issued *The Opinions on Implementation of Deepening Reform of the Personnel Institution in Primary and Secondary Schools*, proposing: "improving and perfecting the institution for selecting and appointing primary and secondary school principals; the active implementation of an institution of appointment for primary and secondary school principals; and the implementation of a tenure institution for primary and secondary school principals." "Gradually abolish the administrative level of primary and secondary schools, and actively carry out the pilot work of the management reform of primary and secondary school principals in accordance with the principle of piloting first and steadily promoting." *The National Medium-and-Long-Term Education Reform and Development Plan Outline (2010–2020)* required "the implementation of the principal ranking institution," and this was closely followed by *The Notice of the General Office of the State Council on Launching a Pilot Program for the Reform of the National Education Institution*, which set "exploring the principal ranking institutions of primary and secondary schools and deepening the reform of the title institution of primary and secondary school teachers" as an important objective. Songyuan City (Jilin Province), Shanghai, Weifang City (Shandong Province), Zhongshan City (Guangdong Province), and Baoji City (Shaanxi Province) became pilot units. *The Professional Standards for Principals of Compulsory Education Schools* issued in 2013 requires "strict qualification standards for compulsory education school principals, improvement in the compulsory education school principal selection and appointment institution, and the implementation of the principal ranking institution …" In 2015, *MOE's Opinions on Deeply Advancing the Separation of Education, Management and Evaluation and Promoting the Transformation of Government Functions* required "comprehensive promotion of the reform of the primary and secondary school principal ranking institution and the realization of the specialization and professionalization of principals." It can be seen that after more than 20 years of development, the principal ranking institution has already acquired the conditions for promotion nationwide.

In 2016, Shandong promoted the comprehensive reform of basic education as a main line, fully implemented the principal ranking institution for primary and secondary schools, and also carried out de-administration reforms. During the 13th Five-Year Plan period, the administration level of primary and secondary school principals will be completely abolished (Wei, 2016). In February of the same year, the Shenzhen Human Resources and Social Security Bureau and the Shenzhen Municipal Education Bureau issued the *Shenzhen Primary and Secondary School Principal Ranking Institution Management Method*, which stipulated that the principal ranking institution consists of two principals, the head principal and the vice-principal. Rankings for head principals were split into the following five (from top to bottom): special, first, second, third, and fourth. Vice principals have four rankings, namely (from top to bottom): first, second, third, and fourth. Since 2016,

Anhui Province has carried out reform of the principal ranking institution across the whole province. Within this reform, Ma'anshan City was the first to carry out reform of the primary and secondary school principal ranking institution in the central region. It is expected that the administration level for principals will be abolished across the whole of Anhui by 2020. In addition, other provinces and cities are also continuously pushing implementation of the principal ranking institution. In short, the principal ranking institution is playing an increasingly important role in promoting the specialization and professionalization of school principals.

SECTION 4 THE EMERGING MODERN SCHOOL INSTITUTION CONSTRUCTION

The 2003–2007 Education Revitalization Action Plan required "deepening the reform of the internal management institution of schools and exploring the establishment of a modern school institution." In December 2004, the first modern school institution experimental research experience exchange meeting was held in Chengdu, after which exchange meetings were held in different regions every year. In 2010, *The National Medium-and-Long-Term Education Reform and Development Plan Outline (2010–2020)* described the construction of modern school institutions in one particular chapter (Chapter 13), making provisions and requirements for the construction of modern school institutions in four main aspects from "promoting the separation of government and schools and the separation of management and administration," "the implementation and expansion of the school's autonomy in running school affairs," "improvement of the modern university institution with Chinese characteristics," to "improvement of the school management institution for primary and secondary schools," and this basically set the tone for the construction of modern school institutions, requiring "construction of a modern school institution that runs school affairs according to law, with self-management, democratic supervision, and social participation, and builds a new type of relationship between the government, schools and society." Specifically, the construction of a school regulations charter is a prerequisite for running a school according to the law. The democratic participation of teachers, students, parents, and society is an important guarantee of the independent management and democratic supervision of the school.

I. Gradually Forming a Structure of "One School, One Regulations Charter"

In 1995, *The Education Law of PRC* clearly stated that it was necessary to formulate school regulations charters. In 2003, MOE issued *The Opinions on Strengthening the Work of Managing Schools According to Law*, proposing that "a school regulations charter must be formulated and improved in accordance with laws and regulations, and serves as an important basis for school-running activities after examination and approval by the education administration department." However, this did not compel schools to attach importance to the construction of a regulations charter in this year. In 2010, *The National Medium-and-Long-Term Education Reform and Development Plan Outline (2010–2020)* considered the construction of a school regulations charter to be an inherent requirement of a modern university institution with Chinese characteristics, running a school in accordance with the rule of law, and as an important part of the modern university institution reform pilot. It required that "higher education institutions of all kinds should formulate a charter according to law and manage the school in accordance with the regulations of the charter." "Schools must establish and improve the school charter and regulations in a way that conforms to legal requirements and that reflects its own characteristics; schools must be run according to law and be strictly managed." Soon after, in *The Notice of the General Office of the State Council on Launching the Pilot Program for the Reform of the National Education Institution*, "26 higher education institutions including Peking University had piloted the establishment of a sound school regulations charter and had improved the internal governance structure of the institution."

In 2012, the MOE issued *The Outline for the Implementation of Comprehensive Promotion of School Management According to Law*, and called for "the lawful formulation of school regulations charters that possess the characteristics of the institution," and hoped to promote the autonomy of schools through the construction of regulations charters, and regulate the internal power structure and power operation rules of schools. At the same time, the school regulations charter construction schedule was once again brought forward, requiring that "by 2015, a comprehensive structure of 'one school, one charter' will be formed." In 2015, *MOE's Opinions on Deeply Advancing the Separation of Education, Management and Evaluation and Promoting the Transformation of Government Functions* once again stated: "All levels and all types of schools must formulate school regulations charters with their own characteristics in accordance with the law and form a structure of 'one-school, one-charter.' Primary schools in the same school district can formulate joint articles of association. Schools should use the charter as a guide, rationalize and improve rules and regulations, formulate and improve management institutions for teaching, scientific research, students, personnel, etc., and establish and improve various procedures, internal organizational rules, rules of procedure, etc., to form a sound, standardized and unified series of institutions." So far, school regulations charter construction has spread across the country's higher education institutions, junior high schools, and primary schools. In December of 2017, *The Notice of MOE on Printing and Distributing "The Management Standards of Compulsory Education Schools*" required "the development and revision of school regulations charters according to law, improvement and perfection of the charter formulation and supervision mechanism, standardization of school-running behavior, and improvement in school governance." Charter construction has become an important criterion for evaluating school management. After more than twenty years of development, especially following active promotion in recent years, school regulations charter construction has made great progress.

II. Advocating a Pluralistic Democratic Participation Institution

Participation is an important symbol of democratic management in schools. In 1999, *The Decision of the Central Committee of the Communist Party of China on Deepening Education Reform and Comprehensively Promoting Quality Education* required "encouraging all sectors of society, parents and students to participate in the evaluation of school work in an appropriate manner." *The 2003–2007 Education Revitalization Action Plan* emphasized deepening the reform of the internal management institution of schools and required "actively promoting the participation and supervision of the community, students and parents in school management." In 2012, *The Outline for the Implementation of Comprehensive Promotion of School Management According to Law* required "expanding orderly participation, strengthening deliberation and consultation, giving full play to the role of the faculty congress, the Communist Youth League, the student union and other mass organizations in democratic decision-making mechanisms, and actively exploring the participation of teachers and students in these mechanisms" and had institutional provisions for the institutions, methods, and specific content of teacher participation in school affairs. It can be seen that the promotion of multi-subject participation has always been an important part of the national education policy document. In 2017, *The Compulsory Education School Management Standards* took "establishing a problem negotiation mechanism, listening to the opinions and suggestions of students, faculty and parents, effectively solving relevant contradictions" and "building a harmonious cooperative relationship between families, schools and communities" as an important management standard for compulsory educational schools. This section reviews the important role of internal institutions and subjects in the democratic management of schools.

(1) Internal Institutions Involved in School Governance

School Committees. In 1985, *The Decision of the Central Committee of the Communist Party of China on the Reform of the Education Institution* stated: "Schools with suitable conditions must establish prestigious school committees with a small number of people chaired by the principal to serve as a deliberative body." After this, school committees were rarely mentioned in policy documents until 2012, when *The Outline of the Comprehensive Promotion of the Implementation of Governing Schools in Accordance with the Rule of Law* required that: "Primary and secondary schools must improve the principal responsibility institution, establish school committees with representative teachers, students and parents, and improve the democratic decision-making process." In 2015, *MOE's Opinions on Deeply Advancing the Separation of Education, Management and Evaluation and Promoting the Transformation of Government Functions* further explained the functions of school committees, requiring "the improvement of the internal governance structure of schools ... Adherence to and improvement of the principal responsibility institution of ordinary primary and secondary schools and secondary vocational schools. Primary and secondary schools are required to set up school committees attended by school leaders, teachers, students and parent representatives, community representatives and so on. Reports are to be made on the school regulations charter, development plans and annual work. Suggestions are to be made on important matters including major education and teaching reforms and work involving students, parents and the community so as to improve the democratic decision-making process." From the policy documents mentioned above, it can be seen that with the development of society, school committees of the present day are very different from those established as stipulated in the 1985 *Decision of the Central Committee of the Communist Party of China on the Reform of the Education Institution*, most basically on the composition of committee members. Later documents contained regulations for a much more diverse range of subjects. In recent years, many cities and counties in China have formulated their own documents on their own school committees or construction of a modern school institution. For example, the Shenzhen Municipal Education Bureau issued *The Guiding Opinions on the Comprehensive Promotion of Modern School Institution Construction in Primary and Secondary Schools in Shenzhen*, and the Ningbo Municipal Education Bureau issued *The Opinions on Promoting the Establishment of a Primary and Secondary Schools Committee Institution*. In addition, Jiangsu, Shandong, and other provinces are also actively exploring school committee construction. Most of these provinces and cities have positioned the nature of the school committees as supervisory bodies, but some cities have defined them as decision-making and supervisory bodies.

Boards of Directors. In addition to school committees, boards of directors/councils are also playing or being asked to play a role in different types of schools. In 2003, *The Opinions of MOE on Strengthening the Work of Managing Schools According to Law* pointed out: "Privately-run schools and educational institutions jointly run by Chinese and foreign organizations must regulate school-running behavior in accordance with 'The Private Education Promotion Law' and 'The Regulations on Sino-foreign Cooperation in Running Schools' as well as relevant state regulations. They must establish and improve the rules of procedure of school boards of directors, councils or other decision-making bodies, and standardize the decision-making process." In 2010, *The National Medium-and-Long-Term Education Reform and Development Plan Outline (2010–2020)* (hereinafter referred to as *The Plan Outline*) continued to emphasize that "privately-run schools should set up councils or boards of directors according to law, guarantee that principals exercise their powers according to law, and gradually promote the supervisory institution," and also required "exploring the establishment of councils or boards of higher education institutions to improve the long-term mechanism for social support and supervision of school development." "[They must] develop and improve the school regulations charter and explore the mechanism by which the school council, board of directors or academic committee plays an active role." In fact, the university board institution originated in the United States. The government of the Republic of China and the Kuomintang Government implemented the board institution before liberation, but it was abolished after liberation. After Reform and Opening Up began, the reform of the economic institution turned the board of directors institution into a vision of the university institution. In 1987, Shantou University first established a board of directors and led other schools in establishing theirs. However, the boards of public universities in China did not change the original institution for universities until 2010, when *The Plan Outline* finally began to increase emphasis of the institution in the hopes of exploring a long-term mechanism. In 2012, *The Outline for the Implementation of Comprehensive Promotion of School Management According to Law* made the following emphases towards boards of directors of vocational schools and privately run schools: "Vocational schools should establish a school council or board of directors with the participation of industry personnel to form a decision-making mechanism where the school and enterprises work together; privately run schools and jointly run Sino-foreign schools must improve the regulations of the board of directors or the council, regularly hold meetings on carrying out statutory duties according to law, and improve decision-making procedures." At the same time, the role of the boards of directors of higher education institutions in decision-making is required to be clarified according to law, and "the scope of authority and regulations on decision making of the Party committee and principal working committee of higher education institutions shall be clarified according to law, making use of the role of academic committees, school councils (boards) and other organizations in decision-making …." In 2015, *MOE's Opinions on Deeply Advancing the Separation of Education, Management and Evaluation and Promoting the Transformation of Government Functions* required for ordinary higher education institutions to also establish school councils and have them play an active role in decision-making consultation and social cooperation.

Teacher Appeal or Mediation Committees. Appeal or mediation committees are the crystallization of the implementation of the spirit of administering schools according to law. In 2012, *The Outline for the Implementation of Comprehensive Promotion of School Management According to Law* required "improving the dispute resolution mechanism within schools according to law. The law should be used as the basic way of resolving contradictions and conflicts within schools, and various dispute resolution mechanisms such as letters and visits, mediation, appeals, arbitration, etc., should be established and comprehensively applied so as to properly and conveniently handle various interest disputes within the school according to the law. "In 2017, *The Compulsory Education School Management Standards* required for: "a specified person to be responsible for a school's legal affairs, for a school legal counsel institution to be established, and for full utilization of legal means as a way of maintaining a school's legitimate rights and interests."

(2) Main Participants in School Governance

Faculty Congress and Teacher Participation. In 1985, *The Decision of the Central Committee of the Communist Party of China on the Reform of the Education Institution* required "the establishment and improvement of faculty congresses represented by school workers with teachers as the main subjects, and the strengthening of democratic management and democratic supervision." In 2003, *The Opinions of MOE on Strengthening the Work of Managing Schools According to Law* pointed out: "For the promotion of democratic construction and improvement of democratic supervision, it is necessary to further improve the faculty congress institution, effectively guarantee the rights of faculty and staff members to participate in the democratic management and democratic supervision of schools, and ensure that faculty and staff have the right to know about and participate democratically in major school decisions." This is only a directional guide on the use of the faculty congress to promote the participation of teachers in democratic management and supervision, and does not make detailed provisions on how to participate. On December 8, 2011, the then MOE Guiren Yuan issued the 32nd *Order of MOE of the People's Republic of China*, issuing *The Regulations of School Faculty Congresses*, stating that "school faculty congresses are a basic form of faculty staff participating in the democratic management and supervision of schools according to law." Detailed provisions on its powers, elections, terms of office, rights, obligations and organizational rules, and working institutions (i.e., trade unions) and other aspects were also given. Teachers have gained an operational reference as a result of participating in school affairs through faculty congresses. In 2012, *The Outline for the Implementation of Comprehensive Promotion of School Management According to Law* proposed: "Implementing 'The Regulations of School Faculty Congresses', giving full play to the role of the faculty congresses as a way of allowing faculty staff to participate in the school's democratic management and allowing them to serve as main channels of supervision. Institutions and affairs related to the personal interests of faculty staff members such as hiring methods for technical posts, income allocation plans etc. should be submitted to the faculty congress for deliberation and approval; major issues involving the development of the school should be submitted to the faculty congress for discussion. The powers of evaluation and assessment over school leaders and management departments should be expanded for faculty members."

Autonomous Student Organizations and Student Participation. In 2012, *The Outline for the Implementation of Comprehensive Promotion of School Management According to Law* clearly stated: "We must actively expand channels for students to participate in the democratic management of schools, further reform and improve the institution of student congresses in higher education and secondary schools, and promote the independent management of students. The opinions of students and their parents should be fully sought when it comes to formulating management regulations that involve student interests …." It can be seen that policies are more concerned with the participation of students in secondary schools and higher education. In 2015, *MOE's Opinions on Deeply Advancing the Separation of Education, Management and Evaluation and Promoting the Transformation of Government Functions* required primary and secondary schools to establish school committees with student participation, "further improvement and implementation of the student congress institution, and guarantees for the expansion of faculty staff and student participation in the democratic management and supervision of schools according to law." In December 2017, *The Compulsory Education School Management Standards* required: "Making full use of the role of the Young Pioneers, the Communist Youth League, the Student Union, and the Student Association to guide students in self-managing or participating in school governance." In summary, the current participation of students in the governance of higher education institutions has aroused the attention of academic circles and policy discourses, but even though the participation of students in primary and secondary schools was mentioned in the policy, the differences have not attracted enough attention.

Parent Committees and Parent Involvement. *The Decision of the Central Committee of the Communist Party of China on Deepening Education Reform and Comprehensively Promoting Quality Education* from 1999 stated: "Actively encourage all sectors of society, parents and students to participate in the evaluation of school work in an appropriate manner." *The 2003–2007 Education Revitalization Action Plan* stated: "Actively promote the participation and supervision by the community, students and parents in school management." In 2003, *The Opinions of MOE on Strengthening the Work of Managing Schools According to Law* pointed out that "primary and secondary schools should actively promote community participation in school management and supervision, promote the establishment of parent committees, clarify the responsibilities of parent committees, and fully listen to the opinions of parent committees when making important decisions on student rights. They should accept supervision from parent committees, and provide institutional guarantees for parents, community support, and participation in school management." However, the establishment of parent committees has not attracted enough attention from schools. Shandong was one of the provinces to attach importance to the construction of parent committees relatively early on. In 2009, the Education Department promulgated *The Regulations on the Establishment and Management of Parent Committees in Primary and Secondary Schools in Shandong Province (Draft)*, requiring regular parent committee meetings in order to establish an institution of regular communication between the committee and the school, to create a favorable environment for school development, to help carry out family education, to send representatives to attend meetings on school affairs and academic affairs, to support and help students in practice outside the school, and to play a role in publicity. Later, in a number of policy documents, the parent committee has always been regarded as an important institution for internal school governance, and is an important force that cannot be ignored in school education. For example, *The National Medium-and-Long-Term Education Reform and Development Plan Outline (2010–2020)* required "improving the management institutions in primary and secondary schools … the establishment of primary and secondary school parent committees." In 2012, *The Outline for the Implementation of Comprehensive Promotion of School Management According to Law* issued by MOE required that "primary and secondary schools and kindergartens should gradually establish and improve the parent committee institution. The parent committee should assume responsibilities such as supporting education and teaching work, participating in and supervising school management, and promoting school and family communication and cooperation. Its members should be democratically elected by all parents." In order to implement the spirit of *The Outline*, *The Guiding Opinions of MOE on Establishing Parent Committees for Primary and Secondary Schools and Kindergartens* from 2012 sets out the meanings, responsibilities, and rules for formation of parent committees. The basic duties of a parent committee include: participation in school management, participation in education work, and communication between schools and families. In October 2015, the MOE promulgated *The Guiding Opinions on Strengthening Family Education Work* with the theme of "Family Education" for the first time, proposing that full play be given to the role that schools play in family education, incorporating parent committees into the daily management of the school, making full use of the role that parent committees play, and having parent committees become an important bridge in connecting school education and family education. In December 2017, *The Compulsory Education School Management Standards* furthered the concepts of "improving and perfecting the parent committee institution, establishing a parent school, establishing school open days, increasing the participation of parents in school governance and forming a joint effort in educating people" as important indicators in evaluating school management.

Social Participation. The emphasis on social participation in the education policy documents began with *The National Medium-and-Long-Term Education Reform and Development Plan Outline (2010–2020)* (hereinafter referred to as *The Plan Outline*) in 2010, which considered social participation to be an important factor in constructing a modern school institution. It also required "the establishment and improvement of a government-led, socially-involved rural left-behind children care service institution and dynamic monitoring mechanism" and "the development of educational quality evaluation activities with the participation of the government, schools, parents and society." In order to implement the spirit of *The Plan Outline*, in 2012, *The Outline for the Implementation of Comprehensive Promotion of School Management According to Law* required "improvement of the social participation mechanism according to law. We must actively explore channels and means to expand social participation in school education and management. Primary and secondary schools must strengthen cooperation with their respective communities, actively develop community services, create conditions for opening up educational resources and public facilities, participate in community building, institutions and mechanisms for cooperation with communities and relevant enterprises, and institutions must be improved. Appointment methods and qualification requirements of part-time vice-principals in charge of legal education and the school's legal affairs must be improved; use of the resources and strengths of society that can strengthen school safety management should be explored; and teaching of the legal institution and other targeted education activities should be carried out to improve the surrounding environment of schools. Vocational schools and higher education institutions should actively expand social cooperation in decision-making consultation, teaching and research, safety management, student internship practice and other aspects to introduce more social resources, improve institutions and expand the breadth and depth of social participation." Although *The Plan Outline* of 2010 did mention social participation in education quality evaluation, it did not expound on it. In 2012, *The Outline for the Implementation of Comprehensive Promotion of School Management According to Law* emphasized the use of social resources to provide assistance and convenience for school security, decision-making, teaching and research, security, student practice, etc., and the scope of social participation was to be more extensive, while the next policy document seems to place more emphasis on social participation in education evaluation. In the context of the separation of education, administration, and evaluation, social participation in education evaluation has become an important part of what the state has given to society in recent years.

In 2014, *The Opinions on Deepening the Reform of Education Supervision and Transformation of Education Management Methods* pointed out the need for "the establishment of a specialized education quality evaluation and inspection institution under the management of an education supervisory department, where professional institutions provide services and various organizations in socicty take part" and "the cultivation and support of a group of professional evaluation agencies to guide social forces to participate in education quality assessment and monitoring." In 2015, *MOE's Opinions on Deeply Advancing the Separation of Education, Management and Evaluation and Promoting the Transformation of Government Functions* provided more detailed descriptions and requirements on the participation of society in education evaluation: "Promoting scientific and standardized education evaluation as a breakthrough point, establishing a comprehensive education evaluation institution with the participation of various parties, including the government, schools, professional institutions and social organizations. By 2020, we will basically form a new structure of education administered by the public in which the government manages according to law, schools operate independently according to law, and all sectors of society participate and supervise according to law. Important institutional guarantees are provided for basically achieving education modernization." Specifically, measures used to support professional institutions and social organizations in regulating education evaluation include the following aspects: "Making great efforts to cultivate professional education service institutions, integrating education quality monitoring and evaluation institutions, improving the monitoring and evaluation institution, and regularly issuing monitoring and evaluation reports; expanding industry associations, professional societies, foundations and other social organizations to participate in education evaluation; formulating qualification certification standards for professional institutions and social organizations to participate in education evaluation; introducing market mechanisms and entrusting professional institutions and social organizations to carry out the incorporation of education evaluation in the scope of government procurement services, and in accordance with the principles of openness, fairness, and impartiality, establishing and improving the bidding institution and performance management institution to ensure the quality and efficiency of education evaluation services; emphasizing the expansion of participation in science and technology, culture and other departments and news media in education evaluation; giving attention to the role of student unions and other student organizations in education evaluation; and encouraging regions with suitable conditions and schools to actively participate in education quality assessment projects implemented by international organizations." In order to better promote the participation of social organizations in school governance, in September 2016, Shandong Province issued the notice *Measures for the Evaluation of Third-Party Education in Shandong Province (Draft)*. Undoubtedly, social participation has become an important part of modern education governance. In 2017, "The Compulsory Education School Management Standards" also considered "actively striving for social resources and social forces to support school reform and development" to be an important indicator in evaluating school management.

In summary, the modern school institution has been established for more than 10 years. It has made many achievements in the development process, but there are also some shortcomings. In terms of achievements, it has improved the school leadership mechanism, strengthened institution construction with regulations charters as the core, optimized the school organizational structure, and deepened the reform of the internal management institution of schools, guaranteed democratic management of schools, and expanded social cooperation. However, at the macro level, problems such as insufficient supply of policy institutions, the need to improve school autonomy, unsound third-party institutions, and insufficient credibility, comprehensiveness, and institutionization of regulations charters are still faced. At the micro level, it is not easy for schools to understand that the participation of the main subjects is not strong, recognition and understanding of pilot projects is insufficient, the concept of student-centered school running has not been sufficiently deepened, and the coordination and balancing of stakeholders is not easy (Xu, 2014). The 2020 Strategic Objectives for Education Governance mentioned in *MOE's Opinions on Deeply Advancing the Separation of Education, Management and Evaluation and Promoting the Transformation of Government Functions* is aimed at "basically forming a new structure of public governance of education, with government administration according to law, school autonomous administration according to law, and participation and supervision by all sectors of society according to law." There may still be tough work ahead and a long way to go. However, *The Qingdao City Primary and Secondary School Management Measures*, is already well on this path,. It has made detailed regulations on teacher recruitment, training, bonus distribution, budget and expenditure, public management of school affairs, school governance structure, etc. in primary and secondary schools, which has effectively promoted the independent operation of schools.

REFERENCES

Basic Education Curriculum and Textbook Development Center, MOE (The Ministry of Education of PRC). (2015). *On the Road to Expert Education — Interpretation of the Reform of the Principal Ranking Institution*. Beijing: Education Science Press (in Chinese).

Beijing Municipal Education Commission, Beijing Municipal Education Bureau, & Beijing Education Union. (1987). The need for "The Principal Responsibility System"—Answering the queries of principals. *Primary and Secondary School Management*, *2*, 21–23 (in Chinese).

Central China Normal University "Study on the Reform of the School Leadership System" Research Group. (1996). Study report on the reform of the school leadership system. *Jiangxi Education and Research*, *5*, 36–40 (in Chinese).

Deng, X. (1994). *Selected works of Deng Xiaoping* (Vol. II) (Edited by the Document Editing Committee of the CPC Central Committee). Beijing: People's Publishing House (in Chinese).

Feng, Z. (1985). The Central Propaganda Department and MOE hold a symposium on the pilot work of the provincial principal responsibility system in certain provinces and cities for higher education institutions. *China Higher Education*, *1*, 23 (in Chinese).

Gong, F., & Wang, B. (2011). An analysis of the leadership system in China's colleges and universities. *Journal of the National Institute of Education Administration*, *1*, 20–24 (in Chinese).

Hao, B. (2016). Analysis of the characteristics and effects of the reform of the principal system in primary and secondary schools. *Chinese Teachers*, *23*, 31–36 (in Chinese).

Li, K. (2016). Reform of the principal ranking system: From administrative to professional. *Education Development Research*, *36*(20), 3 (in Chinese).

Li, G., & Wang, B. (2000). *General history of China's education institution* (Vol. VIII). Jinan: Shandong Education Press (in Chinese).

Liu, C., Chu, H., et al. (eds.) (2014). *Policies and practice of the reform of the principal ranking system: Exploration of Zhongshan City, Guangdong Province*. Beijing: Beijing Normal University Press (in Chinese).

The National Research Centre for Educational Development & MOE. (2013). Weifang, Shandong improves the principal ranking system to ensure the school-running ability of educators. Retrieved from http://old.moe.gov.cn//publicfiles/business/htmlfiles/moe/s6635/201301/146612.html (in Chinese).

Wei, H. (2016). Administration level of Shandong primary and secondary school principals to be abolished. *China Education News*, March 23 (in Chinese).

Xiao, Z. (1985). Why "Gradually Implement the Principal Responsibility System?". *People's Education*, *10*, 10–11 (in Chinese).

Xiao, Z. (1989). Primary and secondary schools should continue to implement the principal responsibility system — Reviews and reflections of management system reform of primary and secondary schools after the founding of the People's Republic of China. *China Education News*, October 17 (in Chinese).

Xiao, Z. (2000). The propositions and connotations of the principal responsibility system. *Primary and Secondary School Management*, *11*, 2–5 (in Chinese).

Xiao, Z. (2002). Questions on the leadership system of primary and middle schools. *Primary and Secondary School Management*, *9*, 49–50 (in Chinese).

Xu, J. (2014). Building a modern university system with Chinese characteristics: Effectiveness, problems, and countermeasures – Based on the exploration and practice of pilot universities. *Educational Research*, *10*, 12–18, 33 (in Chinese).

Zhao, Z. (1987). Advance along the Road of Socialism with Chinese Characteristics: Report to the Thirteenth National Congress of the Communist Party of China. Retrieved from http://www.gov.cn/test/2008-07/01/content_1032279.htm (in Chinese).

CHAPTER THREE

Curricula and Teaching Materials Institutions

LINGCHEN WEN

During the past forty years of Reform and Opening Up, the reform of curricula and teaching materials has always been the main theme of basic education reform. In these past forty years, the transformation from the teaching discourse system to the curriculum discourse system has been basically realized, with the development of teaching materials transforming from standardization to diversification. For students, the selectivity of their curriculum learning is now more guaranteed. Since the new era began, the reform of the curriculum and teaching materials institution has always centered on the fundamental tasks of "establishing morals and cultivating the young" and has headed towards becoming more scientific, institutionalized, and refined. The reform of curriculum materials is not only about "what knowledge is most valuable" but also about "who has the most valuable knowledge," and it relates to the major issues of "what kind of people should we cultivate?" and "who are we cultivating these people for?" In December 2016, the General Office of the CPC Central Committee and the General Office of the State Council issued *The Opinions on Strengthening and Improving the Development of Teaching Materials for Primary and Secondary Schools in the New Situation*. In the following year, the National Textbook Committee was established to guide and coordinate the work on national textbooks; implement the major guidelines and policies of the Party and the state on teaching materials; research and review textbook development planning and annual work plans; research and solve major problems in the development of teaching materials; guide, organize, and coordinate the work of relevant textbooks in various regions and departments; and review national curriculum settings and curriculum standards, and also national plan textbooks with strong ideological attributes. On the basis of combing the historical process of curriculum reform and textbook development in China, this chapter focuses on exploring the power changes in curriculum management, the diversification trends of textbook writing, the more scientific and standardized ways that textbooks are reviewed, and the autonomy and richness demonstrated by the curriculum elective institution.

SECTION 1 THE TRAJECTORY OF CURRICULUM AND TEXTBOOK REFORM

Reform and Opening Up has brought about profound changes in China, and the politics, economy, and culture of society have all made tremendous progress. The field of education, especially the curriculum and teaching materials institution, urgently needs to be replanned and transformed. The institution design at the beginning of Reform and Opening Up aimed to restore the textbook institution that was damaged in the era of turmoil so that education and teaching in schools could get back on to a normal track. In the 1990s, when correcting exam-oriented education and advocating quality education, reform went deep into the structure and content of the curriculum; since the beginning of the new century, it has further penetrated into the fields of curriculum management, curriculum implementation, and curriculum evaluation.

I. Restoration of Curriculum and Textbook Order after the Cultural Revolution

During the Cultural Revolution, the institution for primary and secondary schools was chaotic, the syllabus and teaching plans were mixed, and teaching materials were varied. In the autumn of 1978, curriculum reform actually focused on dealing with educational problems left over from the Cultural Revolution, adopting measures such as bringing about a unified academic institution and syllabus, and standardizing textbook writing, which laid the foundation for the later curriculum reform. By 1981, after two years of restoring order from chaos, curriculum development tended towards normalization.

On May 27, 1985, the Central Committee of the Communist Party of China promulgated *The Decision of the Central Committee of the Communist Party of China on the Reform of the Education institution*, stating: "The fundamental purposes of education institution reform are improving the quality of the nation's people, increasing the number of talents and making good talents," "handing the responsibility for developing basic education over to the localities, and implementing nine-year compulsory education in a step-by-step manner," and "implementing the principles of localities being responsible for basic education and hierarchical management." In response to the problem of "overly controlling policies" in the management of education institutions at the time, the reform measures of decentralization and hierarchical management were adopted.

Against the background of this era, the National Education Commission entrusted Shanghai to first implement curriculum reform of primary and secondary schools in 1988, and put forward clear requirements in special policies, including the preparation of nine-year compulsory education materials suitable for use in economically developed areas and an overall design for the unified system of primary and secondary schools; schools could develop their own curriculum plans, and develop their own syllabuses (Shanghai changed this to curriculum standards), and schools could write their own textbooks (Sun et al., 2016: 25). As a result, Shanghai initiated "first-phase curriculum reform." The curriculum reform determined the objectives of the "two changes" and "three breakthroughs": changing the textbook system of "test-oriented education" curriculum centered on furthering studies and changing the curriculum teaching model with compulsory courses as the main body. Realizing the "three major breakthroughs" means reducing burdens and improving quality; strengthening foundations, cultivating abilities; and improving quality and developing individuality. In order to achieve this goal, the Shanghai Phase I Curriculum Reform Program has completed three tasks after five years of work: formulating a set of primary and secondary school curriculum and teaching plans; writing a set of primary and secondary school textbooks, workbooks, and teaching manuals; and compiling a set of software for auxiliary teaching such as recordings, videos, slideshows, movies, computers, and so on.

II. Curriculum Textbook Reform against the Background of Quality Education

In February 1993, the Central Committee of the Communist Party of China issued *The Outline of China's Education Reform and Development*, proposing that primary and secondary education should be shifted from "test-oriented education" to quality education. Subsequently, in 1996, the State Education Commission promulgated the *Full-time Ordinary High School Curriculum Program (Draft)* linked to the Compulsory Education Curriculum Program. This curriculum reform was a big move, born against the background of China's Reform and Opening Up, and fully absorbed and summarized the curriculum reform experiences and lessons learned since the founding of New China, not only developing a new curriculum plan at the text level but also requiring the changing of "test-oriented education" in the curriculum practice of the past, promoting quality education, and emphasizing the cultivation of students' abilities. This is curriculum reform with real significance (Xie et al., 2013).

The *Nine-Year Compulsory Education Full-time Elementary and Junior High School Curriculum Program* issued in 1992 changed the term "teaching plan" to "curriculum plan" for the first time. The whole curriculum was divided into two main categories: subjects and activities. The basic education curriculum began to transform the traditional segmentation design of "Primary-Secondary," replacing it with a two-stage unified design of "Compulsory Education—High School." Second, the curriculum structure was optimized. Local schools were able to set a localized curriculum structure according to actual local conditions and needs, changing the curriculum structure. For example, comprehensive courses were established in elementary schools, elective courses were established in junior high schools, and activities were also formally included in junior high school teaching plans. In addition, curriculum content was updated to reduce difficulty. The seventh set of national primary and secondary school textbooks, which were newly compiled and revised by the People's Education Publishing House, began to be used in the autumn of 1988.

On the basis of the practice and understanding of the first phase of curriculum reform, Shanghai launched the "Second Phase Curriculum Reform" with the aim of improving the basic quality of citizens, using moral education as the core and focusing on cultivating students' innovative spirit and practical abilities in October 1998. The theme of the second phase of curriculum reform was implementing quality education in depth and focusing on solving three major problems: how to focus on cultivating students' innovative spirit and practical abilities, how to strengthen moral education more effectively, and how to use information technology to promote the modernization of curriculum teaching. In order to solve these three problems, the main tasks of the second phase of curriculum reform included: overall research of curriculum structure, formulation of a *Plan of Action* and *Curriculum Standards* for the reform of various disciplines, the initiation of curriculum reform for early childhood education, curriculum and teaching materials reform of special education, and establishing a research base for curriculum reform (Wang, 2016b).

III. Basic Education Curriculum Reform since the Beginning of the New Century

In preparation for basic education curriculum in the 21st century, some developed countries such as the United States and Japan began in the 1980s. China only began reforming basic education curriculum materials in 1997.

In order to meet the requirements of development in science and technology and progress in society on the quality of citizens, and implement the spirit of the Third National Conference on Education, *The Decision of the Central Committee of the Communist Party of China on Deepening Educational Reform and Comprehensively Promoting Quality Education* proposed that "the implementation of quality education is the full implementation of the Party's education policy, with the improvement of the quality of the people as the fundamental aim, and the focus on cultivating students' innovative spirit and practical abilities." It clarified the basic ideas for the reform of basic education curriculums and teaching materials, namely, "adjusting and reforming the curriculum system, structure, and content, and establishing a new basic education curriculum institution, piloting national courses, local courses and school curricula; curriculum reform overemphasizes the subject system, breaking away from the era and social development, and the actual situations of students; establishing a mechanism for updating teaching content, strengthening the comprehensiveness and practicality of the curriculum, attaching importance to the teaching of experimental courses and cultivating students' practical operational abilities; enhancing the adaptability of the curriculum, teaching materials and local economic and social development in rural areas, especially in poverty-stricken areas; promoting the diversification of teaching materials, and further improving the nation's evaluation institution of basic education teaching materials." The third "National Conference on Education" decision clarified the policy direction of the new round of curriculum reform. After that, the Ministry of Education officially launched the reform of national basic education curriculum textbooks in January 1999, and established a work policy of "proactively enterprising, steadily advancing, 'first establishing then breaking', 'first experimenting then promoting'." In June 2001, with the approval of the State Council, *The Basic Education Curriculum Reform Outline (Draft)* (hereinafter referred to as *The Outline*) was officially issued at the National Basic Education Work Conference.

The Outline proposed six specific objectives for this round of reform of the basic education curriculum: altering the tendency of the curriculum being too focused on knowledge transfer; emphasizing the formation of a proactive learning attitude so that the process of acquiring basic knowledge and basic skills becomes a process of learning and forming correct values at the same time; changing the curriculum structure that places too much emphasis on the subject standards, where there are too many subjects and is a lack of integration. The overall curriculum and class time ratio is set for nine years, and general lessons are set to meet the needs of different regions and students, reflecting the balance, comprehensiveness, and selectivity of the curriculum structure; changing the status quo of curriculum content being overly complex, difficult, partial, old, and too focused on book knowledge, strengthening the connection between course content and student life and the development of modern social science and technology, paying attention to students' interests and experiences in learning, choosing the basic knowledge and skills necessary for lifelong learning; changing curriculum implementation from overly emphasizing the status quo of reception learning, rote memorization, and mechanical training, advocating students to actively participate, be willing to explore and work diligently, cultivating students' abilities to collect and process information, acquire new knowledge, analyze and solve problems and communicate and work together; changing the overemphasis of curriculum evaluation on the functions of examination and selection, making use of the role of evaluation in promoting student development, improving teachers and improving teaching practice; changing the situation of overly concentrated curriculum management, implementing national, local, and school three-level curriculum management, and enhancing the adaptability of the curriculum to the locality, school, and students.

This reform also included requirements for the organization and implementation of a new curriculum structure, curriculum standards, teaching process, textbook development and management, curriculum evaluation, curriculum management, teacher cultivation and training, and curriculum reform of basic education.

SECTION 2 CONCENTRATION AND DECENTRALIZATION OF CURRICULUM MANAGEMENT POWER

Over the past forty years of Reform and Opening Up, the focus of China's curriculum management institution has continuously shifted, and the transition from centralized and unified curriculum management to national, local, and school-level curriculum management models has been gradually realized. The curriculum decision-making mechanism shifted from centralized decision-making to decentralized decision-making. The school-based curriculum institution is a typical representative of one of the decentralized decision-making mechanisms. It can be said that curriculum management shifted from a traditional focus on power constraints and external promotion to "empowerment and raising abilities" and internal drive; curriculum leadership also shifted from transactional leadership to innovative leadership (Yang, 2013a: 51).

I. Centralized and Unified Curriculum Management

Since the founding of the People's Republic of China, in the aspect of primary and secondary school curriculum materials policy, despite the fact that decentralized curriculum settings and the right to compile and choose textbooks have appeared, it is basically the state that unified formulation of teaching plans and outlines, uniformly preparing teaching materials and the textbooks used throughout the country. That is, "the four unifications": "unified curriculum policy, unified curriculum settings, unified curriculum standards, unified teaching materials" (Li, 2010). This is the so-called central management of the curriculum and state formulation of textbooks.

In the early days of the founding of the People's Republic of China, the centralized curriculum management institution was particularly necessary for improving the quality of school education and teaching, and to a certain extent promoted the standardization and improvement of the school curriculum and teaching institution. Generally speaking, the centralized institution can ensure the smooth flow of government orders and standardization, help to realize the overall interests of the country, help maintain the balanced development of education in all regions, eliminate the inequality of educational opportunities, and easily achieve the effects the state expects when it comes to the implementation of curricula (Li, 2010).

II. The Three-Tiered Curriculum Management Model

At the end of the 20th century, the past tendency of the curriculum management institution being overly concentrated was improved. In 1996, the State Education Commission promulgated *The Full-time Ordinary Senior High School Curriculum Program (Draft)*. For the first time, the "Curriculum Management" section was separately listed, clearly stating that "the ordinary high school curriculum is managed at the central, local, and school levels" and stipulated the administrative rights of all levels. The establishment of a three-tiered management model for curriculum materials ensured and promoted the adaptability of the curriculum for different regions, schools, and students, and implemented and guided gradual decentralized empowerment (Shi, 2001: 90).

In June 1999, the Third National Conference on Education Work proposed the adjustment and reform of the curriculum institution, structure, and content; the establishment of a new basic education curriculum institution; and the piloting of a national, local, and school curriculum (MOE, 1999). In 2001, the *Basic Education Curriculum Reform Outline (Draft)* clearly stated: "Change curriculum management so that it is not too concentrated, implement the three levels of curriculum management at the national, local, and school levels, and enhance the adaptability of the curriculum to localities, schools, and students."

The three-level curriculum management institution allocates part of the decision-making power that was originally too concentrated at the central level to localities and schools, and enables localities and schools to participate in curriculum development, thereby leading to a situation of parallel existence in the national, local, and school curriculum, making it more suitable for specific educational and teaching situations at the local and school levels. This current reform of the curriculum management institution reflects the tendency of China's current curriculum policy in moving from centralization to limited decentralization (Zhong & Yang, 2003: 341). In fact, behind this lie the curriculum management concepts of power sharing and responsibility sharing (Wu, 2002: 69).

In reality, setting up the three-tiered curriculum is not just as simple as stratifying the curriculum. To truly implement the three-tiered curriculum institution, the body administering the curriculum needs to be transferred from the education administrative department to the school. The education administration's role in managing the curriculum will gradually change from the control of the curriculum implementation process to macro-adjustment and curriculum evaluation. Appropriate decision-making procedures and internal school curriculum supervision mechanisms are to be established as well as curriculum intermediaries to guide the school in curriculum design, including curriculum theory and technology guidance and specific guidance for the school's curriculum (Chen, 2010: 83).

III. Exploration of the School-Based Curriculum Development Institution

The manifestation of decentralized decision-making in the field of education gives schools sufficient autonomy, and in the field of the curriculum it is manifested in school-based curriculum institutions. *The School Curriculum Management Guide (Discussion Draft)* states that three-tiered curriculum management is a redistribution of authority in China's basic education curriculum institution. Through reforms, schools have gained some power in setting up curricula, but also bear the corresponding responsibilities. Therefore, schools and their related personnel should form the concepts of power sharing and responsibility sharing, clarify the corresponding roles in curriculum management, fulfill curriculum responsibilities, ensure the effective implementation of the national/local curriculum, and rationally develop school-based curricula.

Regarding the proportion of school-based curricula, *The Guide* also states that in the management of school curricula, national curricula cannot be used to encroach on local or school-based curricula, national/local prescribed curriculum standards cannot be arbitrarily raised, nor can school-based curricula be used as an extension or supplement of the cultural curriculum prescribed by the state. Instead, the relationship between these three types of curricula should be properly handled according to the relevant curriculum documents to ensure a reasonable proportioning of various subjects, and to give full play to their various values for student development.

The implementation of the three-tiered curriculum management institution at the school level gave schools the power to "develop or select curricula suitable for the school," which led to an upsurge in school-based curriculum development. In academic discussion, terms such as "school-based curricula," "school curricula," and "school-set curricula" appeared. Related to this is the process of "school-based curriculum development," which is equally ambiguous in concept and gives rise to many interpretations. It can be said that the development of school-based curricula includes both the development of "school-based curricula" and "school-based" curricula development (Lin, 2002). At the beginning, Yunhuo Cui and other scholars started from the Chinese educational traditions and the reality in schools, where the chosen path could only be the development of school-based curricula. This is because school-based curricula development requires rich and shared curriculum resources, as well as relatively high teacher curriculum development skills (Cui, 2000a).

The policy of school-based curriculum development in China is positioned in terms of "non-academic and interest." The reason for choosing such a policy positioning is that it is relatively safe and feasible. It is said to be safe because the decentralization of nonacademic curriculum authority does not affect the academic quality of basic education; it is feasible because academic curricula are developed by experts, nonacademic curricula are developed by teachers, and teachers gradually develop curriculum awareness and improve their curriculum ability during the process of using curriculum decision-making opportunities, exercising curriculum authority, and developing school-based curricula (Cui, 2011: 1–6).

In the field of practice, Xishan High School of Jiangsu Province, which is known as the "origin of school-based curricula" (Huang, 2014; Tang, 2010), carried out school-based curriculum development at the end of the 20th century (Cui, 2000b: 104–119). At the beginning of the 21st century, No. 2 High School Affiliated to East China Normal University also began exploration and practice of school-based curriculum development. At present, it has already formed six major sections, consisting of the national basic curriculum, the large cultural curriculum, the STS series curriculum, the community activity curriculum, the moral education curriculum, and the honorary curriculum, which are related to the three main school curriculum institutions: the basic curriculum, the expanded curriculum, and the research curriculum. By 2015, the school had already constructed and begun running more than 500 extended school-based courses, and about 80 elective courses per semester (No. 2 High School Affiliated to East China Normal University, 2015; He, 2003: 1–10; He & Qi, 2008: 125–157).

Yucai Middle School established six types of school-based courses: physical and mental health courses, subject development courses, general courses, social practice courses, student club activity courses, and life vocational skills courses (Zou, 2007: 232–242).

Table 3.1 Classification and Targeting of Characteristic Courses in Yucai Middle School

Course Group	Objective	Course List
Physical and Mental Cultivation	Developing a healthy personality and a healthy body, as well as a positive attitude towards life; learning to accept one's own identity and social status; being good at controlling one's emotions and learning to recognize and evaluate oneself; creating a healthy personal image; learning to plan one's own life; having the courage to face setbacks and difficulties.	Exceeding IQ, personal career planning, preparatory psychologist speech, debating and oratory skills, social skills and etiquette
Humanities Research	Establishing a correct world outlook, outlook on life and values, and establishing correct moral cognition and political stance; developing good ethics, social responsibility, citizenship and democratic literacy; learning to coordinate, communicate and collaborate and actively participate in collective and public affairs; enhancing one's sense of identity and belonging to the country and the nation; cultivating compassion, responsibility, humanistic literacy and hardship; learning how to care for the weak and human destiny.	Humanities and social studies, the history of Western philosophy, ancient Chinese mythology research, the mystery of history and culture, exploring the mysteries of Chinese characters, introduction to enterprise management
Scientific Exploration	Cultivating scientific literacy and information literacy; mastering the methods of scientific experimentation and cultivating the ability to collect, screen, organize, and summarize information; developing clear logical thinking and accurate written and verbal skills; becoming good at finding, analyzing, and solving problems; cultivating the ability to question, to think, and to explore independently, and form a healthy and critical attitude.	Plant organization, culturing robot experimentation, chemistry and the environment, astronomical observation, introduction to urban rail transit

Table 3.1 Continued

Course Group	Objective	Course List
International Understanding	Having a good national mentality and conservation, with a global vision and a global perspective; actively paying attention to the international community and world affairs, and to the future development conditions and situations of global society; the ability to treat and respect the cultural traditions of all countries, regions, and nations of the world fairly and objectively, and actively drawing on the outstanding achievements of civilization created by mankind; actively, peacefully, and rationally participating in international activities and international competitions, knowing how to respect, understand, and tolerate.	Intercultural communication, cultures of Anglophone countries, cultural conflict and integration, Korean language foundation, Japanese language foundation, French language and French culture
Skills Application	Mastering lifelong learning and life skills; learning how to use a variety of computer application software, skilled use of various network resources; developing good internet ethics.	Digital film production, practical internet technology and troubleshooting experiments

It can be seen that controversy in theoretical circles is particularly prominent compared to the practice of school-based curriculum development. Specifically, the focus of the debate is on whether the school-based curriculum improves existing courses or develops new ones (Li, 2003). This is actually a new topic that China will encounter and have to solve after carrying out reform of the basic education curriculum and realizing the transformation process from teaching to the discourse system of the curriculum. At a deeper level, school-based curriculum development is also connected to the relationship between the expansion of school curriculum autonomy and the implementation of national curriculum programs. It poses new challenges to curriculum experts, education administrations, school leaders, teachers and students, and even parents and society.

As far as teachers are concerned, school-based curriculum development will undoubtedly have the potential to help teachers to re-recover the "reskilling" of curriculum development (Zhong, 2006: 367). For a long time, Chinese schools did not need to consider the question of "what to teach" (curriculum rights), and only had to consider "how to teach" (teaching rights) (Cui, 2011: 1–6).

In addition, although a "school" based curriculum is not completely equivalent to a "local" based curriculum, a school-based curriculum does not necessarily teach local concepts and regional characteristics (local curriculum) (Hong, 2013), but in the process of school-based curriculum development and implementation, to a certain extent, one can pay more attention to the local level and pay attention to local and community knowledge. For example, Shanghai Yucai Middle School, which is adjacent to a grape production base, has launched the school-based course "Grape Research." This will undoubtedly help students overcome their prejudices against local knowledge, and thus achieve a positive interaction between local culture and the national curriculum, local knowledge and universal knowledge.

In reality, both a school's self-developed curriculum and the school-based implementation of the national curriculum belong to the "art of localization" of the curriculum and adhere to the "site-based" stance because "a generalized formula does not, and cannot, translate a rough general understanding into the local knowledge needed for successful, delicate application. If you want to achieve local success, the more generally applicable the rules, the more translation is necessary" (Scott, 2004: 436). Looking from this perspective, in fact, the development and implementation of the school-based curriculum is the process of translating the curriculum. In reality, the authority, guiding significance, and mandatory requirements of the national curriculum do not eliminate the selective and creative space that the curriculum should have.

SECTION 3 INSTITUTIONALIZATION AND DIVERSIFICATION OF TEACHING MATERIAL DEVELOPMENT

Curricula and teaching materials are inextricably linked. As some scholars have suggested, the next step in the curriculum is on the next page of the textbook (Elliott et al., 1990). The reform of the teaching materials institution includes the textbook editing institution, the textbook review institution, and the setting of the textbook management organization. This involves who writes the textbook, who reviews it, and how the review is conducted. By combing through the development of the textbook institution during the forty years of Reform and Opening Up, it is not difficult to find that the reform of the Chinese textbook institution has generally experienced the editorial era, the era of diversification of teaching materials, and the era of teaching materials and institutions development. In the new era, the development of teaching materials has further expanded around the fundamental task of creating talented people with good morals.

I. Development of Teaching Materials in the Era of Editing

During the "Cultural Revolution," China's education industry suffered a huge blow. Primary and secondary school institutions were in chaos, syllabuses and teaching plans were uneven, and teaching materials varied widely. This seriously affected the development of education in China and the improvement of teaching quality.

In this regard, after Xiaoping Deng resumed work in 1977, he convened a national scientific education work conference, personally took the reins of the development of education and teaching materials, and made important instructions regarding the development of primary and secondary school curriculum materials: For primary and secondary school education, the key was teaching materials; teaching materials had to be picked up from primary and secondary schools, and general textbooks had to be printed (Shi, 2001: 85). Since then, the Ministry of Education began to organize the drafting of a unified national teaching plan, the preparation of a unified syllabus, and a national general textbook.

According to Xiaoping Deng's instructions, the Ministry of Education formulated relevant policies and measures for the curricula and teaching materials of primary and secondary schools: establishing a "Leadership Group for Textbook Review and Examination" and leading the compilation of teaching materials; reestablishing the People's Education Publishing House, organizing the "Working Conference on Teaching Materials for Primary and Secondary Schools," and compiling primary and secondary school textbooks; and establishing the primary and secondary school ten-year institution as the basic academic institution, formulating a unified syllabus, and compiling full-time ten-year primary and secondary school textbooks. Since the autumn of 1978, national textbooks have been in use, which has reversed the use of erroneous textbooks and the chaotic unevenness in various places. This has played an important role in gradually bringing back normal teaching order and improving the quality of education in primary and secondary schools.

A nationally unified compilation and unified supply institution has basically been implemented for primary and secondary school textbooks, that is, the nationally designated People's Education Publishing House compiles and publishes textbooks according to the unified syllabus and these are uniformly distributed by Xinhua Bookstore. Primary and secondary school students across the whole country use the same "nationally compiled textbooks." "One syllabus, one book, one review, and one high level of unity" is the outstanding feature of the textbook institution at this stage (Yang, 2013b: 189).

II. Development of Teaching Materials Diversity

In January 1985, the Ministry of Education issued the *Work Regulations of the National Primary and Secondary School Textbook Validation Committee (Trial)*, stating: "In the future, the development of primary and secondary school textbooks will be separated from preparation and examination, and the People's Education Publishing House will be responsible for compiling the textbooks; the education departments, schools, teachers and experts of each province, municipality and autonomous region will be responsible for compiling the textbooks; the National Primary and Secondary School Textbook Validation Committee will be responsible for examination and approval, and revised textbooks will recommended by the Ministry of Education for use by localities" (Shi, 2001: 85).

In September 1986, the National Primary and Secondary School Textbook Validation Committee and the Textbook Review Committee for various disciplines were formally established. This was the first authoritative institution to be responsible for the examination and approval of primary and secondary school textbooks after the founding of the People's Republic of China. It marked that the textbooks of Chinese primary and secondary schools had changed from "nationally set" to "set on approval," from "one syllabus and one textbook" to "one syllabus and multiple textbooks," and formulated the policy for the reform of primary and secondary school curriculum materials: "Under the premise of unified teaching requirements and unified approval, there are leaders who systematically try to diversify the curriculum materials to meet the needs of various schools in different regions of China." The diversification of Chinese primary and secondary school textbooks started from here (Course Teaching Material Research Institute, 2004: 194).

In terms of specific implementation, in 1988, the State Education Commission began to organize the compilation of textbooks suitable for use at the three different levels of "Five-Four" and "Six-Three" schools, historically called "eight sets and a half." The People's Education Publishing House compiled a set of textbooks for the two "Six-Three" and "Five-Four" academic institutions throughout the country; Beijing Normal University compiled a set of textbooks adapted to the "Five-Four" academic institution; Guangdong Province compiled a set of textbooks for coastal areas; Sichuan Province compiled a set of textbooks for inland and western regions; the eight normal universities (Beijing Normal University, Northeast Normal University, Southwest Normal University, Huazhong Normal University, Shaanxi Normal University, Guangxi Normal University, Beijing Normal College, and East China Normal University) jointly compiled a set of high-demand "Six-Three institution" textbooks (unfinished and suspended); Shanghai and Zhejiang each compiled a set of textbooks suitable for curriculum reform in the region; and Hebei Province compiled a set of rural primary school class textbooks, and because this set of textbooks lacked those for use in junior high schools, it was called a "half set."

After this, a series of documents was issued in the fields of textbook compilation and the examination and approval institution. Then in October 1987, the State Education Commission issued *The Working Charter of the National Primary and Secondary School Textbook Validation Committee*, *The Standards for the Validation of Textbooks of Primary and Secondary Schools*, and *The Measures for the Delivery of Textbooks of Primary and Secondary Schools*. In 1996, the new "Working Charter of the National Primary and Secondary School Textbook Validation Committee" was revised and issued.

In general, the transformation from "one syllabus, one textbook" to "one syllabus and many books" and "multiple syllabuses and multiple textbooks" actually reflected the demands of education democracy. The reform of the textbook institution was able to promote the democratization of education, improve the quality of textbooks, promote the transformation of teachers' roles, and promote the reform of the school entrance examination institution. However, there are also some problems, such as the serious problem of cloning of textbooks, the lack of a textbook evaluation institution, confusion regarding the textbook market mechanism, and the increasing burden of learning for students in many schools (Zhong, 2004).

> Reform the current textbook compilation, review and examination institution, separate compilation and validation, and gradually realize the various styles of textbooks under the premise of unifying the basic requirements and unifying examinations. Encourage all localities, institutions of higher learning, research institutes, experts, scholars, and teachers to participate in the compilation of textbooks in accordance with the educational policies and unified basic requirements of the Party and the state, allowing different styles in the content selection and system arrangement of the textbooks.
>
> Curriculum Teaching Material Research Institute (2004), *Textbook institution Evolution* (Volume 1), Beijing: People's Education Press, p. 261.

III. Development of Teaching Institutions and Mechanisms at the Beginning of the New Century

Since the beginning of the new century, the state has made reforms in the compilation, validation, publication, distribution, and selection of existing textbooks, including the approval institution for textbooks (2001–2012), the two-level textbook validation institution, and the establishment of professional textbook institutions.

During this stage, the development of teaching materials for primary and secondary schools implemented a diversified approach to teaching materials under the guidance of basic national requirements. The state encouraged and supported qualifying units, groups, and individuals to organize the compilation of high-quality and distinctive teaching materials in accordance with national curriculum standards, and especially encouraged the compilation of teaching materials suitable for use in rural areas and ethnic minority areas.

Based on this policy, the management of textbook writing changed from the original approval institution to the project approval institution. The so-called approval institution meant that the compilation of primary and secondary school textbooks had to be approved by the education administrative department, and more emphasis was placed on administrative will. The project approval institution, on the other hand, meant that the compilation of teaching materials was managed as a project, where administrative management based on expert argumentation was emphasized. Approval management still adopts two levels of management at the national and provincial education administrative department levels.

In addition, before reform, there were no restrictions on those who participated in the compilation of textbooks, including national civil servants and administrative departments, and this caused large negative impacts. After reform, in order to establish a healthy textbook market that was conducive to fair competition, phenomena such as the use of administrative power to monopolize the textbook market and breeding corruption was eliminated, and it was made clear that the following units and individuals could not participate in the compilation of primary and secondary school textbooks: (1) National civil servants could not participate in the compilation of teaching materials in any form, (2) the educational administrative department could not participate in the compilation of teaching materials in any form, and (3) textbook reviewers could not participate in the compilation of teaching materials during their period of employment (MOE, 2002).

> Chapter V: Validation of Teaching Materials
>
> Article 18: The administrative department of education of the State Council shall establish a national textbook validation committee for primary and secondary schools, which shall be responsible for the preliminary examination and approval of national curriculum materials and the validation of local curriculum materials used by provinces (autonomous regions and municipalities directly under the Central Government).
>
> Article 19: The administrative departments of education of provinces, autonomous regions and municipalities directly under the Central Government shall establish a textbook validation committee for provincial primary and secondary schools, which shall be responsible for the preliminary examination and validation of the textbooks for local curriculums; and shall be authorized or entrusted by the education administrative department of the State Council to undertake preliminary examination work of relevant national curriculum materials.
>
> Article 20: The National Primary and Secondary School Textbook Validation Committee and the Provincial Primary and Secondary School Textbook Validation Committee shall have a textbook review committee (or disciplinary review group) for each subject, which shall be composed of experts in that discipline, teaching researchers in primary and secondary schools, and primary and secondary school teachers. They will be responsible for reviewing the subject textbook and submitting a validation report to the validation committee.

Interim Measures for the Administration of the Compilation of Textbooks for Primary and Secondary Schools (Order No. 11 of the Ministry of Education of People's Republic of China)

The compilation of teaching materials must be approved by the relevant textbook management department in advance, and the completed textbooks must be approved by the textbook validation body before they can be used in primary and secondary schools. Primary and secondary school textbook compilation comes under the authority of the state. According to the *Compulsory Education Law* and related regulations, a two-level management institution has been implemented for primary and secondary schools. National curriculum materials are managed by the education administrative department of the State Council, and local curriculum materials are administered by the provincial education administrative management department.

In February 2010, the Leading Group on National Basic Education Curriculum Teaching Materials, the National Basic Education Curriculum Textbook Expert Advisory Committee, and the National Basic Education Curriculum Materials Expert Working Committee were set up especially. The newly established Leading Group on National Basic Education Curriculum Teaching Materials is the leading decision-making body responsible for the development of basic education curriculum materials. It is composed of comrades in charge of relevant departments of the Ministry of Education, as well as the Central Publicity Department, the Central Party History Research Office, the Ministry of Foreign Affairs, the Ministry of Culture, the State Administration of Press and Publications, the Chinese Academy of Sciences, the Chinese Academy of Social Sciences, the Engineering Institute, and the China Association for Science and Technology. Their main responsibilities are studying and determining basic education curriculum teaching materials development plans and major policies; studying and determining the major issues of the basic education curriculum textbooks, coordinating and solving related problems; reviewing the basic education curriculum program, reviewing results of curriculum standards for various subjects and the results of textbook reviews; and guiding the work of the national basic education curriculum material expert working committee (MOE, 2010).

The Basic Education Curriculum Textbook Expert Advisory Committee is a high-level expert consultation organization that provides consultation for major decision-making in basic education curriculum materials. It consists of forty-one senior experts and scholars with profound academic knowledge, high academic status in the field, or high standing in society. Its main responsibilities are accepting consultations from the Ministry of Education and the National Basic Education Curriculum and Teaching Materials Expert Committee on the development of basic education curriculum materials, and studying and putting forward opinions and suggestions on the development of national basic education curriculum materials.

The Basic Education Curriculum Textbook Expert Working Committee organizes for experts to cooperate with and assist education administrative departments in carrying out professional work around the development of national basic education curriculum materials. It is composed of 116 experts in basic education and experts in the fields of education, curriculum and psychology, and experts in education and teaching. Its main responsibilities are organizing research and development of national curriculum programs for basic education and curriculum standards for various subjects, organizing deliberation and deliberation opinions; organizing reviews of qualifications of textbook writers and submitting audit opinions, organizing review materials, and coordinating the solving of major issues in the review of teaching materials; organizing research and monitoring and evaluation of major issues in curriculum materials; carrying out professional guidance and services for local and primary and secondary school curriculum reform; and receiving special research work assigned by the Ministry of Education and the Leading Group of National Basic Education Curriculum Materials. As a result, the textbook planning and development institution, consisting of decision-making, consulting, and work took shape, and the professional and institutionalized textbook development institution gradually took shape.

In October 2014, the "Leading Group on National Basic Education Curriculum Teaching Materials" was renamed the "Leading Group of the Ministry of Education's Curriculum and Teaching Materials" (MOE, 2014). The Leading Group of the Ministry of Education's Curriculum and Teaching Materials is mainly responsible for making leadership decisions on the development of basic education, vocational education, and higher education curriculum materials. Its specific responsibilities are:

1. Studying and determining the plans and major policies for the development of basic education, vocational education, and higher education curriculum materials;
2. Studying and determining major issues in basic education, vocational education, and higher education curriculum materials and coordinating to solve related problems;
3. Examining basic education curriculum plans, the results of reviews of curriculum standards for each subject, and the results of textbook examinations;
4. Reviewing national-level planning textbook selection plans for general higher education, guiding the selection and recommendation work of national-level planned textbooks, and providing guiding opinions on

the quality supervision of ordinary higher education undergraduate textbooks and the selection of textbooks for ordinary higher education institutions;
5. Studying the curriculum settings and textbook development of ideological and political theory courses in higher education institutions, examining Marxist theoretical research and key development materials for development projects under the Ministry of Education, and guiding the unified use of engineering textbooks;
6. Guiding the work of the Ministry of Education Basic Education Curriculum Materials Expert Working Committee, the Industry Vocational Education Teaching Guidance Committee, and the Higher Education Institution Teaching Guidance Committee.

It can be seen that due to the deepening of the study of curriculum materials and an understanding of the importance of teaching materials, the state is committed to strengthening the development of curriculum materials institution at this stage, having established a framework for the curriculum and textbook development institution with clear division of labor, high authority, and professionalism of the trinity of the Basic Education Curriculum Teaching Materials Leading Group, Expert Working Committee, and Expert Advisory Committee, bringing together experts and scholars to study and formulate curriculum plans and standards, and organize review materials.

IV. The Scientific and Standardized Review of Teaching Materials in the New Era

With the advent of the internet and the social media era, the public is paying more attention to textbooks in primary and secondary schools. Accusations of primary and secondary school textbooks have sometimes come up: education departments removing all texts on revolutionary leaders and heroes such as Zedong Mao, Xun Lu, Feng Lei, and Jiguang Huang from primary and secondary school textbooks (MOE, 2015); Xun Lu 's articles being withdrawn from textbooks (People's education press, 2013); problems such as certain versions of primary school Chinese textbooks having too many foreign themes, and the textbooks having problems such as "demeaning Chinese people" and serious westernization (People's education press, 2016); and a middle school Chinese textbook that included the Christian Bible's story of "God Creating the Universe" in teaching materials as a mythological story. All in all, problems in the field of teaching materials have appeared frequently, to the extent that some scholars have raised the idea that the media is "too concerned" with Chinese language textbooks (Wen, 2013). In fact, despite media reports and online comments either being one-sided or inaccurate, the writing and reviews of textbooks still attracts the attention of the national education department.

In 2014, the Ministry of Education promulgated *The Opinions of the Ministry of Education on Comprehensively Deepening Curriculum Reform and Implementing the Fundamental Tasks of Instilling Morals in Young People* and initiated the ninth curriculum reform (Wang, 2016a). *The Opinions* decided: "The Ministry of Education will organize the compilation and revision of textbooks on moral education, language, history and other subjects in primary and secondary schools."

Since 2012, the Ministry of Education has organized the compilation of textbooks on compulsory education ethics and the rule of law, language, and history. This work began in 2012, and after review and approval by the National Textbook Committee in the first half of 2017, all review work was completed after five years. According to the work schedule, starting from the fall semester of September 1, 2017, all initial grades were to be put into use in all regions of the country. Thus, it marked the official entry of ethics and law, language, and history textbooks on to the track of nationally unified editing, unified review, and unified use.

New attempts have begun not only in the compilation of textbooks but also in the review institution. The examination of textbooks in three subjects of compulsory education were first implemented for the discipline review, comprehensive review, thematic review, and final review institution, as well as the three subjects in the political, conceptual, and scientific aspects. The "four examinations" subject review focuses on textbook content being scientific, systematic, accurate, and appropriate; comprehensive review focuses on interdisciplinary horizontal cooperation and the vertical organic connection of each section; special review focuses on China's sovereignty, maritime borders, major events, famous figures, etc.; and final review focuses on the comprehensive review and implementation of the fundamental task of instilling morals in young people, organic integration of socialist core values, strengthening China's excellent traditional culture and revolutionary traditions, and ensuring the overall quality and level of teaching materials. It is said that the education department will summarize the experience in the next step, further improve and promote the "four-examination" institution, and promote the formation of a review institution for curriculum materials with more Chinese characteristics (Zheng, 2016).

The emphasis on teaching materials work is also reflected in the establishment of teaching material management institutions. In March 2017, the Textbook Bureau of the Ministry of Education was established. Working beneath it is a curriculum textbook planning office, a textbook compilation department for primary and secondary schools, an engineering textbook compilation office, a textbook review management office, and a comprehensive coordination office. In terms of functions, the textbook bureau is responsible for the overall planning, development, and management of curriculum materials, specifically undertaking the work of the National Textbook Committee Office, and formulating the national textbook development plan and annual work plans; it is responsible for organizing the experts to develop curriculum design plans and curriculum standards, formulating and improving the basic institutional norms for the development of textbooks, guiding the management of teaching materials development, and strengthening the development of informatization of teaching materials.

In July 2017, the National Textbook Committee was established. Its main duties are to guide and coordinate national textbook work; implement the major guidelines and policies of the Party and the state on teaching materials; study and review the textbook development plan and annual work plan; study and solve major problems in the development of teaching materials; guide, organize, and coordinate the work of relevant textbooks in various departments of various regions; review the formulation of national curriculum and curriculum standards; and review national planning textbooks with strong ideological attributes (The State Council of PRC, 2017). The Textbook Bureau of the Ministry of Education and the National Textbook Committee have been established in succession, and a textbook management mechanism based on overall planning, unified integration, classified guidance, and clear responsibilities has been determined.

For some subject textbooks, more emphasis is placed on unity. It is mainly textbooks with strong ideological attributes that have returned to one syllabus, many textbooks to one syllabus, one textbook, and these should be viewed rationally. After all, the method for realizing diversification of textbooks in different disciplines should be based on the nature and characteristics of the discipline, and should not just be done in the same way. Discussion on this topic has been around for a long time. Previously, some scholars proposed that the three disciplines of political ideology and morality, history, and geography are political, sensitive, and have more in common. Whether the use of a large amount of human, material, and financial resources is recommended to write a variety of textbooks or the model of "National Unified Textbooks + Local Supplementary Textbooks (or Local Textbook)" is more appropriate (Lv, 2001: 65–66) is worth the further summarizing of experiences and exploring correct and effective methods.

It can be seen that after Reform and Opening Up, in the aspect of the textbook compilation institution, there has been a transformation from unified compilation ("One Syllabus, One Textbook") to "One Syllabus, Multiple Textbooks," "Multiple Syllabuses, Multiple Textbooks," and then a return to unified editing of textbooks for subjects that have strong ideological attributes; while the examination and checking institution underwent a process of continuous improvement from unified compilation and review to separated compilation and review, and then on to the four-review institution; in terms of institution building, from the "Leadership Group for Textbook Review" at the beginning of Reform and Opening Up, to the National Primary and Secondary School Textbook Validation

Committee and textbook review committees of various disciplines of the 1980s, and then on to the Basic Education Curriculum Teaching Materials Leading Group, the Expert Working Committee and the Expert Advisory Committee of 2010, and the establishment of the National Textbook Committee and the Ministry of Education Textbook Bureau in 2017, it can be seen that the professionalism of decision-making advisory institutions in the development of teaching materials has gradually strengthened, and the division of labor has become more and more effective.

SECTION 4 AUTONOMY AND ABUNDANCE OF COURSE ELECTIVES

If it can be said that the curriculum and teaching materials have been focused on solving the problem of "teaching what" and "learning what," then the elective institution can be seen as a way of solving "what I want to learn" from the perspective of students. In recent years, the course elective institution has also added connotations of "how to learn," such as "what time to learn," "where to learn," and "how much to learn." In fact, the selectivity of courses has always been an inevitable topic at the high school stage. For example, at the beginning of the development of mathematics curriculum standards in 2000, Chinese high schools faced a series of difficulties. Among them, the first issue was the question of the selectivity of high school mathematics (Zhang, 2000).

In general, the elective institution is enacting exploratory plans for course selection aimed at expanding the selection available to students at higher education institutions in terms of courses. In the early 1980s, the elective institution at that time was based on a separation of liberal arts and sciences. After curriculum reform in 2000, simple separation of liberal arts and sciences had already been exceeded, giving students the opportunity to combine more subjects. Then in the new era, the elective institution transcended subjects, taking into account the choice of students' time, space, and degree of learning. It can be seen from this that the elective institution of the curriculum has always been designed around giving students more choices.

I. Elective Institution Based on Separation of Liberal Arts and Sciences

In 1981, the Ministry of Education issued the *Full-time Six-Year Key Secondary School Teaching Plan (Trial Draft)*, stating that elective courses for high school second and third grades should be set up for key secondary schools or schools with better conditions in order to adapt to students' hobbies and needs, develop their specialties, and lay better foundations. Specifically, the first option is a single-choice elective, which means having electives for certain courses. During term time, in addition to the 26 required courses in the second and third grades of high school, four electives are arranged for each grade. What elective courses are offered depends on the requirements of the students, the needs of society, and the conditions of the school. New courses (including vocational and technical courses) can be set up, and electives for the deepening and widening of one or more of the compulsory courses can be set up for students to choose from and allow the school to grow its own characteristics. Students can choose one or two electives, or can also choose not to do one.

Option 2 is a sub-disciplinary elective, that is, an elective that students can choose based on their focus on either liberal arts or science. Students who focus on liberal arts should be students with a good foundation and an interest in liberal arts—appropriate improvement in the disciplines of language, history, geography, etc. Requirements on mathematics, physics, chemistry, and other disciplines are shallower, and those on computational and experimental requirements are lower. Students who focus on science should be students with a good foundation and interest in science; they are required to receive training that strengthens basic skills and cultivates abilities in mathematics to an appropriate level and experimentation in physics and chemistry; basic knowledge of language, history, and geography will not be weakened.

The two arrangements for the above electives are chosen by the localities. Both arrangements have a preparation process. For sub-disciplinary electives, provinces, municipalities, and autonomous regions may conduct experiments in some key middle schools. At this point, the closed, rigid, and shrinking state of the Chinese middle school curriculum structure has finally changed. However, experiences that can withstand scrutiny and can be promoted are still very rare (Zhong, 1994). After all, the 1981 elective institution was only guaranteed based on the length of classes.

Since the 1981 plan did not compile the syllabuses and teaching materials of disciplines compatible with the elective teaching of subtopics, added to the influence of college entrance examinations in subtopics, the lack of supervision and inspection in the implementation of teaching plans, and management not being strict enough, many schools focused on liberal arts classes and set up fewer science courses or did not set up any at all, and schools that focused on science set up fewer liberal arts courses or did not set up any at all. This led to the structure of knowledge of students being incomplete, which is not conducive to the overall improvement of student quality.

In order to solve the problem of students learning the liberal arts and not studying any of the sciences and vice versa, the State Education Commission issued *The Adjustment Opinions on the Current Ordinary High School Teaching Plan* in 1990 to serve as a transitional teaching plan before the promulgation of the new general high school teaching plan. The plan stated that elective courses were to be divided into two categories (types), one being a single-choice elective, mainly arranged in the first and second grades. The setting up of single-semester elective courses in the first and second grades could be based on the conditions of the school, the requirements of the students, and the needs of society. Another new course may be set up, or elective courses deepening or widening a certain module or modules of compulsory courses may be set up. Vocational and technical electives can also be offered that students can choose from freely. The other type is a sub-discipline elective, that is, electives in the six aspects of liberal arts, science, foreign languages, art, sports, vocation, and technology, which are to be mainly set up for third-year students (The National Board of Education, 1990).

With a further comparison, it can be seen that the 1990 practice is actually the integration of the two electives method in 1981. That is to say, the first scheme is selected in the first and second grades, and the second scheme is selected in the third grade. This "two-in-one" strategy avoids the emergence of premature division, and at the same time eases the contradiction between the selectivity of the high school curriculum and the division of liberal arts and sciences in college entrance examinations to a certain extent.

Of course, the state also supervised the implementation of elective courses through the general examination institution. In 1991, the National Board of Education issued the notice *Opinions on the Implementation of 'The Adjustment Opinions on the Current Ordinary High School Teaching Plan' and on the Ordinary High School Graduation General Examination institution*, stating that the purpose of simultaneously implementing the *Adjustment Opinions* and "General Examination institution" in ordinary high schools was to comprehensively implement the education policy, effectively strengthen moral education, correct the phenomenon of separation in liberal arts and sciences and irrationalities in the knowledge structures of students, and enable students to develop their interests and specialties on the premise of laying a solid foundation.

In 1991, *The Opinions on Setting Up Electives in Ordinary High Schools* stated that there can be two forms of electives available in ordinary high schools. The elective courses (single-class elective courses) offered in the first and second grades of high school can be divided into the following three types according to current needs and possibilities: 1. Elective courses related to compulsory courses (deepening classes). The content of these elective courses are an expansion and deepening of the corresponding compulsory course content, but cannot be a transfer of third-year high school elective courses. This type of elective is suitable for students who have a good command of compulsory courses. 2. Knowledge-based elective courses not directly related to compulsory courses. The content of these elective courses can be introducing new scientific theories, expanding the students' horizons, improving the student's level of political theory, and enriching the students' knowledge. It can also meet the needs of students' interests, hobbies, and specialties; cultivate students' cultural and artistic accomplishments; nourish their spirits; and so on. 3. Technical elective courses. These elective courses are offered according to the students' hobbies and the needs of society. They are comprehensive technical basic courses, some of which are characterized by initial vocational training. Of course, for the above three elective courses, all localities and schools must make overall arrangements, and offering only one of them is not permitted.

Elective courses offered in the third year of high school are mainly divided into two types: one is a sub-disciplinary elective course, including liberal arts (history, geography), science (physics, chemistry, biology), foreign languages (English, Russian, Japanese), art, and sports; the other is technical and vocational electives.

At present, elective courses in ordinary high schools have two forms of requirements for students. One kind of elective course is one that some students must choose to study, so-called designated elective courses (i.e., mandatory courses). For example, all kinds of elective courses offered in the third year of high school are compulsory for some students. Taking the subject of history as an example, since the autumn of 1993, ancient Chinese history has been added to the curriculum of year three in ordinary high schools as an elective course (there are seven provinces and cities that set up the ancient Chinese history elective course in 1992), and as a liberal arts class "designated elective course" (compulsory course) (Chen, 1999). Another type of elective course is one where students can decide whether to choose them according to their own interests and hobbies under the guidance of teachers. These can be called "optional elective courses" (optional courses). This round of high school curriculum plans includes technical and vocational electives, thereby including employment preparation. It is also worth noting that from the phrase "designated elective courses" (compulsory courses) that appears in the article, it can be seen that there is a dilemma between the "compulsory" subdivision of liberal arts and sciences and "selection" based on interests, hobbies, and specialties at the level of the reconciliation institution.

In 1996, *The Full-time General Senior High School Curriculum Program (Experiment)* divided the general high school curriculum into subject-based courses and activity-based courses, in which the general high school subject courses were divided into compulsory, limited elective, and optional elective courses. A curriculum institution was built based on the principles of optimizing compulsory courses, standardizing elective courses, and strengthening qualifying elective courses (Jin, 1997). Compulsory subjects are courses that every high school student must take, these include the twelve subjects of ideological politics, language, mathematics, foreign languages (English, Russian, Japanese, etc.), physics, chemistry, biology, history, geography, sports, art, and labor technology. Elective subjects are courses that students must study further on the basis of studying compulsory subjects, focusing on preparing for higher education or preparing for employment. These include language, mathematics, foreign languages, physics, chemistry, biology, history, geography, and labor technology. Students can choose these subjects under the guidance of teachers according to their ambitions, hobbies, and needs. Elective subjects are designed to develop students' hobbies, broaden and deepen their knowledge, develop their specialties, and improve their skills in certain aspects. Students can choose any subject that may be offered by the school under the guidance of the teacher according to their personal interests and ambitions (Jin, 1997).

In 2000, *The Full-Time General High School Curriculum Plan (Revised Trial)* was issued. It stipulated that ordinary high school compulsory courses were established to lay a common foundation for students, and each student must take courses. Elective courses are offered on the foundation of compulsory courses to broaden and enhance the knowledge and abilities of students in relevant subject areas. In addition to the elective courses offered in accordance with national regulations, localities and schools should create the conditions to offer flexible and diverse elective courses to meet the diverse development needs of students. Students can choose an elective based on their personal ambitions, interests, and needs.

Based on the above analysis, we can see that the 1981 plan basically only slightly estimates the selectivity of courses under the framework of separating liberal arts and science. The subsequent curriculum plans promulgated in 1990, 1996, and 2000 divided subject courses into compulsory and elective courses, but did not change the basic structure of the separation of liberal arts and sciences. This rigid separation greatly restricted the selectivity and diversity of the curriculum (Zhong et al., 2003: 37). It can be said that breaking the separation between the liberal arts and sciences is crucial to increasing the selectivity of a student's curriculum.

II. Beyond the Liberal Arts and Sciences Separation Elective Institution

In June 2001, the Ministry of Education's *Basic Education Curriculum Reform Program (Trial)* stipulated that "high schools mainly have curriculums that are separated by subject. While establishing compulsory courses, a variety of elective courses are offered, as well as technical courses and credit institution management is actively tested." "Standards for ordinary high school curriculum standards should be based on the premise that students generally meet the basic requirements, have a certain level of stratification and selectivity, and offer elective courses to help students obtain more choices and development opportunities." Shortly after, in 2003, the Ministry of Education promulgated *The Ordinary High School Curriculum Program (Experiment)*. The courses offered are listed in Table 3.2.

Table 3.2 Courses Offered in the Ordinary High School Curriculum Program (Experiment)

Field of Study	Subject	Compulsory Credits (Total 116 Credits)	Elective Credits I	Elective Credits II
Language and Literature	Chinese	10	According to society's demand for talent diversification, adapting to the needs of students' different potentials and developments. On the basis of common compulsory courses, various elective modules are set up in different categories and levels for students to choose from.	Based on the needs of local social, economic, technological, and cultural developments and the interests of students, schools offer a number of elective modules for students to choose from.
	Foreign Language	10		
Mathematics	Mathematics	10		
Humanities and Society	Ideological Politics	8		
	History	6		
	Geography	6		
Science	Physics	6		
	Chemistry	6		
	Biology	6		
Technology	Technology (including Information Technology and General Technology)	8		
Sports and Health	Sports and Health	11		
Arts	Art or Music, Fine Arts	6		
Comprehensive Practice	Research Learning Activities	15		
	Community Services	2		
	Community Practice	6		

Table 3.3 Ratio of Compulsory and Elective Courses among New Courses

	Compulsory Courses	Elective I	Elective II
Credit Score (144)	116	22	6
Percentage	80.5%	15.3%	4.2%
Course Function	Ensure that the common requirements of all high school students are met.	Meet the differences in the development of students on a common basis.	Further meet the differences in students' personal lives, while meeting the differences in school development.

As Table 3.3 shows, Elective I is based on the needs of society for talent diversification, adapting to the different potentials and development needs of students. On the basis of common compulsory courses, several elective modules are set up in different categories and levels for students to choose from. For Elective II, schools set up a number of elective modules for students to choose from according to the needs of local social, economic, technological, and cultural development and the interests of students.

In line with the elective institution, the new curriculum requires schools to establish an effective in-school elective guidance institution to avoid students selecting elective courses arbitrarily. Schools should provide a course description and an elective guidance manual to the students ahead of course selection. Class teachers and other teachers have the responsibility to guide students in class selection, and establish a relatively fixed and long-term contact with students to provide guidance and help for students in forming a reasonable curriculum plan that suits their personal characteristics. It can be seen that compared with the previous stage, there has been development in schools encouraging students in choosing more elective modules in line with their interests and potential, making it so that students are more able to achieve individual development (MOE, 2003).

III. More Selective Elective Institution Attempts

If it can be said that the scope of the previous elective stayed between the arts and sciences, then the room for choice was extended to preparation for further studies (including the separation between liberal arts and sciences) and preparation for employment, then the time and space that students have to choose elective subjects, the degree of mastery, and for study have all undoubtedly further expanded the space that students have for selecting electives.

(1) Reduction of Compulsory Subjects, Increase in Elective Subjects, and the Mobile Learning Institution

In 2012, Zhejiang Province began to deepen reform of ordinary high school curricula. This round of curriculum reform adhered to the concept of "selective education" and adopted the strategy of "reducing compulsory subjects and increasing elective subjects" to increase the selectivity of ordinary high school education and encourage independent choice of study of students on the basis of commonality. This is an inevitable requirement for providing suitable education for each student and promoting the diversification and characteristic development of ordinary high schools. In line with this, Zhejiang Province also set up the teaching organization form of the mobile learning institution and implemented it across the whole province in 2015.

> III. Deepen the Main Content of Curriculum Reform of Ordinary High Schools
>
> (6) Adjusting the Structure
>
> - Adjusting and optimizing course structures. Reducing credits for compulsory courses from 116 credits to 96 credits, and increasing elective credits from 28 credits to 48 credits. Comprehensive practical activities are included in elective courses, and research-based learning permeates into the teaching of various subjects in compulsory courses and elective courses. Thematic education is included in compulsory courses.
> - Increasing the number of elective courses. Elective courses are divided into four categories: knowledge expansion, vocational skills, interests and specialties, and social practice. (1) Knowledge expansion elective courses include compulsory expansion courses, university primary courses, cutting-edge subject development courses, and subject research studies, etc., aimed at forming a thicker knowledge base for students. (2) Vocational skills elective courses include life skills, vocational skills, local economic technology and other courses aimed at improving students' hands-on abilities, mastering certain life skills and vocational skills, and cultivating students' professional inclinations. (3) Interests and specialties elective courses include sports, art, health education, leisure life, knowledge application and other courses aimed at developing students' potential and improving their overall quality. (4) Social practice elective courses include investigative activities, social practice activities, and campus cultural activities, aimed towards guiding students toward paying attention to society and cultivating the students' practical abilities, scientific humanities, and social responsibilities.
>
> Schools should make full use of various social resources according to the actual situation of the school and the region, and set up four types of elective courses, of which the proportion of elective courses for knowledge expansion is not more than 60% and the proportion of elective courses for vocational skills is not less than 10%. The proportion of elective courses per semester is to make up not less than 20% of total class hours.

(7) Reduction of Total Amount
   - Combing through and integrating the subject knowledge system. Clarifying the basic knowledge requirements of compulsory courses, removing repeated content as well as non-mainline and overly complex, overly difficult content, appropriately reducing the necessary content and total amount of learning for all students; the original "elective IA" and "elective IB" course modules are included in the knowledge expansion category of elective courses. Form a curriculum structure with a reasonable and progressive structure of compulsory courses and elective courses.

(8) Excellence Method
   - Implement the credit institution and flexible academic institution. Students should complete regular high school study within three years. Students are allowed to graduate early. Students must take 96 credits in compulsory courses and 48 credits in elective courses (including no less than 6 credits for vocational skills and no more than 8 credits for social practice electives), and 144 credits for total credits. When academic level examinations and comprehensive quality evaluations meet the prescribed requirements, the student may graduate.

   "Plan for Deepening the Reform of Ordinary High School Courses in Zhejiang Province," June 20, 2012

It can be seen that in the process of deepening the reform of the high school curriculum, Zhejiang is striving to optimize its curriculum structure: in terms of quantity, reducing credits for compulsory courses, increasing elective credits, and stipulating the lower limit of various elective courses; and in terms of quality, planning and designing the school elective course institution. In reality, the logic behind these initiatives is lowering the common foundation and thereby enlarging the space for choice that high school students have.

(2) Academic Course Institution

In addition to the reduction of compulsory subjects and addition of optional subjects, high school students can also choose the time, place, and even the study process of the courses, further expanding the time and space of study. For example, Shanghai Yucai Middle School flexibly divides each semester into several learning stages according to the characteristics of students' learning and the internal structure of the subject, and this is called a "study course." There are six courses per academic year and three courses per semester, with two years of schooling (first and second years of high school), totaling twelve courses (see Table 3.4). The teaching time of a course is basically five weeks. The basic points of operation are: one course completes one module of study for each of several subjects, different courses are designed for different subjects, and the number of class hours is the same for the several different subjects in the same course. According to the curriculum settings and class time schedules issued by the Shanghai Municipal

Education Commission, schools have reset various courses for the first and second years of high school.

Table 3.4 A Sketch of Elective Courses in Yucai Middle School

Course One		Course Two		...
Weeks 1—5	Week 6	Weeks 7–11	Week 12	...
Study Module A – 1 Assessment Module A – 1	Study Module A – 2 Making up deficiencies + Foundation examination Module A – 1	Study Module B – 1 Assessment Module B – 1	Study Module B – 2 Making up deficiencies + Foundation examination Module B – 1	...

The eight subjects of Chinese language, mathematics, English, physics, chemistry, sports and fitness, art, and psychology are offered in each course. For the subjects of ideology and politics, history, geography, biology, and information technology, students can choose the time and process of study. Within the same course, students can choose two different subjects, and each subject is four lessons per week. For sports and fitness (special) courses, schools offer tennis, badminton, table tennis, basketball, yoga, aerobics, swimming, and more. Art (special) courses include street dance, engraving, oil painting, drawing, choir, musicals, drama, percussion, and wind and string instruments.

After the completion of the study of three courses in each semester, there is an integration stage targeting the actual teaching situation of the semester and the level of students' learning. The subjects of Chinese language, mathematics, English, physics, chemistry, biology, information technology, politics, history, and geography can be taught with categorical or hierarchical teaching to ensure the relevance and effectiveness of learning.

In general, during the forty years of Reform and Opening Up, the elective institution for secondary schools has been gradually refined and completed. In the early 1980s, the elective institution was nothing more than an initiative to serve the separation of liberal arts and sciences. The flexibility of the elective institution was reflected in the differences in class hours, but it lacked a matching teaching syllabus or curriculum standards. The subsequent elective institution further takes into consideration the preparation for further studies and the preparation for employment.

Since the beginning of the new century, the range of student choices has continued to expand. On the basis of school guidance, students choose subjects, levels, teaching classes, and learning time. The basis of a more selective institution is the internal structure of the elective course, the organization of a logical system, the transformation of the teaching organization, course selection guidance, and career planning, for example, the curriculum structure based on the learning field, subjects, and modules and the hierarchical mobile learning institution.

From a deeper perspective, the elective institution has to deal with the relationship between a common foundation and multiple choices. On the one hand, there is no "mathematics that everyone can learn," but there is "basic mathematics that everyone must learn," and this kind of basic mathematics (the core part) should also be able to be determined according to the standards that most students can achieve. Students who do not reach this scale can learn a little less. In short, this scale should be the scale that the Chinese nation expects middle school students to reach (Cai, 2005). On the other hand, the infinite raising of the common foundation is neither possible (in the case where the objective conditions have not changed much) nor necessary.

In summary, the secondary school elective institution provides students with a more selective curriculum (Chen, 2016) that meets the diverse needs of students, but also tests the students' ability to plan and choose. In other words, there is no choice but to "choose" (Liu, 2001). Students need to make choices on what to learn (choosing the subject), what time to study (the course), where to learn (mobile learning), and to what extent.

It is not just about students and the guidance for them on selecting courses brought about by the institution; the offering of courses at different levels poses a huge challenge to the professionalism and professional competence of teachers. A layered, mobile, personalized, and highly selective curriculum organization has produced nearly a thousand personalized curriculums for each course, which greatly increases the complexity of course organization, and the difficulty of course management is beyond imagination.

However, during the course of implementation, elective courses have shown a tendency towards becoming "compulsory" (Xu, 2016). Some commentators use Zhejiang's "Selected Readings of the Analects" as an example to point out that there is such thing as "compulsory elective courses" in the high school curriculum, that is, the college entrance examination is unified in the province, but under the premise that the province's elective materials are different, in order to save costs, the education administrative department will uniformly designate an "elective" (Cai, 2009: 61–64). The elective institution, which originally aimed to increase the selectivity of students to help them find their own specialties, eventually fell to the point where electives had become mandatory and disguised as compulsory to increase the burden on students (Shen & Lin, 2012).

In the practice of curriculum reform, the development of Chinese language elective courses is still in the trial and exploration stage. Many schools still do not have the ability to develop Chinese language elective courses with school-based characteristics. Schools that offer Chinese language elective courses can only be offered around subjects that may be tested in the college entrance examination and prescribed by the education authorities. The elective courses offered highlight common features and lack individuality. Based on the actual situation of the local college entrance examination, the education administrative department has also established corresponding elective materials, which has led to the upward development of the right to choose textbooks. Teachers also have to teach elective courses as compulsory courses, and the school-based characteristics of elective courses have been diluted. The misplacement of elective course practice and objectives has become a new problem in curriculum reform (Wei, 2006).

There is a close relationship between high school electives and exams. Conceptually, both depend on the student's interests and expertise. Both electives and exams and even professional placements should depend on the student's personal advantages and life planning. However, in a highly selective institutional environment, students are increasingly succumbing to risk assessments of selected subjects (of course, this is also an option). In other words, the interests and specialties give way to the probability of winning, and the intrinsic value of the subject gives way to the input-output benefit. In practice, such a situation has already appeared. In the new college entrance examinations piloted by Shanghai and Zhejiang, the phenomenon of electives and selected examinations and "the shrinking of the liberal arts and science" has already appeared (Pan et al., 2017). If it can be said that the previous predicament was "not testing and not learning" and "what to test and what to teach," then in the face of a more selective institution, it may be "if you don't win, don't learn" and "what is worth learning."

During forty years of Reform and Opening Up, the education sector completed the transition from the teaching discourse system to the curriculum discourse system. The role of the curriculum has become more and more important to people, and it has been artificially exaggerated, even to the extent that the curriculum is equal to education itself in a certain sense. Not only that, the curriculum textbook institution is also involved in many educational roles: education administration, principals, teachers and students, and even parents. Through historical analysis, the trend towards professionalization of textbook development has become more and more intense. It can be said that the shackles of administrative thinking have come off to some extent; the game between unity and pluralism of teaching materials will go on. The curriculum powers and responsibilities of the state, localities, and schools have been redistributed, and the transition from "single-level" management to "three-level management" has been completed. Therefore, the mission of examining curriculum change from a macro perspective is dealing with the distribution of curriculum powers and responsibilities between the central government, local governments and schools, and how to deal with the struggle between professional and administrative aspects. From a micro point of view, the development of school-based curricula has regranted the rights of teachers to develop curricula, and solved the problem of "what to teach." The evolution of the elective institution has gradually given students freedom on "what to learn" and "how to learn." It can be seen that in the era of education decentralization, curriculum reform has gradually pushed the two most important roles in the school system—teachers and students—to the forefront.

Of course, the deeper curriculum reform goes, the more people understand that curriculum change is a systematic project. If the college entrance examination plan cannot be mentioned, the curriculum should not be changed (Shen & Lin, 2012). It is only the combination of curriculum teaching, examination evaluation, student enrollment, and admission (teaching-examination-enrollment) that can drive the comprehensive reform of basic education.

REFERENCES

Cai, S. (2005). On the ten relationships that should be handled in the reform of the middle school mathematics curriculum. *Secondary Mathematics, 05*, 1–4 (in Chinese).

Cai, C. (2009). *Reading resistance absurdity: Cai Chaoyang China education watch.* Taipei, China: Xiuwei Information Technology Co (in Chinese).

Chen, G. (2010). *Curriculum truth.* Shanghai: East China Normal University Press (in Chinese).

Chen, H. (1999). Review and analysis of China's ordinary high school history curriculum reform in the past 20 years. *Journal of Southwest China Normal University (Philosophy and Social Sciences Edition), 05*, 130–135 (in Chinese).

Chen, Q. (2016). Shanghai Yucai middle school: Curriculum-based and organizational models based on academicization. *People's Education, 14*, 57–61 (in Chinese).

Course Teaching Material Research Institute (ed.) (2004). *Textbook institution evolution* (Vol. 1). People's Education Press (in Chinese).

Cui, Y. (2000a). From "Elective Classes and Activity Classes" to "School-Based Curricula". *Education Development Research, 02*, 47–49 (in Chinese).

Cui, Y. (2000b). *School-based curriculum development: Theory and practice.* Beijing: Educational Science Press (in Chinese).

Cui, Y. (2011). Exploring the development of school based curriculum with Chinese characteristics. In Y. Cui, X. Xia, & Z. Wang (Eds.), *School-based curriculum development: The Shanghai experience* (pp. 1–4). Shanghai: East China Normal University Press (in Chinese).

Elliott, D. L., Woodward, A., & Rehage, K. J. (1990). *Textbooks and schooling in the United States.* Chicago: National Society for the Study of Education.

He, X. (Ed.). (2003). *School-based curriculum of No. 2 High School affiliated to East China Normal University.* Shanghai: East China Normal University Press (in Chinese).

He, X., & Qi, Y. (Eds.). (2008). *School-based curriculum development for high schools based on enhancing international competitiveness.* Shanghai: East China Normal University Press (in Chinese).

Hong, R. (2013). Exploration of local pedagogy: Analysis of the views of Sobel, Theobald and Smith. *Curriculum and Teaching, 16*(1), 115–138 (in Chinese).

Huang, S. (2014). Analysis of school cases in the development of school-based curricula in ordinary high schools – Taking Xishan high school in Jiangsu Province as an example. *New Curriculum Research, 01*, 68–71 (in Chinese).

Jin, X. (1997). Introduction to the "Full-time General Senior High School Curriculum Program (Experiment)". *People's Education, 09*, 30–32 (in Chinese).

Li, S. (2010). Recognition of the three-level curriculum management institution. *Modern Education Science, 06*, 20–22, 107 (in Chinese).

Li, Z. (2003). School-based curriculum development: Theory and orientation. *Curricula and Teaching, 03*, 105–127 (in Chinese).

Lin, Y. (2002). Is a school-based curriculum an "Elective Curriculum or Activity Curriculum"? *Shanghai Educational Research, 09*, 47–49 (in Chinese).

Liu, L. (2001). There is no choice but "to Choose" – Thinking about strengthening the structural selectivity of China's ordinary high school curriculum. Master's Thesis of Hunan Normal University (in Chinese).

Lv, D. (2001). Thoughts on the reform of teaching materials for basic education in China. In National Curriculum Professional Committee Secretariat (Ed.), *21st century Chinese curriculum research and reform* (pp. 33–70). Beijing: People's Education Press (in Chinese).

MOE (The Ministry of Education of PRC) (Ed.). (1999). *Deepening education reform, comprehensively promoting quality education, compilation of the third national conference on education work.* Beijing: Higher Education Press (in Chinese).

MOE. (2002). *China education yearbook 2002.* Retrieved from http://www.moe.edu.cn/jyb_sjzl/moe_364/moe_302/moe_368/tnull_4408.html (in Chinese).

MOE. (2003). *Notice of the Ministry of Education on the Printing and Distribution of "The Ordinary High School Curriculum Program (Experiment)"and The Course Standards (Experiment) of 15 Subjects Including Chinese Language* (Jiao Ji [2003] No. 6). Retrieved from http://www.moe.gov.cn/srcsite/A26/s8001/200303/t20030331_167349.html (in Chinese).

MOE. (2010). *Notice of the Ministry of Education on Establishing a Leading Group for the Teaching of National Basic Education Curriculum Materials* (Teacher's Letter [2010] No. 2). Retrieved from http://old.moe.gov.cn//publicfiles/business/htmlfiles/moe/A04_zcwj/201005/xxgk_87809.html (in Chinese).

MOE. (2014). *Notice of the General Office of the Ministry of Education on Adjusting the Leading Group on National Basic Education Curriculum Teaching Materials* (Education Office Letter [2014] No. 21). Retrieved from http://old.moe.gov.cn//publicfiles/business/htmlfiles/moe/s7051/201411/178342.html (in Chinese).

MOE. (2015). Statement on the Relevant Situations of Revolutionary Traditional Education in Primary and Secondary School Textbooks. Retrieved from http://www.moe.gov.cn/jyb_xxgk/s5743/s5746/201512/t20151217_225311.html (in Chinese).

No. 2 High School Affiliated to East China Normal University. (2015). School-based Curriculum of No. 2 High School Affiliated to East China Normal University. Retrieved from http://www.hsefz.cn/school-of-excellence/elective-courses/ (in Chinese).

Pan, K., Liu, J., & He, Z. (2017). Inquiring into the phenomenon of "The Shrinking of the Liberal Arts and Science" of High School Students Under New College Entrance Examination Reform. *China Education Journal, 08*, 31–36 (in Chinese).

People's Education Press. (2013). The People's Education Publishing House's Official Reply to the Issue of the Removal of The Works of Xun Lu from People's Education Publishing House Seventh Grade (Chinese Language) Textbooks. Retrieved from http://www.pep.com.cn/rjdt/jqgg/201309/t20130906_1164895.shtml (in Chinese).

People's Education Press. (2016). Declaration on the Relevant Situations of Selected Subjects of Foreign Languages in the Primary School Chinese Textbook for People's Education. Retrieved from http://weibo.com/2173867535/DsWeqhDkF?type=comment#_rnd1520843839388 (in Chinese).

Scott, J. C., Translated by Wang, X. (2004). *Seeing like a state: How certain schemes to improve the human condition have failed.* Beijing: China Social Sciences Publishing House (in Chinese).

Shen, W., & Qu, L. (2012). Reflections and Prospects of China's Ordinary High School Curriculum Reform – Interview with Professor Zhang Hua of Hangzhou Normal University. *Global Education Outlook*, *12*, 3–14, 55 (in Chinese).

Shi, J. (2001).The development of curriculum and textbook policy of basic education in China for 50 years. In National Curriculum Professional Committee Secretariat (Ed.), *21st Century Chinese curriculum research and reform* (pp. 78–99). Beijing: People's Education Press (in Chinese).

Sun, Y., et al. (Eds.). (2016). *25 years of Shanghai curriculum reform (1988–2013).* Shanghai: Shanghai Education Press (in Chinese).

Tang, J. (2010). Looking back and thinking: How to build a high-quality school-based curriculum. *Basic Education Curricula*, *Z1*, 157–160 (in Chinese).

The National Board of Education. (1990). Notice of the National Board of Education on the Printing and Distribution of "The Adjustment Opinions of the Current Ordinary High School Teaching Plan". *People's Education*, *06*, 9–10 (in Chinese).

The State Council of PRC. (2017). *Notice of the General Office of the State Council on the Establishment of the National Textbook Committee* (Guo Ban Fa [2017] No. 61). Retrieved from http://www.gov.cn/zhengce/content/2017-07/06/content_5208390.htm (in Chinese).

Wang, W. (2016a). Classroom teaching reform: Taking the high-speed train to informatization. *China Education News*, January 13 (in Chinese).

Wang, Y. (2016b). Curriculum reform: Transforming Shanghai's education from quantitative to qualitative. *People's Education*, *08*, 44–47 (in Chinese).

Wei, B. (2006). High School elective Chinese language courses: Change, confusion and reflections. *Courses, Teaching Materials and Teaching Methods*, 04, 40–44 (in Chinese).

Wen, R. (2013). Calm down and discuss language. *Shandong Business Daily*, December 19 (in Chinese).

Wu, G. (2002). *School-based curriculum development.* Chengdu: Sichuan Education Press (in Chinese).

Xie, Y., Ma, Y., & Zhang, Z. (2013). Have there really been eight curriculum reforms in New China? *Education Research*, *34*(02), 125–132, 146 (in Chinese).

Xu, M. (2016). Studies on the phenomenon of elective courses tending towards "Compulsory Courses" in ordinary high schools. Master's Thesis of Shanxi Normal University (in Chinese).

Yang, D. (Ed.). (2013a). *Four discussions of basic education: Authority, objects, tools and vessels.* Beijing: Beijing Press (in Chinese).

Yang, J. (Ed.). (2013b). *Ability building of the school curriculum: A study based on the cultural transformation of ordinary high school curricula.* Nanjing: Jiangsu Education Press (in Chinese).

Zhang, D. (2000). 15 topics currently undergoing study in the National High School Mathematics curriculum standards. *Mathematics Teaching*, *06*, 2 (in Chinese).

Zheng, F. (2016). Firmly grasping the correct political direction of basic education curriculum materials. *China Education News*, January 15 (in Chinese).

Zhong, Q. (1994). The elective institution and personality development: Comment on the standards of Shanghai secondary school elective courses. *Comparative Education Research*, *03*, 19–23 (in Chinese).

Zhong, Q. (2004). One syllabus, multiple textbooks: The demands of education democracy – A review of China's textbook policy. *Education Development Research*, *04*, 1–6 (in Chinese).
Zhong, Q. (Ed.). (2006). *Modern curriculum theory.* Shanghai: Shanghai Education Press (in Chinese).
Zhong, Q., & Yang, M. (2003). Curriculum policy and practice in China. In Q. Zhong & H. Luo (Eds.), *The transformation of curriculum paradigm: Curriculum reform in Shanghai and Hong Kong* (pp. 335–360). Shanghai: Shanghai Science and Technology Education Press (in Chinese).
Zhong, Q., Cui, Y., & Wu, G. (Eds.). (2003). *Introduction to the new general senior high school curriculum program.* Shanghai: East China Normal University Press (in Chinese).
Zou, S. (Ed.). (2007). *School-based curriculum development and management.* Beijing: Science Popularization Press (in Chinese).

CHAPTER FOUR

The Institutions of Teachers Development and Appointment

MINGFENG DU

The teacher institutions is an important part of the reform of the education institutions and mechanism. The key to cultivating a team of highly qualified teachers depends on institutional support. During the past forty years of Reform and Opening Up, China has made great achievements in institutions construction and reform of teacher cultivating, the teacher personnel institutions, teacher training, teacher development, and so on. This chapter starts from the macro background of the reform of the education institutions and mechanism, then combs through the history of the reform of the Chinese teacher institutions in the forty years of Reform and Opening Up, refines the major issues of concern to the reform of the Chinese teacher institutions, and provides historical references and rational resources for the reform and optimization of the Chinese teacher institutions in the new era.

SECTION 1 THE INSTITUTIONS OF TEACHER CULTIVATING

Normal education (teacher training education) is the main channel for cultivating teachers and an important part of improving the overall quality of teachers. Since Reform and Opening Up began, the Chinese teacher training institutions have undergone a series of reforms, but its fundamental nature has not changed, and it still emphasizes the adjustment of the institutions under the guidance of the state.

From normal education to teacher education and creating a more open teacher training institutions, it is a major choice for the reform of the contemporary Chinese teacher institutions.

I. Establishing "The Four-Level Teacher Education Institutions"

As early as the founding of the People's Republic of China, China learned from the Soviet education experience and established a socialist teacher education institution on the basis of reforming "old education." It mainly included four levels: junior normal schools, secondary normal schools, teacher's colleges, and higher normal schools. Therefore, it was also called "the four-level teacher education institutions." On August 10, 1951, *The Decision on Reforming the School Institutions* adopted by the Government Administration Council was the first school institutions promulgated by China after the founding of the People's Republic. It systematically designed China's early childhood education, primary education, secondary education, and higher education reform. Among them, secondary education was the most diverse form, including secondary schools (junior high schools and high schools), vocational and agricultural secondary schools, amateur secondary schools, and secondary specialized schools. Normal schools had a three-year period of study, recruiting junior high school graduates or equivalent students; junior normal schools had a three-to-four-year period of study, recruiting primary school graduates or equivalent students; the age of kindergarten teachers and the enrollment conditions were equivalent to normal schools; normal schools and junior normal schools had to be equipped with early childhood teachers; graduates of junior normal schools, normal schools, and kindergarten normal schools had to serve in primary schools or kindergartens. After expiration, they were to be promoted to normal schools, high-level middle schools, teacher's colleges, or other institutions of higher learning (The Government Administration Council of PRC, 1951). Normal schools here were to be the prototypes for the "middle teachers" in the future. On August 26, 1951, in his opening speech for "The First National Primary Education and Teacher Education Conference," Xulun Ma stated: "To determine the guidelines and tasks of various types of normal schools at all levels … We should clearly define the tasks of secondary normal schools, which is to train teachers in primary schools and kindergartens and some teachers in the schools of industry and agriculture. The task of higher normal schools is training teachers in ordinary middle schools, fast-growth middle schools for workers and farmers, teachers in normal schools, and teachers of other subjects in other secondary schools." "In the setting up of higher normal schools, each Greater Administrative Region must set up a teacher college directly under the leadership of MOE of the Greater Administrative Region; each province should set up a normal college or a teacher's college; the original university education department should be based on the principle of adjustment and transformation. At present, there is no additional establishment. All kinds of secondary normal schools should strive for development, and pay attention to correcting the phenomenon of unbalanced development in the past. In particular, more short-term teacher training courses and crash courses should be set up to meet the needs of gradually popularizing primary education" (He, 1988: 109).

On September 11, 1951, Junrui Qian further stated in "Running the People's Education Using Revolutionary Methods": "Schools that train primary education teachers are normal schools and junior normal schools, and schools that train kindergarten teachers are kindergarten teachers' schools. As for the task of training secondary school teachers, in addition to part of the responsibility being undertaken by the universities, the teachers of secondary schools are mainly the normal colleges and normal vocational colleges. The teachers of higher education institutions are mainly trained by the research departments of higher education institutions …." "On the adjustment and setting of higher education normal schools, each Greater Administrative District shall establish at least one sound normal school, which is to be directly led by MOE (or the Ministry of Culture and Education) of the Greater Administrative Region, with the main task of cultivating teachers of senior secondary schools. In principle, all provinces and major cities should establish one sound teacher's college. It is up to the education departments and bureaus of each province (or city) to directly lead the training of junior middle school teachers; if conditions permit, they must also set up teacher colleges." "On the adjustment and setting of normal schools and junior normal schools, we should strive to set up one normal school in each prefectural district and provincial city. When conditions do not permit, a junior normal school can be established. Larger counties should strive to set up a junior normal school, and smaller counties should jointly establish a junior normal school or a normal school" (He, 1998: 115). In this way, the prototype of China's three-level teacher education institutions will basically take shape.

On July 16, 1952, the MOE issued two draft bills: *The Provisional Regulations for Normal Schools (Draft)* and *The Provisions on Higher Normal Schools (Draft)*, which formally established the normal education institutions in China. *The Interim Procedures for Normal Schools (Draft)* stipulates: "The length of schooling for normal schools is three years, recruiting junior high school graduates or equivalent students. The age of enrollment is tentatively set at 15 to 30 years old; normal schools that train kindergarten teachers are called kindergarten normal schools; normal schools must attach intensive teacher's courses, recruit junior high school graduates or those with equivalent academic qualifications, and schooling is limited to one year" (MOE, 1952a). *The Regulations on Higher Normal Schools (Draft)* state: "Higher normal schools are divided into two categories: normal colleges and normal vocational colleges. Higher normal schools enroll graduates of higher secondary schools and normal schools (expiration of service) or equivalent students; the length of schooling for normal colleges is limited to four years, and schooling for normal vocational colleges is limited to two years" (MOE, 1952b:112). Thus, at the beginning of the establishment of the People's Republic of China, a relatively sound institutional institutions of teacher education was established.

II. Restoring "The Three-Level Teacher Education Institutions"

After the decade of stagnation of the "Cultural Revolution," a multitude of reforms were enacted in the field of education in the early days of Reform and Opening Up. In order to restore order to teaching as quickly as possible and solve the problem of teachers having low statuses and there being a serious shortage in the number of teachers, the state first restored the reputation of teachers, affirmed the class attribute of "intellectuals are part of the working class," and proposed to "respect knowledge and respect talents," improving the social status of teachers (Deng, 1994: 41, 108). After that, normal schools were restored and reestablished to train primary and secondary school teachers. After the 1960s, junior normal schools were gradually replaced by middle normal schools, and the center of the hierarchical structure shifted upwards, forming the three levels of middle, vocational, and undergraduate normal schools. On October 12, 1978, the MOE issued *The Opinions on Strengthening and Developing Normal Education*, proposing to "coordinate planning and establish a normal education network." The main contents were as follows: First, ordinary regions rely on current middle normal schools with good conditions to establish a normal vocational college. While training junior high school teachers, it also undertakes the training tasks of some junior high school teachers. The length of schooling is three years. Second is working hard to properly set up middle normal schools. The task of middle normal schools is training primary school teachers and undertaking the training tasks of some primary school teachers. The academic institutions of the middle normal schools is divided into two forms: two-year and three-year normal education. Third, the six higher normal colleges under the MOE should be responsible for cultivating teachers for normal colleges, normal vocational colleges, normal middle schools, and key middle schools for all regions (He, 1998: 1649). This is the earlier clarification of the specific duties and tasks of the three-level normal colleges after Reform and Opening Up, and it is also a relatively comprehensive planning and arrangement.

On June 15, 1980, the state convened a national normal education work conference, proposing to establish a sound normal education institution: First, the MOE should properly establish normal universities and teacher's colleges that are directly subordinate. Each province, city, and autonomous region should have one or several higher normal schools; second, relevant business departments gradually restore and establish some necessary professional normal schools, or establish additional normal departments in some colleges in a planned fashion; third, relevant provinces and autonomous regions should pay attention to appropriate development and vigorously establish national normal schools; fourth, provinces and localities (cities) should each set up an education college (teacher training college) and the county should set up a teacher training school, dividing up the work in training working teachers and school administrators (The Department of Normal Education of the National Education Commission of PRC, 1997: 136–137). This meeting corrected the chaotic situation of normal education in the "Ten Years of Unrest," comprehensively summed up the historical experiences and lessons of Chinese teacher education over the previous 30 years, formulated a series of documents, clarified the future guidelines and tasks, and pointed out training objectives of normal schools at all levels (Wang, 2009).

In terms of secondary normal education, on August 22, 1980, the National Normal Education Working Conference discussed and approved *The Opinions of MOE on Further Strengthening the Training of In-service Teachers in Primary and Secondary Schools*, *The Opinions of MOE on Running Secondary Normal Education*, and *The Regulations for Secondary Normal Schools (Trial Draft)*. Among these, *The Opinions of MOE on Running Secondary Normal Education* (hereinafter referred to as *The Opinions*) on the basis of affirming the important role and significance of secondary normal education established regulations on the problems of tasks, academic institutions and enrollment, teaching plans and teaching materials for secondary normal education, properly carrying out leadership and management for teacher training of kindergarten normal schools, ethnic normal schools, blind, deaf, and mute teacher training, and secondary normal education. *The Opinions* further clarified the mission of secondary normal education: to train qualified teachers for primary schools. Secondary normal schools have a three-year and four-year academic institutions, both of which recruit junior high school graduates and social youth with equivalent academic strength (He, 1998: 1834–1869). Subsequently, the *Regulations for Secondary Normal Schools* and the *Teaching Plan for Secondary Normal Schools (Draft)* were successively issued, and basic work was done on the restoration and reconstruction of secondary normal education.

In the aspect of higher normal education, on September 29, 1980, the MOE issued a *Report Request on Several Issues Concerning Normal Education*, emphasizing that normal education is the "working machine" in education and is the talent base for cultivating talents. It is necessary to establish a sound normal education institutions and make it a foundation for cultivating qualified teachers of various medium and primary schools and kindergartens. The report stated: "The basic mission of normal education is training teachers. The undergraduate courses of higher normal colleges mainly train middle school teachers; normal vocational colleges train junior middle school teachers; middle normal schools and kindergarten normal schools train primary school teachers and kindergarten teachers" (The Department of Normal Education of the National Education Commission of PRC, 1997: 131–132). On October 27, 1980, the MOE issued the *Opinions on Vigorously Running Higher Normal Vocational Colleges*, which standardized the management institutions, academic institutions, professional setup, and teaching work of higher normal vocational colleges, and believed higher normal vocational colleges to be an important part of China's higher normal education institutions, its main task being "training qualified teachers for junior high schools in the region" (Su & Zhang, 1996: 41). In this way, China restored and preliminarily established a teacher training institutions based on normal universities, normal vocational colleges, secondary normal schools, and a teacher-in-service training institutions in about 1980.

In May 1985, *The Decision of the Central Committee of the Communist Party of China on the Reform of the Education Institutions* fully affirmed the established normal education institutions and called for the development of normal education and the training of in-service teachers as strategic measures for the development of education. In short, through recovery and development in the ten or so years after the initiation of Reform and Opening Up, China had further improved the "three-level normal education institutions" by the mid-to-late 1980s, forming a relatively complete structure and relatively positive institutions.

III. The Construction of an Open Normal Education Institution

The traditional "three-level normal education institutions" emphasizes the full status of "normal" colleges in cultivating teachers. However, with the continuous development of economic and social development and education, especially the gradual opening of reform of China's education institutions in the late 1980s, the normal education institutions began to face some new situations: In one aspect, basic education had grown stronger thanks to education reform. The demand for quality education in society grew more and more, and high-quality education required high-quality teachers. Therefore, it was imperative to adjust and reform the teacher training institutions. In another aspect, normal colleges, especially national key normal universities, began to actively expand their methods of running schools. In order to improve the competitiveness of normal colleges and comprehensive colleges, non-normal degrees began to be set up on a large scale, and the idea of normal colleges and ordinary universities jointly cultivating normal students was advocated. To this end, the National Education Commission issued *The Opinions on Basic Education Teachers and Normal Education Planning* (hereinafter referred to as *The Opinions*) on March 10, 1986, in addition to further clarifying the existing three-level institutions of middle normal, normal vocational, and university undergraduate degrees in China's normal colleges, it was also emphasized that secondary normal schools should undertake on-the-job training and further training tasks for primary school teachers. Kindergarten normal schools should cultivate and train teachers for early childhood education. Normal vocational colleges are responsible for a portion of on-the-job training for junior high school teachers. Normal undergraduate colleges train teachers at an undergraduate level for basic education. *The Opinions* creatively proposed that the sources of secondary school teachers should be diversified, and it was necessary to consider normal colleges and ordinary comprehensive colleges in meeting the needs of educational development. The enrollment, distribution, and treatment of teachers of non-normal colleges had to be treated equally with normal colleges in accordance with the plan; graduates of non-normal colleges could also be assigned to teach secondary schools as needed, and incentive measures had to be adopted in policies (Su & Zhang, 1996: 19–20). In this way, on the issue of teacher training, the important role of comprehensive universities and other non-normal colleges in teacher training began being considered, opening up new ways of teacher training.

It was also during this period that some debates appeared in the field of academic research. The main worry was whether such an open and diverse teacher training path would weaken the status of normal education.

In this context, the issue of the development and orientation of normal schools became a big problem in the development of teacher education. In order to further consolidate and train teachers and improve the quality of the teaching staff, Lanqing Li, then Vice Premier of the State Council, stated in a speech at the 1996 National Normal Education Conference: "The next 20 or 30 years or even longer will be China's golden age for normal education. We must unswervingly do a good job with normal education in China" (The Department of Normal Education of the National Education Commission of PRC, 1997: 178). On March 16, 1999, the MOE issued the *Several Opinions on the Adjustment of the Structure of Teachers' Colleges*, arguing that the development trend of normal education in China was as follows: normal colleges as the main body with the active participation of other institutions of higher learning, diversification of sources for primary and secondary school teachers, a gradually increasing focus on the normal education hierarchy structure, a linking up of pre-employment and post-employment education, the continuance of education on the legal track, a reliance on modern education technology and information communication technology, and the continued initial establishment of an open primary and secondary school teacher education network. The goal of hierarchical structural adjustment is to be gradually advanced from urban to rural areas, and from coastal areas to inland areas. There will be a transition from three-level normal education (higher undergraduate, high-level vocational, and medium-level teachers) to two-level education (higher undergraduate and higher vocational). By 2010, the newly added elementary and junior high school teachers had basically reached vocational college and undergraduate degree levels of education.

On September 9, 1996, Kaixuan Zhu further emphasized in the report *Vigorously Carrying Out Normal Education, Strengthening the Construction of Teaching Teams and Struggling to Develop Cross-Century Education*: "We must continue to maintain an independent normal education institution and make it so there is a stable base for the training of the huge amount of new teachers in primary and secondary education and the training of in-service teachers. It is necessary to adhere to the independent setting of various levels and types of normal colleges and universities as the main body, and give full play to the synergistic role of non-normal colleges to train teachers. Non-normal colleges participating in the training of primary and secondary school teachers is an inevitable requirement for the development of the social economy, culture and education." "The hierarchical structure of normal education should still be stable at three levels: middle normal, normal vocational, and undergraduate. Appropriate development of undergraduate, development of vocational as needed, adjustment and strengthening of middle normal." "Gradually changing the situation of only training teachers in teacher training institutes and the separation of pre-employment and post-employment teacher training, and further improving the training network of provinces, cities (prefectures), counties, and townships. While giving full play to the main role of teacher training institutes (training centers), the positive role of ordinary normal colleges and post-employment teacher schools in teacher training work should be fully utilized, and through joint and collaborative education and other forms, the link between pre-employment and post-employment education should be strengthened, and conditional locations should gradually realize the integration of cultivation and training" (The Department of Normal Education of the National Education Commission of PRC, 1997: 187–188).

In the mid-to-late 1990s and especially at the beginning of the 21st century, there was a situation across the whole of China where normal schools and non-normal schools either combined or were upgraded into comprehensive universities. Many normal schools, especially normal vocational schools and non-normal colleges, combined and upgraded to become comprehensive universities or colleges. Some vocational level normal schools or education colleges were merged with normal colleges and upgraded to become normal universities. In this context, in order to ensure the strategic position of prioritized development of normal education in the development of education, Bin Liu, deputy director of the State Education Commission, stated in the *Summary Report of the National Normal Education Conference*: "All levels and types of normal colleges must unswervingly serve primary and secondary schools. This is an important criterion for us in evaluating the quality of the running of a normal college. To enter the '211', normal colleges must first look at this article and see if their guiding ideology for the running of a school is correct" (The Department of Normal Education of the National Education Commission of PRC, 1997: 200).

As such, after more than a decade of development, by the end of the 20th century China had already formed a network structure combining cultivation and training using various types and levels of normal colleges and universities as the main body. Pre-employment training uses general normal colleges at all levels as its main channel, including undergraduate level normal universities (normal colleges), vocational and technical normal colleges, high level specialist schools such as specialist normal colleges, vocational and technical normal specialist colleges, and middle-level general secondary normal schools, kindergarten normal schools, and special education normal schools; with general higher education institution classes, education faculties, and TV university teacher classes used as auxiliary channels (Chen et al., 1996).

After entering the 21st century, the state began to guide the establishment of an open teacher education institutions from the policy level, and realized the transformation from normal education to teacher education. This has been a major transformation of the development of the Chinese teacher institutions since Reform and Opening Up began. On December 24, 1998, the MOE promulgated *The Action Plan for Education Revitalization for the 21st Century*, proposing to implement the "Cross-Century Gardening Project," while emphasizing the need to strengthen and reform normal education and improve the cultivation quality of new teachers. Stronger institutions of higher learning should contribute to the cultivation of new teachers and teacher training.

On March 16, 1999, the MOE issued *The Several Opinions on the Adjustment of the Layout of Normal Colleges and Universities*, proposing: "From the perspective of China's national conditions, adhere to the independent role of the main body of the normal colleges, and at the same time further broaden the source channels of primary and secondary school teachers. Encourage a group of high-level comprehensive universities to participate in the training of primary and secondary school teachers; actively promote the reorganization of normal education resources in large and medium-sized cities with relatively concentrated teacher resources, and form a group of normal universities with high level, large scale and comprehensive strength across the country; a number of normal universities are to be jointly established by MOE and local governments. One normal university is to be established in provinces, autonomous regions, and municipalities directly under the Central Government with a basis in undergraduate education. They shall also undertake postgraduate education and establish teaching centers and research centers that serve primary and secondary education. They will play a leading, backbone and demonstrative role in the development of normal education; with provinces, autonomous regions and municipalities directly under the Central Government as the mainstay, the integration of normal specialist colleges, education colleges and secondary normal schools will be promoted in qualified cities (districts) to build a group of normal colleges or normal specialist colleges that will undertake the cultivation and training tasks for primary and secondary school teachers; and school adjustment work for secondary normal schools will be carried out in an active and reliable manner. A number of secondary normal schools will continue to be established to train primary school teachers for areas that are underdeveloped economically and in education" (He, 2003: 241).

On June 13, 1999, *The Decision of the Central Committee of the Communist Party of China on Deepening Educational Reform and Comprehensively Promoting Quality Education* proposed: "Strengthening and reforming normal education, vigorously improving the quality of teacher training, adjusting the level and layout of normal schools and encouraging comprehensive higher education schools and non-normal colleges and universities to participate in the cultivation and training of primary and secondary school teachers, and explore the trial of normal colleges in comprehensive higher education institutions with the right conditions. By 2010, qualifying regions will strive to upgrade the academic qualifications of teachers in full-time education in primary and secondary schools to the specialist level and undergraduate level respectively. The proportion of full-time teachers and principals in high school education in economically developed areas with masters degrees should be raised. The proportion of school teachers in higher education institutions with PhDs is to be raised." This is a major document on education reform released from the highest decision-making level in the country. It proposes to encourage comprehensive institutions of higher learning and non-normal colleges to participate in the training of primary and secondary school teachers, and to test out normal colleges, marking an important step in building an open teacher education institutions.

On May 29, 2001, the State Council issued *The Decision of the State Council on the Reform and Development of Basic Education*, proposing to improve the teacher education institutions and strengthen the construction of primary and secondary school teachers: "improve the open teacher education institutions with the existing normal colleges and universities as the main body and other higher education institutions participating in cultivation and training; strengthen the subject construction of normal colleges and universities, and encourage comprehensive universities and other non-normal colleges to hold educational institutions departments or open up courses that teachers require to obtain teacher qualifications." "Relying on normal universities and comprehensive universities that meet conditions, build a group of open teacher education network colleges; promote the adjustment of the teacher education structure, and gradually realize the transition from three-level normal education to two-level normal education; qualifying areas should train primary school teachers with specialist college degrees and junior high school teachers with undergraduate degrees, gradually improve the qualifications of high school teachers, expand the training scale and enrollment scope of masters of education; and enhance the education and lifelong development ability of normal graduates" (He, 2003: 890). This was the first time that the concept of "teacher education" was used at the national level. At the same time, it proposed that Chinese teacher education had gradually realized the transition from three-level normal education to two-level normal education.

In 2002, the MOE issued *The Opinions on the Reform and Development of Teacher Education during the Tenth Five-Year Plan*, which stated: "Teacher education is a general term for pre-employment cultivation, job-entry education and post-employment training of teachers under the guidance of lifelong education ideology, in accordance with the different stages of professional development of teachers." Accelerating the development of teacher education is an inevitable trend in the reform and development of normal education in the new situation. It is necessary to "preliminarily form an open teacher education institution that manifests the idea of lifelong education with the existing normal colleges and universities as the main body and other higher education institutions participating in cultivation and training" (He, 2003: 1146–1148).

In 2003, the MOE proposed to "accelerate the establishment of an open and flexible education institutions, improve the level of running schools, promote the reform of normal colleges and universities, and encourage comprehensive universities to carry out teacher education" (MOE, 2003). From this perspective, the upgrading from normal specialist colleges to comprehensive universities or normal universities, and the upgrading from specialized normal schools or middle normal schools to normal colleges or normal universities have in itself already improved the level of Chinese normal colleges. In 2004, *The 2003–2007 Education Revitalization Action Plan* proposed to "reform the teacher education model, gradually integrate teacher education into the higher education institutions, and build a modern teacher education institutions with normal universities and other universities that carry out teacher education leading the way, with coordinated development between the three levels of specialist, undergraduate, and research education, back and forth communication between pre and post-employment teacher education, and a combination of academic and non-academic education, where the teacher's professional development and lifelong learning are promoted."

In order to further improve the quality of teacher training, the state decided to implement free education for normal students in the six normal universities directly under the MOE starting from 2007. The purpose was to form an atmosphere of respect for teachers and education, attracting outstanding students to find jobs in education, and making education the most respected cause in the whole of society. In May 2007, the General Office of the State Council forwarded *The Notice of MOE and Other Departments on The Measures for Implementing Free*

Education for Normal Students of Normal Universities under MOE (Trial), and decided to provide free education for normal students of Beijing Normal University, East China Normal University, Northeast Normal University, Huazhong Normal University, Shaanxi Normal University, and Southwest University (all directly under the MOE) from the autumn of 2007. Students were to be exempted from tuition and accommodation fees during the schooling period and receive a living allowance.

While striving to adjust the level and mode of running normal schools, the state also actively encourages non-normal colleges to participate in teacher education and promote the integration of normal colleges. In order to improve the quality of their own schools, each school began to construct a teacher education institutions that was compatible with China's economic and social development and the development of education, such as the "university + normal" teacher education model implemented by Beijing Normal University, the academy institutions implemented by East China Normal University, and the "2+2" model implemented by Shaanxi Normal University (i.e., general training for the first two years and professional training for the second two years). With the advent of the era of higher education popularization, China's normal education institutions also begun to change; schools where teachers were taught were no longer limited to the level of graduate schools. Graduates of many comprehensive universities or research-based universities in developed regions also went to primary schools to work in education, and even masters and doctors went to work in primary and secondary schools. Schools were not limited to cultivating primary and secondary school teachers at the undergraduate or specialist level, and more and more were training primary and secondary school teachers at the master's or doctoral level.

In 2010, *The National Medium-and-Long-Term Education Reform and Development Plan Outline (2010–2020)* put forward: "Strengthening teacher education, building an open and flexible teacher education institutions with normal colleges and universities as the main body and comprehensive university participation; deepening teacher education reform, innovating training modes, strengthening the practice internship stage, strengthening the training of teacher morality and teaching ability, and improving the quality of teacher training." In 2012, the MOE, the National Development and Reform Commission, and the Ministry of Finance jointly issued *The Opinions on Deepening Teacher Education Reform*. With regard to the reform of teacher education and the design of the teacher education construction institutions, it was proposed to further improve the open and flexible teacher education institutions: "Leveraging the main role of normal colleges in teacher education, focusing on the construction of normal universities and normal colleges; encouraging comprehensive universities to make use of their comprehensive advantages in disciplines and participation in teacher education; local comprehensive colleges, higher specialist normal schools, and secondary normal schools should actively adjust the professional structure and strengthen the training of primary and kindergarten teachers according to the requirements of teacher training. MOE and each of the provincial people's governments should jointly build a group of normal universities and vocational technology normal institutions. Supporting affiliated normal universities in establishing regional teacher education alliances in cooperation with local normal colleges and universities."

On August 19, 2014, MOE issued *The Opinions on the Implementation of the Excellent Teacher Training Plan* (hereinafter referred to as *The Opinions*), proposing to deepen the reform of teacher training models, establish cooperation of universities and local governments, and primary and secondary schools (kindergartens, secondary vocational schools, special education schools, as below) in cultivating new mechanisms to train a large number of high-quality professional primary and secondary school teachers with noble teacher ethics, a solid professional foundation, and outstanding teaching and self-development capabilities. *The Opinions* advocates the reform of training models for outstanding teachers, including the training of excellent middle schools, primary schools, kindergartens, secondary vocational schools, and special education teachers. Through collaboration of universities, local governments, and primary and secondary schools, a long-term cooperation and win-win mechanism was established to jointly formulate training goals, design curriculum institutions, build curriculum resources, organize teaching teams, build practice bases, conduct teaching research, and evaluate the quality of training.

In short, after 2003, the political discourse of teacher education gradually assumed a dominating position, practical discourse was pushed forward comprehensively, the closed and targeted normal education institutions was gradually broken, and a diverse, open, and comprehensive teacher education institutions was gradually established.

SECTION 2 THE INSTITUTIONS OF TEACHER MANAGEMENT

The teacher management institutions is an important part of the teacher institutions, and it is also an important support point ensuring the construction of teaching teams. The teacher management institution mainly refers to teacher personnel management, including comprehensive affairs such as teacher qualifications, teacher positions, teacher quota, and teacher salary. The consolidation and improvement of the teacher management institutions is an important guarantee in the reform and development of primary and secondary schools. The teacher management institutions has also undergone major changes and development in the forty years of Reform and Opening Up.

I. The Professional-Oriented Teacher Qualification Institutions

The requirements for teachers' professional qualifications have undergone a process of continuous professionalization from the teacher qualification certificate institutions implemented in the 1980s to the professional standards of teachers since the beginning of the new century.

(1) The Standard-Based Teacher Qualification Institutions

Since the founding of the People's Republic of China, China has never established a teacher qualification institution from the institutional and legal level. This is because China has long implemented an independent, closed normal education institutions, the so-called three targeted and one guaranteed teacher training policy, with targeted enrollment, targeted training, targeted allocation, and a guaranteed living allowance security institution. Under this institutional arrangement, normal students are considered qualified after graduation, and all are allocated to primary and secondary schools for education and teaching activities. Therefore, no necessary link to teacher qualifications was ever established. After Reform and Opening Up began, especially in the late 1980s, with the participation of non-normal schools and non-normal degree courses in the training of normal students as well as education and teaching activities, and the influence of foreign teacher qualification institution, the country began to consider establishing a teacher qualification institution. In May 1985, the General Office of the Central Committee of the Communist Party of China promulgated *The Decision of the Central Committee of the Communist Party of China on the Reform of the Education Institutions (*hereinafter referred to as *The Decision*), proposing: "Only those with a qualifying education background or examination qualification certificate can become teachers. Normal education at all levels from kindergarten normal education to higher normal education must be vigorously developed and strengthened. Normal colleges and universities must adhere to the idea of serving primary and secondary education, and graduates must be assigned to teach in schools, and a certain proportion of other higher education graduates should also be assigned to schools to serve as teachers." Guided by the spirit of *The Decision*, China began the construction of a teacher qualification institutions.

On April 12, 1986, the Fourth Session of the Sixth National People's Congress passed *The Compulsory Education Law of the People's Republic of China*, of which Article 13 stipulates: "The state adopts measures to strengthen and develop normal education and accelerate the cultivation and training of teachers. The situation of primary school teachers having a level of graduation above secondary normal schools, and teachers in junior middle schools having a level of graduation above higher normal schools will be realized in a planned manner. The state establishes a teacher qualification assessment institutions and issues qualification certificates to qualified teachers" (He, 1998: 2415). On September 6 of the same year, The State Education Commission's *Notice on the Printing and Distribution of "The Provisional Measures for Assessment Qualification Certificates for Primary and Middle School Teachers"* (hereinafter referred to as *The Provisional Measures*) proposed that the implementation of the assessment qualification certificate institutions is not a temporary measure but a long-term method. "The Provisional Measures" stipulates that assessment qualification certificates are applicable to primary and middle school teachers who do not have the qualifications required by the state. Assessment qualification certificates are temporarily categorized into "qualification certificates for teaching materials and teaching methods" and "professional qualification certificates." "The Certificate of Assessment Qualification for Teaching Materials and Teaching Methods" marks the teacher's preliminary study and mastery of the syllabus, textbooks, and basic teaching methods of the teaching subject; "The Professional Qualification Certificate" indicates that the teacher has the cultural majors knowledge and ability necessary for teaching a certain subject, and is basically able to do the teaching work of the teaching subject. Teachers of primary and secondary schools who do not have the qualifications required by the state and have worked for more than one year can apply to take an examination for "The Teaching Material Teaching Method Examination Qualification Certificate"; those who have worked for more than two years and have obtained "The Teaching Material Teaching Method Examination Qualification Certificate" can apply to take "The Professional Qualification Certificate" cultural professional knowledge exam (He, 1998: 2492).

On February 13, 1993, *The Outline of China's Education Reform and Development* issued by the Central Committee of the Communist Party of China and the State Council stated: "By the end of this century, most teachers in primary and secondary schools must meet nationally-recognized qualification standards through replenishment and on-the-job training. The proportion of teachers with vocational and bachelor's degrees in primary and junior high schools has increased year by year." *The Law of Teachers of the People's Republic of China*, which came into effect on January 1, 1994, stipulates that the state implements a teacher qualification institutions. On December 12, 1995, the State Council issued *The Regulations on Teacher Qualifications* (hereinafter referred to as *The Regulations*), which clearly stipulates the established basic measures on the nature, qualification classifications, qualification conditions, teacher qualification examinations, and qualification establishment of Chinese teacher qualifications. *The Regulations* stipulates that "teacher qualifications are divided into kindergarten teacher qualifications, primary school teacher qualifications, junior middle school teachers and junior vocational school culture classes, professional class teacher qualifications, senior middle school teacher qualifications, secondary professional schools, technical schools, vocational senior middle school cultural classes, professional teacher qualifications, secondary professional schools, technical schools, vocational senior high school internship instructor qualifications, and higher education teacher qualifications." "Teacher qualification examination subjects, standards and examination outlines are reviewed by the State Council's education administration; preparation and examination of teacher qualification examination papers and the issuance of examination results certificates is down to kindergarten, primary school, junior middle school, senior middle school, secondary vocational school teacher qualification examinations and secondary vocational school internship teacher qualification examinations shall be organized and implemented by the education administrative department of the People's government at or above the county level; qualification examinations for teachers in higher education institutions shall be organized and implemented by the education administration department of the State Council or the higher education institutions are entrusted by the education administration department of the People's government of the province, autonomous region, or municipality directly under the Central Government."

Following the promulgation of *The Regulations on Teacher Qualifications* in 1995, the MOE issued *The Measures for Implementing "The Regulations on Teacher Qualifications"* (hereinafter referred to as *The Implementing Measures*) on September 23, 2000, stipulating that: "The State Council's education administration department is responsible for the organization, implementation, coordination and supervision work of the national teacher qualification institutions; the education administration department of the local people's government at or above the county level shall be responsible for the organization, guidance, supervision and implementation of the qualification and management of local teacher qualifications in accordance with the provisions of *The Regulations on Teacher Qualifications*; education administration departments of the local people's government at or above the county level that deal with applications for teacher qualification certification according to law should be an established teacher qualification certification institution." The promulgation and implementation of *The Implementation Measures* marked the initial establishment of a legally regulated teacher qualification institutions in China.

On May 14, 2001, the MOE issued *The Opinions on Several Issues Concerning the Qualification of Teachers for the First Time* (hereinafter referred to as *The Opinions*), proposing that: "Teacher qualifications are the basic requirements of the state for those who carry out specialized work in education and teaching. After the teacher qualification institutions is fully implemented, only those who have obtained teacher qualifications in accordance with the law can be employed as teachers by schools and other educational institutions of all types and levels approved by the education administration department. Once the teacher qualifications are obtained, they cannot be lost or revoked unless required by law. After being formally hired by a school or other educational institution in accordance with legal appointment procedures, a person with teaching qualifications has the obligations and rights of a teacher." On August 8, 2001, *The Regulations on the Management of Teacher Qualification Certificates* were issued, in which the purpose, management organization, accreditation organization, main content, certificate specifications, conditions for withdrawing the certificate, and numbering methods were specified in detail. With this as a sign, China's teacher qualification institutions was officially implemented throughout the country.

(2) The Nationally Unified Teacher Qualification Institutions

In 2010, *The National Medium-and-Long-Term Education Reform and Development Plan Outline (2010–2020)* (hereinafter referred to as *The Plan Outline*) put forward: "Improving and strictly implementing the teacher access institutions and strictly controlling the entrance of teachers. The state formulates teacher qualification standards, improves teachers' academic qualification standards and moral requirements, establishing a regular registration institutions for teacher qualification certificates. Provincial education administration departments uniformly organize primary and secondary school teacher qualification examinations and qualifications, and county education administration departments carry out management functions such as primary and secondary school teacher recruitment, job qualification evaluation (title), training and assessment according to the regulations."

In accordance with the spirit of *The Plan Outline*, China has implemented a national unified examination institution for teacher qualifications since 2011. In 2013, the MOE issued *The Notice on Printing and Distributing "The Interim Measures for the Examination of Primary and Secondary School Teacher Qualifications" and "The Interim Measures for the Periodic Registration of Qualifications for Primary and Secondary School Teachers." The Interim Measures for the Examination of Primary and Secondary School Teacher Qualifications* stipulates: "Passing the teacher qualification examination is a prerequisite for professional admission of teachers. Teacher applicants for kindergarten, primary, junior high school, ordinary senior high school, secondary vocational schools and secondary vocational school internship teacher qualifications must take the teacher qualification examinations of the corresponding category respectively." Teacher qualification examinations include written and interview sections. The written test mainly examines the basic abilities of the applicant that those in the teaching profession should have including educational philosophy, professional ethics, knowledge of laws and regulations, scientific and cultural literacy, reading comprehension, language expression, logical reasoning, and information processing; basic knowledge about education and teaching, student guidance and class management; basic knowledge in the proposed subject area, knowledge and methods of implementation evaluation of teaching designs, and the ability to analyze and solve practical problems in education and teaching using knowledge learned. The interview mainly examines basic teaching qualities such as the applicant's professional cognition, psychological quality, appearance and bearing, speech expression, and thinking quality as well as basic teaching skills including teaching design, teaching implementation, and teaching evaluation. *The Interim Measures for the Periodic Registration of Qualifications for Primary and Secondary School Teachers* explains the conditions and procedures for the registration of teacher qualifications for primary and secondary schools: "Periodic registration for a period of five years for primary and secondary school teachers is to be implemented. Those who fail to register regularly or fail to register after the deadline shall not engage in education and teaching work." This breaks the "permanent and valid" institutions of teacher qualification certificates, and emphasizes that through regular registration, the management and identification of teacher qualifications are strengthened to ensure the improvement of the quality of teaching staff.

II. The Standard-Oriented Appointment Institutions

China has implemented a institutions of professional and technical positions in primary and secondary schools since 1986. It has experienced a process of transformation from the appointment institutions to the employment institutions and of continuous improvement in the method of appointing professional teaching positions.

(1) Appointment of Teachers Based on "The Appointment Institutions"

Implementing the teacher appointment institutions for primary and secondary schools was a major measure in teacher team building for China's primary and secondary schools, and was conducive to the cultivation, use, assessment, and promotion of teachers, and to the stability of teaching teams. In the early days of Reform and Opening Up, the appointment of Chinese teachers was based on the employment distribution institutions for graduates of normal universities. On October 12, 1978, the MOE issued *The Opinions on Strengthening and Developing Normal Education*, which stated: "In order to run normal education and consolidate and improve the teaching staff in primary and secondary schools, the quality of recruiting freshmen in normal colleges and universities at all levels should be effectively guaranteed; all higher normal and middle normal school students enjoy people's grants; all higher normal and middle normal school graduates are allocated by the state and should be allocated to the front lines of education work."

In 1986, the state began to pilot teachers in primary and secondary schools. On May 19, 1986, *The Notice of the Leading Group of Central Professional Title Reform Work on Forwarding Documents from the State Education Commission Including the Trial Regulations for Primary and Secondary School Teacher Posts* proposed that in principle the National Education Commission's *Trial Regulations for Secondary School Teacher Posts, Trial Regulations for Primary School Teacher Posts, Opinions on the Implementation of the Trial Regulations for Primary and Secondary School Teacher Posts*, and other documents had stipulated on such issues as the job grades, job responsibilities, employment conditions, and assessment of primary and secondary school teachers. Among them, *The Trial Regulations for Secondary School Teacher Posts* stated: "The positions of secondary school teachers are job positions set up in accordance with the needs of the school's education and teaching work. Secondary school teacher positions include senior secondary school teachers, grade one secondary school teachers, grade two secondary school teachers, and grade three secondary school teachers. The appointment or employment institutions is enacted for secondary school teacher positions. Appointment or employment of teacher positions must be reviewed by the teacher position review committee taking into consideration political thought, cultural expertise, education and teaching ability, work performance, performance of duties and other such aspects, and it is determined whether or not the candidate meets the conditions for the corresponding position. The appointment or employment of a teacher is to be done by schools or education administration departments above the county level. There should be a set term of appointment or employment for teachers, with each term generally being from three to five years with renewal or reappointment possible" (He, 1998: 2403–2440).

The Trial Regulations for Primary School Teacher Posts states: "Primary school teaching posts are jobs that are set up in accordance with the needs of school education and teaching. Primary school teachers are composed of senior primary school teachers, grade one primary school teachers, grade two primary school teachers, and grade three primary school teachers. The appointment or employment institutions is enacted for primary school teacher positions. Appointment or employment of teacher positions must be reviewed by the teacher position review committee taking into consideration political thought, cultural expertise, education and teaching ability, work performance, performance of duties and other such aspects, and it is determined whether or not the candidate meets the conditions for the corresponding position. The appointment or employment of a teacher is to be done by schools or education administration departments above the county level. There should be a set term of appointment or employment for teachers, with each term generally being from three to five years with renewal or reappointment possible" (He, 1998: 2441). Thereinto, *The Implementation Opinions on the Trial Regulations for Primary and Secondary School Teacher Posts* provides detailed interpretations and stipulations of the employment of primary and secondary school teachers. "According to the actual situation regarding the teaching staff in primary and secondary schools, the appointment institutions for teachers in primary and secondary schools is generally appropriate. Districts or schools where conditions permit may use the appointment institutions." "Every elementary and middle school teacher who currently does not have the level of education stipulated by the state, should generally pass an assessment test, obtain a professional qualification certificate or a textbook teaching method examination qualification certificate, and have the corresponding teacher position qualifications before they can be appointed or employed for the corresponding teacher position. Teachers who have passed the textbook teaching method examination certificate can only be appointed or employed for grade three teacher positions, and it is only after obtaining a professional qualification certificate that they can be hired or appointed for positions at grade two and above" (He, 1998: 2442–2443). On October 22, 1986, the State Education Commission issued *The Notice on the Pilot Work on the Reform of Teachers' Professional Titles in Primary and Secondary Schools and Secondary Professional Schools* to carry out pilot work for primary and secondary school teacher titles.

(2) Teacher Position Institutions Based Mainly on "The Appointment Institutions"

On July 16, 1991, the State Education Commission and the Ministry of Personnel issued *The Several Opinions on Properly Carrying Out Job Appointment of Teachers in Primary and Middle Schools*, proposing that employment of elementary and middle school teachers should continue to be done properly, and insisting on the correct political direction; appointing or employing teachers should be done in accordance with the requirements of Article 8 of the Trial Regulations for Teachers in Primary and Middle Schools, the political performance and ethics of the teacher should be assessed, and the ideological and political conditions must be strictly controlled with appointments made only where the candidate is morally upright and the choices are made based on merit; in combination with the needs of the development of local basic education and factors such as the structure, staffing, and teacher growth of the teaching team, attention should be paid to the employment of teachers in primary and secondary schools while properly carrying out a series of job appointments in higher education and scientific research; education administration departments and schools should actively create conditions for the growth of outstanding young and middle-aged core teachers (He, 1998: 3180).

In September 2003, the Ministry of Personnel and the MOE jointly issued *The Implementation Opinions of the Ministry of Personnel and Education on Deepening the Reform of the Personnel Institutions in Primary and Secondary Schools*, which proposed that the overall objectives of deepening the reform of the personnel institutions in primary and secondary schools were: focusing on enacting the appointment institutions and position management, with rationally allocating human resources, optimizing the structure of teachers and staff in primary and secondary schools, and comprehensively improving the quality of education and management as the core, accelerating the reform of the employment institutions and distribution institutions, establishing a personnel management operation mechanism that meets the characteristics of primary and secondary schools, and building a high-level professional and qualified team of teachers and managers. The main tasks are: to strengthen staff hiring management, adjust and optimize the structure of teaching staff in primary and secondary schools; further improve the principal responsibility institutions, progress and improve the institutions of selecting and appointing principals; implement the appointment institutions for hiring teaching staff; improve the salary guarantee mechanism for primary and secondary school teachers, establish a healthy distribution and incentive mechanism; and promote the rational flow of talents.

On March 3, 2004, *The Notice of the State Council on Re-approval of MOE's "The Action Plan for the Rejuvenation of Education 2003–2007"* stated that it is necessary to actively promote the full appointment institutions. The state should strengthen the hiring management of schools, set up school institutions and posts scientifically in accordance with the requirements of "leanness and efficiency"; and implement a teacher qualification institutions. In accordance with the principles of on-demand posts, open recruitment, equal competition, merit-based appointments, strict assessment, and contract management, we will implement a institutions of appointing teachers and staff in primary and secondary schools and secondary vocational schools, and implement the policy of "only appointing those who are qualified, competitive employment, and full employment."

On August 28, 2015, the Ministry of Human Resources and Social Security and the MOE issued *The Guiding Opinions on Deepening the Reform of the Title Institutions for Teachers in Primary and Middle Schools* (hereinafter referred to as *The Opinions*), which requires organized and effective reform implementation work. *The Opinions* points out that the basic spirit of the reform is establishing a unified primary and secondary school teacher title (position) institutions in accordance with the direction and overall requirements for deepening the reform of the professional title institutions, which is consistent with the employment institutions and post management institutions of public institutions and consistent with the professional characteristics of teachers; fully mobilizing the enthusiasm of the majority of primary and secondary school teachers; providing a foundation and basis for the employment of teachers in primary and secondary schools; and providing a institutions guarantee and talent support for the comprehensive implementation of quality education.

One of the aspects of the reform is strengthening the institutional institutions: Reforming the originally independent job title (post) institutions of primary and middle school teachers, and establishing a unified institutions of teacher titles in primary and secondary schools. Teacher titles are divided into junior, intermediate, and senior titles; and job title (post) levels and titles are unified. Junior level will be set as staff level and assistant level, senior level will be set as deputy senior and full senior level; staff, assistant, intermediate, deputy senior, and full senior titles (positions) are in turn named level three teachers, level two teachers, level one teachers, senior teachers, and full senior-level teachers. The unified job titles (positions) of teachers in primary and secondary schools after unification correspond to these former professional and technical positions of primary and secondary school teachers: former senior middle school teachers (including senior middle school teachers employed in primary schools) correspond to senior teachers, former level one middle school teachers and senior primary school teachers correspond to level one teachers, former level two middle school teachers and level one primary school teachers correspond to level two teachers, and former level three middle school teachers, level two and level three primary school teachers correspond to level three teachers. The job titles (positions) of teachers in primary and secondary schools after unification correspond to these levels of professional and technical posts in public institutions: Full senior teachers correspond to professional technical positions from level one to four, senior teachers correspond to professional technical positions from level five to seven, and level one teachers correspond to professional technical positions from level eight to ten, level two teachers correspond to professional technical positions from level eleven to twelve, and level three teachers correspond to professional technical positions at level thirteen.

On June 7, 2017, *The Notice on Properly Carrying Out Evaluation Work of Primary and Secondary School Teacher Titles in 2017* jointly issued by the General Office of the Ministry of Human Resources and Social Security and the General Office of the MOE emphasized that all localities should fully consider the characteristics and requirements of different regions, different semesters, and different disciplines to further progress and improve the evaluation standards of professional titles in accordance with the actual education and teaching work of primary and secondary schools in the region; the industry evaluation mechanism should be adhered to based on peer expert review, focusing on reference to work unit assessment recommendations, exploring the participation of schools, students, and parents in forms of evaluation; properly assessing the titles of full senior teachers in primary and secondary schools, with high standards and strict requirements, and setting benchmarks and models for the development of teachers in primary and secondary schools; primary and secondary schools affiliated to universities should undertake evaluation of teacher titles in accordance with the requirements of the state to deepen the reform of the teacher title institutions for primary and secondary schools.

III. The Equity-Oriented Teacher Quota Institutions

In order to strengthen teacher management and provide excellent teacher resource guarantees for the promotion and development of quality education, the state has implemented and continuously improved the teacher quota institutions. During this process, the transfer of private school teachers was a transitional event in which teacher quota management was gradually formalized in the early stages of Reform and Opening Up.

(1) Transfer of Private School Teachers

After "The Cultural Revolution," with the continuous strengthening of China's primary and secondary school teachers and the continuous improvement of their academic qualifications, the state began to emphasize the formalization of teaching teams, and gradually eliminated private school teachers. At the same time, it strengthened the construction of teacher job appointment institution and teacher qualification institution to improve the quality of the teaching staff and promote the reform and development of education. On October 31, 1979, the MOE, the Ministry of Finance, the Ministry of Food, the State Civil Affairs Commission, and the State Administration of Labor jointly issued *The Several Provisions on the Conversion of Private School Teachers to Public School Teachers in Frontier Counties (Banners) and Municipal Primary and Secondary Schools* (hereinafter referred to as *The Regulations*). Since 1979, all private school teachers (including employees) in primary and secondary schools in 136 counties (borders) and cities on the border have been converted to public school teachers after passing assessment. These teachers had to be "serving private school teachers who were engaged in teaching before the end of 1978. They had to have a clear political history, honest and upright ideology, good moral qualities, and support the Communist Party of China. They had to love the socialist motherland, be loyal to the Party's education cause, be competent in teaching and have a healthy body." The audit methods included political review, professional inspection, cultural examination, professional ability inspection, and health checks. "The Regulations" opened the prelude to the state's response to and resolution of the private school teachers issue.

On August 6, 1992, *The Opinions of the State Education Commission, the State Planning Commission, the Ministry of Personnel, and the Ministry of Finance on Further Improving and Strengthening the Work of Private School Teachers* (hereinafter referred to as *The Opinions*) were issued, in which it was proposed that after a certain period of time the guiding ideology of the work of private school teachers had to meet the needs of the development of education, reduce numbers, improve quality, improve treatment, strengthen management, solve the problems of private school teachers, further mobilize the enthusiasm of private school teachers to teach and educate people, and promote the development of rural basic education in China. At the same time, *The Opinions* proposed further advancing the adjustment and rectification of private school teachers teams, gradually reducing the number and improving overall quality; further improving the qualification and assessment institutions, appointment institutions, and file management institutions of private school teachers; greatly strengthening the training of private school teachers, continuously improving the political ideology and professional quality of private school teachers; further improving the status and treatment of private school teachers, and gradually realizing equal pay for equal work for public school teachers as that for state school teachers; and recruiting public school teachers from outstanding private school teachers.

In 1997, *The Notice of the General Office of the State Council on Solving the Problems of Private School Teachers* was issued, which put forward ten opinions on solving the problems of private school teachers, including: implementing a local responsibility institutions for the overall solution to the problems of private school teachers, with all relevant output departments actively cooperating; comprehensively implementing the "close, transfer, recruit, resign, retire" policy step-by-step with planning in each district, reducing the number of private school teachers year after year; resolutely shutting down newly added private school teachers; converting qualified private school teachers into public school teachers in a planned manner; further expanding the number of private school teachers targeted by normal schools; dismissing non-qualified private school teachers; establishing private insurance and welfare funds for private school teachers, improving measures for leaving and retiring private school teachers, and ensuring the livelihood of elderly private school teachers who are sick and disabled; making it so private school teachers and public school teachers receive the same pay for equal work; ensuring that private school teachers are assured of their jobs after they are converted into public school teachers; and finally, under the unified leadership and overall coordination of the government, education, personnel, planning, finance, public security, and other departments must work in a coordinated manner. Through the advancement of these measures and policies, by the end of the 20th century, private school teachers had basically all been converted into public school teachers, and private school teachers withdrew from the stage of history.

(2) The Teacher Quota Institutions of Urban-Rural Differences

On December 27, 1984, the MOE issued *The Opinions on the Standards for the Quota of Teaching Staff in Secondary Normal Schools and Full-time Primary and Secondary Schools,* which clarified the standards for the quota of teaching staff: "The quota of teaching staff in secondary normal schools and full-time primary and secondary schools shall be calculated by class with schools as the unit (including separate and combined quotas). For the quota standards, refer to *The Standard Reference Table for the Quota of Teaching Staff of Secondary Normal Schools and Full-time Primary and Secondary Schools*; experimental primary and secondary schools can be appropriately increased according to the item of experimentation; in areas where conditions permit, according to the size of the school, etc., set staffing standards for teaching staff of different functions; and the number of students in each class is to be determined according to the source of students within the school's operations radius. The number of students in each class in sparsely populated areas such as pastoral areas, mountain areas, lake areas and islands can be appropriately reduced according to actual conditions or multiple classes can be held" (He, 1998: 2403–2448).

On October 11, 2001, *The Notice of the General Office of the State Council on Forwarding the Opinions of the State Commission Office of Public Sectors Reform, MOE, and the Ministry of Finance on the Establishment of Standards for the Quota of Primary and Secondary School Teaching Staff* proposed that the quota of primary and secondary school teaching staff is an important part of China's quota undertaking. It is necessary to formulate scientific quota standards and implementation methods for teaching staff of primary and secondary schools, and reasonably verify the quota of primary and secondary school staff. Teaching staff of primary and secondary schools include teachers, office workers, teaching assistants, and work staff. Specifically, teachers refer to professionals directly engaged in education and teaching in schools, office workers refers to personnel engaged in school management, and teaching assistants refers those in schools who are mainly engaged in teaching auxiliary work such as teaching experiments, books, e-education, and health care. Work staff refers to staff engaged in school logistics services. The quota of teaching staff in primary and secondary schools is checked and ratified subject to a certain percentage of students based on the different levels of education, that is, high school, junior high school, and elementary school, and different regions, that is, cities, county towns, and rural areas. As much as possible, the management of primary and secondary schools should be done by teachers part-time, and logistics services should be gradually implemented in a socialized way. Where it is really necessary to have staff, teaching assistants, and work staff, their proportion of teaching staff should generally not make up more than 16% of a high school, 15% of a junior high school, and 9% of a primary school. The quota of full-time faculty and staff is determined in accordance with the quota standards for senior and junior high schools, respectively. Nine-year schools are approved according to the junior high school and primary school quota standards. The quota of rural teaching sites is calculated in township central primary schools. The quota standards for teaching staff of special education schools, vocational middle schools, elementary schools with preschools, and work schools can be determined by reference to the staffing standards for primary and secondary schools, which will be specifically determined by localities based on actual conditions. The quota of adult junior and secondary schools is determined by each locality according to the actual situation. Due to the large regional differences in China and the uneven level of economic development in various regions, provinces, autonomous regions, and municipalities may adjust the standards up and down when formulating implementation methods for the quota of primary and secondary school teaching staff based on the status of the local supply of students, economic and financial conditions, transportation conditions, population density, and so on.

In 2002, *The Implementation Opinions of MOE on "The Notice of the General Office of the State Council on Forwarding the Opinions of the State Commission Office of Public Sectors Reform, MOE, and the Ministry of Finance on the Establishment of Standards for the Quota of Teaching Staff in Primary and Middle Schools"* (hereinafter referred to as *The Implementation Opinions*) stated that it is the responsibility of the administrative department of education at the county level, together with the staff quota and finance departments, to propose a staff quota plan for primary and secondary schools in the region according to the implementation methods and development plans for education in the provinces, autonomous regions and municipalities. *The Implementation Opinions* stipulates that primary and secondary schools set up management institutions according to the type, size, and task of the school, and key middle schools and schools with more than twenty-four classes may add one to two institutions. The functional institutions of complete primary schools set up a teaching office (room) and a general affairs office (room). Specifically, primary schools with less than 12 classes will only have management positions and no functional institutions, and can be staffed by one teaching director and one general affairs director. It is necessary to strictly control the number of primary and secondary school leadership positions. There will be one or two school-level leaders in ordinary middle schools with less than twelve classes; two or three school-level leaders in those with thirteen to twenty-three classes; and three school-level leaders in those with twenty-four to thirty-six classes. For complete primary schools with fewer than twelve classes, one to two school leaders will be assigned; two to three school leaders will be assigned for those with thirteen to twenty-three classes; three school leaders will be assigned for those with twenty-four to thirty-six classes. For ordinary middle schools and complete primary schools with more than thirty-six classes, one or two school leaders may be added as appropriate. Rural primary schools (grades 1–3) or branch schools and teaching points designate a teacher responsible for schoolwork. Elementary and secondary schools arrange classes according to the laws and requirements of education and teaching, and organize teaching classes according to the number of students in classes. In principle, there are forty-five to fifty students per class in ordinary middle schools, forty to forty-five students in urban primary schools, and a reduced number in rural primary schools. The specific standards are determined by the provinces (autonomous regions and municipalities) according to actual conditions. Effective measures will be taken to solve the problem of there being classes with more than fifty-five students. Ordinary high schools can be staffed with 3.0 teachers per class; ordinary junior high schools can be staffed with 2.7 teachers per class; urban elementary schools and county township primary schools can be staffed with 1.8 teachers per class; staffing per class for rural elementary schools can be equipped determined according to the actual circumstances by the local provinces (autonomous regions, municipalities). After the number of teachers is determined, the staff, teaching assistants, and work staff are calculated based on a certain percentage of the total number of teaching and administrative staff, and will be uniformly approved by the education administration department at or above the county level. When specifically approving the staffing of primary and secondary schools, inland ethnic primary and secondary schools, urban ordinary middle schools that hold ethnic classes and bilingual classes, boarding elementary and middle schools, township central primary schools, and teachers are scheduled to take time off for further education. Modernized schools of a certain size that reach a certain scale of teaching facilities shall undertake demonstration and experimental tasks. Schools in mountain, lake, island, and pastoral regions, and areas with more teaching sites, shall increase staff quota as appropriate according to strict and rigorous principles based on the calculation of student proportions. Arrange for teachers to increase the number of establishments for off-the-job training and a small number of logistics service establishments approved by the school-run factory (farm) that undertakes the tasks of student work, study, and internship, and shall be uniformly arranged and used by the education administrative department at or above the county level according to the affiliation.

(3) Urban-Rural Integrated Teacher Quota Institutions

On September 17, 2003, *The Implementation Opinions on Deepening the Reform of the Personnel Institutions in Primary and Secondary Schools* (hereinafter referred to as *The Implementation Opinions*) proposed that the employment (hiring) institutions for teaching staff in primary and secondary schools should be fully implemented. This was a major breakthrough for the teacher quota institutions which was originally based around the appointment institutions. "The Implementation Opinions" proposed that the overall goal of deepening the reform of the personnel institutions in primary and secondary schools is: focus on implementing the employment (hiring) institutions and position management to rationally allocate talent resources, optimize the structure of primary and secondary school teaching and administrative staff, comprehensively improve the quality of education and management levels at the core, accelerate the reform of the employment institutions and the distribution institutions, establish a personnel management operation mechanism that meets the characteristics of primary and secondary schools, and build a high-quality and professional team of primary and secondary school teachers and management staff.

On March 12, 2009, *The Notice Regarding Problems Related to Further Implementing "The Notice of the Opinions of the General Office of the State Council Forwarded to the State Commission Office of Public Sectors Reform, MOE, and the Ministry of Finance on the Establishment of Standards for Teaching Staff Quota in Primary and Middle Schools"* stated: It is necessary to effectively strengthen the overall control and use of the total number of teaching staff in primary and secondary schools; further improve verification work of staff quota in rural primary and secondary schools, implement a "county-based" management institutions, and solve the problem of tight staffing of primary and secondary schools in some rural areas; conscientiously implement the addendum factors stipulated in the State Council Release [2001] No. 74, continuously improve the dynamic management mechanism for the quota of teaching staff in primary and secondary schools, adjust the staff quota of schools that receive more children from floating populations, and strictly regulate the management of staff quota in primary and secondary schools.

On November 13, 2014, *The Notice of the State Commission Office of Public Sectors Reform, MOE, and the Ministry of Finance on Unifying the Standards for Staffing in Urban and Rural Primary and Secondary Schools* stated that it was necessary to unify staffing standards for education workers in urban and rural primary and secondary schools. On the basis of following the principles for staffing primary and secondary schools in *The Notice of the Opinions of the General Office of the State Council, Forwarded to the State Commission Office of Public Sectors Reform, MOE, and the Ministry of Finance on the Establishment of Standards for Staffing of Primary and Secondary Schools* and *The Notice on Problems Regarding the Further Implementation of 'The Notice of the Opinions of the General Office of the State Council, Forwarded to the State Commission Office of Public Sectors Reform, MOE, and the Ministry of Finance on the Establishment of Standards for Staffing of Primary and Secondary Schools* and relevant work requirements, the county, township, and rural primary and secondary teacher staffing standards were unified to urban standards, whereby the ratio of teaching staff to students is 1:12.5 in high schools, 1:13.5 in junior high schools, and 1:19 in primary schools. To implement urban-rural integrated teacher staffing standards for primary and secondary schools, it is necessary to resolutely implement the spirit of the central government's strict control of organizational staffing and the current government's financial support for reducing and not increasing staff, and in accordance with the requirement to strictly control the total amount, revitalize the inventory, optimize the structure, and increase or decrease the balance, the provincial government bears the overall responsibility and carries out control of the total to ensure that the total number of authorized primary and secondary school teaching staff does not exceed the existing total. At the same time, emphasis is given to the need to consider actual needs and give appropriate leeway to remote rural areas, deepen logistics reform, increase government purchasing power of services, continue to deepen the socialized reform of logistics services in primary and secondary schools, and gradually reduce the non-teaching staff make-up.

IV. The Incentive-Oriented Teacher Salary Institutions

A scientific and rational salary distribution institutions is an important guarantee for encouraging motivated and creative work from staff. Since Reform and Opening Up, China has continuously explored and improved the teacher salary institutions, and gradually shifted from a structured salary institutions to a performance-based salary institutions that embodies excellent compensation for excellent work.

(1) Structured Wage Institution

The formation of a wage institutions is an important part of a country's socio-political and economic institutions, and it is also a concrete manifestation of a country's national income redistribution policy. The teacher salary institutions is an important part of the national wage institutions. It refers to the state's implementation of teachers' salary levels, wage standards, wage forms, and other relevant wage regulations and methods. The salary level and structure of teachers are not only important factors affecting the supply of primary and secondary school teachers but also critical to attracting, cultivating, and retaining high-quality teachers, and thus affecting the overall quality and efficiency of education and teaching in schools. A reasonable wage structure helps to enhance the motivation of teachers, attract outstanding talents to teach for life, and form a good incentive mechanism, thereby improving the overall quality and efficiency of education and teaching in schools (An, 2014).

After Reform and Opening Up, with the comprehensive advancement of the reform of the national political and economic institutions, the salary of teachers improved. The Central Committee of the Communist Party of China and the State Council issued *The Notice on Issues Regarding the Reform of the Wage Institutions of Staff in State Organs and Institutions* in June 1985, in which it was decided that ordinary primary and middle schools will implement the new wage institutions, that is, a structured wage institutions with post wages as the main content, from January 1, 1985. The most important change in this reform of the wage institutions was the abolition of the hierarchical wage institutions and the gradual implementation of a structured wage institutions consisting of four parts: basic wages, post wages, length of service allowances, and bonus wages. The basic salary is based on maintaining the basic living needs of teachers, and an equal salary is stipulated regardless of post level; post wages are mainly determined according to the technical, business requirements and responsibilities of the job, and is divided into several levels; the length of service allowance wage is based on how long the staff member has been in the job; and the bonus wage is mainly determined in conjunction with attendance and performance. This not only emphasizes the post wage, making staff remuneration closely related to the work, but also makes use of the different functions of various components of the salary, embodies the principle of "the equal importance of fairness and efficiency," and overcomes certain disadvantages of egalitarian distribution methods. Since then, the state has repeatedly issued documents relating to increasing the salary of teachers, such as: *The Notice on Raising the Salary of Primary and Secondary School Teachers*, issued by the State Council on November 28, 1987; *The Implementation Measures for Raising the Salary Standards of Teachers*, issued by the Ministry of Labor and Personnel and the State Education Commission in January 1988, where it was proposed that starting from October 1987, the current salary standards of all middle school teachers (the sum of the basic salary and post salary) should be increased by 10% (Tian & Yang, 2008).

(2) Post-Rank Salary Institution

Following the gradual deepening of the state's reforms in the field of income distribution, the original wage institutions needed to be further reformed. In November 1993, the Central Committee of the Communist Party of China and the State Council formulated and implemented *The Implementation Measures for the Reform of the Staff Wage Institutions of Public Institutions* and *The Implementation Measures for the Allowances of Agencies and Public Institutions in Hard and Remote Areas*, where according to the work characteristics of public institutions, the education industry implements a post-rank salary institutions for professional and technical positions. Wages are mainly divided into two parts: professional and technical salaries and allowances, which are, respectively, linked to the level of the job and the actual workload. On February 5, 1994, the Ministry of Personnel and the State Education Commission jointly issued *The Opinions on Implementing "The Reform Plan for the Wage Institutions of Staff in Public Institutions" for Primary and Secondary Schools*, which states that the general term for the new salary institutions for primary and secondary schools will be the primary and secondary school duties (technical) hierarchical wage institutions. Staff salary consists of two parts: post (technical)-rank salary and allowance. The post (technical)-rank salary is the fixed part of the salary, which mainly reflects work ability, contribution, and complexity of labor; the subsidy mainly reflects the job characteristics of various types of personnel and the quantity and quality of labor. In the composition of the total wages of each unit, the post (technical)-rank salary makes up 70% and allowances make up 30%. A nationally unified post-rank salary standard will be implemented for teachers in primary and secondary schools. This wage reform is based on scientific classification and the principle of distribution according to work. It establishes a new wage institution that is decoupled from the wage institutions of state agencies mainly based on the different types of units and the characteristics of different industries. The institutions should introduce competition and incentive mechanisms to increase the motivation of employees, and introduce different subsidy and reward institutions for various industries and types (Tian & Yang, 2008). However, this reform of teacher wages has also brought new injustices. For example, the difference in wage levels between regions due to differences in the level of economic development in different regions, the problem of low teacher salaries has not been resolved, egalitarianism has not been completely broken, and many more problems still exist.

(3) Performance-Based Wage Institution

In 2006, *The Opinions on Implementing "The Reform Plan for the Wage Institutions of Staff in Public Institutions" for Primary and Secondary Schools* stipulated that: Primary and secondary schools should implement a post-performance wage institution; the average salary level of teachers in compulsory education schools should not be lower than the average salary level of local civil servants; in areas where the reform of the compulsory education funding guarantee mechanism is implemented, subsidies that are introduced locally and should be enjoyed by teachers should be included in the scope of performance salary verification. Post-performance salary consists of four parts: post salary, grade salary, performance salary, and subsidy. Post salary and job grade salary make up the basic salary. Post salary mainly reflects the duties and requirements of the position the teacher was hired for. Corresponding post salary standards are enacted for the position the teacher was hired for. Grade salary mainly reflects the performance and qualifications of staff. There are sixty-five salary levels for primary and middle school teachers, with each level corresponding to a salary standard, and different starting salary levels are set for different positions. Primary and secondary school staff will have a salary level that corresponds to the number of years they have been in the job and current position they hold in combination with their performance. Performance salary mainly reflects the actual performance and contribution of staff members. The state conducts regulation and guidance on the allocation of performance wages to public institutions. Public institutions shall, within the approved total amount of performance wages, independently allocate in accordance with standardized procedures and requirements. This part of the salary will "implement the policy of high limit, middle stable, and low compensation on a trial basis, so as to limit the excessively large inter-school gap." This policy first entered the implementation phase in compulsory education schools on January 1, 2009. Primary and secondary school allowances are divided into hard and remote area allowances and special post allowances. Hard and remote area allowances are mainly defined based on differences in physical geography and environment, social development, etc., and appropriate compensation is given to staff working and living in hard and remote areas. Allowances for staff in primary and secondary schools in hard and remote areas are enacted in accordance with unified national regulations. The special post allowance mainly reflects the preferential policies for staff working hard, dirty, tiring, dangerous, and other special jobs in public institutions. The state exercises unified management over special post allowances. The new salary institution consists of two parts: basic salary and performance salary. Performance salary is further divided into basic performance salary and reward performance salary. Basic performance salary highlights the "health" effect of salary; reward performance salary focuses on the "incentive" function of performance salary, promotes the school's internal distribution, encourages teachers to perform well, gives favor to outstanding talents, gives favor to key positions, and opens up a reasonable and appropriate income gap (Tian, 2012; Tian & Yang, 2008).

SECTION 3 THE INSTITUTIONS OF TEACHER DEVELOPMENT

On-the-job teacher training is an important part of the teacher education institutions. China has always attached importance to teacher training. After Reform and Opening Up, the primary focus of normal education reform has been strengthening on-the-job training for primary and secondary school teachers. With the transformation from normal education to teacher education, teacher training has also shifted from "compensatory" and "universal improvement" training to "integrated cultivation and training" of teachers. Contemporary teacher training has gone beyond the training of teachers' knowledge and skills, paying more attention to teachers' professional development and practical wisdom.

I. The "Compensatory" On-the-Job Teacher Training Institutions

On December 10, 1977, the MOE issued *The Opinions on Strengthening the Training of In-service Teachers in Primary and Secondary Schools*, which proposed to expose and criticize "the gang of four," correctly implement the Party's policy on intellectuals, and mobilize the enthusiasm of teachers for socialism; strive to bring most primary school teachers who have a low level of cultural and professional skills up to secondary school graduation levels, most junior high school teachers up to teacher's college level in their teaching subjects, and most high school teachers up to teacher's college graduation in their teaching subjects within three to five years; propose that all teachers should continue to strengthen the study and exercise of basic skills that teachers should have; they must learn Standard Mandarin Chinese (Putonghua), and be able to write on a blackboard and mark schoolwork properly (Liu, 1993: 1049). This was a policy aimed at teachers in hard conditions in primary and secondary schools early in Reform and Opening Up. The goal was to make teachers competent in basic teaching work. Then, in order to allow teachers to participate in training, with the approval of the State Council, the MOE issued "The Notice on Approval Procedures for Resumption or Establishment of Education Colleges or Teacher Training Colleges" in April 1978. Teacher training institutions have been restored or established in various parts of the country (He, 1998: 1606).

On August 23, 1980, *The Opinions of MOE on Further Strengthening the Training of In-service Teachers in Primary and Secondary Schools* (hereinafter referred to as *The Opinions*) proposed that, by 1985, best efforts would be made to bring the majority of primary school teachers with low cultural and professional skills to secondary school graduation level, junior high school teachers to teacher college graduation level in the subject they teach, and high school teachers to normal college graduate level in the subject they teach. *The Opinions* emphasizes the need to give full play to the role of teacher "training colleges, normal colleges, and teaching research offices (departments) at all levels." The main task of provincial, prefectural (municipal) education colleges, and teacher training colleges is to train middle-school teachers and administrative cadres, county-level advanced schools mainly train in-service teachers and administrative cadres in primary schools, and commune training stations do a good job at training in-service teachers in the commune; focus on running relatively large education colleges and teacher training colleges in provinces, municipalities, and autonomous regions; and have them play a key role and demonstrative role in training in-service teachers in primary and secondary schools; normal colleges and universities at all levels must make greater contributions to the training of politically conscious, professionally competent, and qualified primary and secondary school teachers; normal colleges and universities at all levels must properly carry out correspondence education or face-to-face guidance. *The Opinions* also emphasizes the need to gradually implement a unified national teaching plan and improve the construction of further teaching materials and establish and improve the assessment mechanism for in-service teachers' further education, and any trainee must undergo a strict culture and professional knowledge assessment for admission; those who have completed the prescribed courses and passed all the assessments will be issued a graduation certificate by the training unit in recognition of their education (He, 1998: 1832–1833).

Subsequently, on June 7, 1982, the MOE issued *The Notice on the Trial Implementation of Higher Normal Specialization and Undergraduate Teaching Plans for Middle School Teacher Training*, requiring teachers to pass higher normal education institutions training and master the basic theory, basic knowledge, and basic skills of the subject they study; improve their ability to analyze and solve problems; and to reach the level of two-year higher normal college graduates; teachers participating in advanced education must have a high school graduation education level or equivalent academic ability; training mainly includes three forms: leave training, amateur training, and correspondence education (He, 1998: 2016). On August 20, 1982, the MOE issued *The Primary School Teachers' Training Program for Secondary Normal School Teachers*. The training objectives clearly state that students should be improved in terms of education theory, cultural knowledge, and teaching ability. This is mainly to allow them to reach a secondary normal graduate level in their subject and make them competent at primary school teaching. The enrollment targets are mainly in service primary school teachers (He, 1998: 2036). On January 20, 1983, the MOE issued *The Opinions on Strengthening Training Work of In-Service Primary School Teachers* (hereinafter referred to as *The Opinions*), and proposed to revise the training plan for primary school teachers, endeavor to bring most primary school teachers up to secondary school graduate level so that most of them are competent and basically qualified for teaching work by 1985, and train a group of key teachers in a planned way; in another three to five years, the vast majority of primary school teachers should reach the level of secondary school graduates, and be fully competent in teaching. *The Opinions* also proposes adherence to the principle of classified guidance, carrying out targeted education and training according to the actual cultural knowledge of teachers and the level of teachers in different regions, and effectively improving the quality of training (He, 1998: 2068).

In May 1985, the General Office of the Central Committee of the Communist Party of China promulgated *The Decision of the Central Committee of the Communist Party of China on the Reform of the Education Institutions* (hereinafter referred to as *The Decision*) and proposed the establishment of a sufficient number of qualified and stable teachers. This is the basic plan for implementing compulsory education and improving basic education. To this end, it is necessary to carry out serious training and assessment of existing teachers, and make the development of normal education and training of in-service teachers a strategic measure for the development of education. We must strongly promote and encourage teachers to closely integrate teaching with self-learning and mutual education; organize correspondence education and radio and television lectures for in-service teachers; effectively run teacher training colleges, and use existing facilities to train teachers in groups; and mobilize, select, and organize some teachers and senior students in colleges and universities, researchers in research institutes, and qualified cadres in party and government agencies to participate in helping to train primary and secondary school teachers in a planned manner. In short, we must strive to make the vast majority of teachers competent for teaching in five years or more. *The Decision* clearly defines the importance of teacher training, training methods, training targets, training organizations, and the source of teachers. It also focuses on the issue of teacher standards and requires a qualified education achievement or a certificate of assessment of them before they are qualified to teach. On November 12 of the same year, Dongchang He stated in a speech at the National Primary and Secondary School Teachers' Work Conference that it was necessary to build a qualified team of primary and secondary school teachers with sufficient numbers. It was emphasized that there are "three steps" in the construction of teachers in primary and secondary schools: First, through training and adjustment of teachers, the vast majority of in-service teachers can be basically competent when it comes to their education and teaching tasks; second, on this basis, further supplementation and training ensures that teachers of all subjects are basically equipped, and most teachers are qualified for education and teaching. Third, after the nine-year compulsory education has been basically realized, the political professional qualifications or academic qualifications of primary, junior, and senior high school teachers should generally transition to higher requirements (Liu, 1993: 1050).

On December 21, 1986, the State Education Commission's *Opinions on Strengthening the Training of In-service Primary and Secondary School Teachers* pointed out that of the 8.02 million primary and middle school teachers and agricultural vocational middle school teachers, about half do not have the academic qualifications stipulated by the state. A large proportion of teachers work in teaching, and a considerable number of teachers urgently need to improve their training. For this reason, in the next five years or more, the focus of teacher training work is making the vast majority of teachers who do not have a qualified education record or are not competent to teach obtain a certificate or qualifications through serious training. For the few teachers who do not have the most basic cultural knowledge and preliminary teaching ability, arrangements should be made for them to participate in teaching materials and teaching methods so that they are familiar with the syllabus and teaching materials of the taught subject, master the basic teaching principles and methods, and have preliminary teaching skills. In order to meet the requirements of the "three orientations" and further improve the level of basic education in China, arrangements should be made for teachers who already have qualifying education records and teaching competence to learn new knowledge; learn and master new educational theories and teaching methods; summarize their education and teaching experiences; continuously improve their levels of politics, culture, and business; and train a group of leaders in various disciplines and experts in education and teaching. Teacher training mainly includes multi-level and multi-form training through teacher training colleges, higher schools, secondary professional schools, and radio, television, and electronic education institutions and various forces in society (He, 1998: 2732–2733). In general, from the beginning of Reform and Opening Up to the mid-to-late 1980s, the state mainly provided primary and secondary schools with compensatory training, emphasizing the training of teachers' basic knowledge and basic abilities in order to make them competent for basic education and teaching work to ensure the quality of primary and secondary education.

II. The "Universal Improvement" Teacher Training Institutions

In the 1990s, with the continuous advancement of the reform and development of basic education in China, the construction of teacher training institutions for primary and secondary schools began to move towards standardization and entered the stage of "government-led, systematically planned, and generally advanced." In October 1990, the State Education Commission held *The National Symposium for Continuing Education of Primary and Secondary School Teachers* in Zigong, Sichuan Province, and issued *The Minutes of the National Symposium for Continuing Education of Primary and Secondary School Teachers* in December of the same year, proposing that China had already "established a teacher training base and training network with the teacher training college as the main body, built a team of teachers from factual training, and actively carried out multi-level, multi-channel, and multi-form teacher training, which improved the quality of a vast number of primary and secondary school teachers" (He, 1998: 3060). The meeting emphasized the need to gradually shift the focus of teacher training in primary and secondary schools to continuing education. Continuing education refers to the training of teachers who have reached the nationally required academic qualifications with the main goal of improving their political and ideological quality and education and teaching abilities. It marks the beginning of a shift in Chinese teacher training policies and the beginning of a focused and targeted shift making up academic qualifications to continuing education for teachers.

On December 3, 1991, *The Opinions on Carrying Out Continuing Education for Primary School Teachers* issued by the National Education Commission pointed out that the main objective of continuing education of primary school teachers is improving the political ideology, teaching ethics, educational theories, and education and teaching abilities of teachers who have obtained teacher qualifications. The task of continuing education is continuously improving the political and professional quality of every teacher through education and teaching practice and training, developing a group of backbone teachers in education and teaching, with some gradually becoming experts in primary school education and teaching (He, 1998: 3060). It is mentioned here that it is necessary to train primary school teachers to become experts in primary education and teaching. It is clear that the basic requirements for teachers at the beginning of Reform and Opening Up have already been exceeded. On July 26, 1993, *The Opinions on Strengthening the Training of Backbone Teachers in Primary Schools* issued by the State Education Commission also stated: "The overall goal of backbone teacher training is training carried out for young and middle-aged teachers who have training prospects according to the requirements of backbone education and the teaching of existing backbone teachers according to even higher standards" (He, 1998: 3537–3538).

On February 13, 1993, the Central Committee of the Communist Party of China and the State Council promulgated *The Outline of China's Education Reform and Development* (hereinafter referred to as *The Outline*), which was proposed from the perspective of educational development planning to further strengthen the training of teachers. Normal education is the mothership from which primary and secondary school teachers are trained. Governments at all levels must work hard to increase investment, do a good job in normal education, and encourage outstanding middle school graduates to apply for normal colleges. Teacher training plans should be formulated to promote continuous improvement of teachers, especially young and middle-aged teachers, so that the vast majority of primary and secondary school teachers are better qualified for education and teaching. By the end of this century, through supplementary teaching and on-the-job training, the vast majority of primary and secondary school teachers must meet the national qualification standards. The proportion of primary and junior high school teachers with college and bachelor degrees has increased year after year, and the construction of the primary and secondary school teacher qualification institutions has been clarified since then. In order to implement the provisions on teacher training in *The Outline*, the State Council formally implemented *The Teachers Law of the People's Republic of China* on January 1, 1994, establishing a series of legal institutions for teacher qualification, appointment, cultivation, training, and assessment. It is clearly stipulated that "participation in further education or other training is the right of teachers; teachers' training schools at all levels assume the task of training primary and secondary school teachers; education administrative departments, school authorities and schools of People's governments at all levels should formulate teacher training plans. Teachers undergo various forms of ideological, political, and professional training." *The Education Law of the People's Republic of China* and *The Teacher Qualification Regulations* were promulgated and implemented in 1995 and 1996, respectively, putting the training of teachers in primary and secondary schools on track towards a scientific, standardized, and legal institutions.

Facing the new situation of educational development, the MOE promulgated *The Action Plan for the Revitalization of Education for the 21st Century* on December 24, 1998, and proposed the implementation of "The Cross-century Gardener Project," emphasizing the need for full-training and continuing education for current primary and secondary school principals and full-time teachers in different ways within three years; full-time teachers in primary and secondary schools and students in normal schools must receive basic computer training; specifically, it is proposed to strengthen the construction of key teachers in primary and middle schools, and to select and train 100,000 middle and primary school and vocational school teachers across the country, of which 10,000 will be organized for key training by the MOE. Through carrying out activities including centralized training, tour lectures, teaching research, and field observation training, they play a leading and radiating role in local teaching reform. From this it can be seen that teacher training pays more attention to the construction of teacher ethics, and training targets have been extended to primary and secondary school principals and full-time teachers. The construction of teaching materials for teacher training has also been put on the agenda, focusing on teachers' abilities in using advanced technology, and putting more emphasis on pre-service teacher training. The training of key teachers also reflects the implications of "universal improvement," which is in sharp contrast to the "compensation and emergency" teacher training used previously. Using the "Cross-century Gardener Project" as an opportunity, the MOE held a "National Conference on Continuing Education of Primary and Secondary School Teachers and Principals' Training" in Shanghai in June 1999, and decided to implement *The Continuing Education Project for Primary and Secondary School Teachers* nationwide. The task of "putting 10 million elementary and middle school teachers through training in five years to improve the overall quality of the teacher teams and basically meet the needs for implementing quality education" was put forward. After the meeting, the MOE promulgated *The Provisions for Continuing Education of Primary and Middle School Teachers*, and incorporated ideological and political education and teacher moral education into the content of continuing education for primary and secondary school teachers (He, 2003: 371). Since then, special policies and regulations have been formed for continuing education of primary and secondary school teachers in China, and an institutional framework for primary and secondary school teacher training has gradually formed.

III. The Integrated Institutions of Teacher Cultivation and Training

Upon entering the 21st century, teacher professional development and teacher professionalization became the main theme of teacher institutions reform. On May 29, 2001, the State Council issued *The Decision of the State Council on the*

Reform and Development of Basic Education, which proposed to improve the teacher education institutions and strengthen the development of teachers in primary and secondary schools. "Focusing on changing education concepts, improving professional ethics and education and teaching levels, we will closely integrate curriculum reform in basic education, strengthen the continuing education of primary and secondary school teachers, improve the teacher training institutions, and strengthen the construction of training bases." In addition, teacher training programs such as the "Cross-century Gardener Project" must be implemented to train a large number of outstanding teachers who play a backbone and demonstration role in education and teaching and a group of well-known teachers. In supporting education counterparts, schools should cultivate and train key teachers for schools in the aided areas.

In February 2002, the MOE issued *The Opinions on the Reform and Development of Teacher Education During "The Tenth Five-Year Plan"* period, which further adjusted the goal of teacher training towards developing teachers' innovative spirit and practical abilities. On February 10, 2004, the MOE promulgated "The 2003–2007 Education Revitalization Action Plan," and further proposed new requirements for teacher training in elementary and secondary schools with "new concepts, new courses, new technologies, and teacher ethics training." *The Technical Education Ability Standards for Primary and Secondary School Teachers* was promulgated in 2005. Its overall purpose was to improve the ability and level of primary and secondary school teachers in educational technology application, establish primary and secondary school teachers' educational technology training and examination certification institutions, and organize educational technology training with effective implementation of information technology and subject teaching integrated as the main content to further improve the ability of many teachers in implementing quality education.

In 2004, *The Opinions of MOE on Accelerating the Promotion of the National Teacher Education Network Alliance Program to Organize and Implement a New Round of Teacher Training for Primary and Secondary School Teachers* (hereinafter referred to as *The Opinions*) proposed that the teacher network plan should be accelerated to build an open and effective lifelong learning institutions for teachers. In accordance with the "three steps" development policy, strive to take about five years to construct a teacher and education network institutions that covers urban and rural areas across the country with normal colleges and other higher education institutions and education bodies that carry out teacher education as the mainstay, high level universities as the guide and core, regional teacher learning and resource centers as the support, research in primary and secondary schools as the basis, with integration of pre-service and post-service education, and communication of diploma education and non-diploma education, sharing high-quality education resources, and improving the quality of teacher training. *The Opinions* proposes that the main task of the National Teacher Networking Plan in the next five years is to organize the implementation of a new round of all-round training for primary and secondary school teachers with a focus on new ideas, new courses, new technologies, and teacher ethics in accordance with the principle of "facing all employees, highlighting key teachers, and putting more emphasis on the countryside," organizing high-level training of outstanding teachers and training of key teachers, and continuously improving the education achievements and degree levels of the majority of primary and secondary school teachers and ability levels in implementing quality education, promoting the significant improvement of the overall quality of teachers, including the implementation of a new round of training for 1 million primary and secondary school teachers, significantly improving the teaching ethics and professional levels of many teachers; the implementation of degree improvement training for 2 million primary and secondary school teachers, promoting the overall improvement of national teacher education qualifications and levels; and the implementation of teacher training for 1 million key teachers, forming a team of key teachers for primary and secondary schools.

The National Medium-and-Long-Term Education Reform and Development Plan Outline (2010–2020) from 2010 specifically emphasizes the need "to improve the professional level of teachers, improve the cultivation and training institutions, properly carry out cultivation and training planning, optimize the structure of teachers, and improve the professional and teaching levels of teachers." At the same time, the central government financially supported the launch of the "*National Training Program for Primary and Secondary School Teachers*" (referred to as *The National Training Program*), which implemented exemplary training of outstanding key teachers, training of rural teachers in the central and western regions, training of teachers in weak subjects, training of class teachers, preschool teacher training, special education teacher training and other important projects, to promote education reform and development in all regions to carry a batch of "seed" teachers, and explore innovative teacher training models, develop high-quality teacher training resources, build key teacher training bases, create more and better training opportunities, and provide quality training services for primary and secondary school teachers, especially rural teachers in central and western China.

In January 2011, the MOE issued *The National Medium-and-Long-Term Education Reform and Development Plan Outline (2010–2020)* (hereinafter referred to as *The Opinions*), proposing that the general requirements for primary and secondary school teacher training in the new period are to implement the outline of education planning and focus on education reform and development. The central task is closely related to the strategic goal of cultivating a high-quality professional teacher team, focusing on improving teachers' moral literacy and professional levels, with improving the quality of training as the main thread, carry out training of all primary and secondary school teachers with a focus on rural teachers, striving to build an open and flexible lifelong learning institutions for teachers, increase support for teacher training, comprehensively improve the quality of teachers, and provide teacher guarantees for the basic realization of education modernization and the construction of a country with strong human resources. *The Opinions* further suggests that the overall goal of the current and future period of China's primary and secondary school teacher training work is to implement the "National Training Program" as the starting point and promote various effective ways for all places to purposefully and systematically train primary and secondary school teachers split into type, level, and post. In the next five years, more than 10 million teachers nationwide will be trained with each member receiving no less than 360 hours; 1 million key teachers will be supported for national training; 10,000 outstanding key teachers will be selected for overseas research and training; arrangements will be made to improve the academic qualifications of 2 million teachers; training, academic exchanges, project funding, and other methods will be used to promote the training of famous teachers and educators in primary and secondary schools, and the overall quality and professionalism of primary and secondary school teachers will be comprehensively improved. At the same time, provisions were also made on training content optimization, training method application, training institutions establishment, training result evaluation, and other aspects.

On October 8, 2011, the MOE issued "*The Opinions on Vigorously Promoting the Reform of the Teacher Education Curriculum* and *The Teacher Education Curriculum Standards (Trial)*" (hereinafter referred to as *The Curriculum Standards*). *The Curriculum Standards* is based on the concept of "education-based, practical orientation, and lifelong learning." It regulates the teacher training process from three dimensions: educational beliefs and responsibilities, educational knowledge and abilities, and educational practices and experiences, and puts forward framework recommendations on curriculum setting for in-service teacher education, requiring non-educational teacher education curriculum plans to be formulated to meet the special needs of teachers at different stages of development, to provide flexible, diverse, novel, practical, and targeted courses to meet the diverse needs of teachers' professional development. This is a landmark policy in the construction of teacher teams in China. In November 2011, the General Office of the MOE also issued *The Notice on the Evaluation and Accreditation Work of Model County-level Teacher Training Institutions* and *The Standards for Evaluation and Accreditation Work of Exemplary County-level Teacher Training Institutions*, raising various standards requirements for county-level teacher training organizations.

In 2012, *The Opinions of MOE, the National Development and Reform Commission and the Ministry of Finance on Deepening the Reform of Teacher Education* proposed that a school-based teacher training institution be established with normal colleges as the main body and teacher training institutions and modern distance education as the support. All localities should promote the integration and union of county-level teacher training institutions and departments of teaching and research, scientific research, and audio-visual education; standardize the development of county (district) teacher development platforms; and coordinate the training work of all teachers in the county. Relying on existing resources, the construction of training bases for kindergarten teachers, vocational school teachers, special education teachers, and bilingual teachers in ethnic regions will be strengthened.

On December 15, 2016, *The Guiding Opinions of MOE on Vigorously Promoting the Management of Training Credits for Primary and Secondary School Teachers* proposed that a teacher training credit management institution should be implemented in primary and secondary schools, including ordinary primary and secondary schools, kindergartens, special education schools, and secondary vocational schools. Provincial education administration departments shall establish a teacher training curriculum institutions with different levels, classifications, and subjects in accordance with the relevant national regulations for teacher professional standards, teacher education curriculum standards, and teacher training curriculum standards, and in combination with the actual needs of local primary and secondary education and teaching and teacher professional development needs, set compulsory courses and elective courses reasonably, and assign corresponding credits to different levels and types of training courses; local education administration departments at all levels should formulate teacher training plans according to the standards for teacher training credits, and core training courses for training should be defined. The organization is provided with a basis for serial and periodic training courses for teachers at different levels; the provincial education administrative department shall scientifically determine the structure of the credit institutions for teacher training, clarify the total number of credits, propose requirements for credit ratios for training at different levels such as national, provincial, municipal, county, and school and self-training by teachers, standardize and guide local education administration departments and primary and secondary schools to provide diversified and personalized training services for teachers, and rationally formulate training hour and training credit conversion methods; provincial education administration departments should explore the establishment of a teacher training credit bank, record and store the results of teachers' participation in training and independent training, support query, accumulation and conversion of training credits, provide services for higher education institutions to recognize training credits, and incorporate diploma education; support higher schools and teacher training institutions through curriculum connection, credit recognition and other methods, establish a connection mechanism between non-diploma training and diploma education, build an "overpass" for teachers' professional growth, expand teachers' life-long learning channels, and promote the construction of a learning society.

In summary, in forty years of reform, we have seen that teacher training has moved from a relatively closed training mechanism to a more open and flexible teacher education institutions; the level of teacher training institutions has continued to move up from the original secondary normal, normal vocational, and normal colleges to the current normal colleges and normal universities; the teacher qualification examination is more stringent and complete, and the general ability of teachers is more comprehensively examined; the appointment of teachers is more standardized, and the dual choice of teachers and schools is emphasized; the teacher staffing institutions is fairer, encouraging education to develop more efficiently; teacher salaries pay more attention to mobilizing teachers' enthusiasm, and teacher training has also moved to a higher level, from a "standard level" to a "lifelong learning" level. This chapter mainly focuses on the policy institutions of normal student training, teacher personnel and teacher training. It roughly summarizes and presents the development context and main reform content of the Chinese teacher institutions over the past 40 years of Reform and Opening Up, and strives to reflect the major progress and important achievements made in the construction of the teacher institutions. In reality, the content of the teacher institutions does not stop there. It is difficult to say that the teacher institutions has made significant progress in one specific aspect and slow progress in other aspects, nor is it that some aspects are important and others are not. This is also not the case in practice: the reform of the teacher institutions is a holistic, continuous, and systematic practice. For example, teacher cultivation is always combined with teacher training, and teacher training is closely linked to teacher positions and teacher qualifications. Teacher qualifications are largely determined by teacher training. In other words, institutional change is a systematically change where a change in one aspect will affect the overall situation. The future reform of the teacher institutions should also pay more attention to advancing as a whole, cultivating better teachers, and providing impetuses and guarantees for the development of fair and quality education.

REFERENCES

An, X. (2014). Study on the changes and differences of the salary levels of primary and secondary school teachers in China. *Educational Research, 35*(12), 44–53 (in Chinese).

Chen, G., Hu, H., & Wang, J. (1996). China normal education: 1981–1996. *Journal of East China Normal University (Educational Science Edition), 03*, 2–6 (in Chinese).

Deng, X. (1994). *Selected works of Deng Xiaoping* (Vol. 2) (Edited by the Editing Committee of the Central Committee of the Communist Party of China). Beijing: People's Publishing House (in Chinese).

He, D. (Ed.). (1998a). *Important education documents of the People's Republic of China (1949–1975).* Haikou: Hainan Publishing House (in Chinese).

He, D. (Ed.). (1998b). *Important education documents of the People's Republic of China (1976–1990).* Haikou: Hainan Publishing House (in Chinese).

He, D. (Ed.). (2003). *Important education documents of the People's Republic of China (1998–2002).* Haikou: Hainan Publishing House (in Chinese).

Liu, Y. (Ed.). (1993). *China educational events (1949–1990) (I).* Hangzhou: Zhejiang Education Press (in Chinese).

MOE (The Ministry of Education of PRC). (1952a). *Provisional regulations for normal schools (Draft).* In B. Qu, Y. Lei, G. Yu, & R. Huang (Eds.) (1991). *China education reform* (Selected Papers on Education, Vol. 17, pp. 94). Beijing: People's Education Press (in Chinese).

MOE. (1952b). *The regulations on higher normal schools (Draft).* In B. Qu, Y. Lei, G. Yu, & R. Huang (Eds.) (1991). *China education reform* (Selected Papers on Education, Vol. 17). Beijing: People's Education Press (in Chinese).

MOE. (2003). MOE main working points 2003. Retrieved from http://www.moe.edu.cn/jyb_xwfb/moe_164/201002/t20100220_1517.html (in Chinese).

Su, L., & Zhang, G. (Eds.). (1996). *15 years of Chinese normal education.* Changchun: Northeast Normal University Press (in Chinese).

Tian, D. (2012). *Research on the performance wage institutions reform of primary and secondary school teachers in China.* Master's Degree Thesis, Zhengzhou: Henan Normal University (in Chinese).

Tian, Z., & Yang, Y. (2008). The reform of the salary institutions of middle school teachers since the founding of the People's Republic of China. *Educational Review, 06*, 158–161 (in Chinese).

Wang, L. (2009). Reflections and prospects of China's teacher education policy development over the past thirty years. *Journal of the National Academy of Educational Administration, 01*, 30–35 (in Chinese).

CHAPTER FIVE

The Education Evaluation Institutions

MINGHAO LIU

Since Reform and Opening Up, many achievements have been made in the theoretical research and institutional construction of educational evaluation in China. The concept of multiple educational evaluations has been widely recognized, the educational value of educational evaluations has been valued, multi-subjects and multi-ways participation in educational evaluations has become increasingly recognized, the education evaluation index institutions and evaluation procedures are becoming more and more standardized, and the application of modern technology in education evaluation has attracted attention. This chapter focuses on reviewing and sorting out the reform process of China's developmental student evaluation institutions, education quality monitoring institutions, and third-party education evaluation institutions after Reform and Opening Up, reflecting the basic path and basic strategy of the development of China's education evaluation institutions over the past forty years.

SECTION 1 DEVELOPMENT HISTORY OF THE EDUCATION EVALUATION INSTITUTIONS

Since the 1960s, educational evaluation has attracted the attention of the majority of educators, and relevant research results are quite abundant. Compared with theoretical research, the establishment of an educational evaluation institutions came a bit later. Since Reform and Opening Up, the development of China's education evaluation institutions has roughly gone through three stages: the reconstruction stage of the education evaluation institutions, and the formation of an examination evaluation institutions with selection and screening as its core function, with a strong atmosphere of test-orientated education evaluation; the adjustment stage of the education evaluation institutions, reflecting on the disadvantages of test-oriented education evaluation, actively exploring the establishment of an education evaluation institutions that meets the needs of quality education development and promotes the all-round development of all students; and the stage of diversified development of the education evaluation institutions, which has gradually enriched the macro, meso, and micro education evaluation institutions. The developmental and educative functions of education evaluation have been widely affirmed, and the comprehensive education evaluation mechanism with multi-subjects and multi-ways participation has gradually improved.

I. Reconstruction of the Education Evaluation Institutions

On October 12, 1977, the State Council approved the Ministry of Education's *The Opinions on Enrollment Work for Higher Education in 1977*, stating: "The enrollment of colleges and universities has a direct bearing on the quality of colleges and universities training senior professionals, affects primary and secondary education, and relates to all industries and households. It is a major event." The Ministry of Education's *The Opinions on Enrollment Work for Higher Education in 1977* stipulated: "This year's enrollment is postponed to the fourth quarter, and freshmen in 1977 will be enrolled before the end of February next year. From 1978, general colleges and universities will begin enrolling students in June and begin the first term in early September" (Yang, 2003). The introduced of these documents marks the restoration of the college entrance examination institutions and also the reconstruction of the education evaluation institutions.

The restoration of the college entrance examination institutions has effectively promoted the development of education in China. Primary and secondary education, which was severely damaged before, has also rapidly expanded because of this, and an orderly and harmonious education institutions is rapidly forming. The college entrance examination has built a bridge between basic education and higher education, and has produced an important impact on the basic education concept, teaching methods, and even curriculum settings (Wei, 2008). In the context of the restoration of the college entrance examination institutions, China's education industry has begun to flourish, various tasks have been gradually carried out, and theoretical research and practical exploration of education evaluation has also begun.

"At present, China has initially established some learning level examination institutions for the purpose of achieving standards or selections (such as the provincial middle school entrance examinations, the unified national college entrance examinations, the national university foreign language grading examinations, etc.)" (Zhang and Guo, 1994). After Reform and Opening Up, for a considerable period of time, China's education evaluation institutions was dominated by examination evaluation institutions, and exam-oriented education evaluation contained many elements. An important function of the examination evaluation institutions is selecting and screening students, taking the quality of subject learning as an important evaluation object, distinguishing and screening students through examination results, and achieving the connection between different semesters. In this context, an important role of school education is improving students' test scores and meeting their needs for further studies. Overemphasis on academic performance and progression rates are the most obvious characteristics of educational evaluation. "Now it is popular in society to use the level of higher education as the sole criterion for evaluating schools. The ensuing various higher education examinations, especially the higher education entrance examination, have become the batons for running a school" (Liu, 1989). "Especially after the restoration of the higher education entrance examination institutions, given the influence of the pursuit of higher education rates, society and schools almost unilaterally used the higher education admission rates as the sole criterion for measuring the school's running level and quality of education. Schools are graded according to the higher education admission rates, and students are lined up according to test scores. As a result, leaders only value high schools with better higher education admission rates, teachers only pay attention to those students who have high scores, and students only pay attention to the courses that they have to take" (You and Hou, 1986).

During the reconstruction stage, the unique value of education evaluation was widely recognized, but the development of the education evaluation institutions was relatively slow. "In 1985, the State Education Commission proposed putting the education evaluation institutions into legislation between 1987 and 1988, but so far the status, procedures, and guidelines of China's education evaluation institutions have yet to be clearly specified in the law" (Chen, 1999). The National Education Commission has also not yet provided provisions and guidance on the development of the evaluation institutions. Education evaluation activities are mostly carried out at the micro level, and there is a lack of meso and macro education evaluation. "It is generally believed that at present, our evaluation of education in the macro area has not yet begun, and only discussing school education is not sufficient" (Wang, 1988).

At the practical level, the form of educational evaluation is relatively narrow, and most of it is carried out from top to bottom. The main body of educational evaluation is the relevant government functional departments. The main function of educational evaluation is selection and screening. Students are differentiated and classified based on their scores. The selective value of educational evaluation is obviously higher than its developmental and educative value. The content of educational evaluation is relatively narrow. Most of them focus only on the academic performance of students, and lack attention on students' physical and psychological qualities, emotions, moral qualities, and personality qualities. Educational evaluation methods are relatively narrow. Most of them use paper-and-pen tests to evaluate the learning effects of students, so the results of educational evaluations are usually presented in the form of quantitative rankings, and it is difficult for objects of evaluation to obtain detailed feedback from evaluation activities.

II. Adjustment of the Education Evaluation Institutions

"Before 1990, China's education evaluation work was only in a preliminary and exploratory research stage, and a formal, orderly, and institutionalized education evaluation institutions had not yet been formed" (Zhang, 2001). With the development of education, people are becoming more and more aware of the many shortcomings of examination-oriented education evaluation based on academic performance and education progression rates as core indicators, changing the existing education evaluation institutions, making full use of the educational value of evaluation, and helping evaluation promote the positive development of education and the healthy growth of individuals, and is gradually obtaining more and more recognition. The 1990s was the exploratory period for China's education evaluation institutions. On the basis of reflecting on the shortcomings of examination-oriented education evaluation, the majority of educators have made relevant explorations to establish an education evaluation institution that meets the needs of quality education development.

In October 1990, the former National Education Commission promulgated *The Interim Provisions on Education Evaluation in General Higher Education Institutions*. This is a regulatory document in China's higher education evaluation. It is a sign that China's higher education evaluation work has begun to standardize. It has established the basic framework of China's higher education evaluation institutions and marks China's entrance into a new education evaluation stage (Chen, 1999). In March 1995, the Eighth National People's Congress passed *The Education Law of the People's Republic of China*, which stipulated in the basic institutions chapter: "The state implements education supervision institutions and other education evaluation institutions for schools and other education institutions." In June 1999, *The Decision of the CPC Central Committee and the State Council on Deepening Education Reform and Comprehensively Promoting Quality Education* clearly stated: "Establish a mechanism for evaluating schools, teachers, and students that meets the requirements of quality education. Local People's governments at all levels may not issue further education indicators, and may not use the education progression rates as a criterion for evaluating school work. Encourage all sectors of society, parents and students to participate in the evaluation of school work in an appropriate manner." The promulgation of a series of documents has prompted people to continuously reflect on the existing education evaluation institutions and actively explore new education evaluation institutions that meet the needs of the development of the times. Positive changes in education concepts provide the soil for development and the space for the development of new education evaluation institutions.

The emergence of many regulatory documents has provided strong guarantees for the construction of the education evaluation institutions, provided necessary impetus for the development of the education evaluation institutions in related explorations, and positively changed educational evaluation activities at the practical level. The narrow content institutions of examination-oriented education evaluation has gradually broken, and education evaluation pays more attention to the multifaceted development of students. For example, Beijing has explored and formulated a comprehensive education evaluation plan for the quality of primary and secondary schools based on the overall situation of students' comprehensive development based on the actual conditions of primary and secondary schools and the age characteristics of students. The standard institutions for comprehensive evaluation of student (education) quality is divided into six first-level indicators including ideological and political level, knowledge and ability level, physical health level, and aesthetic consciousness level, and thirteen second-level indicators, with twenty-three evaluation elements for middle schools, and twenty-two for primary schools (Mei, et al., 1992). During the process of exploring compulsory education reform, Zhejiang Province actively established a compulsory education evaluation institutions and divided the evaluation content into multiple aspects (Table 5.1) (Dai, 1992). Educational evaluation methods have gradually diversified, breaking the past situation where written tests dominated. The value of self-evaluation in education evaluation has been affirmed, the developmental function of education evaluation has been strengthened, and the discriminative function has weakened.

Table 5.1 Evaluation Content and Methods in Various Fields of Compulsory Education

Evaluation Area		Evaluation Content	Evaluation Method
Ideology and Morals		Ideology, Morals, and Behavior	Comments and conduct level, rewards and punishments
Subject Knowledge	Citizen ideology and morals	Display of citizen consciousness, political common sense, moral knowledge, and behavior	Knowledge point achievement test; combination of written and behavioral tests, score, and grade
	Sports and health	Basic activity skills, sport and health knowledge, attendance, learning attitude, and skill level	Knowledge point achievement tests; scores, grades, and competitive rankings
Ideology and Morals		Ideology, Morals, and Behavior	Comments and conduct level, rewards and punishments
	Chinese Language	Listening, speaking, reading, writing; noble thoughts and sentiments, aesthetic taste and language communication ability	Knowledge point achievement tests; combination of written and oral examinations; combination of open and closed examinations; combination of knowledge and writing compositions; scoring and commenting; competitive rankings
	Mathematics	Quantitative relationships, basic knowledge of geometric figures, basic skills and basic abilities, as well as personality qualities and learning habits	Knowledge point achievement tests; written tests, oral tests, practical operations; scoring; competitive rankings
	Foreign Languages	Master phonetic transcription, spell and memorize words, look up words, writing habits, listening and speaking simple daily expressions	Knowledge point achievement tests; written tests, oral tests, practical operations; scoring; competitive rankings

Evaluation Area		Evaluation Content	Evaluation Method
	Common Knowledge	Life, common knowledge regarding nature and society, and ability to participate in practical activities	Knowledge level achievement tests; written tests, oral tests, practical operation inspection; and scoring, comments, or ratings
	Natural sciences	Recognize natural phenomena and laws, as well as ability to use knowledge to solve simple problems	Knowledge point achievement tests; written tests, operation experiments, internships; scoring or ratings; competitive rankings
	Society	Understand social phenomena and laws of social development and the ability to participate in social activities and adapt to social life	Knowledge point achievement tests; written tests, social practice tests, survey reports, small essays, debates; combination of open and closed exams; scores, ratings, or comments
	Music	Appreciation, skills, music theory	Knowledge achievement tests; individual singing (playing) performances, written tests, oral tests, observations; ratings and comments; competitive rankings
	Art	Appreciation, skill, art principles	Knowledge point achievement tests; paintings, oral tests, written tests, exhibitions, ratings and comments; competitive rankings
	Agricultural Technology Foundation	Production knowledge, labor practice and investigations	Knowledge point achievement tests; oral tests, written tests, investigative reports, operation skill tests; reviews, ratings
Ideology and Morals		Ideology, Morals, and Behavior	Comments and conduct level, rewards and punishments

(*Continued*)

Table 5.1 Continued

Evaluation Area		Evaluation Content	Evaluation Method
Subject knowledge	Life and labor technology	Basic knowledge, operational skill level, working attitude	Operational skills examinations, speaking and written examinations; ratings with additional comments
	Family Life	Application of knowledge, operational skills, and daily behavior	Rating, grading and additional comments
	Career guidance	A summary of local urban and rural industries, the students' own abilities and tendencies, as well as the correct attitude towards employment and further education	Comments
Physical and mental condition		Routine physical examinations such as height, weight, vision, etc., as well as observations of mental state	Table of records as well as grades and comments
Work and attendance		Work attendance, working attitude, disciplinary status, whether or not there have been absences or late arrivals	Table of records, comments, praise, and rewards
Extracurricular activities and social practices		Frequency, content, attitude, performance, specialties	List of records, comments

III. Diversified Development of the Education Evaluation Institutions

In the process of advancing quality education, the educational value of education evaluation has been increasingly affirmed, and the education evaluation institutions is developing towards diversification. In 2001, the Ministry of Education issued *The Outline of Basic Education Curriculum Reform (Trial)*, stating: "Changing curriculum evaluation overemphasizes the function of assessment and selection, and exerts the functions of promoting student development, teacher improvement and teaching practice." "Establish an evaluation institutions that encourages the all-round development of students. Evaluation should not only focus on students' academic performance, but also discover and develop students' multiple potentials, understand the needs of student development, help students understand themselves and build self-confidence. Make use of the educational function of evaluation to promote student development on the original level. Establish an evaluation institution that promotes the continuous improvement of teachers. Emphasize teachers' analyses and reflections of their own teaching behaviors. Establish an evaluation institution with teacher self-evaluation as the main point and the participation of principals, teachers, students, and parents to enable teachers to obtain information from multiple channels and continuously improve the level of teaching. Establish an evaluation institution to promote the continuous development of the curriculum." The promulgation of this document highlights the developmental value of evaluation and points out the direction and path for the reform of education evaluation and the beginning of the establishment of the developmental education evaluation institutions.

In 2004, the Ministry of Education promulgated *The Action Plan for the Rejuvenation of Education 2003–2007*, which stated: "With comprehensively promoting quality education as the goal, accelerate reform of the examination evaluation institutions. Actively explore the reform of enrollment methods in high schools with a combination of junior high school graduates' academic examinations as the basis along with comprehensive evaluations." "Establish a project evaluation institution that combines administration, experts, and social intermediaries." Education evaluation methods have been developed, and in addition to the top-down evaluation activities carried out by administrative departments, third-party evaluations and self-evaluations have received attention. *The National Medium-and-Long-Term Education Reform and Development Plan Outline (2010–2020)* is China's first outline for medium-to-long-term education plan in the 21st century, and therein it is clearly stated: "Develop education quality evaluation activities involving government, schools, parents, and all sectors of society, make a record of student growth, improve comprehensive quality evaluation, explore a variety of evaluation methods to promote student development, and encourage students to be optimistic, independent, and to work hard to become successful."

From this series of documents, it can be seen that China's education evaluation institutions in the new period has the characteristics of developmental functions and diversified development. Since the beginning of the 21st century, the education evaluation institutions of achievement and progression rates as core factors have been gradually torn down, and the comprehensive education evaluation mechanism with multi-subjects and multi-ways participation has been gradually improved. The formation of the developmental student evaluation institutions has enhanced the educational value of the education evaluation institutions. The education quality monitoring institutions, county education evaluation institutions, and rural basic education evaluation institutions have gradually developed, making the education evaluation institutions much richer in content. Administrative departments, education experts, social intermediary agencies, and other parties participated in educational evaluation activities, and the evaluation subjects showed diversified characteristics. The formation of the third-party education evaluation institutions and the development of school-based evaluation have greatly increased the effectiveness of education evaluation.

SECTION 2 THE DEVELOPMENTAL STUDENT EVALUATION INSTITUTIONS

The developmental student evaluation institutions aims to promote the all-round development of students through dynamic and diversified evaluation, and contains the important educational concept of "the student is the center." Critical reflections on the traditional student evaluation institutions and the educational practice calling for the birth of a new student evaluation institutions are the inevitable foundations for the emergence of a developmental student evaluation institutions. Since the 1980s and 1990s, during the process of constructing and improving the developmental student evaluation institutions, relevant policy guarantees have gradually transitioned from idea advocacy to active guidance, providing a solid impetus for the educational practice of developmental student evaluation. During the process of putting the developmental student evaluation institutions into practice, it has become more and more diverse.

I. The Traditional Student Evaluation Institutions Shifts to the Developmental Student Evaluation Institutions

After the beginning of Reform and Opening Up, China's education industry was restored, and various areas of education work were steadily advanced. During the 1980s and 1990s, the focus of education was mainly on improving the quality of the nation, producing more and better talents, and changing the original face of education as a whole. At that time, China's understanding and researching on student evaluation had certain limitations, and was influenced by Western educational evaluation concepts, which led to the traditional student evaluation institutions, and this was dominated by examination evaluation institutions, occupying an important position in this historical period. As an important practice orientation of the examination evaluation institutions, discriminative evaluation usually uses a single evaluation method to evaluate students' academic performance and uses quantitative evaluation results to distinguish students. It meets the needs of selecting talents, but ignores the developmental function of evaluation.

The traditional student evaluation institution ignores the students' individual differences and the multiple possibilities of development, and to a certain extent, it is contrary to the law of education and human development, which is not conducive to the overall development and healthy growth of students. On the basis of critical reflection of the traditional student evaluation institutions, a developmental student evaluation institution has been vividly portrayed. The shift from the traditional student evaluation institutions to the developmental student evaluation institutions is an important innovation in the reform of the student evaluation institutions. The focus of evaluation has shifted from focusing on screening and selection to promoting development. These changes are mainly reflected in the positive changes in the views of students, values, processes, and methods.

(I) View of Students: Eliminating Abstract Individuals and Treating Students as Individuals of Development

Traditional student evaluation regards students as abstract individuals, and personality characteristics are often ignored. Under the influence of the traditional view of students, the students' initiative and personality are constrained, and individual creativity is difficult to show. Due to the closed and limited nature of student evaluation content and subjects, the space for individual development is greatly restricted. Developmental student evaluation regards students as individuals with unique personalities and believes that each student has development potential. Students are all equal subjects, and they all have the right to be evaluated fairly. They will not be treated differently because of their different external attributes and are considered to be living individuals. They have their own inner worlds and rich emotional experiences, as well as various development needs. Knowledge is only part of an individual's development needs, so the content of student evaluation not only focuses on academic performance but also pays attention to changes in students' various abilities, emotional experiences, and space for progress. At the same time, students are regarded as individuals with the potential for development and creativity. Through appropriate methods they are to be given guidance and encouragement so that they can achieve their own progress and creativity. Focus on discovering the unique personalities of students from the perspective of appreciation, respecting individual differences, and affirming the students' own interests, hobbies, specialties, ideals, and so on. Emphasize experiencing and understanding the students' true feelings and inner worlds from their perspective, understand students' thoughts and actions, and then discover and tap the space for further development of students.

(II) Values: Weakening the Value of Selection and Highlighting the Value of Motivation and Development

Promoting the comprehensive development of each student is the fundamental value pursuit of developmental student evaluation. Developmental student evaluation dilutes the value of selection of traditional student evaluation and highlights the value attributes of motivation and development.

First, developmental student evaluation focuses on the vertical comparison of individual learners and breaks the previous horizontal student comparison mode. Through continuous comparison of individual learning statuses before and after, students are provided with objective evaluation information, and points of strength for the next stage of learning. Encourage students to reasonably arrange their own learning process based on evaluation feedback information and choose the learning method that suits them.

Second, developmental student evaluation aims to promote student development, rather than using evaluation as a mean of selection to screen students. Pay attention to the diversity of student development. Evaluation should understand and analyze the development statuses of students from multiple perspectives. Students obtain feedback information and improvement suggestions through developmental evaluations, and find that they have made progress, advantages and accumulations, as well as existing deficiencies and room for improvement.

Finally, developmental student evaluation can promptly encourage students, sincerely affirm their progress and achievements, enhance their self-confidence, and help them to maintain a positive and aggressive attitude during their growth process. When students encounter difficulties, timely encouragement can motivate students to take reasonable measures to solve them. Guide students to correctly understand setbacks and actively respond to them, turn experiences of failure into stepping-stones for growth, and draw valuable nutrients from experiences and lessons.

(III) View of the Process: Breaking the Barrier of Static Result Evaluation and Treating It as a Dynamic and Continuous Process

Traditional student evaluation focuses on the measurement and evaluation of students' learning conditions after a certain learning stage. Evaluation activities rarely appear in the process of student learning. Developmental student evaluation is very different. It regards student growth as a continuous and dynamic process. Therefore, student evaluation also exists in an institutional process.

First, it no longer focuses merely on student development at a certain static point in time, but extends student evaluation to the entire learning process. The time sample for traditional student evaluation is one time point after another (Figure 5.1), while the sample for developmental student evaluation is a time interval (Figure 5.2), which is dedicated to collecting and analyzing development information throughout the entire process. Pay attention to the development status of students in each specific development stage. The process evaluation information can provide more comprehensive data so that individuals can understand their own changes over the course of the entire process.

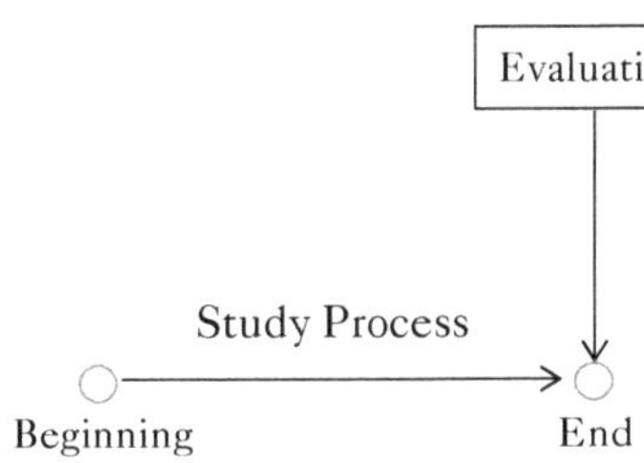

Figure 5.1 Time Sampling of Traditional Student Evaluation

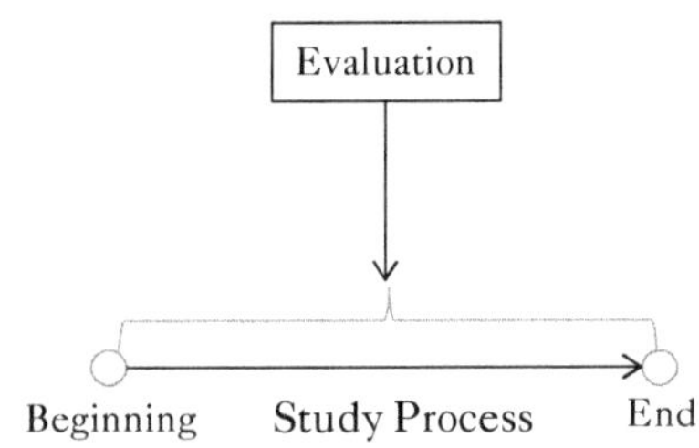

Figure 5.2 Time Sampling for Developmental Student Evaluation

Second, developmental student evaluation activities have a certain degree of continuity, and the student evaluation activities before and after are related to each other. The development proposal at one stage not only refers to the comprehensive development status of the previous stage but also points out a clear direction and possible action plans for progress in the following stage and these are interconnected with each other. It can form a database that reflects the development status of students in various aspects. Continuous and interconnected data analysis can clearly indicate the space for student progress and development, and can provide targeted help for student growth.

Finally, the process of developmental student evaluation possesses systematic characteristics. This is mainly reflected in the fact that evaluation content is comprehensive. Different evaluation content is connected to form a systematic evaluation content institution; from student learning to life, from knowledge and ability to attitudes, emotions, values, etc., evaluation activities cover all aspects of student growth. The evaluation process runs through all topics of student life, changing the monotony of previous evaluation activities.

(IV) Methodology: Change the Monotony of Previous Evaluations and Focus on Multiple Evaluations

Compared with the traditional evaluation method, the developmental student evaluation method has distinctive characteristics. First, it enables different subjects to participate in actual evaluation activities. In the past, the main subject of student evaluation was teachers or administrators. Developmental student evaluation can absorb the students themselves, peers, teachers, school administrators, parents, and communities into evaluation activities to obtain rich development information through multiple channels. Analyze and understand various behaviors and events in the developmental status of students in a comprehensive way, and exert the advantages and functions of various evaluation resources. Second, use a variety of evaluation methods to observe or investigate student activities, collect data, analyze data, and provide information feedback and guidance suggestions. All methods that are conducive to student progress and conform to individual physical and mental laws can be used for student evaluation. Traditional student evaluation considers examinations to be an important mean, while developmental student evaluation adopts multiple evaluation methods. Different evaluation methods are balanced with each other and complement each other. Through this combined effect, the positive role of evaluation activities is enhanced to promote student growth.

II. The Construction of the Developmental Student Evaluation Institutions

Facing the situation of accelerating reform, opening up and modernization, the development of education has become the most important way of promoting the enhancement of comprehensive national strength and the improvement of national quality. Many disadvantages arising in the development of traditional education became increasingly prominent. Schools were lacking in vitality, classroom teaching was boring, teaching methods were monotonous, there was insufficient student motivation, lack of interest, weak willpower, one-sided abilities, and so on. With the interaction of many factors changing the face of traditional education, reforming traditional education and teaching have become important issues, and quality education has become the focus of education reform. During the process of promoting quality education, the importance of constructing a developmental student evaluation institutions has been highlighted, and related explorations have gradually become richer.

After the 1990s, the introduction of relevant educational documents provided a strong policy guarantee for the construction and improvement of the developmental student evaluation institutions. For example, in June 1999, *The Decision of the Central Committee of the Communist Party of China on Deepening Education Reform and Comprehensively Promoting Quality Education* clearly states: "Accelerate the reform of the admissions examination and evaluation institutions and change the status of 'one exam for a lifetime'. Establish an evaluation mechanism for schools, teachers, and students that meets the requirements of quality education. Local people's governments at all levels may not issue education advancement indicators, and may not use the education advancement rate as a criterion for evaluating school work. Encourage all sectors of society, parents and students to participate in the evaluation of school work in an appropriate manner." Dilute or eliminate the screening function of student evaluation, and promote the all-round development of students as a new value orientation of student evaluation, providing a basic impetus for the construction of a developmental student evaluation institutions. At the same time, relevant guidance opinions and representations in documents are different at different stages of development (Table 5.2).

Table 5.2 Provisions on Developmental Student Evaluation in Relevant Educational Documents since the 1990s

Year of Release	Education Document	Summary of Relevant Content
1993	*The Outline of China's Education Reform and Development*	Primary and secondary schools should shift from "examination-oriented education" to the track of comprehensively improving the quality of the nation, comprehensively improving students' ideology and morals, culture and science, labor skills and physical and psychological qualities, and promoting students' lively development.
1999	*The Decision of the Central Committee of the Communist Party of China on Deepening Education Reform and Comprehensively Promoting Quality Education*	Accelerate the reform of the admissions examination and evaluation institutions, and change the situation of "one exam for life." Establish an evaluation mechanism for schools, teachers, and students that meets the requirements of quality education.
2001	*The Outline of Basic Education Curriculum Reform (Trial)*	Change course evaluations placing too much emphasis on the functions of screening and selection. Make use of the functions of evaluation to promote student development, teacher improvement, and improving teaching practice.

(*Continued*)

Table 5.2 Continued

Year of Release	Education Document	Summary of Relevant Content
2002	*Notice of the Ministry of Education on Actively Promoting the Reform of the Evaluation and Examination Institutions in Primary and Secondary Schools*	The content of student evaluation must be diversified. It is necessary to attach importance to the academic performance of students, as well as the development of students' ideological and moral qualities, as well as the development of multiple potentials, and to focus on students' innovative and practical capabilities. Explore evaluation methods that help guide students, teachers, and schools to conduct positive self-evaluation and other evaluations; formative assessment and summative assessment must be combined so that the process of development and change becomes an integral part of assessment.
2010	*The National Medium-and-Long-Term Education Reform and Development Plan Outline (2010–2020)*	Carry out educational quality evaluation activities with participation of the government, schools, parents, and all sectors of society. Keep a record of student growth and improve comprehensive quality evaluation. Explore a variety of evaluation methods to promote student development, and encourage students to be optimistic, independent, and hard-working.
2013	*Opinions of the Ministry of Education on Promoting the Comprehensive Evaluation Reform of Primary and Secondary Quality Education*	Use the students' moral development level, academic development level, physical and mental development level, interest development, academic burden status as the main content to evaluate the quality of school education, strive to build a comprehensive evaluation index institutions of primary and secondary education quality; combine formative and summative evaluations, pay attention to examining student progress and school efforts; combine quantitative evaluation with qualitative evaluation, and internal evaluation with external evaluation.

Table 5.2 Continued

Year of Release	Education Document	Summary of Relevant Content
2017	*13th Five-Year Plan for National Education Development*	Establish student volunteer service records and archives, and incorporate volunteer services into the comprehensive quality evaluation of students; comprehensively improve the educational evaluation institutions at all levels and types, focus on examining students' ability to adapt to social development and lifelong development, and prevent students from being evaluated solely by marks. Explore and implement open evaluation with the participation of stakeholders, improve the mechanism for publicizing evaluation results, and promote reform of comprehensive evaluation of basic education quality. Facing the future, clarify the core literacy of student development in each semester, implement teaching evaluation based on core literacy, and promote the all-round and sustainable development of students.

Although in different historical stages, people's levels of understanding of developmental student evaluation and the expression of related education documents are different; however, on the whole, the policy guarantee of the developmental student evaluation institutions has continuity, and the policy's leading role in building a developmental student evaluation institution is gradually becoming apparent. From concept advocacy to active guidance is the main trend of its policy guarantee.

(I) Continuity of Policy Guarantees

In earlier education documents, the important guiding idea of education promoting the multifaceted development of students was explicitly put forward. For example, *The Outline of China's Education Reform and Development* stated: "Primary and secondary schools should shift from 'examination-oriented education' to the track of comprehensively improving the quality of the nation, and comprehensively improve the students' ideology and morals, culture and the sciences, labor skills and physical and psychological qualities to promote the active development of students." Although terms such as "developmental student evaluation" or even "education evaluation" do not appear, to a certain extent, the educational concept of promoting students' all-round development has implied that student evaluation must be carried out from multiple aspects and has developmental, practical expectations. Subsequently, *The Decision of the Central Committee of the Communist Party of China on Deepening Education Reform and Comprehensively Promoting Quality Education* clearly stated: "Establish an evaluation mechanism for schools, teachers, and students that meets the requirements of quality education," advocating changing the traditional student evaluation institutions during the process of promoting quality education, and actively building a new student evaluation institutions with the core of promoting student development.

Since the beginning of the new century, concepts such as "developmental student evaluation," "formative evaluation," and "comprehensive quality evaluation" have been clearly put forward in relevant documents, and the concept of the developmental student evaluation institutions has gradually reached consensus. Developmental student evaluation has been presented in a series of education documents in different ways, but the important ideas are the same. The promulgation of a series of documents has provided a continuous policy guarantee for the construction of a developmental student evaluation institutions. With students as the center, the promotion of student development as the fundamental purpose, a variety of dynamic evaluation methods and so on have been adopted to constitute the basic essence of the developmental student evaluation institutions.

(II) The Guiding Nature of Policy Has Gradually Become Prominent

During the process of promoting the active construction of the developmental student evaluation institutions, the guiding role of policy has become increasingly prominent. It is mainly reflected in the following aspects. First, as policies advance, "developmental student evaluation" clearly appears in relevant educational documents. In earlier documents, the concept of developmental student evaluation was implicit in the corresponding educational guiding ideology and was not explicitly proposed. Since the beginning of the new century, the relevant concepts have been clearly presented in the documents. For example, from "establishing an evaluation mechanism for schools, teachers, and students that meets the requirements of quality education" to "making use of the function of evaluation to promote student development, the improvement of teachers and the improvement of teaching practices," the expression of developmental student evaluation has become clearer. Second, the relevant regulations on developmental student evaluation are becoming increasingly abundant, for example, from advocating for the establishment of a student evaluation institutions consistent with the concept of quality education, to proposing that the student evaluation institutions should focus on developmental functions, and then to guiding developmental student evaluation from the aspects of student evaluation content, evaluation subjects, and evaluation methods. Guiding opinions on developmental student evaluation in the documents have gradually increased, and the developmental student evaluation institutions has become more institutional. Third, the operability of the developmental student evaluation institutions is gradually increasing. Specific operational regulations have provided a path for putting the concept of developmental student evaluation into educational practice, and the role of policy-led practice has been significantly enhanced. For example, it is clearly stated in *The Notice of the Ministry of Education on Actively Promoting the Reform of the Evaluation and Examination Institutions in Primary and Secondary Schools* that "the content of student evaluation must be diversified, and students' academic achievements must be valued as well as their ideological and moral qualities and multi-faceted development potential, and focus should be put on students' innovative and practical abilities." "Explore evaluation methods that are helpful to guiding students, teachers, and schools in carrying out active self-evaluation and other evaluations." "We must combine formative evaluation and final evaluation so that the process of development and change becomes an integral part of evaluation." This document provides institutional guidance for advancing developmental student evaluation from many aspects such as evaluation methods and evaluation content, giving practice a solid focus.

III. Practical Reform Orientation of the Developmental Student Evaluation Institutions

After decades of exploration, the developmental student evaluation institutions has been gradually constructed, and the transformation from the conceptual level to the practical level has been realized. During the process of putting the concept into practice, developmental student evaluation has shown diversified characteristics.

First, the content of student evaluation has shown the characteristic of diversity. In addition to academic indicators, student evaluation is also concerned with changes in nonacademic aspects. The student evaluation institutions is becoming more and more complete. Students' moral qualities, academic level, physical and mental health, artistic literacy, and life skills are all elements that constitute a comprehensive evaluation institution. Evaluation indicators reflect the development status of students from multiple aspects. One survey showed that in addition to academic performance evaluation, the majority of front-line teachers began to gradually evaluate students' learning hobbies, interests, abilities, motivations, thinking processes, learning methods, and practical skills (Yin, 2011).

Second, the subjects of student evaluation are continually increasing. Detailed survey data on evaluation subjects shows that more than half of teachers choose multiple subjects to participate in the evaluation process. When evaluating students, it is hoped that teachers, parents, and students can all actively participate in evaluation activities (Yin, 2011). With the development of practice, in addition to teachers, parents, and students, education administrators, school administrators, and third parties in society have gradually come to be participants in student evaluation activities, which has enhanced the comprehensiveness, effectiveness, and development of evaluation results.

Third, the methods of student evaluation are flexible and diverse. Different evaluation methods cooperate with each other and play a role together. During the explorative process, developmental student evaluation has gradually started to pay attention to the feelings and opinions of those evaluated, and the evaluation of others has been closely integrated with self-evaluation. Singular evaluation methods have certain limitations: Quantitative methods occupied a considerable proportion in early evaluations; however, through the deepening of investigation, quantitative research and qualitative research are now usually combined. Combining formative assessment with summative assessment focuses on both results and the students' changes throughout the process.

Finally, in the specific educational context, a rich developmental student evaluation method institution has been formed. In addition to the traditional test methods, other methods that have become important for student evaluation include situational test methods, self-reporting methods, activity expression methods, dialogue methods, and portfolio evaluations. After practical accumulations, the evaluation method possesses rich characteristics in the specific application process.

SECTION 3 EDUCATION QUALITY MONITORING INSTITUTIONS

With the advent of the knowledge economy era, the quality of education and the role of talents in social development have become increasingly important. Meanwhile, the issue of quality of education has come to be valued, and the unique value of education quality monitoring institutions has begun to receive attention. For example, the National Assessment of Education Progress (NAEP) of the United States was launched in 1969 as a voluntary cooperative program and began conducting evaluation (Zhou, 2005). It is committed to establishing a national student performance evaluation institutions and getting the overall academic performance of students across the country, and also promoting the progress of education through targeted measures.

Since China's Reform and Opening Up, people have gradually come to realize the practical significance of education quality monitoring institutions in promoting the positive development of education. As early as the 1990s, the Ministry of Education introduced *The China Education Monitoring and Evaluation Statistical Indicator Institutions (Trial)*, which provides a good basis for scientific monitoring and evaluation of the development of education. At the same time, some scholars have proposed the establishment of China's education quality monitoring and evaluation institutions. During its process of progression, China's education quality monitoring institutions achieved a leap from initial exploration to gradual implementation, completing the transformation from concept to practice. With the development of practice, the education quality monitoring institutions has gradually extended from the basic education field to preschool education, higher education, vocational education, and many other fields, and is realizing its second leap from stable results to active improvement.

I. The Necessity of Constructing an Education Quality Monitoring Institutions

The education quality monitoring institutions has its own unique attributes, which are quite different from the traditional school evaluation institutions, and play an important role in improving the quality of education. It is quite necessary to build an education quality monitoring institution, which is of great significance in promoting the comprehensive development of students, improving the quality of school education, and enhancing overall national strength.

First, constructing an education quality monitoring institution can build a step for students in their progression, create a positive and healthy growth environment, and promote the all-round development of students. Students are the core group in education quality monitoring, and the main content of monitoring centers around the development of students. Individuals can learn about their own development status through specific tests or surveys, learn about their current level in various aspects, as well as find their own advantages, disadvantages, and areas of improvement. Students are encouraged to find areas of progress in many aspects, and positive factors are added to their growth through environment safeguards and external motivation.

Second, the construction of an education quality monitoring institution can provide school development momentum, enhance the vitality of school education, and promote the improvement of school education quality. School managers and the majority of teachers have a wealth of practical experience in education and teaching, but they lack academic analysis and strategic considerations compared to experts and scholars in the face of certain problems in education and teaching, and in response to school changes and development. The development of schools needs the support of external forces, and education quality monitoring institutions just so happen to provide academic wisdom and intelligence teams. Monitoring teams are composed of professional staff. Professional education quality assessment can provide detailed school development reports so that the majority of school educators can understand their own development resources, subject advantages, and existing problems. On the basis of clear questions, they can formulate substantive development plans and ways to improve the quality of school education.

Finally, building an education quality monitoring institution is an important guarantee for building a country with strong human resources, enhancing the overall strength of the country, and enhancing international competitiveness. The improvement of overall quality of the people and the formation of an innovative country depend fundamentally on the cultivation and generation of talents. To some extent, the quality of education determines the quality of talents. The establishment of an education quality monitoring institution, through scientific empirical analysis, diagnoses problems in the development of education, gets a hold on various contradictory relationships in education issues, and deepens understanding of the laws of education development, which is conducive to promoting real changes in government and schools, making use of the value of education, cultivating talents that meet the needs of social progress, and consolidating the foundation for the construction of a country with strong human resources through the norms of educational development and talent training.

II. Development History of the Education Quality Monitoring Institutions

Changes in the concept of education and positive reforms of education practice are necessary foundations for the development of the institutions, and attaching importance to the improvement of education quality is a precondition for the formation of an education quality monitoring institutions. The 1980s was an important stage in the development of China's education industry; various causes were steadily advanced, laying a practical foundation for the construction and improvement of the education institutions in the future. However, new assumptions and investigations on education quality monitoring during this period seldom appeared. During the development process, how to measure and evaluate the state of education development, and how to ensure the improvement of education quality through supervision, evaluation, monitoring, and other means became topics of increasing concern. Since the 1990s, the education quality monitoring institutions has gradually been established. In the course of practice, it has achieved a leap from preliminary exploration to gradual implementation.

(I) Preliminary Explorations of the Education Quality Monitoring Institutions

The 1990s were a critical period in the development of China's education industry in terms of advancing the orderly realization of nine-year compulsory education, promoting the optimization and adjustment of the education structure, reforming traditional education, and implementing quality education to meet the demand for talents and making progress in society in the new period. These tasks were important goals in education development at this stage. With the vigorous development of education, the quality of education has also become the issue that has attracted the most concern from all sectors of society. The initial conception of the education quality monitoring institutions began to brew in this period.

In 1991, the Ministry of Education issued *The China Education Monitoring and Evaluation Statistical Indicator Institutions (Trial)*, which provided the necessary prerequisites for education administration departments and schools at all levels to carry out scientific education development monitoring and evaluation, and also laid the foundation for the development of the education quality monitoring institutions. In February 1993, the Central Committee of the Communist Party of China and the State Council issued *The Outline of China's Education Reform and Development*, which stated: "Establish quality standards and evaluation index institutions for all types of education at all levels. Education departments in all regions should make inspection and evaluation of school education quality as a recurring task." Regarding the evaluation of school education quality as a recurring task initially reflects the normal thinking of education quality monitoring. In 1994, *The State Council's Implementation Opinions on "The Outline of China's Education Reform and Development"* proposed that in accordance with Xiaoping Deng's requirement and guideline that "education should be orientated towards the modern, the world and the future," basic school running conditions and quality standards were to be studied and formulated for schools of all levels and types. Education monitoring, evaluation, and supervision institutions were to be established and improved to clearly improve the quality of educated people, and better meet the needs of economic construction and social development. "Establishing an education monitoring and evaluation institutions" was clearly put forward, the idea of education quality monitoring gradually developed, and related explorations gradually began. For example, some studies began to put forward ideas of establishing a compulsory education quality monitoring institution that explores the functions, value standards, quality indicators and quality standards, information collection methods, and data processing of education quality monitoring institutions. It is clearly pointed out that the establishment of a compulsory education quality monitoring institutions is a complex process, and the design of related quality monitoring programs has only just begun (Cai, 2007).

In the 1990s, the education quality monitoring institutions was in the preliminary exploration stage, and the concept of constructing an education quality monitoring institution began to emerge. In the preliminary exploration stage, it was mainly the following features that were presented: First, the series of educational policy documents issued by the state reflects the country's high level of emphasis on the evaluation and development of education quality, and this has enlightened and guided the development of education quality monitoring ideas.

Through the policy text, some concepts related to education quality monitoring can be seen, such as the normality of education quality monitoring, and implementing education quality monitoring through social supervision mechanisms. Second, the education quality monitoring institutions has not yet been truly established, and preliminary exploration is still being carrying out at the conceptual level. The responsibility for the inspection and evaluation of education quality is mainly attached to the education supervision department. Education supervision departments of all levels and types are responsible for evaluating the quality of school education. However, as relatively uniform quality evaluation standards and procedures have not yet been formed, relatively large differences exist in the actual operations of various regions and the quality of assessments is also uneven. Finally, the concept of constructing an education quality monitoring institution put forward by related research has a certain promoting effect on practically promoting education quality monitoring. Preliminary explorations made in some regions in relevant aspects have accumulated some practical experience for the development of the education quality monitoring institutions.

(II) Gradual Implementation of the Education Quality Monitoring Institutions

Since the beginning of the new century, the idea of education quality monitoring has been further developed. The relevant education documents have stipulated and guided the construction of education quality monitoring institutions (Table 5.3), which has greatly promoted the education quality monitoring institutions moving from concept to practice.

Table 5.3 Provisions on the Education Quality Monitoring Institutions in Relevant Education Documents from 2000 to 2010

Year	Education Policy	Summary of Relevant Content
2004	"2003–2007 Education Revitalization Action Plan"	Establish tracking, monitoring, evaluation, and feedback mechanisms for national and provincial level curriculums to strengthen the quality of basic education.
2005	"Opinions of the Ministry of Education on Further Promoting the Balanced Development of Compulsory Education"	Education administration departments at all levels shall gradually establish standardized, scientific, and institutionalized compulsory education teaching quality monitoring and evaluation institutions and teaching guidance institutions.

Table 5.3 Continued

Year	Education Policy	Summary of Relevant Content
2006	"Key Work Points of the Ministry of Education in 2006"	Study and establish a national education supervision report institutions and a national education quality monitoring and evaluation institutions. Strengthen the evaluation of ordinary primary and secondary schools, and guide schools in implementing quality education in an all-round way.
2007	"Key Work Points of the Ministry of Education in 2007"	Establish a national education quality monitoring center, and carry out monitoring and testing points for the academic situation of primary and secondary students.
2008	"Key Work Points of the Ministry of Education in 2008"	Draw up a work plan for implementing quality education supervision in primary and secondary schools, conduct pilot evaluations for the balanced development of compulsory education, conduct basic education quality monitoring, and carry out special supervision and inspection work such as sunshine sports, and carry out national primary and secondary school students' mathematical learning quality and mental health status monitoring work.
2009	"Key Work Points of the Ministry of Education in 2009"	Establish and improve the basic education quality monitoring institutions, improve the standards and indicator institutions for students' mathematical learning and psychological status monitoring, and carry out quality testing of Chinese language and scientific learning at the compulsory education stage.
2010	"The National Medium-and-Long-Term Education Reform and Development Plan Outline (2010–2020)"	Improve the quality of compulsory education. Establish basic standards and monitoring institutions for national compulsory education quality; establish and improve basic standards for national education. Integrate national education quality monitoring and evaluation institutions and resources, improve the monitoring and evaluation institutions, and regularly issue monitoring and evaluation reports.

In 2015, *The National Compulsory Education Quality Monitoring Program* was introduced, which made detailed provisions on the implementation of the compulsory education quality monitoring institutions in terms of its purposes, principles, disciplines, objects, cycles, and content. A series of released education documents fully affirmed the value and importance given to the education quality monitoring institutions, and the guiding opinions on the implementation of the education quality monitoring institutions became more abundant. Under the strong guarantee of the policy, the education quality monitoring institutions has been gradually implemented, which is mainly reflected in the following aspects:

First, education quality monitoring work is gradually being carried out in the field of education. In practice, different regions have actively explored the monitoring of education quality. For example, Shunyi District of Beijing has issued *The Shunyi District Primary School Education Quality Monitoring and Evaluation Program*, which has four aspects of monitoring and evaluation: the development level of primary school students' academic achievements, physical development, ethics cognition and behavioral habits, and personality development. Zhengzhou City in Henan Province has issued a basic education teaching quality monitoring and evaluation plan. The quality monitoring and evaluation content has three aspects: student growth, teacher progress, and school development. The main monitoring and evaluation points of student growth are divided into comprehensive student quality and the student's academic performance. The main monitoring and evaluation points of teacher progress are divided into overall quality, performance of duties, and teaching performance. The main monitoring and evaluation points of school development are divided into daily management of school teaching, classroom teaching, school-based teaching research, and quality management (Zeng, 2007).

Second, national and local education quality monitoring institutions have been gradually established to provide professional assistance for the implementation of the education quality monitoring institutions. For example, in 2005, the Ministry of Education relied on the Shanghai Academy of Educational Sciences to set up a basic education monitoring center of the Ministry of Education. It focuses on the monitoring of macro-development of education, mainly through the processing of large amounts of data to monitor the development of education in various places (Chen, 2008). In 2007, the Quality Monitoring Center for Basic Education of the Ministry of Education was formally established. The center is a professional institution established by Beijing Normal University under the leadership of the Ministry of Education. It mainly monitors the learning quality and physical and mental health of students at the basic education stage and related factors affecting student development, and reports the status of basic education quality to the country in order to provide information, evidence, and recommendations for decision-making in education. Through the release of monitoring data and results, parents, schools, and society are guided in establishing a correct view of education quality and the healthy growth of young people is promoted (Liu, 2007).

Finally, the education quality monitoring institutions has achieved a transition from pilot exploration to gradual implementation. From "developing monitoring pilot for primary and secondary school students' academic situation" to "establishing basic standards and monitoring institutions for the quality of compulsory education in the country," the education quality monitoring institutions has been gradually implemented in more regions, and in practice has gradually taken on local characteristics. For example, since the first implementation of basic education quality monitoring in 2009, Chongqing has been committed to analyzing and researching education data, developing tools for monitoring the quality of basic education, constructing analysis platforms and institutions, forming a set of more complete education data collection and processing models or methods based on the analysis results of big data, processing diagnosis and evaluation for school development and regional education development, and formulating multiple educational administration documents (Gong, et al., 2015).

III. The Future Direction of the Education Quality Monitoring Institutions

With the deepening progression of the institutions, people's understanding of education quality monitoring has deepened, relevant beneficial experiences have continued to increase, and the education quality monitoring institutions has gradually improved. In the latest relevant education documents, relevant instructions indicate that the education quality monitoring institutions will enter a stage of vigorous promotion and active improvement, and relevant guidance opinions provide a clear idea for the development of the next stage of education quality monitoring. In 2017, *The 13th Five-Year Plan for National Education Development* clearly stated: "Improve the education quality monitoring institutions. Improve national education quality assessment and monitoring institutions and continue to implement national compulsory education quality monitoring. Explore the establishment of preschool education and special education quality monitoring evaluation institutions. Encourage industry enterprises to carry out vocational education quality monitoring according to vocational skills standards, regularly monitor and evaluate vocational education quality by industry, and establish and improve the vocational education quality assurance institutions." The scope of education quality monitoring has been further expanded, and the monitoring institutions has been gradually improved. In the same year, the General Office of the Central Committee of the Communist Party of China and the General Office of the State Council issued *The Opinions on Deepening the Reform of Education Institutions and Mechanisms*, which clearly stated: "We must establish and improve an education evaluation institutions, establish an education quality monitoring and evaluation institutions that extends to children in primary, middle and high schools, and establish an education quality monitoring and evaluation institutions with full standards, tiered objectives, multi-level evaluation, participation from multiple parties, and that is complete at the academic level."

The improvement of the institutions is a gradual process, as is the education quality monitoring institutions. From initial formation to vigorous advancement, from solid results to active improvement, these are the future development directions of China's education quality monitoring institutions. Education quality monitoring will extend from basic education to preschool education, higher education, as well as vocational education, special education, and many other fields. Constructing an education quality monitoring institutions that penetrates primary, secondary, and high schools has become an important goal for the next stage of work. Education institutions of all types and at various levels carry out education monitoring work in accordance with the characteristics of their own field and actual conditions, and enrich and improve the entire education quality monitoring institutions. Education quality monitoring standards will be more scientific and objective, and education quality monitoring procedures will become more standardized. Education quality monitoring institutions will be further improved to provide more robust guarantees for the implementation of the institutions. The main subject of education quality monitoring will be more diversified. Relevant education functional departments at the national level, local education administration departments, education quality monitoring centers, college education research institutions, industries in society, third-party institutions, etc., will participate in education quality monitoring work. These forces work together to promote the improvement of education quality monitoring. The methods of education quality monitoring will be more diversified, and the role of modern information technology in education quality monitoring will be more prominent.

SECTION 4 THIRD-PARTY EDUCATION EVALUATION INSTITUTIONS

The participation of third-party institutions in education evaluation has a value that other evaluation subjects cannot provide. Actively absorbing third-party social forces to participate in educational evaluation has become the consensus of many countries. The UK has established the Higher Education Quality Assurance Agency (QAA), an evaluation agency that conducts unofficial third-party evaluations of higher education institutions. "Finland has been conducting third-party education evaluations for many years. In the '2012–2015 Education Evaluation Plan', Finland also made participation in international third-party evaluation projects an important part of the plan" (Li, 2017). In addition, "since 1991, when Japan's Department of Education Regulations launched two reforms, its education evaluation has also achieved a transition from self-evaluation to third-party evaluation" (You, 2006).

There is a strong need to build a third-party education evaluation institution that can promote the improvement of education quality to a certain extent. China's exploration of third-party education evaluation can be traced back to the 1990s. Earlier explorations appeared in the field of higher education. After decades of gestation and development, the third-party education evaluation institutions has completed transitions such as those from promotion of ideas to education practice and from research in specific fields to multi-field exploration and has realized the phased change from initial exploration to vigorous advancement. Under the strong protection of relevant policies, the independence, objectivity, and professionalism of third-party education evaluation is being greatly enhanced, and the third-party education evaluation institutions with Chinese characteristics is gradually being improved.

I. The Necessity of Building a Third-Party Education Evaluation Institution

Since China's Reform and Opening Up, within a certain historical period, education evaluation activities have usually been carried out by people within the education institutions. With the advancement of education, people have continued to explore the law of education evaluation, gradually realized the limitations of existing education evaluation, and the need to attract social forces to participate in education evaluation. Third-party education evaluation is conducive to enhancing the objectivity and scientific nature of education evaluation and improving the effectiveness of education evaluation. The construction of a third-party education evaluation institutions can reduce the government's workload in education evaluation and promote effective changes in school education and teaching, which has important practical significance for educational practice.

First, building a third-party education evaluation institution is conducive to promoting the transformation of the functions of relevant government departments and providing realistic possibilities for the separation of education management evaluation. It can promote the separation of education management and evaluation from idea to practice, relevant government departments manage education, schools are responsible for carrying out specific education activities, and third-party education evaluation agencies implement education evaluation. The three have clear responsibilities, are interconnected with each other, and jointly promote the improvement in quality of education. Third-party education evaluation can use the advantages of professionalism to play a greater role in education evaluation activities. Some of the education evaluation responsibilities originally undertaken by the government can be undertaken and performed by it, which is beneficial to the transformation of government functions and enhances the vitality of government work.

Second, the construction of a third-party education evaluation institutions will help relevant subjects make reasonable education decisions. By providing scientific and objective evaluation and analysis, a true and effective reference for education reform is provided. There is no complicated interest relationship between it and what is being evaluated. During the evaluation process, an objective and neutral attitude can be maintained, ensuring the objective authenticity of the data and increasing the credibility of the analysis results. At the same time, third-party education evaluation is a professional evaluation carried out by professionally qualified personnel. It has clear evaluation goals and evaluation standards, and a detailed evaluation plan and uses standardized evaluation procedures and scientific data collection methods to obtain real information, and finally conduct reasonable data processing and analysis on the basis of a large amount of data to form an evaluation result. When government departments formulate related education policies, the results of third party education evaluation can be used as an effective reference to enhance the rationality and feasibility of the policies. Through educational evaluation activities, schools can comprehensively understand development information, diagnose development problems systematically, and strengthen educational reflections within the school. Parents and other parties in society can better understand the actual situation of the school through relevant evaluation information released by third-party education evaluation agencies, thereby reducing the asymmetry of information between the school and the external environment and increasing the possibility of the outside world rationally participating in education, promoting mutual understanding between different subjects, and jointly promoting the development of education.

Finally, building a third-party education evaluation institution is conducive to improving the quality of school education. Third-party education evaluation is committed to promoting the reform and development of school education through real, effective, and professional scientific evaluation analysis. The evaluation results are not a tool for dividing school echelons, and supervision and inspection are not the ultimate goals. Evaluation is only a mean of promoting development, and guiding and promoting the development of schools is its core. Due to many subjective and objective reasons, the effect of educational evaluation activities carried out by schools themselves are not ideal. When a government department implements education evaluation, because it has a certain affiliation with the school, the school is usually in a passive state of "being checked" and "being evaluated," which may cause the school to have concerns about the evaluation activities, and the education evaluation atmosphere is relatively tense. Third-party education evaluation has the characteristics of independence, professionalism, and autonomy. It can better solve the problems encountered by other evaluation subjects in the evaluation process, create an equal and relaxed evaluation atmosphere, and objectively and truthfully carry out evaluation of the state of a school's development in a standardized manner and diagnose problems in the development of the school. Suitable entry points for promoting the effective reform of school education are searched for through detailed cause analysis and suggestion guidance, thereby promoting the improvement of education quality.

II. Vigorously Promoting the Third-Party Education Evaluation Institutions

China's earlier exploration of third-party education evaluation appeared in the field of higher education, but the concept of "third-party evaluation" did not appear explicitly at first. Since the 1990s, related explorations have gradually increased. In the course of practice, third-party education evaluation institutions have realized an important shift from preliminary exploration to vigorous promotion.

(I) Preliminary Exploration of Third-Party Education Evaluation Institution

In October 1990, the National Education Commission promulgated *The Interim Provisions on Education Evaluation in General Higher Education Institutions*, which clearly stated: "Based on school self-assessment, with organizing social evaluations carried out by the Party and government departments and education, intellectual and personnel departments as the focus, on the principles of differential treatment through policy, rewarding good and punishing bad, academic institutions and social groups are encouraged to participate in educational evaluation." Although there is no mention of the term "third-party evaluation," academic institutions and social groups are encouraged to participate in educational evaluation activities, which implies that the concept of school education evaluation had begun to change, the significance of social evaluation had gradually been realized, and this was an initial reflection of the idea of third-party education evaluation.

In February 1993, *The Outline of China's Education Reform and Development* was promulgated. In the guidance on the development of higher education, "higher education must adopt a combination of leadership, experts and employment departments, and quality assessment and checks must be conducted through various methods." "We must attach importance to and strengthen decision-making research, establish consultation, review, evaluation and other institutions with participation from experts from all walks of life in education and society, and provide advice on development strategies and plans for higher education policies to form a democratic and scientific decision-making process." The thinking that promoted the participation of social forces outside the education institutions in the evaluation of higher education and even in development planning became clearer, and the role of social organizations in education development, especially in education evaluation, was highlighted. In June 1999, *The Decision of the Central Committee of the Communist Party of China on Deepening Education Reform and Comprehensively Promoting Quality Education* was issued, affirming the role of social supervision mechanisms and evaluation institutions in the evaluation of higher education quality. This decision clearly stated: "Strengthen the supervision and quality checking of school running, and gradually form a social supervision mechanism and evaluation institutions for school running behavior and education quality."

In the 1990s, the third-party education evaluation institution was in the preliminary exploration stage, and mainly had the following characteristics: First, the important ideas of third-party education evaluation germinated in the field of higher education, and the role of social organizations in the evaluation of higher education quality was valued. Second, during this period, although the concept of third-party education evaluation was not explicitly put forward, expressions similar to the meaning of "third party," such as "social groups" and "social intermediary organizations," clearly appeared in relevant education documents, providing a good foundation for the development of third-party education evaluation in the future. Third, third-party education evaluation agencies had not yet appeared on a large scale. Most of the explorations on third-party education evaluation remained at the level of ideas and strategies. Most studies recognized and promoted third-party education evaluation at a macro level, but there was a lack of exploration on specific operating procedures, practices, and institutions guarantees. Finally, the promulgation of a series of education documents during this period provided important policy guarantees for the practical implementation of third-party education evaluation activities in the field of higher education, laying a solid foundation for the development of third-party education evaluation institutions.

(II) Vigorous Promotion of Third-Party Education Evaluation Institutions

In the 21st century, third-party education evaluation has developed rapidly. Many education evaluation institutions have appeared in the field of practice. For example, in 2000, the Shanghai Education Evaluation Institute was formally established and Guangdong Province established the Education Development Research and Evaluation Center; in 2002, the Jiangxi Higher Education Evaluation Institute was established; in 2003, the Fujian Province Education Evaluation Institute was established; in 2005, the Heilongjiang Higher Education Teaching Evaluation Center was established; in 2006, the Beijing Education Evaluation Institute, and the Education Policy and Evaluation Research Center under the Chongqing Academy of Educational Sciences were established. The emergence of third-party educational evaluation institutions has greatly promoted the practical development of third-party education evaluation activities in the field of education.

After 2010, many relevant education documents clearly stipulated and guided the third-party education evaluation institutions (Table 5.4). Under the continuous and effective guarantees of the policy, the third-party education evaluation institutions has achieved a transition from initial exploration to vigorous promotion.

Table 5.4 Provisions on Third-Party Education Evaluation Institutions in Relevant Education Documents from 2010 to 2017

Year	Education Policy	Summary of Relevant Content
2010	*The National Medium-and-Long-Term Education Reform and Development Plan Outline (2010–2020)*	Launches education quality evaluation activities involving government, schools, parents, and all sectors of society; promotes professional evaluation; encourages specialized agencies and social intermediary agencies to evaluate the level and quality of disciplines, majors, courses, etc., in colleges and universities.
2011	*The Opinions of the Ministry of Education on Fully Utilizing the Guiding Role of the Industry*	It is necessary to establish a vocational education quality evaluation institutions that involves the participation of society, industry, enterprises, education administration departments, and schools and is based on ability levels and contribution levels. Industry norms and vocational standards should be used as an important basis for school teaching quality evaluation. The opinions of employers are important indicators of the quality evaluation of vocational education. Gradually establish a third-party evaluation mechanism for vocational education led by industry companies.
2013	*The CPC Central Committee's Decision on Comprehensively Deepening the Reform of Certain Major Issues*	Further promotes the separation of management and evaluation, expanding the provincial government's right to coordinate education and school autonomy, and improving the internal governance structure of schools.

(*Continued*)

Table 5.4 Continued

Year	Education Policy	Summary of Relevant Content
2015	*The Ministry of Education's Opinions on Deeply Advancing the Separation of Education, Management and Evaluation and Promoting the Transformation of Government Functions*	With the promotion of scientific and standardized education evaluation as the breakthrough point, establishes and improves an education evaluation institutions with multiple parties participating such as government, schools, professional institutions, and social organizations; supports professional institutions and social organizations in conducting education evaluation in a standardized manner; expands industry associations, professional societies, foundations and other social organizations to participate in educational evaluation. Sets qualification standards for professional institutions and social organizations to participate in education evaluation. Introduces market mechanisms, entrusts professional institutions and social organizations to conduct education evaluation into the scope of government purchasing services, and establishes and improves the bidding institutions and performance management institutions in accordance with the principles of openness, fairness, and impartiality to ensure the quality and effectiveness of education evaluation services. Attaches importance to expanding the participation of science and technology, culture and other departments and news media education evaluation. Attaches importance to the role of student organizations such as student unions in educational evaluation. Encourages qualified regions and schools to actively participate in education quality assessment projects implemented by international organizations.
2017	*The 13th Five-Year Plan for National Education Development*	Strengthens the supervision and guidance of third-party education quality assessment, and cultivate professional education evaluation institutions. Encourages industry enterprises, professional institutions and social organizations to carry out education evaluation and decision-making consultation in a standardized manner, vigorously cultivates professional service institutions, and entrusts professional institutions and social organizations to carry out evaluations.

The value of the third-party education evaluation institutions has been fully affirmed in many of the issued education documents, and guidance on the operation of institutions has gradually been enriched, providing a clear direction for the practical promotion of third-party education evaluation institutions. During the process of the central government's vigorous promotion of third-party education evaluation institutions, local governments have also kept pace with active exploration and putting in effort to make advancements. For example, in July 2012, Xi'an introduced a social third-party intermediary agency, Shan'xi Advanced Talent Office Limited Company, to conduct a social evaluation of the development of education reform (Deng, 2013). In May 2014, Henan Education Evaluation Center was established. Since its establishment, the evaluation center has actively explored the methods of third-party education evaluation, and has actively and steadily carried out evaluations. It has achieved the beginning of operations and made them bigger, and has experienced the process of moving from initial trial and small to steady advancement and has initially set up an education evaluation institution with a more complete institution (Wen, 2015). In June 2015, the leading group of Sichuan Provincial Education Institutions Reform issued *The Guiding Opinions on Promoting the Separation of Education Management and Evaluation and Promoting the Transformation of Government Functions*, which clearly stated that "third-party evaluation should be vigorously promoted."

During the stage of vigorous promotion, the development of third-party education evaluation institution has the following characteristics. First, the value and role of third-party education evaluation has been recognized by the government, schools, and society. The government actively guides all parties in strengthening the exploration of third-party education evaluation and, through a series of documents, provides a strong policy guarantee for the practice of third-party education evaluation. The number of third-party education evaluation institutions has continued to increase and actively participate in education evaluation activities, with significant changes in both quantity and quality. Schools also strive to change the concept and practice of education evaluation, actively integrating a variety of social forces to participate in school education evaluation activities, and are committed to promoting the effective reform of the school education evaluation institutions. Second, the scope of application of third-party education evaluation has been further expanded. From initial exploration in the field of higher education, it has gradually expanded outwards. It has also gradually been applied in areas such as preschool education, basic education, and vocational education. Finally, the practice of third-party education evaluation has become richer and richer, which has enhanced the effectiveness of education evaluation activities and provided a strong basis for improving the scientific nature of education decision-making. According to the concepts and principles of third-party education evaluation in different regions, combined with the actual situation and using available resources, flexible evaluation methods are used to carry out specific evaluation activities, and the practice is quite abundant (Ye, 2017).

III. The Practice Reform Orientation of the Third-Party Education Evaluation Institutions

Vigorously promoting the third-party education evaluation institutions is conducive to promoting the reform of the separation of education management and evaluation, and is an important guarantee for pushing forward the scientific development of education. After years of active exploration, China has accumulated a lot of useful experience, laying a good foundation for the improvement of the institutions and the development of practice in the future. But at the same time, third-party education evaluation has also come to face some challenges in the development process. For example, the professional authority of third-party education evaluation results has not been widely recognized, and the independence of third-party education evaluation institutions still needs to be further improved. As the quality of third-party education evaluation is continuously improved, its positive effects on educational practice become greater. Further improving the independence and professionalism of third-party education evaluation will become an important orientation for its practical change.

First, improving the independence of third-party education evaluation has become a key orientation of reform in practice. Third-party education evaluation organizations should be professional service organizations independent of the government and schools, and have the autonomy to carry out education evaluation activities independently. Independence is an important prerequisite for its own survival and development. In the past 10 or so years, various third-party organizations such as educational intermediaries, educational professional societies, or industry associations have been established, but most of them have been established or promoted by government authorities, and are not only used to following the instructions and requirements of government authorities to carry out work, but they are also reliant on the government administration department's project arrangements, capital investment, process leadership and management, leading to them having a lack of independent development capabilities and poor independence (Tang, 2016). The lack of independence limits the actual effects of third-party education evaluation and causes it to be unable to make full use of its unique value. During the process of vigorously promoting the development of third-party education evaluation institutions, full attention should be paid to the independence of third-party education evaluation institutions. The government and society need to vigorously nurture and actively support, bear the responsibilities they should bear, actively create an atmosphere conducive to the development of third-party evaluation agencies, provide them with solid policy guarantees, and give them sufficient independence and autonomy.

Second, during the development process, evaluation agencies should focus on enhancing their professionalism. Professionalism is the main support point for the existence of third-party educational evaluation institutions and an important reflection of its unique value. Third-party education evaluation is actually a complex activity; the establishment of evaluation goals and evaluation standards, the development of evaluation tools, the standardized operation of the evaluation process, the scientific analysis of evaluation data, the objective presentation of evaluation results and so on, all of these are permeated with professional factors. Only a professional third-party education evaluation can accurately diagnose education problems, scientifically analyze the development status of education, and provide clear recommendations for promoting the improvement of education quality. High-quality third-party education evaluation requires not only the support of many theories such as pedagogy, psychology, and test theory but also accumulation of relevant experience. In the final analysis, the degree of professionalism determines the survival status and social recognition of third-party education evaluation institutions. There are currently many third-party education evaluation institutions in society, but due to the differences in the comprehensive literacy of their constituents, the actual quality of services is also uneven, and people have mixed opinions on third-party education evaluation. Some third-party assessments done as a mere formality will not bring substantial benefits to the development of schools, nor will they be conducive to the professionalization of the evaluation agency itself. Improving the professionalism of third-party education evaluation is an inherent need for ensuring sustainable development. Evaluation agencies should strive to improve their professionalism, actively recruit high-quality talents with relevant subject backgrounds, strengthen relevant training to increase business training opportunities, continuously summarize practical experience, reflect on deficiencies in the evaluation process, and strengthen the standardization of evaluation procedures.

REFERENCES

Cai, W. (2007). Conceptions on establishing a quality monitoring institutions for compulsory education. *Education Guide*, *04*, 10–12 (in Chinese).

Chen, R. (1999). On the construction of an educational evaluation institutions in China. *Education Exploration*, *06*, 22–23 (in Chinese).

Chen, X. (2008). Establishing a quality monitoring institutions for basic education with Chinese characteristics. *Scientific Consulting (Education and Scientific Research)*, *01*, 2 (in Chinese).

Dai, L. (1992). Establishment of a compulsory education evaluation institutions – Two of Zhejiang Province's compulsory education curriculum reform explorations, curriculum. *Teaching Materials and Teaching Methods*, *06*, 26–31 (in Chinese).

Deng, Y. (2013). Annual results of third party evaluation of education reform in Xi'an. *Shaanxi Daily*, October 24 (in Chinese).

Gong, C., He Huaijin, J., & Lujinyun, et al. (2015). Chongqing model: Big data evaluation promotes scientific education decisions. *Primary and Secondary School Management, 08*, 7–10 (in Chinese).

Li, Y. (2017). *Practical Research on Third-Party Institution Evaluation Schools*. Master's Degree Thesis of Sichuan Normal University (in Chinese).

Liu, B. (1989). Management of educational evaluation. *Educational Theory and Practice, 01*, 10–13 (in Chinese).

Liu, Q. (2007). Basic Education Quality Monitoring Center of the Ministry of Education Established in Beijing. *People's Education, 24*, 5 (in Chinese).

Mei, K., Xiuniu Zhang, J. L., et al. (1992). Beijing's comprehensive evaluation scheme for primary and secondary school education quality (Part 1) … *Education Science Research, 06*, 9–17 (in Chinese).

Tang, Z. (2016). Promoting the healthy and orderly development of third-party education evaluation. *Nanfang Daily*, January 16 (in Chinese).

Wang, R. (1988). Summarization of domestic general education evaluation research. *Jiangxi Educational Research, 01*, 68–70 (in Chinese).

Wei, G. (2008). *Research on the reform of China's college entrance examination institutions since 1977*. Doctoral Dissertation of Hebei University (in Chinese).

Wen, Z. (2015). Quick, small steps and solid progress: Third-party education Evaluation in Henan Province. *Henan Education* (Higher Education), *01*, 30–31 (in Chinese).

Yang, X. (2003). *College entrance examination documents (Part 2)*. Beijing: Higher Education Press (in Chinese).

Ye, Y. (2017). Your prospects are good, 'My Son'. *China Youth Daily*, September 22 (in Chinese).

Yin, H. (2011). *Research on the developmental student evaluation institutions in rural high schools against the background of the new curriculum*. Master's Degree Thesis of Shaanxi Normal University (in Chinese).

You, B. (2006). The changing Japanese academic evaluation institutions: The transition from self-evaluation to third-party evaluation. *Journal of National School of Education and Administration, 12*, 86–89 (in Chinese).

You, X., & Hou, X. (1986). Summary of general education evaluation symposium. *Educational Research and Experimentation, 03*, 59–62 (in Chinese).

Zeng, X. (2007). *Research on 'Monitoring Indicators for Teacher Growth' in quality monitoring of ordinary high schools*. Master's Thesis of Fujian Normal University (in Chinese).

Zhang, X. (2001). The significance, types and features of education evaluation institutions. *Journal of Fujian Education Institute, 03*, 25–28 (in Chinese).

Zhang, L., & Guo, G. (1994). Establishment and improvement of the national education evaluation institutions: A summary of 'The International Symposium on a National Education Evaluation Institution'. *Educational Research, 02*, 74–75, 69 (in Chinese).

Zhou, H. (2005). The emergence and development of the national assessment of education progress. *Foreign Education Research, 02*, 77–80 (in Chinese).

CHAPTER SIX

The Examination and Admission Institutions

YONG SUN

The examination and admission institution is the country's basic education institution. Reform of the examination and admission institution, especially the reform of the college entrance examination, is a key area and a key link in China's education reform. It can be said that the reform of the examination and admission institution is a "crucial area," where even a slight adjustment affects the overall situation. It has a huge leading effect on deepening the comprehensive reform of education. During the past forty years of Reform and Opening Up, China's examination and admission institution has been continuously improved. Since China's college entrance examination institution was restored in 1977, it has been continuously adjusted and optimized. The content and form of examinations have paid more attention to abilities and comprehensive qualities. Admissions have gradually moved from "one test for a lifetime" to exploring the idea of "admissions based on multiple factors," initially forming a modern education examination admission institution with Chinese characteristics. The main content of this chapter reflects the major reforms and major advances in China's examination and admission institution, especially the college entrance examination institution and admission institution over the past forty years of Reform and Opening Up.

SECTION 1 RECOVERY AND REFORM OF THE COLLEGE ENTRANCE EXAMINATION INSTITUTION

Throughout the history of the college entrance examination institution, we can see that the college entrance examination has been constantly changing and improving since the day it was restored, thus gradually forming an examination admission institution with Chinese characteristics. As the most important and influential examination in China, the college entrance examination continues to advance in reform, and is constantly improved amid controversy. During these reforms and improvements, the history of the college entrance examination institution has continuously changed, and the design of the college entrance examination institution has become more and more perfected. The choice of colleges and universities is increasing, and the content and scope of the college entrance examination institution are becoming increasingly rich. It is in this process that the vitality of the college entrance examination institution constantly flourishes, strongly proving the importance and necessity of its existence.

I. Establishment and Abolition of the College Entrance Examination Institution

When New China was established in 1949, education entered a new period of development and in order to ensure its smooth connection and transition, the enrollment methods of the past continued to be used. Each university set their own questions and carried out enrollment independently, giving rise to an imbalance between the universities. For this reason, in 1950, the Ministry of Education of the Central Government began to make adjustment, attempting to unify and standardize admissions examinations. Major administrative regions regularly implemented all or part of the joint or unified admissions at appropriate locations, and allowed each school to enroll their own students. In 1951, the Ministry of Education required college admissions to continue using the 1950s approach, emphasizing the implementation of all or partial joint admissions and the nationwide unified examination, and unified admissions had to be held before separate admissions. In 1952, the Ministry of Education clearly stipulated that starting from this year, except for individual schools approved by the Ministry of Education, all other institutions of higher learning were to participate in nationally unified admissions examinations and various requirements were stipulated such as enrollment quota, application conditions, examination content, questions, grading, admission, and deployment. In 1959, with the establishment of the Chinese socialist institution and the formation of the socialist planned economic institution, the unified examination institution was finally established and stabilized as a basic institution. At this point, the unified college entrance examination institution had basically been formed and continued until just before "The Cultural Revolution." It should be said that the establishment of a unified national college entrance examination institution was the product of a combination of the social needs and the development of the exam itself in this particular historical period. This made great efforts towards selecting qualified freshmen for colleges and universities at that time, balancing out the level of higher education in various regions, improving the overall composition of higher education, improving the overall quality of higher education, and achieving equality of opportunity for national education (Liu et al., 2002: 338).

After the admissions examination became unified, it inevitably brought about the problems of student burden and the myopic pursuit of increasing higher education admission rates. In July 1955, the Ministry of Education issued New China's first "burden reduction" document, *The Instructions on Reducing the Overburden of Primary and Secondary School Students*, proposing to strengthen the usual performance assessment and improve the examination institution (He, 1998a: 476). In January 1966, the Central Committee of the Communist Party of China forwarded *The Three Documents of the Party Committee of the Ministry of Education and the Party Committee of the Ministry of Higher Education on Reducing the Burden of Students*, and put forward clear requirements for reducing the burden on students in primary and secondary schools and colleges with unprecedented force (He, 1998a: 1390). In April, the Ministry of Education held a seminar on enrollment of colleges and universities, and the participants had a fierce debate on the issue of the college entrance examination and college admissions. On June 13, the Central Committee of the Communist Party of China and the State Council approved *The Report of the Party Leadership Group of the Ministry of Education on Reform of the Enrollment Measures for Senior Middle Schools*, abolishing the existing admission measures for senior middle schools, and implementing a combination of recommendation and selection (He, 1998a: 1402). On the same day, the Central Committee of the Communist Party of China and the State Council issued *The Notice on Postponing the Enrollment of Colleges and Universities for Half a Year*, carrying of the postponement of enrollment of colleges and universities for half a year in 1966 (He, 1998a: 1402). On June 27, the Ministry of Higher Education issued *The Notice on Suspension of Postgraduate Enrollment in 1966 and 1967*, suspending the admission of graduate students in 1966 and the formulation of a postgraduate admissions plan in 1967 (He, 1998a: 1403). On July 24, the Central Committee of the Communist Party of China and the State Council issued *The Notice on Reforming the Enrollment Work of Higher Education Institutions* and decided that starting from that year, admission examinations would be cancelled and a combination of recommendation and selection was to be adopted for students admitted to higher education institutions (He, 1998a: 1404). Subsequently, all tertiary institutions stopped enrolling students, and higher education entered a state of full paralysis.

In August 1971, the Central Committee of the Communist Party of China approved "The Minutes of the National Education Work Conference." The enrollment targets of colleges and universities were outstanding workers, peasants, and soldiers with junior high school education or above and two to three years of practical experience. Higher education enrollment had to strictly abide by the idea of "voluntary signing up, recommended by the masses, approved by the leaders, and reviewed by the school" (i.e., the "16-character" enrollment method) (He, 1998a: 1481). The promulgation of this document marked the complete abolition of the unified national college entrance examination institution.

II. The Restoration of the College Entrance Examination Institution

The college entrance examination institution was abolished and the disadvantages of the "combination of recommendation and selection" enrollment method quickly appeared and became increasingly prominent. For this reason, with the official end of the ten years of turmoil, the restoration of the college entrance examination was put on to the agenda.

On May 24, 1977, Xiaoping Deng, speaking with Zhen Wang and Liqun Deng, said: "After passing a rigorous examination, the best people will be concentrated in key middle schools and universities" (He, 1998b: 1573). In July, the Third Plenary Session of the Eleventh Central Committee was successfully held. From August 4th to 8th, Xiaoping Deng personally hosted a symposium on science and education. Thirty-three renowned scientists, professors, and heads of science and education departments from across the country participated. The attendees generally called on the country to take firm measures. From the beginning of the year, the method of enrolling college and university students was to be reformed and the quality of students recruited was to be ensured. Xiaoping Deng agreed to restore the college entrance examination. In view of the 1977 meeting of student admissions, Xiaoping Deng proposed another meeting and the college entrance examination was restored in 1977. On August 8, the Symposium on Science and Education Work concluded. Xiaoping Deng delivered the famous speech "Several Opinions on Science and Education Work" and formally proposed the restoration of the college entrance examination.

> There are many specific issues in the education institution. ... One is the problem of recruiting fresh graduates from high schools. This year, we will be determined to resume recruiting students directly from high school graduates. Direct enrollment from high school, I think, may be a good way to produce talents and produce results early.
>
> Deng, Xiaoping (1977),"Several Opinions on Science and Education Work"

From August 13 to September 25, the National Admissions Conference was held in Beijing. On September 19, Xiaoping Deng summoned the Minister of Education Xiyao Liu and sharply criticized the unliberated mindset of the Ministry of Education. Speaking about enrollment, the question of direct enrollment from new high school graduates was raised again (He, 1998b: 1577).

> I know that science and education are difficult, but I offer to undertake the task of putting it in order. Without science and education, there is no hope for the four modernizations, and it becomes empty talk. … The admissions documents you drafted are hard to understand and are also tedious. Regarding the admissions conditions, I have changed some of them. Political review mainly depends on political performance. A clear political history, a love for socialism and labor, observance of discipline, and a determination to learn for the revolution. These are all we need. In short, there are two main points of enrollment that need to be put in order: the first is that the person performs well, and the second is selecting based on merit.
>
> "The Issue of Bringing Out Order from Chaos on the Front Line of Education"

Under the personal guidance of Xiaoping Deng, enrollment work achieved significant results in terms of bringing about order from chaos. The unified enrollment and examination institution that was gradually established after the founding of New China in line with China's national conditions and the needs of socialist construction was fully restored. Subsequently, at the request of Xiaoping Deng, the Ministry of Education revised admissions work documents. On October 5, the Politburo of the Central Committee discussed and approved in principle the Ministry of Education's *Opinions on Enrollment for Colleges and Universities in 1977*. On October 12, the State Council approved the Ministry of Education's *Opinions on Enrollment for Colleges and Universities in 1977*, stipulating that starting from 1977, the college admissions institution should be reformed and the unified examination institution restored (He, 1998b: 1579–1581). On October 21, *The People's Daily* published "Enrollment for Higher Education Institutions Undergoes Major Reform" (Xinhua News Agency, 1977) and issued the editorial "Proper University Admissions is the Hope of People Across the Country," interrupting the eleven-year restoration of the college entrance examination institution.

The restoration of the college entrance examination in 1977 was neither a simple repetition of the college entrance examination institution before "The Cultural Revolution" nor was it just a matter of restoring cultural examinations, rather, it was a complex social institution project. In the context of "The Cultural Revolution" having just ended, there being many abolished policies waiting to be resurrected and there being many difficulties to solve, the restoration of the college entrance examination was related to the direction of society and the way out, future and destiny of the tens of millions of educated youth who had accumulated over the previous ten years. Many of these policy issues were extremely sensitive and complicated, where the adjustment of one factor could affect the whole situation. Even today, the documents related to enrollment from that year still shine with the glory of history, such as the changing of the admissions ratio, expanding the enrollment scope, relaxing the admission age, marriage restrictions, modifying cumbersome political review conditions, and implementing merit-based admissions.

> I. Enrollment Targets and Conditions
> All workers, peasants, and educated youth who went to the countryside and have returned home (including those who have stayed in the city according to the policy but have not yet been assigned work), demobilized soldiers, cadres and recent high school graduates, who are about 20 years old, not more than 25 years old, and are unmarried. For those who have rich practical experience and have achievements or expertise in studying, the age can be relaxed to 30 years old, whether they are married or not (focus on recruiting high school graduates from 1966 and 1967). Those who meet the following conditions can apply for registration:
>
> 1. Have clear political history, support the Communist Party of China, love socialism, love labor, observe revolutionary discipline, and determined to learn for the revolution.
> 2. Have graduated from high school or have an equivalent level of schooling (high school students still in school with particularly good results can apply for themselves, be introduced by the school, and take the test).
> 3. Have good health.
>
> II. Enrollment Methods
> In order to ensure the quality of recruitment of new students, under the leadership of Party committees at all levels, implement the mass line, select the best admissions based on the principle of comprehensive evaluation of morality, intelligence, and physical fitness, implement voluntary registration, unified examinations, initial selection at the local and municipal level and school admissions, with methods approved by provinces, cities and autonomous regions. … Political review is carried out by the commune or the party organization of the factory, mine, institution, or school. Political performance will be mainly looked at. … with reference to the person's own aspirations, a comprehensive evaluation of morals, intelligence, and physical fitness to determine the admissions list, … This year's enrollment is postponed to the fourth quarter, and freshmen in 1977 will be enrolled before the end of February next year. From 1978, regular colleges and universities are to begin enrolling students in June and start in early September.
>
> "The State Council's Endorsement of the Opinions of the Ministry of Education on Enrollment for Higher Education Institutions in 1977"

The news of the resumption of the college entrance examination came, and the whole country was jubilant. The college entrance examination became the biggest focus of society at that time, and the backlog of candidates who had accumulated over the previous ten years flooded into exam rooms. In the winter of 1977, 5.7 million candidates across the country participated in the college entrance examination and 278,000 new students were admitted; in the summer of 1978, a total of 6.1 million candidates across the country participated in the college entrance examination and 402,000 new students were admitted. In 1977, the college entrance examination was originally expected to reach more than 20 million people, and the original plan was to recruit 200,000 students, with an admission rate of 1%. Later, many provinces and cities adopted the use of a regional preliminary test, and 2–5 times the planned admission number of students were selected and then participated in the formal college entrance examination. As a result, the actual number of candidates nationwide reached 5.7 million. Later, as proposed by Xiaoping Deng, the State Planning Commission and the Ministry of Education decided to expand enrollment. After the expansion, the number of undergraduates was 23,000, and the number of those enrolled in junior college classes was 40,000, with a total enrollment of 63,000 people and expansion rate of 29.3%. In the end, 272,971 people were admitted. The ratio of candidates was 21:1, and the acceptance rate was 4.8%. This was the lowest admission rate in China's college entrance examination history (Liu, 2017).

The restoration of the college entrance examination institution was the beginning of China's path towards a new order in terms of higher education, the entire education institution, and society as a whole after "The Cultural Revolution." The restoration of the college entrance examination has played a vital role in enabling Chinese education and Chinese society to constantly develop rapidly all the way to today. The significance of the restoration of the college entrance examination institution far exceeds the field of education. It was a revolution in the real sense. It was not only a restoration but also a breakthrough. It has become a typical representation of reversing "leftist" thought and breaking the "Two Whatevers," playing the prelude to breaking the shackles of the "two estimates," establishing an ideological line of seeking truth from facts, becoming the starting point of negating "The Cultural Revolution," and bringing about order from chaos. It wiped out the turbulence caused by "the theory of the uselessness of study" and "the theory of the unique importance of class origin," blowing the first spring breeze of respect for knowledge and talents for the vast land of China, for which many abolished things were waiting to be reinstated. Since then, the term "college entrance examination (gaokao)" has entered the lives of Chinese people and influenced every aspect of social process with unparalleled importance and particularity. Its significance is profound and far-reaching. The journey of China's modernization, the revival of Chinese education, and the rise of contemporary China almost all start with the restoration of the college entrance examination. The restoration of the college entrance examination turned over a new page in the history of Chinese society (Liu, 2007).

III. Reform and Improvement of the College Entrance Examination Institution

If it can be said that the restoration of the college entrance examination institution in 1977 played the prelude to the symphony of Reform and Opening Up, the continuous improvement of the college entrance examination institution over the past forty years has been a strong witness to the continuous wave of reform. Almost all subsequent education reforms have seen the reform of the examination and admission institution as a breakthrough point. In May 1985, the Central Committee of the Communist Party of China issued *The Decision on the Reform of the Education Institutions*, proposing to reform the enrollment plan and graduate distribution institution of colleges and universities, change the method of uniform enrollment of colleges and universities in accordance with the national plan and all graduates being allocated by the state, and implement the three methods of state-planned enrollment, enrollment entrusted by employers, and enrollment of a small number of self-financed students outside the state plan (He, 1998b: 2288). In April 1987, the State Education Commission issued "The Provisional Regulations on Enrollment for Ordinary Colleges and Universities," which made clear regulations on registration, political and ideological assessment, physical examination, test examinations, planning, and admission (He, 1998b: 2600–2604).

In February 1993, the Central Committee of the Communist Party of China and the State Council issued *The Outline of China's Education Reform and Development*, which proposed reform of the enrollment and employment institution for graduates of universities, changing the institution of enrolling all students in accordance with the unified national plan, and implementing the combined state mission plans and regulatory plans (He, 1998c: 3476). In June 1999, *The Decision of the Central Committee of the Communist Party of China on Deepening Education Reform and Comprehensively Promoting Quality Education* proposed to accelerate the reform of the admissions examination and evaluation institution and change the status of "one examination determining a lifetime." Reforming the college entrance examination institution is an important measure in promoting the comprehensive implementation of quality education in primary and secondary schools. The reform of the college entrance examination institution has been actively promoted in accordance with the principles of helping colleges and universities select talents, implementing quality education in primary and secondary schools, and expanding the autonomy of colleges and universities. Pilots for admission examinations for colleges and universities are held twice a year. The reform of the college entrance examination subject setting and content should further highlight the examination of ability and comprehensive quality. Provincial people's governments with the right conditions are encouraged to carry out various forms of college entrance examination institution reform experiments to expand the school's enrollment autonomy and candidates' choice opportunities.

A more scientific and fair college admissions selection institution with multiple choices was established (He, 2003: 288).

In the same year, universities began to expand the scale of enrollment and kicked off a new round of college entrance examination reform. In 2001, the Ministry of Education introduced a new policy that allows citizens over the age of 25 to participate in the college entrance examination, completely liberalizing the age limit for college admissions. In the same year, three colleges and universities in Jiangsu Province took the lead in implementing the "independent enrollment" pilot. In 2003, twenty-two universities, including Peking University and Tsinghua University, were granted 5% autonomy in enrollment. In the same year, the Ministry of Education allowed Hong Kong universities to independently recruit students in the Mainland. The implementation of the July college entrance examination institution for more than twenty years has ushered in changes. The college entrance examination has been brought forward by one month, and is fixed on the 7th and 8th of June each year. In 2007, Guangdong, Shandong, Ningxia, and Hainan, as the first experimental areas of the national high school new curriculum reform, ushered in the first college entrance examination after curriculum reform.

Subsequently, reform of the examination admission institution was gradually put on the agenda, and the pace of reform was accelerated. In July 2010, the Central Committee of the Communist Party of China and the State Council issued *The National Medium-and-Long-Term Education Reform and Development Plan Outline (2010–2020)*, which proposed that the reform of the examination admission institution should be used as a breakthrough point for overcoming the shortcomings of one exam determining a lifetime, promoting the implementation of quality education and training innovative talents. In November 2013, The *CPC Central Committee's Decision on Comprehensively Deepening the Reform of Certain Major Issues* proposed to deepen comprehensive reforms in the field of education, promote reform of the examination and admission institution, explore the running mechanism of relative separation of admissions and examinations, students having the choice to take examinations multiple times, independent enrollment of students by schools in accordance with the law, organization implementation by professional organizations, macro management by the government, and participation and supervision by society, fundamentally solving the disadvantages of one exam determining a lifetime. The reform of the college entrance examination institution had taken another giant step forward.

IV. The New Round of Reform of the College Entrance Examination Institution Is Fully Launched

In September 2014, *The State Council's Implementation Opinions on Deepening the Reform of the Examination Admission Institution* was officially released, marking the start of a new round of reform in the admission institution for examinations, which was "the largest, most extensive and most difficult since the restoration of the college entrance examination" (Wu, 2017), making a systematic deployment of a new round of examination and admissions institution reform, including improving the distribution methods of admissions plans, reforming the form and content of examinations, reforming the admissions mechanism, reforming the supervision and management mechanism, and launching a comprehensive reform test for college entrance examinations. In 2014, the pilot reform of the examination admission institution was launched, and it was comprehensively pushed forward in 2017.

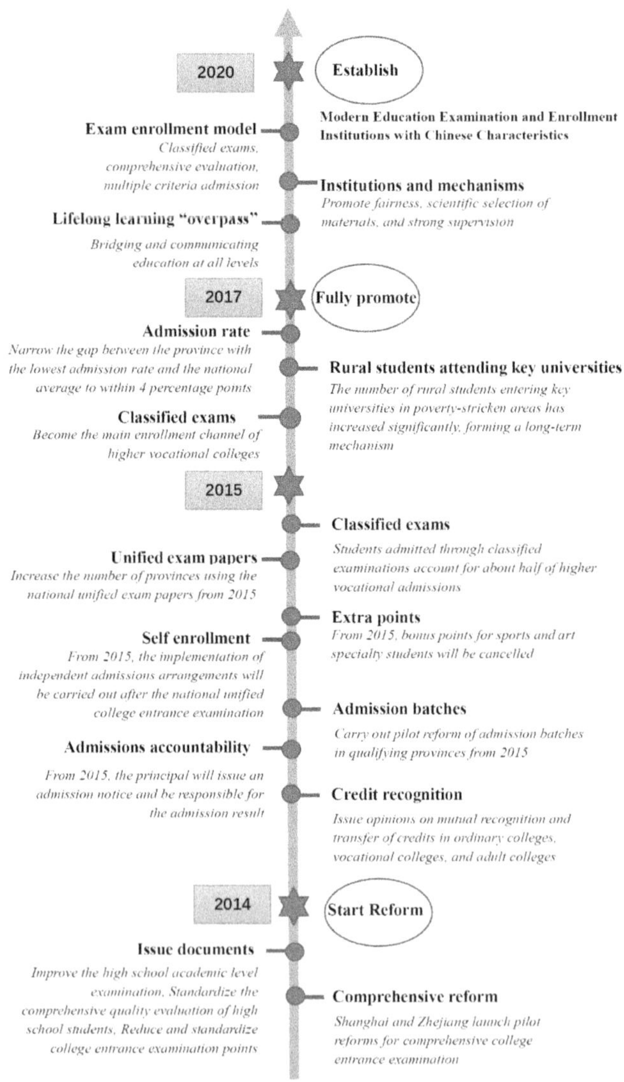

Figure 6.1 The Reform Course of China's Educational Examination and Enrollment Institutions

By 2020, the modern education examination admission institution with Chinese characteristics will be basically established to form an examination admission model for classified examinations, comprehensive evaluations, and multiple admissions, and to promote fair, scientific selection, and institutions and mechanisms with effective supervision. An "overpass" for lifelong learning that connects education at all levels and types and recognizes multiple learning outcomes will be built. Subsequently, the Ministry of Education successively issued documents including *The Opinions on Strengthening and Improving the Comprehensive Quality Evaluation of Ordinary Senior Middle School Students*, *The Opinions on the Implementation of General Senior High School Academic Level Examinations*, *The Opinions on Further Improving and Standardizing the Pilot Work of Independent Enrollment of Colleges and Universities*, and *The Opinions on Further Reducing and Standardizing College Entrance Examination Bonus Points and Credits*, and a new round of reform in the examination admission institution had been fully launched.

(1) Launch of Comprehensive Reform of the College Entrance Examination

Taking into account the importance and complexity of college entrance examination reform, in accordance with the principles of overall planning, pilot advancement, step-by-step implementation, and orderly advancement, *The State Council's Implementation Opinions on Deepening the Reform of the Examination Admission Institution* required Shanghai Municipality and Zhejiang Province to each bring out a pilot scheme for comprehensive reform of the college entrance examination in 2014, and provide a basis for reform of the college entrance examination in other provinces (autonomous regions and municipalities).

According to the unified deployment of the state, Zhejiang Province and Shanghai Municipality successively issued *The Implementation Plan for Deepening Comprehensive Reform of Higher Education Examination and Enrollment in Shanghai* and *The Comprehensive Plan for Deepening the University Examination Admission Reform Pilot Program in Zhejiang Province* to begin comprehensive reform of the college entrance examination. The pilot scheme for comprehensive reform of the college entrance examination in Shanghai Municipality and Zhejiang Province began from the two aspects of examination subject setting and the admissions mechanism. In terms of the examination subject setting, the connection between the college entrance examination and high school learning was enhanced. The total score of candidates was made up of the results in three of the unified college entrance examination subjects of Chinese language, mathematics, and foreign languages and their results in those three subjects at the high school vocational level. Academic level exam subjects were chosen independently from ideology and politics, history, geography, physics, chemistry, biology, and other subjects according to the requirements of colleges and universities and their own specialties; maintaining unity in Chinese language, mathematics, and foreign language subjects of the college entrance examination has remained unchanged, the scores remain unchanged, and there is no distinction between liberal arts and science. Foreign language subjects provide two opportunities for examinations. In terms of the enrollment and admissions mechanism, a multifaceted admissions mechanism is explored based on the unified college entrance examination and high school examination results and with reference to comprehensive quality evaluation; colleges and universities should study candidates' requirements for high school examinations and the use of comprehensive quality evaluation methods, and announce them to society in advance.

In terms of the pilot schemes in Shanghai and Zhejiang, choice will be expanded and emphasis put on making different developments on a common basis, strengthening comprehensiveness, and changing the phenomenon of evaluation forms being too monotonous. Both places have incorporated the results of high school examinations into the unified evaluation institution for college entrance examinations, and implemented a combination of final and procedural examinations. At the same time, colleges and universities can make demands on the evaluation of middle school quality to make the evaluation more comprehensive.

Both places have implemented a combination of a unified college entrance examination, high school vocational level examination, and comprehensive quality assessment, a combination of cultural lessons and vocational skill examinations (vocational adaptability tests), which reflects the process nature, weakening the phenomenon of one examination determining a lifetime. Both places have incorporated the high school examinations into the unified college entrance examination evaluation institution, and changed the one-time assessment of the college entrance examination to a procedural assessment, making the connection between the unified college entrance examination and high school learning stronger. Two opportunities are provided each year for the foreign language subject of each place and the selected subject in Zhejiang Province, where each student can take the exam twice, which is conducive to weakening the impact of accidental factors in one exam, and it is also conducive to dispersing and alleviating the test pressure of candidates (Bian, 2015). Some commentators have pointed out that the reform of the college entrance examination has begun a transformation from "cold scores" to "living people" (Hu, 2014).

With the gradual progress of the comprehensive pilot reform of the college entrance examination, in order to ensure the orderly progress of reform, Shanghai also issued a series of supporting documents related to the ordinary senior high school vocational level examination, comprehensive high school student quality evaluation, higher vocational education examination, and social candidates participating in the college entrance examination. At the same time, high school curriculum standards and curriculum plans are being revised, and high school curriculum plans are being adjusted. In 2017, pilot reforms of the comprehensive college entrance examinations in Shanghai and Zhejiang were successful after evaluation and the smooth implementation of the pilot reforms for college entrance examinations was successfully achieved (Xiong, 2017). Looking at the college entrance examination schemes in both places, whether it was candidates or universities, the two-way choice space generally increased. Students have unprecedented choices in what subjects to choose, how many times to take exams, and which grades to use. Colleges and universities have greater autonomy in terms of enrollment modes, selection criteria, and the scope of professional elective subjects. For example, during the enrollment stage, the number of volunteers reported by candidates in the new admission schemes in Shanghai and Zhejiang increased significantly, and ordinary undergraduate groups in Zhejiang can report eighty professional volunteers. Shanghai general undergraduate groups can report a maximum of twenty-four college professional group volunteers, and each group can report four majors.

The successful implementation of pilot comprehensive reforms for college entrance examinations in Shanghai and Zhejiang has explored experiences for the improvement of the examination admission institution, and is of great significance for the provinces that have entered college entrance examination reforms in succession. Based on the first batch of trials in Shanghai and Zhejiang, in 2017, Beijing, Tianjin, Shandong, and Hainan launched the second batch of pilot comprehensive reforms for the college entrance examination. In 2018, Fujian, Hubei, Chongqing, Jilin, Sichuan, Guizhou, Heilongjiang, Liaoning, Tibet, Shanxi, Anhui, Hebei, Jiangsu, Guangdong, Hunan, Jiangxi, Henan, Xinjiang, and Fujian launched college entrance examination reform. In 2019, Qinghai, Gansu, Shaanxi, Ningxia, Guangxi, and Yunnan launched college entrance examination reform. In 2020, a new college entrance examination reform institution was fully established (Zhang, 2017).

At present, all provinces have successively introduced reform plans for the college entrance examination. From the plans published in each place, the overall reform direction is generally consistent. Most provinces have clearly reformed the college entrance examination subject setting and candidate admission mechanism to promote the comprehensive and individual development of students. Many localities have also introduced specific implementation measures based on local conditions. Although the college entrance examination reform plans for thirty-one provinces, municipalities, and autonomous regions have been released, it will still be a while before full implementation is achieved. Many provinces have clearly stated that, while leaving the overall framework unchanged, they will follow the principle of "first reform special items and conduct exploration with pilots, and then comprehensively reform and fully advance" to conduct step by step reform. On the basis of referring to and learning from the experiences of the pilot projects in Shanghai and Zhejiang, the plans for each province may be adjusted and improved based on actual experience and the actual situation.

(2) Deepening Pilot Reform of the College Entrance Examination

At the same time, with the smooth completion of the first round of the "one province, one city" comprehensive pilot reform of the college entrance examination, breakthroughs have been made in many different kinds of reform work and milestones have been achieved. During the process of deepening the reform of the college entrance examination, some new situations and problems have been encountered. For example, the number of candidates for the subject of physics was too small, and further reforms were needed. For this reason, Zhejiang Province and Shanghai Municipality successively introduced a number of opinions on pilot projects to further deepen the comprehensive reform of the college entrance examination, promote the development of college entrance examination reform in depth, and explore more replicable and expandable experiences for the country. For example, Zhejiang Province issued *The Several Opinions of the People's Government of Zhejiang Province on Further Deepening the Comprehensive Reform of the College Entrance Examination*, which adjusted and improved the elective subjects, examination time, and registration requirements for students, further improved the elective mechanism, and established the elective subject guarantee mechanism, and in accordance with the actual student elective subjects was the first to establish a physical elective subject guarantee mechanism (The People's Government of Zhejiang Province of PRC, 2017).

Shanghai Municipality also issued *The Several Opinions on Further Deepening the Pilot Work of Comprehensive Reform of the College Entrance Examination in this Municipality*, which improved the further deepening of the comprehensive pilot reform of the college entrance examination in three aspects. The first was to establish a guiding mechanism to guide colleges in accurately and reasonably proposing elective subjects. For science and engineering majors that really need a foundation in physics, admissions institutions in Shanghai must reflect clear requirements for guiding candidates in choosing physics subjects. The second was to establish a guarantee mechanism to promote the unification of student selection and national professional talent selection and training requirements, and clearly establish a basic guarantee mechanism for elective subjects to serve as an "adjusting lever" by first establishing a guarantee mechanism for physics elective subjects, and recruiting students and implementing it during admission from the 2018 college entrance examination. The third was to perfect the education model and cultivate socialist builders and successors who have developed morally, intellectually, physically, and in terms of work; further deepen the reform of the teaching content of the curriculum and the reform of the comprehensive quality evaluation mechanism for high school students, and guide the promotion and optimization of the mechanism for selecting and cultivating talents in colleges and universities (The People's Government of Shanghai Municipal of PRC, 2018).

In addition, the Ministry of Education also proposed to actively and steadily advance the reform of the admissions institution for examinations. Guide Shanghai and Zhejiang in implementing pilot comprehensive reform plans for the college entrance examination. Guide Beijing, Tianjin, Shandong, Hainan, and other pilot provinces and cities in the second batch in formulating and implementing comprehensive pilot reform plans for the college entrance examination. Guide relevant provinces in strengthening the construction of basic conditions, and actively and steadily initiate the comprehensive reform of the college entrance examination. In addition, *The Guidelines for Requirements in Selecting Examinations for Undergraduate Enrollment in Ordinary Colleges and Universities (Trial)* was issued to guide universities in optimizing requirements for electing subjects in the provinces where comprehensive pilot reforms of college entrance examinations are taking place.

During the process of deepening the comprehensive reform of the college entrance examination, due to the different levels of economic development in various parts of China, differences in education were great, with problems such as hardware construction and the teaching staff during the college entrance examination reform process, as well as some objective problems encountered by Shanghai and Zhejiang during progress. At present, some provinces and cities that originally planned to initiate reform have clearly suspended the implementation of college entrance examination reform.

SECTION 2 REFORM OF EXAMINATION FORM AND CONTENT

The form and content of the examination is the core of the reform of the examination admission institution, in which it plays an important guiding role. The form and content of the examination are concentrated on the setting of examination subjects and questions. Based on this, since Reform and Opening Up, after forty years of continuous adjustment and improvement of examination subject setting in China's college entrance examination, there has been a continual move from the separation of subjects to integration, the questions being more scientific and standardized, and examination content paying more attention to ability and comprehensive quality.

I. The Transition of Examination Subjects from Separation to Integration

Subject setting for the college entrance examination is one of the core elements of college entrance examination reform. The optimized combination of subjects has an extremely important impact on the function of the college entrance examination. Subject setting for the college entrance examination can regulate the teaching activities of middle schools. It has a certain impact on various aspects including candidates' learning direction and methods, the choice of courses and content, as well as various teaching activities in middle schools. The strength and role of this kind of regulation, by virtue of the authority of the college entrance examination, in terms of quickly internalizing the actions of schools, teachers, and students is self-evident (Chen, 2005). Since Reform and Opening Up, according to the needs of socioeconomic and educational development, the college entrance examination has made unremitting reforms in terms of subject setting, content, and forms, which has improved the college entrance examination institution in exploration.

(1) Separation of Liberal Arts and Sciences

In 1977, when the college entrance examination was reinstated, the examination was divided into two categories: liberal arts and sciences. Liberal arts examination subjects included politics, Chinese language, mathematics, history, and geography. Science examination subjects included politics, Chinese, mathematics, physics, and chemistry. An additional foreign language exam was added for those applying for a foreign language major (He, 1998b: 1580). Since then, subject setting has been gradually improved. First of all, for foreign language subjects, in order to gradually improve the foreign language level of college students and promote foreign language teaching in primary and secondary schools, in May 1979, the State Council approved the Ministry of Education's "Report on the Enrollment Work of Higher Education Institutions in 1979," which stipulated: "For those who apply to key colleges and universities, 10% of foreign language scores will be incorporated into the total score, and this percentage will be increased year by year in the future. For those who apply to ordinary higher education institutions, the score will only be used as a reference point in admission."

In 1980, provinces, municipalities, and autonomous regions with a large number of candidates were required to carry out preselection before the unified exam; Arabic was removed as a foreign language subject; 30% of candidates' foreign language scores for undergraduate institutions were counted towards the total score. In 1981, 50% of foreign language scores of students applying for undergraduate colleges were counted towards the total score, and whether or not vocational training schools were to be counted in the total score was left to be determined by each province, municipality, and autonomous region. The second was the entry of biology subjects. In 1982, when applying to undergraduate colleges, 70% of foreign language scores were counted towards the total score and whether or not vocational training schools were to be counted in the total score was still left to be determined by each province, municipality, and autonomous region. Since 1983,

100% of foreign language scores have been counted towards the total score, with 120 points each for Chinese language and mathematics, 50 points for biology, and 100 points for every other subject. Since 1984, several additional questions have been added to subjects such as mathematics, physics, chemistry, English, Russian, etc., not counting towards the total score, but to be used as a reference for admission to key colleges and universities (Wei, 2008). Since then, separate liberal arts and sciences examinations and separate subject admissions gradually formed. However, it also objectively brought problems such as irrational knowledge structures of students and students favoring one subject over others.

(2) The "3 + 2" Plan

In 1985, with the approval of the Ministry of Education, Shanghai began to carry out an experiment of reforming college entrance examination subjects based on the senior high school entrance examination, that is, the "3 + 1" mode. The college entrance examination subjects included the three mandatory subjects of Chinese language, mathematics, and foreign languages, with an additional test in politics, history, geography, physics, chemistry, or biology depending on the requirements of the major. In 1987, the State Education Commission agreed for Shanghai to begin carrying out independent question setting in 1988, and based on the high school entrance examination, only relevant subjects would be tested on the college entrance examination. After several years of adjustments and additions, the college entrance examination subject settings stabilized locally. In April 1987, the State Education Commission issued *The Provisional Regulations on Enrollment for Ordinary Colleges and Universities*. Among the examination subjects, literature and history (including foreign languages)–type exams tested politics, Chinese language, mathematics, history, geography, and foreign languages; science-, technology-, agriculture-, and medicine-type exams tested politics, Chinese language, mathematics, physics, chemistry, biology, and foreign languages. The above two types of foreign language examinations were divided into six languages: English, Russian, Japanese, French, German, and Spanish. Candidates could choose any one of these. Candidates who apply to do a major in a foreign language college or department should take an oral test in addition to the written test (He, 1998b: 2601–2602).

In October 1990, the State Education Commission issued *The Notice on Reforming the Subject Setting of College Entrance Examinations*, stating that reforming the subject setting of college entrance examinations on the basis of provincial ordinary senior high school entrance examinations is an overall reform of the ordinary senior high school graduation examination and the college entrance examination. The purpose is separating level tests and selection tests so that they each perform their respective functions, which is not only conducive to middle school teaching and overcoming the phenomenon of students having an incomplete knowledge structure caused by the separation of arts and sciences or partiality towards some subjects, but also to helping ordinary colleges and universities select new students according to the requirements of the major, removing the pitfall of current college entrance examination subjects being too numerous, and some subjects having little to do with the majors of students after admission, but playing a decisive role in determining whether students can enter the school.

The new subject groups are:

Group one: politics, Chinese language, history, foreign languages
Group two: mathematics, Chinese language, physics, foreign languages
Group three: mathematics, chemistry, biology, foreign languages
Group four: mathematics, Chinese language, geography, foreign languages.

According to the department and major, each college and university can choose a group of college entrance examination subjects for examination candidates according to the setting of the college entrance examination subject group and its respective characteristics. The new subject first started trials among qualified graduates from Hunan, Yunnan, and Hainan provinces, referred to as the "Sannan Plan." Due to the low level of high school graduation examinations, more than 95% of students could pass the exam in one go. The test results lacked the necessary level of differentiation, and it was difficult to meet the admission requirements of colleges and universities. Therefore, these examination results cannot be used as a reference for admission. At the same time, the college entrance exam questions for the "Sannan Plan" were independently set by the Ministry of Education, the absolute difficulty of the test papers was significantly reduced, and there was not much difference in student performance, which made it difficult to accurately screen the students' levels. In view of this, in November 1991, the State Education Commission issued *The Notice on Continuing the Trial Reform of College Entrance Examination Subject Setting in Hunan, Yunnan, and Hainan in 1992 and Related Issues*, requiring all scores of political subjects of the high school graduation examination to be based on the original scores and included in the total score of the college entrance examination for candidates in the second, third, and fourth groups.

Fresh graduates of ordinary high schools applying for admission to ordinary colleges and universities must pass the high school graduation examination. Each province should formulate reasonable examination standards based on the teaching syllabus issued by the State Education Commission and implement them carefully. In July 1992, on the basis of summing up the trial experience of the "Sannan Plan" and extensively soliciting opinions from various quarters, the former State Education Commission solicited opinions from various provinces and divided the examination subjects into two categories: liberal arts and sciences. Common examination subjects were Chinese language, mathematics, and foreign languages; politics and history examinations were added for the liberal arts, and physics and chemistry examinations were added for science. According to the characteristic of colleges and university majors roughly dividing into natural sciences and social sciences, the new scheme is still divided into two test subject groups, including the subjects necessary for college teaching, whereby majors leaning more towards the liberal arts require examinations in Chinese language, mathematics, history, politics, and foreign languages, and majors leaning more towards science require examinations in Chinese language, mathematics, physics, chemistry, and foreign languages, and the maximum score for each subject was originally 150 points. This is the "3 + 2" plan that people are familiar with. The plan received the support of most provinces, autonomous regions, municipalities, and universities.

In December 1992, the former General Office of the State Education Commission issued *The Notice on the Trial Implementation of the 1993 Trial Program of the National Education Commission's New Subject Group for the College Entrance Examination*, which officially confirmed the "3 + 2" plan. By 1995, all regions except Hong Kong, Macao, and Taiwan had implemented the "3 + 2" college entrance examination reform based on the general examination (Wei, 2008). The "3 + 2" plan brought about a serious phenomenon of subject partiality in liberal arts and sciences, and it was also unscientific to set college entrance examination subjects simply by distinguishing between natural sciences and social sciences for higher education institution majors.

(3) "3 + X" Plan

Although the "3 + 2" plan received support from most provinces, autonomous regions, municipalities, and universities, the number of examination subjects was reduced from seven to five, namely Chinese language, mathematics, and foreign languages, with politics and history added for the liberal arts, and physics and chemistry added for the sciences. Geography was removed from the liberal arts and biology was removed from sciences. The issue of the relatively simple geography and biology subjects taught for the college entrance examination was resolved by putting them on the senior high school exam. This alleviated students' learning burdens to a certain extent, but problems soon appeared. Liberal arts students barely studied physics, chemistry, and biology, which were not included in the liberal arts college entrance examination, and the subjects of geography, history, and politics, which were not included in the science college entrance examination, were abandoned by science students. Since neither liberal arts nor science college entrance examinations tested geography or biology, these subjects became pure furnishing in high school teaching. In 1998, the Ministry of Education carried out a pilot test of comprehensive ability to protect students in some provinces and cities, accumulating experience for question setting in comprehensive subjects. On the basis of summing up many years of experience and conducting a large number of investigations, the Ministry of Education put forward the idea of setting up comprehensive subjects in the college entrance examination subjects.

In February 1999, the Ministry of Education issued *The Opinions of the Ministry of Education on Further Deepening the Reform of the Enrollment Institution of Ordinary Colleges and Universities*, which proposed a "3 + X" reform plan for college entrance examination subject setting, and planned to implement it in about three years. The "3" referred to Chinese language, mathematics, and foreign languages, which are the required subjects for each candidate. Listening tests gradually increased for English. Mathematics would no longer fall into sciences or liberal arts in the future. The "X" refers to colleges and universities determining one or more examination subject from physics, chemistry, biology, politics, history, geography, or comprehensive subjects according to the level and characteristics of the school. Candidates take the exams of the subjects determined by the majors of the college or university they wish to apply to.

Comprehensive subjects refer to comprehensive ability tests based on cultural subjects in middle schools. According to the situation of the time, comprehensive subjects were divided into comprehensive liberal arts, comprehensive sciences, comprehensive liberal arts and sciences, or comprehensive specialist subjects. It is not a "combination" of subjects such as physics, chemistry, biology, politics, history, and geography in a certain proportion, but a test of a students' ability to understand, master, and apply knowledge learned in middle schools (He, 2003: 232–233).

In 1999, the "3 + X" plan was piloted by Guangdong Province. In 2000, the five provinces of Guangdong, Jiangsu, Zhejiang, Shanxi, and Jilin carried out reform experiments in accordance with the plan. By 2001, eighteen provinces across the country had implemented the "3 + X" college entrance examination reform plan. In 2002, the Ministry of Education began to implement the "3 + X" plan throughout the country, and most provinces and municipalities continue to use it today. The purpose of the "3 + X" plan is making the college admissions institution actively adapt to the characteristics of the times and its requirements for the structure of talents' quality and capabilities, and striving to guide the improvement of the overall quality of talents and the cultivation of innovative talents, so as to further improve the role of the college entrance examination. However, though it had the intention of changing the single structure of knowledge by allowing students to choose subjects, in the greater context of the college entrance examination, the desired result was not achieved, and the phenomenon of students favoring some subjects over others became even more serious. At the same time, coupled with the question setting methods of comprehensive subjects, student burdens and other issues, whether or not the "3 + X" plan can achieve its original intention has begun to be widely discussed.

(4) Non-separation of Liberal Arts and Sciences

With the improvement of the college entrance examination reform, the non-separation of liberal arts and sciences has become a trend. In July 2010, *The National Medium-and-Long-Term Education Reform and Development Plan Outline (2010–2020)* proposed to deepen the reform of examination content and form, focusing on the examination of comprehensive quality and ability. Based on the talent selection requirements of colleges and universities and the national curriculum standards, the national examination subject question database was improved to ensure the scientific nature, orientation, and standardization of the national examination. Ways of taking exams in individual subjects more than once a year and ways to implement socialized exams were explored. In September 2014, *The State Council's Implementation Opinions on Deepening the Reform of the Examination Admission Institution* clearly stated the reform of examination subject settings: strengthen the correlation between the college entrance examination and high school learning. The total score of the candidates consists of the three unified college entrance examination subjects of Chinese language, mathematics, and foreign languages, and in the three subjects of the high school examination. The three subjects of Chinese language, mathematics, and foreign languages of the unified college entrance examination remain unchanged, the scores remain the same, no distinction is made between science and liberal arts subjects, and foreign language subjects provide two examination opportunities. The subjects of the senior high school examinations that are included in the total score are selected independently by the candidates from ideology and politics, history, geography, physics, chemistry, biology, and other subjects according to the requirements of the colleges and universities they wish to apply to and their own specialties.

At the same time, in accordance with unified national deployment, Shanghai and Zhejiang took the lead in launching a comprehensive pilot reform of the college entrance examination. Subsequently, *The Implementation Plan for Deepening Comprehensive Reform of Higher Education Examination and Enrollment in Shanghai* and *The Comprehensive Plan for Deepening the University Examination admission Reform Pilot Program in Zhejiang Province* were officially announced. In the Shanghai plan, starting from 2017, the unified college entrance examination subjects were to be Chinese language, mathematics, and foreign languages, with no separation in liberal arts and sciences, and foreign language examinations were to be held twice a year to deepen the reform of foreign language examinations. Foreign language examinations include written, listening, and speaking tests, guiding foreign language teaching to focus on the development of application skills. High school students take a maximum of two foreign language exams, and the one with the better score can be included in the total college entrance examination score. A foreign language standardized examination question bank and standardized examination room were to be established. Foreign language examinations should accumulate experience for gradually implementing standardized examinations in other subjects in the future. In the Zhejiang plan, Chinese language, mathematics, and foreign languages are compulsory subjects. Candidates choose three subjects from the seven high school examination subjects with additional questions in ideology and politics, history, geography, physics, chemistry, biology, and technology (including general technology and information technology) for the college entrance examination based on their interests and specialties, and the requirements of the school and major they apply for.

Subsequently, according to the unified requirements of the Ministry of Education, all provinces across the country successively launched college entrance examination reform. From the perspective of examination subjects, "3 + 3" has become a new model for the future college entrance examination in each province. College entrance examination results are composed of the results of the three subjects of Chinese language, mathematics, and foreign languages plus the three elective subjects selected by the candidates. There is no longer a division between liberal arts and sciences, and students can choose their own subjects.

Table 6.1 Changes in College Entrance Examination Subjects since Reform and Opening Up

Year	Type	Exam Subjects
1977	Liberal arts, sciences	Liberal arts examination subjects include politics, Chinese language, mathematics, history, and geography. Science exam subjects include politics, Chinese language, mathematics, and physics and chemistry. Those applying to do a foreign language major take an additional foreign language exam.
1980		Foreign language exam added
1981		Biology added to science exam
1984		Certain number of questions added to mathematics, physics, chemistry, English, Russian, and other subjects not counted towards total score, but used as a reference for key colleges and universities.
1985	3+1	For Shanghai pilot there were the three compulsory exam subjects of Chinese language, mathematics, foreign languages, and then one more subject to be selected from politics, history, geography, physics, chemistry, or biology depending on the requirements of the major.

Table 6.1 Continued

Year	Type	Exam Subjects
1987	Literature and history, science, technology, agriculture, and medicine.	Examination in politics, Chinese language, mathematics, history, geography, and foreign languages in literature and history (including foreign languages); Examination in politics, Chinese language, mathematics, physics, chemistry, biology, and foreign languages in science, engineering, agriculture, and medicine.
1990	Sannan Plan	"Sannan Plan," Chinese language, politics, history, foreign languages; mathematics, Chinese language, physics, foreign languages; mathematics, chemistry, biology, foreign languages; mathematics, Chinese language, geography, and foreign languages. One group can be chosen for the major enrolled.
1992	Literature and history, science and technology	"3 + 2" plan, examinations on Chinese language, mathematics, history, politics, and foreign languages for liberal arts type majors; examinations on Chinese language, mathematics, physics, chemistry, and foreign languages for those with science type majors.
1999	3 + X	In the Guangdong pilot, "3" referred to the compulsory exam subjects of Chinese language, mathematics, and foreign languages for each candidate. Listening exams were gradually added for English, and mathematics was no longer to be divided into liberal arts and sciences. "X" referred to colleges and universities determining one or more test subjects from the six subjects of physics, chemistry, biology, politics, history, or geography or a comprehensive subject according to the requirements of the level and characteristics of the school.
2002	3 + X	Implemented across the country.
2014	Liberal arts and science subjects not differentiated.	Shanghai and Zhejiang pilots. Results of a unified college entrance examination made up from scores in the three subjects of Chinese language, mathematics, and foreign languages and three subjects in the high school examination.
2017	Liberal arts and science subjects not differentiated.	Gradually extended to the whole country.

*Source of data: Compiled by the author based on relevant data.

II. Examination Content from Knowledge to Ability

The reform of examination content is the focus on the reform of the college entrance examination admission institution and also where the difficulty lies. After the resumption of the college entrance examination in 1977, the content and form of the examination still used the model from before "The Cultural Revolution." With the passage of time, its shortcomings became more and more obvious, and the issues relating to the how scientific and fair the original cultural examination itself was attracted more and more attention. The absence of examination theory as a guide led to the lack of clear test objectives and quality evaluation standards for college entrance examination question setting, and subjective randomness of score assignments. At the same time, there was no full-time institution studying and implementing the examinations, and in particular, there was a lack of relatively stable question setting and test paper analysis teams, resulting in test questions emphasizing knowledge and deemphasizing ability, making it critical for students to rely on rote memorization; subjective questions had large scores and small coverage, which in practice not only induced the appearance of guessing answers to questions but also led to increased scoring errors. These problems caused the difficulty of test papers to be unstable, which was not conducive to testing the actual level of students. In 1980, the Ministry of Education realized that in 1979 some of the questions were beyond the scope of the review outline, and there were too many chemistry test questions, which departed from the reality of middle school. Resuming the college entrance examination question setting work at the beginning of the college entrance examination institution not only failed to achieve the expected purpose of scientifically guiding middle school teaching but also severely hindered the improvement of students' comprehensive quality (Wei, 2008).

In March 1982, the Ministry of Education required that in addition to conducting research on the college entrance examination admission policy and admissions institution, the reform of examination content should also be specially studied and included in future work as a focus point. Required points of discussion included "how are examinations classified, which subjects should be tested for each, as well as scoring proportions and scoring methods for each subject," "how can question setting deal with the relationship between the requirements of freshmen in colleges and universities and the impact of college entrance examinations on middle school teaching," "how does question setting and grading test the ability of students and help overcome the phenomenon of rote memorization among candidates," and so on. In addition, there was a requirement to research foreign admissions institutions and examination theories. This was the first time since the founding of the People's Republic of China that top-down scientific research on the admissions examination itself had been organized (The Hebei Provincial Education Examination Institute, 1998: 127).

In August 1983, the Ministry of Education clarified that starting from 1984, the college entrance examination would focus on assessing students' basic knowledge, skills, and ability to analyze and solve problems according to basic textbook questions (He, 1998b: 2114). In December 1992, the State Education Commission proposed a national unified examination for enrollment of ordinary colleges and universities after the senior high school examinations, while reforming subject setting, content, and form of the examinations were to be reformed accordingly. On the basis of testing knowledge, there was to be a focus on examining ability, and on the premise of selecting the best, the difficulty of the test questions was to be adjusted to achieve examination standardization.

In February 1999, the Ministry of Education pointed out that, for the content requirements of examinations, on the whole, more attention is paid to the examination of candidates' abilities and quality; the scope of the question setting followed the middle school syllabus, but was not limited to the syllabus; the design of the test questions increased knowledge-application questions and ability-type questions. Question setting had to be transformed from testing knowledge to ability, and the traditional closed discipline concept had to be transformed. While examining ability in the subject, there was to be a focus on examining the candidate's comprehensive ability across different disciplines (He, 2003: 233). In June 1999, *The Decision of the Central Committee of the Communist Party of China on Deepening Education Reform and Comprehensively Promoting Quality Education* proposed that the reform of the setting and content of college entrance examinations should further highlight the examination of abilities and comprehensive qualities (He, 2003: 288).

In July 2010, *The National Medium-and-Long-Term Education Reform and Development Plan Outline (2010–2020)* was officially released, and proposed to deepen the reform of examination content and form, with a focus on the examination of comprehensive quality and ability. In September 2014, the State Council's *Implementation Opinions on Deepening the Reform of the Examination Admission Institution* were issued, and clearly stated that the reform of the content of the college entrance examinations should be deepened. In accordance with the requirements for talent selection in colleges and universities and national curriculum standards, the content of questions had to be scientifically designed, strengthening foundational and comprehensive knowledge, and focusing on the ability of students to independently analyze and use the knowledge they have learned to analyze and solve problems. Scoring methods were to be improved, scoring management was to be strengthened, and performance reports were to be improved. The construction of national education examination institutions, national question banks, and foreign language proficiency assessment institutions was to be strengthened, and the number of provinces using the national unified proposition test papers was to be increased from 2015.

In addition, Shanghai clearly implemented qualification and grade tests. The content of qualification tests was based on the basic curriculum requirements in the ordinary high school curriculum standards. Passing the examination results is a necessary condition for high school students to obtain graduation qualifications; the content of the level examinations is based on the basic and extended curriculum requirements in the general high school curriculum standards. Starting from 2017, the unified college entrance examination subjects are Chinese language, mathematics, and foreign languages, with no distinction between liberal arts and sciences. Foreign language examinations are held twice a year to deepen the reform of foreign language examinations. Foreign language examinations include written, listening, and speaking tests, and foreign language teaching is guided to focus on the development of application skills. Foreign language examinations should accumulate experience for gradually implementing standardized examinations in other subjects in the future. Zhejiang Province also proposed to scientifically design the content of questions in accordance with the requirements for talent selection in universities and national curriculum standards in order to enhance the foundational and comprehensive nature of knowledge, and to highlight the ability of students. What should be mainly tested is the ability of candidates to independently think and analyze problems and solve problems through using the knowledge they have gained.

It is worth noting that Shanghai Municipality carries out question setting and examination strictly following the principles of "what to teach and what to test," and clearly determines the difficulty, content, type of test papers, test time, etc. Shanghai focuses on strengthening the reform of examination question setting and on improving stability in the degree of difficulty and the appropriateness of the content to the curriculum standards in order to better promote the lifelong development of each student, promote the scientific selection and training of talents in universities, and maintain social fairness and justice. To this end, Shanghai has also established an education exam question setting committee composed of experts from all walks of life, clarifying the guiding ideology and basic ideas for reform of exam question setting, adhering to the orientation of quality education, focusing on passing on and promoting the outstanding traditional culture of China in exam questions, and focusing on examining a student's ability to think and apply what they have learned to analyze and solve problems to greatly reduce rote memorization. In the subject of Chinese language, increase the amount and score of open test questions, pay more attention to the examination of students' abilities of all kinds, stimulate the potential of students' creative thinking, and set up open test review groups in the college entrance examination papers. In the subject of English, a new listening and speaking test is added. The total score of the listening and speaking test is 10 points, and is recorded in the English college entrance examination score. The listening and speaking test focuses on the ability of students to "speak" English, and emphasizes that English teaching must not only enable students to memorize and write but also to listen and speak, and guide students from "not daring to speak" to "speaking" and "speaking confidently." In addition, a summary writing project was added to the English written exam, which examines the overall English reading and writing ability of candidates, and promotes English as a language to return to the standard of a tool for communication.

Table 6.2 Changes in the Content of College Entrance Examinations since Reform and Opening Up

Year	Exam Content
1977	The exam is mainly used to understand and master the status of basic knowledge and the ability to analyze and solve problems.
1984	Not going outside the scope of the middle school syllabus, and the requirements of exam question content does not exceed the scope of the unified textbooks used in middle schools.
1989	According to the syllabus, determine the reasonable knowledge level requirements, the difficulty of the test questions, and the proportion of various types of questions. Announcing the "examination instructions" for each subject and establishing a question bank for each subject.
1991	According to the syllabus of each middle school subject, the "exam instructions" are formulated as the basis for college entrance examination question setting. While examining basic knowledge, attention is put on testing ability, and the difficulty of test questions is adjusted without affecting the selection of the best students.
1999	Pay more attention to testing the candidates' abilities and quality. The scope of question setting follows the middle school syllabus, but is not limited to the syllabus. The design of the question setting for the exam increases applicability and ability. Question setting should transform from testing knowledge to testing ability, and the traditional closed discipline concept should be transformed. While examining ability in a particular discipline, there should be a focus on examining comprehensive ability across disciplines.
2010	Focus on the examination of comprehensive quality and ability. Based on the talent selection requirements of colleges and universities and the national curriculum standards, the national examination subject database is improved to ensure the scientific, guiding, and standardized nature of the national examination.

(Continued)

Table 6.2 Continued

Year	Exam Content
2014	In accordance with the requirements for talent selection in colleges and universities and national curriculum standards, scientifically design question setting content, strengthen foundational and overall knowledge, and focus on the ability of students to independently analyze and use the knowledge they have learned to analyze and solve problems. Qualification and grade tests were implemented on a pilot basis in Shanghai. The content of the qualification test is based on the basic curriculum requirements in the ordinary high school curriculum standards. Qualification examination results are a necessary condition for high school students obtaining graduation qualifications; the content of the level examinations is based on the basic and extended curriculum requirements in the general high school curriculum standards. Based on the requirements for talent selection in universities and national curriculum standards, Zhejiang Province designed the content of the proposition scientifically, strengthened its foundational nature and comprehensiveness, and emphasized its approach towards testing ability, mainly testing the ability of candidates to independently think and analyze problems and solve problems using the knowledge they have learned.

*Source of data: Compiled by the author based on relevant data.

III. Standardization of Examination Forms

The "standardization" of the college entrance examination is essentially a transformation from the traditional examination to the modern examination. It involves the content, form (question type), management, technology, and statistical analysis of the examination and is the overall reform of multiple working institutions within the exam. Through making exam question setting more scientific, the standardization of management, and the modernization of methods, the blindness and randomness of management of traditional exam question setting is overcome, minimizing errors and obtaining a true reflection of the candidates' grasp of exam content as fairly and accurately as possible (Han, 2009).

(1) Examination Standardization

In April 1978, Xiaoping Deng pointed out at the National Education Work Conference: Exams are an important method for testing the learning situation and effect of teaching, just as testing product quality is a necessary institution for ensuring the production level of a factory. It is necessary to earnestly study, test, and improve the content and form of examinations and improve their usefulness (He, 1998b: 1606). Since then, the Ministry of Education has held many domestic and foreign seminars on the reform of the college entrance examination. Experts have been invited to hold workshops to introduce the ideas and methods relating to making examinations more scientific and standardized. In 1985, the Ministry of Education began experimenting with reforming the college entrance examination in Guangdong Province to make it more standardized. The experiment started with mathematics and English, and gradually expanded to other subjects. In 1986, Guangdong, Shandong, Liaoning, and Guangxi jointly tested the standardized college entrance examination. In 1987, seven provinces participated in the trial. In 1988, this was expanded to sixteen provinces. In 1989, the standardized examinations introduced from the United States gradually summarized their characteristics after trials in Guangdong Province. After four years of successful tests, results were achieved in stages, initially showing the superiority of standardized examinations, and this was gradually promoted across the country.

To this end, in 1989, the State Education Commission issued "*The National Uniform Examination Standardization Implementation Plan for General Colleges and Universities*" (hereinafter referred to as *The Plan*), stating that this was an important reform and should be guided by educational measurement and educational statistics. Computers and other means were to be used to strictly control examination errors, examinations were to be made a more scientific and accurate measurement of candidates' knowledge and ability level, services were to be provided for colleges and universities to select the best students, information was to be provided for improving teaching, and a basis for educational decision-making was to be provided. *The Plan* also clarified the goals in two stages: 1989–1991, achieve initial goals based mainly on machine test papers; 1992–1995, meet the basic requirements of standardized examinations (He, 1998b: 2870–2871). In 1990, *The People's Daily* reported on the standardized examinations that began to be widely implemented that year, stating "this is the biggest reform in examination and marking methods in China since the Sui and Tang dynasties" (Xinhua News Agency, 1990). Since then, the standardized college entrance examination institution has gradually taken shape.

(2) Scientific Propositions

In 1987, in order to strengthen the management of test questions, the National Education Commission Examination Management Center was established. In 1990, it was renamed the National Education Commission Examination Center. According to the requirements of *The Plan* on standardization of college entrance examination question setting, a group of subject question setting experts hired by the Examination Center of the Ministry of Education set up question setting committees in English, physics, chemistry, Chinese language, mathematics, and other subjects starting from 1989. The duties of the question setting committee are: to make plans and suggestions for question setting work in that subject, recommend question setting and review experts, and preside over participating in scientific research topics related to the reform of college entrance examination question setting. Under the guidance of the subject's question setting committee, a relatively stable question setting group was formed. While completing the question setting tasks of a given year, the question setting groups for each subject thoroughly study the theory of educational measurement, and apply the results of the scientific research to question setting. At the same time, combined with the characteristics of the subject, it puts forward the objectives and requirements of examination for the subject, and constantly uses feedback information from the examinations to perfect the question setting scheme, and has achieved significant results in improving question setting technology and the quality of questions set.

In addition, the organization and management of question setting continues to be standardized. In 1995, the Examination Center worked out and formulated *The Regulations on Question Setting Work for National Uniform Examinations for General Colleges and Universities (Trial).* Afterwards, following continuous research on educational measurement theory, technology, and methods, on the basis of practice, the charter underwent improvement. After provincial question setting in 2004, based on a summation of the national and provincial question setting organization and management experience, the Ministry of Education promulgated *The Interim Administrative Measures for Question Setting in Different Provinces of the National Uniform Examinations for Ordinary Colleges and Universities* in 2006, controlling criteria for important indicators such as question setting principles, question setting guides, exam question difficulty, degree of differentiation, exam paper reliability, and validity (Han, 2017).

In July 2012, the National Education Examination Guidance Committee, composed of twenty-six experts in education, science and technology, economics, law, management, and other fields, was formally established. This was the first national-level education exam guidance committee established since the founding of the People's Republic of China (Han, 2017). New steps have been made once again in making exam question setting more scientific.

(3) Modernization of Methods

To achieve the standardization of examinations, we must also modernize the methods. After years of hard work, China's college entrance examination has made great progress in terms of modernization of methods. Beginning in 2001, online admission work was fully implemented for all ordinary universities and colleges across the country. After several years of exploration and practice, online admission has become the only way for colleges and universities to conduct admissions. In 1999, Guangxi took the lead in the nationwide trial of online assessment of the subject of English. Using computer network technology and electronic scanning technology, paper exams were scanned to generate electronic images. Multiple-choice questions were automatically scored based on information points filled in by candidates. Non-Multiple choice questions were reviewed manually on a computer. In 2012, all thirty-one provinces in China realized online scoring for all subjects in the college entrance examination, adopting unified national standards and norms, effectively reducing scoring errors. In 2007, the National Education Examination Guidance Platform for the College Entrance Examination was officially launched, and nearly half of the provinces and cities across the country conducted video communication, and the examination management platform began to initially take shape.

In 2011, the Ministry of Education and the Ministry of Finance issued *The Notice on Vigorously Promoting the Construction of National Education Examination Standardization Exam Sites*, which proposed that: by the end of 2012, 13,000 standardized exam sites, 3,500 secret exam paper rooms, and 365 examination command centers were to be completed nationwide. The main tasks included: construction and improvement of comprehensive exam business institutions, candidate identity verification institutions, cheat prevention and control institutions, video and network monitoring institutions, emergency command institutions, construction of standardized test site-related facilities, strengthening of institution construction, and team building. Through institution construction, a safe, real-time, and efficient national education examination operation institution was to be formed to comprehensively improve the national education examination management level and service quality. Subsequently, the Ministry of Education officially required that college entrance examinations located where the People's governments were located at the county level and above normally had to be set in a national education examination standardized exam site. The 2012 college entrance examinations were conducted in standardized examination rooms for the first time. Ever since, with the successive completion of standardized examination rooms in various places, the college entrance examination has been carried out in standardized examination rooms, an important step in the modernization of examination organization and management.

In 2006, the Ministry of Education formally established a network platform for the supervision and inspection of national education examination test rooms, and established video connections with provinces and cities across the country, and a nationwide unified examination management platform was initially formed. At the same time, most provinces and municipalities across the country began to use modern technical means to strengthen the management of test rooms, and the management of college entrance examination services gradually modernized.

SECTION 3 REFORM OF THE ENROLLMENT AND ADMISSIONS INSTITUTION

As a key part of college entrance examination reform, the reform of the enrollment and admissions institution plays a very important role in the reform of the college entrance examination. As early as March 1982, the Ministry of Education began to explore how to gradually combine the selection of freshmen in high schools and the delivery of graduates in middle schools to make up for the shortcomings of the chance nature of a single exam. The most widely criticized institution of China's college entrance examination is its "one exam determines a lifetime" mechanism. For a long time, test scores were the sole basis for admission. Since Reform and Opening Up, with the reform of the examination form and content, the enrollment and admissions institution has gradually changed from a method of solely looking at test scores to looking at multiple aspects. It is gradually exploring a multifaceted admissions mechanism based on the unified college entrance examination and high school academic examination results, and is based on comprehensive quality evaluation. The model of one exam score determining a person's life has started to be broken.

I. Reform of the Admissions Institution

Since the restoration and reconstruction of the college entrance examination institution, China's college entrance examination institution has gradually evolved from a single national unified enrollment method to a method of multiple aspects including unified enrollment, targeted students, commissioned students, and self-financing students, thereby merging the "dual-track institution" of the charging institution and admission score line into a "single-track institution" to define uniform admission scores and eliminate differences in charging standards.

When the college entrance examination was resumed in 1977, the Ministry of Education stipulated in *The Opinions on Enrollment Work for Higher Education in 1977* that after graduation, students would be uniformly distributed by the state except for "from the commune, back to the commune."[1] The State Planning Commission was responsible for formulating the distribution plan, while the Ministry of Education was responsible for formulating the allocation institution. In principle, the province, city, or autonomous region distributed the graduates from universities of that particular province, city, or autonomous region, and the state made appropriate adjustments as needed (He, 1998b: 1580). In 1983, enrollment work of higher education institutions gradually began to break the single national entrance examination mode, and implemented two kinds of plan forming including national task and regulatory plan entrustment and cultivation, gradually forming two different scoring standards and charging standards for admitting new students that are suited to the two different forms of plan. In May 1985, the CPC Central Committee issued *The Decision on the Reform of the Education Institution*, which clearly put forward the planning institution and the assignment of graduates to reform university enrollment, changing all colleges and universities uniformly carrying out enrollment according to the national plan and the method of graduates being allocated by the state, implementing the three methods of state planned enrollment, employer entrusted enrollment, and enrolling a small number of self-financed students outside the state plan. Students had to pay a certain amount of training fees. After graduation, they could be recommended by the school for employment, or they could work for themselves (He, 1998b: 2288). The purpose of this reform was changing the national uniform planned enrollment institution of the past, implementing the merging of national task plans and adjustment plans to gradually increase the percentage of commissioned recruitment and training and self-financed students at their own expense under the premise of ensuring the completion of the national task plan. The "dual track" enrollment institution had been formally established.

The "dual-track institution" has played a certain role in promoting the tapping of potential of schools, improving the conditions for running schools, and solving the urgent need for social talents. However, with the gradual establishment of the socialist market economy institution and the reform of the personnel institution, the disadvantages of the "dual-track institution" have become increasingly prominent. In April 1994, the State Education Commission pointed out in *The Opinions on Piloting Further Reform of the Enrollment and Employment Institution for Graduates of Ordinary Colleges and Universities* that when enrolling students, higher education institutions should announce their enrollment plans by province, municipality, school, and degree major before candidates submit their wishes and clearly announce the setting of school, and degree major fee standards and student awards and loans for candidates for candidates to use as a reference. Only one minimum control score line is defined for the same school, and score lines are no longer delineated based on the national task and regulatory plan. At the same time, it was pointed out that the pilot colleges and universities that carry out the "combination" pilot reform of enrollment must be in step, and cannot recruit new students using both new and old forms at the same level (He, 1998c: 3633). In July of the same year, the Central Committee of the Communist Party of China and the State Council issued *The Outline of China's Education Reform and Development*, which clearly stated that the reform of enrollment fees and graduate employment institutions for colleges and universities, secondary schools, and technical schools should be actively promoted, gradually realizing the institution of students paying their own fees for university and most graduates choosing their own profession. In 1997, most colleges and majors fully implemented enrollment consolidation and fees. After 2000, normal colleges and majors also began to charge fees, and the admissions reform was fully completed.

II. The Establishment of a Diverse Admissions Model

With the development of the economy and society and the continuous updating of educational concepts, the disadvantages of China's current admissions method, which uses the college entrance examination score as its sole criterion, have gradually become apparent. With the gradual improvement of the admissions institution, the "have the last word" admission model has been gradually broken, and the multi-entry admission mode has been gradually established and the college entrance examination admission mode has changed from a "lone wooden bridge" into an "overpass."

In 2001, the State Council issued *The Decision of the State Council on the Reform and Development of Basic Education*, which proposed that in order to reform the examination evaluation and admissions selection institution, it is necessary to strengthen the examination of students' abilities and qualities; reform the content of college entrance examinations; explore multiple opportunities, two-way choices, comprehensive evaluation examinations, and selection methods; and promote reform of college admissions examinations and selection institutions according to the principles of helping colleges select talents, helping middle schools implement quality education, and helping expand the autonomy of colleges and universities in student enrollment examinations. Students with special talents and outstanding achievements in scientific research, invention, and other fields can study at colleges and universities without needing to sit the entrance examination (He, 2003: 890).

In 2004, the State Council approved the Ministry of Education's *The Education Revitalization Action Plan 2003–2007*, and proposed to promote the reform of the college entrance examination institution, and further establish an admissions institution for colleges and universities combining unified examination-oriented, diversified examinations and diverse selection and admission, school self-discipline, government macro guidance, and effective social supervision (He, 2010: 336). In July 2010, *The National Medium-and-Long-Term Education Reform and Development Plan Outline (2010–2020)* proposed that, in accordance with the principles of being conducive to the scientific selection of talents, promoting the healthy development of students, and maintaining social equity, explore relatively separate methods for admissions and examinations with the government managing at the macro level, professional organizations organizing and implementing, schools enrolling students independently in accordance with the law, students making choices on multiple occasions, and gradually forming a classification examination, comprehensive evaluation, and multiple admissions examination admission institution. The allocation method of enrollment quotas and enrollment methods for colleges and universities will be improved, and a multifaceted admission mechanism that is conducive to the fairness of admission opportunities and the selection of outstanding talents will be established and improved. Undergraduate enrollment in ordinary colleges and universities uses a unified entrance examination as its basic method, combined with the academic level examination and comprehensive quality evaluation, and selects the best for admission. For those who have clear specialties and who meet the requirements of school training, they will be admitted on the basis of the results of interviews or tests; those who are fully developed in high school and perform well are recommended for admission; those who meet the requirements and voluntarily find employment in industries and regions required by the state shall sign an agreement to implement targeted admission; establish special procedures for talents who have made outstanding contributions or have special talents in practical positions, and make exceptional admissions. In November 2013, *The Decision of the Central Committee of the Communist Party of China on Several Major Issues Concerning Comprehensively Deepening Reform* once again proposed that a comprehensive evaluation and admission mechanism for ordinary colleges and universities based on the unified assessment of college entrance examination and senior high school academic performance exam should be gradually implemented.

In 2014, *The State Council's Implementation Opinions on Deepening the Reform of the Examination Admission Institution* clearly stated that the admissions mechanism should be reformed. A multifaceted admission mechanism based on the results of the unified college entrance examination and senior high school proficiency examination was to be explored with reference to comprehensive quality evaluation. Colleges and universities should, according to their own school running positioning and professional training goals, study and put forward high school subject examination registration requirements for candidates and comprehensive quality evaluation and use methods, and announce to them to society in advance; improving admission methods; and promoting the method of filling in voluntary reports after the college entrance examination results are announced; create conditions to gradually cancel college admissions groups; improve the method of file acceptance; advance and improve the method of parallel voluntary file submission; and increase the two-way choice opportunities for colleges and students. From 2015, batch reform pilots will be conducted in provinces that meet the conditions. According to the unified deployment of the state, Shanghai and Zhejiang announced reform plans for the college entrance examination and conducted useful explorations in the admissions mode.

> Reform and unify the admissions model for college entrance examinations and subject requirements for college and university admissions. Ordinary undergraduate colleges and

universities can independently propose a range of elective subjects, but no more than three, from the six major high school level examination subjects of ideology and politics, history, geography, physics, chemistry, and life sciences according to the characteristics and positioning of the school and the training needs for professional talent in each subject. Students who meet the requirements in any one of the elective subjects are eligible for admission. When it comes to colleges and universities that do not require elective subjects, there will be no restrictions on which subject the student can choose when applying for that school. For students who meet the application requirements and meet the school's submitted score line, colleges and universities can propose priority admission conditions by subject (or degree majors). The unified admissions model of colleges and universities can be improved. Starting from 2016, the first and second batches of undergraduate students will be combined, and parallel voluntary submission and admission will be implemented by schools according to the student's total college entrance examination score and the college or university applied for. On this basis, explore the feasibility of students choosing multiple times and being admitted to multiple colleges and universities, and increase the two-way choice opportunities between colleges and students.

"Implementation Plan for Comprehensive Reform of University Deepening Examination Admission in Shanghai"

Colleges and universities determine the range of elective subjects according to their own school orientation and professional training goals, but this cannot exceed three subjects, and they are to be announced to society two years prior to enrollment; candidates need only one elective within the scope of those required by the college or university to apply for a major (subject). If the university does not determine the scope of elective subjects, candidates have no subject restrictions when applying. Colleges and universities can put forward requirements for candidates' comprehensive quality evaluation at the high school stage as a reference for admission. The candidate's aspiration consists of "degree major + school". Admission is not split into groups, and professional parallel submission is implemented. The filling in of aspiration and submission files will be conducted in stages according to the results of the candidates.

"Zhejiang Province Pilot Scheme on Deepening the Comprehensive Reform of the College Entrance Examination Institution"

One of the highlights of the new college entrance examination plan is the implementation of a "two bases, one reference" multifaceted admissions mechanism, which is based on unified college entrance examination results, high school academic proficiency test results, and reference to high school students' comprehensive quality evaluation information for admission. For candidates, there is an expanded choice in the admissions process and candidates are allowed to "be admitted to a college or university according to their wishes" to the greatest extent possible, and for colleges and universities, from "admitting students according to test scores" to "admitting students based on scores + what they are like as a person" to achieving "precise matching" between colleges and candidates.

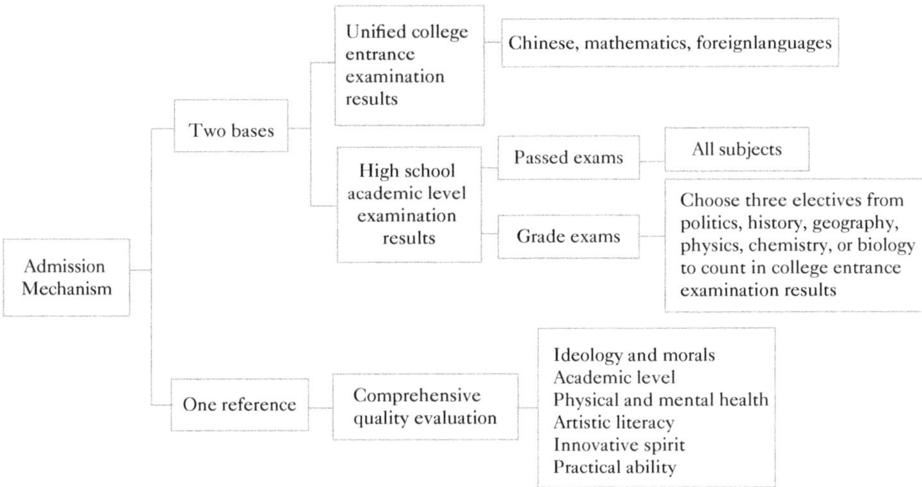

Figure 6.2 Multiple Admission Mechanism

From the perspective of Shanghai, admissions colleges and universities will conduct undergraduate admissions in groups in accordance with the "professional group of colleges" method. Colleges and universities form a number of "academic professional groups" according to the elective subject requirements for each degree major. An "academic professional group" includes a number of different degree majors. As a result, the number of candidates in regular groups of aspiring undergraduates has changed from a maximum of ten "academic" volunteers in the past to a maximum of twenty-four "academic professional group" volunteers. From the perspective of Zhejiang, colleges and universities will not be applied for and students will not be admitted in batches, and applications and admissions will be made in a segmented manner in accordance with the candidate's exam results. General aspirations will be filled in in three segments from high to low scores based on the candidate's exam results. The top 20% of the candidates are classified as the first segment, and the top 60% and the top 90% are classified as the second and third segments, respectively. Candidates can apply for no more than eighty majors at a time.

III. Improvement of the Independent Admissions Institution

In order to further explore a diverse and flexible admissions institution, in January 1993, the State Council approved the State Education Commission's *Opinions on Accelerating Reform and Actively Developing General Higher Education*, proposing: After approval, schools or degree majors with special requirements in terms of training talents may organize admissions examinations by institution or region either jointly or separately, and enroll new students in accordance with relevant regulations (He, 2010: 3452). In the same year, the Shanghai University of Technology and other universities started pilot reform in accordance with the purpose of "expanding the autonomy of college and university admissions and implementing diversified selection of freshmen," with content including: Under the macro control of the state and Shanghai admissions scale, schools may independently determine and adjust the school's admissions plan and the number of students in each major according to the needs of society, school running conditions and the status of student sources; based on the unified college entrance examination, schools may independently determine examination subjects according to the requirements of different majors, with no less than three; based on the principles of comprehensive examination of moral, intellectual, and physical, admission by merit, fair competition, and fair selection, the admission standards and methods are determined independently. While insisting on using the college entrance examination results as the main admission basis, the school may use the results of the high school examination, additional examinations, etc., and certificates that reflect a kind of ability the candidate has as a multivariate basis for admission, and students with special talents can be admitted in exceptional circumstances (Jin & Hu, 1993).

Since then, the Ministry of Education and some provinces and cities have also started similar pilot reform work. On the basis of the previous reforms, in 2003, the Ministry of Education approved twenty-two colleges and universities including Peking University to begin pilot programs for independent selection and admission reform. Colleges and universities conduct initial selection based on independent examinations and interviews. Candidates who have been selected participate in the national unified exam and if their score exceeds the school's admission control score of the same batch, the school may enroll them. The enrollment ratio is within 5% of the school's annual undergraduate admissions plan (He, 2010: 47). In 2004, there were six new autonomous admissions institutions: Xi'an Jiaotong University, Dalian University of Technology, Northeastern University, Wuhan University, Central China Normal University, and South China University of Technology. In 2005, fourteen new admissions institutions were added. In 2006, eleven autonomous colleges and universities were added. In 2007, six autonomous colleges and universities were added. In 2017, ninety-five colleges and universities nationwide had the qualifications for autonomous admissions pilots. This reform has given universities more autonomy in enrollment, expanded the operating space for selecting talents, and at the same time has had a positive guiding effect on the implementation of quality education in middle schools. In addition to exploring the enrollment of outstanding students, autonomous enrollment has also conducted reform experiments at college-level vocational colleges. In 2006, Beijing and Shanghai piloted independent enrollment in a number of higher vocational colleges, using the "written test + interview" method, relying completely on independent question setting and independent determination of admission results. This truly is independent selection and admission with real significance. The admission criteria are completely different depending on the school and major.

In 2014, the Ministry of Education issued *The Opinions on Further Improving and Standardizing the Pilot Work of Independent Enrollment of Colleges and Universities*, calling for further improvement of admissions procedures, reasonable determination of assessment content and form, standardization and disclosure of autonomous admissions methods, assessment procedures, and admission results. The scale of autonomous enrollment was to be strictly controlled so that the scope of pilot universities and the enrollment ratio was not expanded in the current period. Starting from 2015, all pilot colleges and universities' independent admissions assessments are carried out after the college entrance examination ends and before the results of the college entrance examination are announced. From 2016, all colleges and universities' independent enrollment registrations must be registered on the Sunshine College Entrance Examination platform. Independent admission has gradually realized transparency and standardization.

NOTE

1 "From the commune, back to the commune" was the idea that students returned to the commune that they went to university from after graduation.

REFERENCES

Bian, X. (2015). A comparative study of the new round of college entrance examination reform in Zhejiang and Shanghai. *China Examination*, *02*, 3–7 (in Chinese).

Chen, W. (2005). Practice and exploration of the reform of college entrance examination subject setting. *Theory and Practice of Education*, *20*, 24–26 (in Chinese).

Han, J. (2009). China's college entrance examination from traditional to modern – Reform and development of "Standardized Examinations ". *Examination Research*, *04*, 30–41 (in Chinese).

Han, J. (2017). Fair and scientific: The pursuit for value in the reform of college entrance examination question setting. *China Examination*, *06*, 6–11, 43 (in Chinese).

He, D. (Ed.) (1998a). *The educational documents of the People's Republic of China (1949–1975)*. Haikou: Hainan Publishing House (in Chinese).

He, D. (Ed.) (1998b). *Important education documents of the People's Republic of China (1976–1990)*. Haikou: Hainan Publishing House (in Chinese).

He, D. (Ed.) (1998c). *The educational documents of the People's Republic of China (1991–1997)*. Haikou: Hainan Publishing House (in Chinese).

He, D. (Ed.) (2003). *The educational documents of the People's Republic of China (1998–2002)*. Haikou: Hainan Publishing House (in Chinese).
He, D. (Ed.) (2010). *The educational documents of the People's Republic of China (2003–2008)*. Beijing: New World Press (in Chinese).
Hu, H. (2014). From looking solely at "Cold Scores" to focusing on "Living People": China's education reform begins. Retrieved from http://edu.people.com.cn/n/2014/1216/c1053-26219405.html (in Chinese).
Jin, B., & Hu, R. (1993). Unified examination independent enrollment: Reflections on the reform of the enrollment examination system in ordinary Shanghai Universities. *Shanghai Higher Education Research*, *04*, 46–50 (in Chinese).
Liu, H. (2007). The college entrance examination of 1977, an unprecedented admissions test. *Education Development Research*, *13*, 1–5 (in Chinese).
Liu, H. (2017). The college entrance examination of 1977, an unprecedented admissions test. Retrieved from http://www.edu.cn/gaokao30_5897/20070717/t20070717_243323.shtml (in Chinese).
Liu, H., et al. (2002). *The history of examination development in China*. Wuhan: Central China Normal University Press (in Chinese).
The Hebei Provincial Education Examination Institute (Ed.). (1998). *30 Years of the College Entrance Examination in Hebei* … Beijing: Social Science Literature Press (in Chinese).
The People's Government of Zhejiang Province of PRC. (2017). *Several opinions of the People's government of Zhejiang province on further deepening the comprehensive reform of the college entrance examination* (Zhejiang Government [2017] No. 45). Retrieved from http://www.zj.gov.cn/art/2017/11/29/art_32431_295370.html (in Chinese).
The People's Government of Shanghai Municipal of PRC. (2018). *Notice on printing and distributing "The Several Opinions on Further Deepening the Pilot Work of Comprehensive Reform of the College Entrance Examination in this Municipality"* (Shanghai Government [2018] No. 14). http://www.shanghai.gov.cn/nw43425/20200824/0001-43425_55801.html (in Chinese).
Wei, G. (2008). Research on the reform of China's college entrance examination system since 1977. Doctoral Dissertation of Hebei University (in Chinese).
Wu, Q. (2017). Baosheng Chen, Minister of Education: The College Entrance Examination System Will Usher in its Largest Reform in History. Retrieved from http://www.sohu.com/a/199147912_118622 (in Chinese).
Xinhua News Agency. (1977). The major reform of the enrollment of colleges and universities is undergoing. *The People's Daily*. October 21 (in Chinese).
Xinhua News Agency. (1990). China's major changes in examination and marking methods: The first comprehensive implementation of standardized examinations in the college entrance examination in 1990. *The People's Daily*, July 6 (in Chinese).
Xiong, B. (2017). College entrance examination reform: From 'Cold Scores' to 'Living People'. Retrieved from http://www.ce.cn/xwzx/gnsz/szyw/201710/21/t20171021_26600457.shtml (in Chinese).
Zhang, J. (2017). The 2018 Jiangxi college entrance examination reform plan: Liberal arts and science not separate, English exams taken twice Retrieved from http://edu.people.com.cn/n1/2017/1019/c1053-29597282.html (reading time: October 15, 2017) (in Chinese).

CHAPTER SEVEN

The Education Supervision Institution

WENJIE YANG

The focus on the quality of education and supervision and evaluation of schools has aroused more and more attention in many countries and regions in the world including China (Lee et al., 2008). In the UK, education supervision is committed to "pursuing excellence in supervising and managing social care and education for children and adolescents, and providing skills training for students of all ages to raise standards and improve lives" (The Office for Standards in Education, 2009: 4). The function of education supervision has changed from inspection and supervision to providing services to schools and teachers. In the United States, the role of education supervision has changed from inspection and supervision to providing services to schools and teachers since the 1930s. Unlike many developed countries, where school self-assessment is more important than administrative supervision, since the restoration and reconstruction of the education supervision institution in 1986, China has established a supervisory institution with functions of supervision and direction. Over the past forty years of Reform and Opening Up, the content and scope of education supervision has gradually expanded, the supervision function has been continuously strengthened, education supervision organizations have moved from dependency to independence, the professional quality of education supervision personnel has continued to improve, education supervision has extended from education results to the education process, and the authority of education supervision has gradually strengthened. With the continuous advancement of China's education governance institution and governance modernization, the functions and mission of education supervision have been undergoing unprecedented changes. In September 2017, the General Office of the Central Committee of the Communist Party of China and the General Office of the State Council issued *The Opinions on Deepening the Reform of Education Institutions and Mechanisms*, proposing: "To improve the education supervision institution, encourage education supervision institutions to perform their functions independently, implement the statutory responsibilities of supervision and evaluation, inspection and acceptance, and quality monitoring, improve the supervision management institution, improve the level of supervision performance, strengthen the supervision of local governments at all levels in accordance with the law, strengthen the supervision of schools in carrying out standardized school running, and strengthen the use of supervision results." However, education supervision itself still has many problems and insufficiencies: Against the background of education governance ability and institution construction, there is still a long way to go in terms of building an education supervision and evaluation institution that focuses on education supervision and has multiple participants.

The content of this chapter is an analysis of the historical changes that have taken place in the education institution since Reform and Opening Up began by looking at a large number of policy texts to straighten out the process of continuous improvement of the education supervision institution with Chinese characteristics; recognizing the importance of supervisory status and reform in the new era through changes in the content, functions, and institutional settings of education supervision at different stages; against the background of advancing the modernization of the education governance institution and education governance capacity, perfecting the current mechanism of education supervision, and helping the education supervision institution better serve the development of education through the reform of the mechanisms of the education supervision institution.

SECTION 1 DEVELOPMENT HISTORY OF EDUCATION SUPERVISION REFORM

China's education supervision institution began with modern inspection institution. At the beginning of the 20th century, China's modern education supervision institution began to take shape. After the Revolution of 1911, the state institution was restructured, and the Ministry of Learning became the MOE. In 1913, MOE published *The Education Supervision Regulations* and other documents. In April 1918, China's earliest unified local inspection regulations, *The Provincial Inspection Regulations* and *The County Inspection Regulations* were issued. Inspection institutions were set up at the central, provincial (municipal), and county levels, and education inspection networks at three levels were gradually established.

In 1926, the National Government set up an Education Administration Committee with an Administrative Affairs Bureau. A proposal to create an "Education Inspection Office" within the bureau was made, but this was not realized for some reason. School inspection workers were then formally known as "inspectors," and the term "inspector" has been formally used since then. In 1927, the MOE was replaced by a college institution, and supervision was temporarily abolished. In 1929, the supervision institution and institution were restored and established again. From 1929 to 1931, the National Government promulgated *The Supervision Regulations* and *The Details of the Supervision Regulations*, and gradually formed a relatively complete supervision institution. After the founding of the People's Republic of China, the Party and government attached great importance to education supervision. In 1949, the newly established the MOE of the Central People's Government set up a special supervision department and set up education supervision offices or supervision and guidance offices (sections, groups) in education administration departments at all levels in all provinces, municipalities, and counties. In April 1955, the MOE issued a notice on strengthening supervision and guidance. However, due to political interference and the influence of "leftist" ideology, education supervision was weakened or even abolished. Since the restoration and reconstruction of China's modern education supervision institution began in 1977, an education supervision institution with Chinese characteristics gradually formed with a combination of administration and education supervision, focusing on evaluation and monitoring, and covering all types of education at all levels. A complex process played out over this period, which can be roughly divided into the following stages.

I. Recovery and Reconstruction of the Education Supervision Institution

After the Third Plenary Session of the 11th Central Committee of the Communist Party of China, China's economic and political situation gradually improved, and the education institution was restored and developed. This made more and more education managers realize the importance of restoring the education supervision institution. In September 1977, Comrade Deng Xiaoping clearly stated in a conversation with comrades at the head of MOE: "We need to improve the institutions of MOE. We need to find some people around the age of 40 to go to schools every day. We should get 40 people, with at least 20 walking around the school. It will be just like being a soldier in an army; they need to go to school and understand the situation, monitor the implementation of plans, policies and the like, and then come back and make a report. This is the only way to get a reflection of the situation so that problems can be solved swiftly" (He, 2003: 1344). In order to implement Comrade Deng Xiaoping's instructions, in early 1978, on the recommendation of the then Deputy Prime Minister Wang Zhen, the four senior comrades Wang Jiqing, Su Lingyang, Yao Wen, and Yang Bin went to the MOE to serve as supervisors, which was directly led by the Minister of Education. At this time, the inspection and guidance department was set up in the general education bureau, office, and department. Although some education inspection and guidance work was carried out, it was mainly responsible for piecemeal work, making it difficult to systematically control and deal with the problems that arose in practice in education in a targeted manner. At the same time, inspection and guidance personnel were set up only in the central government. Limitations in numbers and regions made work inefficient, making it impossible to conduct comprehensive inspections of education in other provinces, municipalities, and counties. In order to improve the shortcomings of inspection and guidance work at that time, and to further promote the restoration and construction of the education supervision institution, in July 1983, at the National General Education Work Conference, the MOE came up with *The Opinions on Establishing a General Education Inspection Institution* and requested for education administration departments at all levels above the county level to set up supervision agencies, which were to be piloted first and then gradually implemented.

From 1984 to 1985, Guangzhou, Gansu, Shenyang, Chongqing, Nanjing, and other provinces and cities successively established or restored inspection (supervision) guidance bureaus, and also carried out some inspection (supervision) and guidance work. During this period, Comrade Deng Xiaoping contributed to the restoration of the education supervision and guidance institution and became the founder of building an education supervision institution with Chinese characteristics. Although work at this stage was focused on restorative work, public opinion and politics made the necessary preparations for the establishment of an educational supervision institution with Chinese characteristics and laid an important foundation for the reconstruction of the education supervision institution (MOE, 2003).

On the basis of restoring the education supervision and guidance institution, and in accordance with the needs of China's socialist education institution construction and the development of education, China began to rebuild its education supervision and guidance institution. In the five years from 1986 to 1991, the Education Supervision and Guidance Department was established; *The Interim Provisions on Education Supervision* were issued as the first departmental regulatory document after the reconstruction of the education supervision and guidance institution; the issue of team building for supervision was also put on the agenda.

In September 1986, the General Office of the State Council approved *The Opinions on Certain Problems Regarding the Implementation of The Compulsory Education Law* of the National Education Commission, the National Planning Commission, the Ministry of Finance, and the Ministry of Labor and Personnel, clearly stating that "basic education supervision (inspection and guidance) shall be gradually established" and further stipulated: "The state and local governments will gradually establish basic education supervision (inspection) institutions to be responsible for comprehensive inspection, supervision and guidance on the implementation of compulsory education nationwide or in the region, and coordinate with the local people's government to handle issues related to the implementation of compulsory education." In October of the same year, the State Council approved the renaming of the Inspection and Guidance Department to the National Education Supervision Department, marking the beginning of the official reconstruction of China's education supervision institution.

In order to promote the establishment of education supervision institutions in various places, at the end of 1986, the State Education Commission convened a supervision work seminar and issued the (87) Education Supervision 001 document, which clearly stated that the current main task is promoting the establishment of a national education institution supervision mechanism. At the same time, the nature and tasks of the supervisory organization, the conditions for the appointment of supervision, the functions and powers of various supervision personnel, the establishment of supervision organizations at all levels, the training of supervision personnel, and other detailed provisions were made. In September 1988, the State Education Commission and the Ministry of Personnel jointly issued "The Notice on Problems with Establishing Education Supervision Institutions," requiring all People's governments at or above the county level to establish education supervision institutions or provide full-time education supervision personnel in their education administration departments. Corresponding provisions have also been made for measures used to resolve the establishment of educational supervision institutions. The issuance of the above two important documents has deepened the understanding of education supervision work in various places, and has also promoted the establishment of education supervision organizations at all levels and the development of supervision work in various places. Subsequently, all provinces, municipalities, and counties, in accordance with local conditions, carried out a series of explorations that yielded fruitful efforts.

At the same time, in order to ensure that education supervision had laws and rules to follow, legislation was made to promote education supervision. In April 1991, the State Education Commission issued *The Interim Provisions on Education Supervision*. As the first regulatory document on the education supervision institution since the founding of the People's Republic of China, *The Interim Provisions* clarified that the essential attribute of education supervision is administrative supervision over education work, and unified and improved awareness of supervision by government at all levels, education administration departments, and schools (Tu, 2015: 57).

II. The Preliminary Formation of the Education Supervision Institution with Chinese Characteristics

After the 1990s, with the transformation of the government's public functions and the people's increasing attention to the quality of education and teaching, marked by the establishment of the "two basics" and "two comprehensives" supervision and evaluation mechanism, this stage was the period when the construction of the education supervision institution was very productive and had the widest social impact since the Reform and Opening Up. At the same time, it was also the key period for continuous growth and development of education supervision institutions and teams and the construction of a socialist education supervision institution with Chinese characteristics.

Different from Western developed countries, in accordance with the circumstances of education in China, China constructed a supervision institution with Chinese characteristics, which mainly involves supervision of administration and learning. Since the restoration and reconstruction of the supervision institution, supervision dominated for a period of time. After the 1990s, a transition from extended supervision mainly based on supervision of administration to intensive supervision mainly based on supervision of learning began. In February 1993, the Central Committee of the Communist Party of China and the State Council issued *The Outline of China's Education Reform and Development* proposing: "Governments at all levels must conscientiously implement *The Compulsory Education Law of the People's Republic of China* and its detailed provisions, and establish inspection, supervision, and reward and punishment institutions to ensure the implementation of the compulsory education law. Education administrations at all levels should consider inspection and evaluation of school quality to be a regular task. They must strengthen the supervision team, improve the supervision institution, and strengthen the inspection and guidance of the work and education quality of primary and secondary schools." This period of supervision was based on working with the National People's Congress to check the implementation of *The Compulsory Education Law*. It examined the problems in compulsory education across the country, including the wages of teachers in rural compulsory education, the cost of enrolling children from poor families, and guarantees of education funding. Supervision and guidance played an important role in this.

After 1994, with the development of education and the prominent role of education supervision, the number of forms of education included in the scope of supervision continued to increase, extending from a relatively monotonous stage of compulsory education to all types of secondary and lower schools. For example, the 1996 "Kindergarten Work Regulations" clearly states that kindergartens receive inspection, supervision, and guidance from education supervisors higher up. At the same time, with the gradual recovery and development of higher education, the evaluation of higher education was also included in the scope of supervision, evaluation, and monitoring. *The Higher Education Law of the People's Republic of China*, promulgated in 1998, clearly states that the level of education and quality of higher education receives supervision and evaluation from education administration departments.

In 1993, institutions of the State Council underwent reform, the Central Compilation Committee approved the establishment of the Education Supervision and Guidance Group of the State Education Commission, and the Education Supervision and Guidance Group Bureau attached to the Department of Basic Education. The following year, with the review of the Central Compilation Committee and the approval of the State Council, a national education supervision group was formally established to strengthen the macro management and supervision of education in various regions and departments, and the status of education supervision work continuously improved. In July 1998, the State Council approved and issued *The Provisions on the Functional Allocation, Internal Organizations, and Staffing of MOE*, and approved the establishment of an independent Education Supervision and Guidance Office by MOE, one of the eighteen functional divisions of the MOE.

In addition to this, the construction of local education institutions and teams has also been continuously strengthened. By 1998, China had basically formed an education supervision network institution covering the central, provincial, municipal, and county levels. A combination of full-time and part-time education supervision teams opened a new chapter in the construction of China's education supervision institution.

III. Building a Comprehensive Education Supervision and Guidance Institution with Chinese Characteristics

After entering the 21st century, the state has attached importance to the reform and development of basic education. In order to further strengthen and improve the education supervision institution, education supervision has entered a stage of comprehensive development. The content of education supervision has undergone a new change, and the scope of supervision has achieved full coverage. Specifically, in October of 2012, the State implemented *The Education Supervision Regulations*, which fully reflected the idea that "a strong country must strengthen education, a strong country first strengthens education." The state's will to give priority to the development of education and the deepening of education institution reform, and the determination to deepen reform of the education institution and promote managing education in accordance with the law, signifies that the construction of an education supervision institution with Chinese characteristics reached a new height (Zhang, 2012).

The content of education supervision realized a new transformation from supervision of education to a combination of administration and education supervision with an emphasis on evaluation and monitoring. In 2003, the Basic Education Curriculum and Textbook Development Center of the MOE launched "The Establishment of an Analysis, Feedback and guidance institution for Academic Quality of Primary and Middle School Students," and established a set of three level institutions for provincial-, municipal-, and county-level report feedback institutions to comprehensively and systematically improve the monitoring of academic quality of primary and secondary school students (Fu, 2008). The Third Plenary Session of the 18th Central Committee of the Communist Party of China made the decision to deepen comprehensive reform in the field of education, clearly requiring the strengthening of national education supervision, and entrusting social organizations to conduct education evaluation and testing. Correspondingly, in 2014 the Education Supervision Committee Bureau of the State Council issued *The Notice on Deepening Educational Supervision Reform and Transforming the Education Management Method.* On the basis of education administration and learning supervision, it was clearly stated that another work content of education supervision—evaluation and monitoring—requires the establishment of a professional education quality evaluation and monitoring institution under the centralized management of education supervision departments, the provision of services by professional institutions, and the participation of various social organizations for scientific, systematic, and authoritative evaluation and monitoring of all types of education at all levels in order to provide a basis and support point for improving education and teaching, management, and decision-making. In 2017, *The State Council's Notice on Printing and Distribution of 'The Thirteenth Five-Year Plan' for National Education Development* and *The Notice of the General Office of the State Council on the Printing and Distribution of the Evaluation Methods for Provincial People's Governments to Perform Responsibilities in Education* further proposed a comprehensive evaluation and monitoring institution. As a result, education assessment and monitoring, as a "member" of education supervision, was defined in the education supervision institution by policy documents and became an integral part of the education supervision institution.

At the same time, the scope of supervision covered all types of schools at all levels. *The Education Supervision Regulations* clearly stated that all types of education at all levels are included in the scope of supervision, and the targets of supervision are extended to lower-level governments and their functional departments, schools, and educational institutions at all levels. Regulations for other forms of education each use supervision and evaluation as an important means of supervising the quality of a school's education and detailed explanations are given. For example, in 2011, the MOE issued *The Measures for Supervision and Evaluation of Secondary Vocational Education*, which elaborated detailed regulations on the indicators system, standards, policies and institutions, funding, and conditions for running schools for secondary vocational schools. In 2013, *The Private Education Promotion Law* (2013 amendment) pointed out that the education administration department and relevant departments should guide the education and teaching work and teacher training of private schools. At the same time, the education administration department and relevant departments supervise private schools in accordance with the law to promote the improvement of school running quality; social intermediary organizations are organized or entrusted to evaluate the level of running schools and the quality of education, and the results of the evaluation to society are announced. In addition, in July 2016, documents such as *The Notice of MOE on Printing and Distributing "The Interim Measures for the Supervision of School Management"* and other documents were issued, and the construction of the education supervision team was improved further.

Since 2001, the state has focused on building an education supervision institution with Chinese characteristics from the aspects of the internal mechanisms of the supervising and guiding institutions. In 2016, with the approval of the Office of the Central Organization Staffing Committee, the Education Supervision and Guidance Group Office was renamed the Education Supervision and Guidance Bureau, and the Education Supervision and Guidance Committee Bureau of the State Council was added. With the establishment of an institution of education supervision, starting from the aspects of improving education supervision institutions in accordance with the law, improving the mechanism of access to supervision, assessment, appointment management and other aspects, and strengthening the construction of education supervision teams, a supervision institution for local governments was established to perform education duties and improve a special supervision institution for major education policies. At the same time, the education supervision report release institution has been improved to make education supervision and guidance more open and accountable. The supervision and guidance institution was to be further improved and full play given to the role of supervision and guidance in promoting education reform and development. At present, China has formed a network of education supervision at the central, provincial, municipal, and county levels, with 17,500 full-time supervisors, 103,700 part-time supervisors, and 14,500 supervisors. Supervision functions have been gradually improved (Lu, 2017), leading education work at all stages, with an education supervision institution based on the three major institutions of supervision of administration, supervision of learning, and evaluation and monitoring.

SECTION 2 THE STRATEGIC POSITION OF EDUCATION SUPERVISION AND GUIDANCE

Since Reform and Opening Up, the education supervision and guidance institution has continuously changed and improved with the progress of society and the development of education. Education supervision and guidance practice and exploration has achieved remarkable results and accumulated rich experience. As an important measure in improving the efficiency of education management and promoting the improvement of education quality, in the current new era of education reform, the status of the education supervision and guidance institution cannot be shaken. Specifically, during the process of advancing the education governance institution and the capacity building of education governance, the construction of an education supervision and evaluation institution that focuses on education supervision and governance and the participation of multiple parties ensures the scientific nature, standardization, and objectification of education evaluation results, and is an important means in the democratization and socialization of participating subjects.

I. Education Supervision and Guidance in Transformation

Since the reconstruction of the education supervision and guidance institution, with the continuous deepening of education reform, the education supervision and guidance institution has been continuously improved in its transformation. Education supervision and guidance institutions are becoming independent, education supervision and guidance personnel are more specialized, education supervision is more focused on the education process, the authority of education supervision is further strengthened, and various changes have underscored that the education supervision and guidance institution is constantly moving towards professionalism, standardization, and a more scientific nature. This has provided important support in constantly promoting education management for the government, improvement in school running for schools, and improvement in teaching for teachers.

(1) The Path of Education Supervision and Guidance Organizations from Dependency to Independence

Strengthening education supervision and guidance is a necessary part of reforming and developing basic education (Chen, 1995). As a key part of the education institution, the reasonable formation of institutions directly affects the implementation and effectiveness of education supervision and guidance and has an important role in deepening education governance reform (Le, 2015). Since Reform and Opening Up, China has gradually established a relatively complete network of supervision agencies at the central, provincial, municipal, and county levels. In general, the construction of China's supervision and guidance institutions has continued to advance, and education supervision and guidance institutions have gradually become independent from education administration departments, which has strengthened the execution of supervision and ensured the smooth development of supervision and guidance work.

Since the Third Plenary Session of the Eleventh Central Committee of PRC in 1977, education supervision and guidance institutions at the central level have been through five important successive changes. The first time was in 1984 when the State Council approved the establishment of an inspection and guidance office by the MOE, which was mainly responsible for inspecting and guiding general education work across the country (Huang, 2011: 30). The second time was in 1986 when the MOE's Inspection and Guidance office was renamed the Supervision and Guidance Division of the State Education Commission, and the status of supervision and guidance agencies was improved. The third time was in 1993 when the Education Supervision and Guidance Bureau of the State Education Commission was established, the Education Supervision and Guidance Group Bureau was set up, and it was linked to the Basic Education Division. The fourth time was in 2000 when the State Commission Office for Public Sector Reform issued *The Reply on the Renaming of the Education Supervision and Guidance Committee of the State Education Commission*, in which it agreed to rename the Education Supervision and Guidance Committee of the State Education Commission as "The National Education Supervision and Guidance Group" (MOE, 2003) and used the seal of the "National Education Supervision and Guidance Group" with the national emblem (Tu, 2015: 59). In 2015, *The Compulsory Education Law of the People's Republic of China* (2015 Amendment) clearly stated: "Education supervision and guidance organizations of the People's government supervise and guide the implementation of laws and regulations on compulsory education, the quality of education and teaching, and the balanced development of compulsory education and publish a report on supervision and guidance to society." This revised version of *The Compulsory Education Law* clarified that education supervision and guidance agencies at all levels were no longer to be internal institutions under education administration. The fifth time was in 2016. With the approval of the Office of the Central Organization Staffing Committee, the Education Supervision and Guidance Group was renamed the Education Supervision and Guidance Bureau, and the Education Supervision and Guidance Committee Bureau of the State Council was added. Looking back at these five reforms, education supervision and guidance organizations have gradually separated from certain departments of the MOE, and have established themselves under the authority of various levels of government. The education supervision and guidance organizations of the People's government under the same levels of government are parallel to the education administration departments, and the establishment of education supervision and guidance organizations has continued to tend towards independence.

Education Supervision and Guidance Regulations of 2012 clearly stated: "Education supervision and guidance organizations of the State Council undertake the jobs of implementing education supervision and guidance nationwide, formulating basic guidelines for education supervision and guidance, and guiding local education supervision. Education supervision and guidance organizations of local People's governments at or above the county level undertake the task of implementing education supervision and guidance in the region. Education supervision and guidance organizations of the State Council and local People's governments at or above the county level (hereinafter referred to as education supervision and guidance organizations) independently carry out supervision and guidance functions under the leadership of the People's government at the same level." *The Education Supervision and Guidance Regulations* clarifies that supervision and guidance organizations are institutions of the People's government, which provides a legal basis for changing the situation whereby most education supervision and guidance organizations are merely institutions within education administration departments. At the same time, it was made clear that supervision and guidance organizations independently exercise their education supervision and guidance functions. Education supervision and guidance organizations exercise their functions independently under the leadership of the People's government at the same level, which strengthens the relative independence of education supervision and guidance organizations and functions, and provides a legal basis for the establishment of an education administrative supervision institution that is mutually restrictive and coordinated with educational decision-making and implementation.

(2) The Professionalism of Education Supervision and Guidance Personnel Has Been Continuously Improved

In the forty years since the restoration and reconstruction of China's education supervision and guidance institution, the construction of central and local supervision and guidance organizations teams has been continuously strengthened. At present, China has formed a four-level education supervision and guidance network at the central, provincial, municipal, and county levels, and has built an education supervision and guidance team of nearly 80,000 full-time and part-time members (MOE, 2012a). People are the foundation for making a cause succeed. Supervision and guidance personnel are responsible for supervising, inspecting, and guiding the development of education and the implementation of policies. They are the "leaders" of teachers, the "partners" of school administrators, and "the think tanks" of higher level government and education administration departments (Lu, 2014). They must have strong professional skills and professional qualities.

Since the restoration of the education supervision and guidance institution, China has attached great importance to the professional competence and quality of education supervision and guidance personnel. First, China has continuously increased the requirements on them, put strict controls on their appointment and assessment, and ensured their quality at the source. In March 1987, the State Education Commission in the notice of *The Minutes of the Supervision and Guidance Work of the State Education Commission* clearly stated that "in order to ensure that education supervision institutions play a useful role, supervisors must be strictly selected in accordance with the prescribed conditions, and quality must be guaranteed." At the same time, it required that "the principle that supervisors carry out supervision and guidance work only after having had professional training must be adhered to." At that time, it was stipulated that supervisors should meet requirements in four aspects including political quality, education level, work ethic, and health status. In 1991, *The Interim Provisions on Education Supervision and Guidance* added requirements for professional competence and familiarity with educational policies to the conditions of supervisors. On May 29, 1996, the State Education Commission issued *The Several Opinions on Strengthening the Construction of Education Supervision and Guidance Teams* and *The Code of Conduct for Supervisors*, reaffirming that the selection of supervisors must comply with five basic conditions. These five conditions are roughly the same as the five items proposed in 1991, except in terms of teaching time, which changed from "experience in education of more than 10 years" to "experience in education of more than seven years." On July 19, 2006, the MOE revised *The Interim Measures for the Appointment of Supervisors in the State Education Commission* formulated in 1991 to further standardize and strengthen the appointment management of supervisors in accordance with the practical exploration in various localities and issued *The Management Methods for Employing State Education Supervisors (Provisional)*, increasing the conditions for appointment of state education supervisors from five to seven, including political quality, policy and task level, organization and coordination and expression ability, education history and teaching time, positions and titles, work style, and physical condition. The two newly added conditions of "organization and coordination and expression ability" and "positions and titles" pay more attention to actual work ability and work experience. In 2012, *The Education Supervision and Guidance Regulations* set requirements for full-time supervisors in the aspects of ideological and political quality, professional integrity, legal literacy, and policy and task abilities, and for the first time, it was clarified that they must be "qualified through professional examination of education supervision and guidance institutions." In 2016, *The Interim Measures for Supervision of School Management* was promulgated and proposed the establishment of a management institution for school supervision. In addition to meeting the requirements of Article 7 of chapter 2 of *The Education Supervision and Guidance Regulations*, supervision should also meet the needs of reform and development and education supervision and guidance, and achieve the following requirements: passion for education supervision and guidance work, able to conduct education supervision and guidance work with deep involvement with the front line, schools, teachers and students; familiar with education supervision and guidance operations, a mastery of the required knowledge for inspection and guidance, assessment acceptance and monitoring expertise and technology; and able to ensure the work time of education supervision. At the same time, the assessment, duties, and training of supervision and guidance teams at all levels are stipulated.

Second, *The Interim Measures for Education Supervision Management* mention that education supervision and guidance organizations at all levels are responsible for organizing pre-post and on-the-job training in accordance with their responsibilities, and newly recruited supervisors should receive training before taking up their posts. By carrying out various forms of training activities, the professional knowledge of supervision and guidance personnel is expanded and their level of professionalism is increased. During the year of 2016, four provincial, municipal, and county education supervision training courses were held, and research on *The Education Supervision Training Outline* was conducted to strengthen education supervision training and improve the ability and level of supervision performance. A supervision information institution was researched and established (MOE, 2017a). On this basis, various measures were adopted in various places to improve the professionalism of supervisors, and a team of supervisors was built to meet the needs of education supervision and guidance in the new era. For example, in order to promote the professional development of supervision and guidance teams, Chongqing Municipality relies on Chongqing Second Normal University to establish an education supervision training center and carry out training for all supervision staff. The municipal government arranges a special fund of 1.5 million yuan for supervisory training each year to hold on-the-job training and improve training to help supervisors realize a change in job roles. Advanced seminars are held for supervisors and experts and scholars are invited to hold special lectures to improve the theoretical accomplishment and professional quality of education supervisors. Special training such as supervision and guidance of balanced development of compulsory education, supervision and guidance of quality education is held in primary and secondary schools, supervision and guidance of preschool education, supervision and guidance of secondary vocational education, as well as supervision and guidance of "burden reduction and quality improvement" to improve professional skills in supervision and ensure the professionalism and authority of education supervision (MOE, 2014).

(3) Education Supervision and Guidance Extends from Education Results to Education Processes

The implementation of education supervision and guidance is a systematic project, which involves multiple interrelated and mutually restricting processes and stages. It is extremely complicated and challenging work (Su, 2012: 252). Results supervision and guidance reflects the effectiveness and results of school running, while process supervision and guidance reflects the subjective behavior and effort of the school in the school running process. With the change in education evaluation methods, the focus of education supervision and guidance has also been slanted.

In the 1940s, Taylor developed a goal-based evaluation method. As the world's earliest proposed evaluation model, it became an important model for education evaluation. At the level of supervision, guidance, and evaluation, what was emphasized was the evaluation of the extent to which the primary and secondary schools reached school running goals and standards. In the practice of education supervision and evaluation, first, education supervision and guidance organizations shall determine the supervision, guidance and evaluation standards as the development goals of primary and secondary schools; second, supervision and guidance personnel should design appropriate and feasible assessment methods to collect data and information; finally, the collected data, information and established goals are compared, the degree of achievement of school running goals is examined, and further rectification measures and suggestions are proposed. This kind of evaluation method was also one of the main evaluation methods of China's education supervision and guidance for a period of time. However, due to various internal and external reasons for China's education, the tendency to evaluate the quality of primary and secondary education simply based on students' academic test results and school enrollment rates has not yet been fundamentally transformed and prominently manifests itself as: emphasis on test scores in evaluation content, neglecting students' comprehensive quality and personality development; emphasis on final results in evaluation methods, neglect of school progress and effort; and emphasis on identification certificates in the use of evaluation results, and neglect of diagnosis and improvement. These problems have seriously affected students' all-round development and healthy growth, and restricted the cultivation of students' social responsibility, innovative spirit and practical ability. To solve these outstanding problems and adapt to the new situation and requirements of the development of economic society and education, it is necessary to vigorously promote the reform of comprehensive evaluation of primary and secondary school education quality (MOE, 2013). In 2013, the MOE issued the document *Opinions on Promoting the Comprehensive Evaluation Reform of Primary and Secondary Quality Education*, emphasizing people-oriented education and focusing on the learning process and effectiveness. In 2015, the Office of the State Council's Education Supervision and Guidance Committee issued *The National Compulsory Education Quality Monitoring Program*, which aims to correct the practice of using school enrollment rates as the sole criterion for evaluating schools and students, focusing on process-based education quality assessment and monitoring. Due to the shift in evaluation methods, education supervision has also extended from focusing on education results to the educational process.

The main achievement that school education provides to society is talented individuals, and education achievements are formed in the education process. If we only measure the quality of talents provided by a school for society from the perspective of results supervision and guidance, it cannot properly guide the development of school education. Because results are established as facts, they cannot be changed (Huang, 2011: 28). In specific supervision and guidance practice, the focus of supervision and guidance personnel will shift from the results of school development to the process of implementing quality education in schools. Through monitoring the process evaluation, they will collect relevant data and information to provide help and guidance in practical and feasible methods for improving and optimizing school work.

(4) The Authority of Education Supervision and Guidance Is Gradually Being Strengthened

As an important supervision institution of modern education administration, the authority of education supervision and guidance is mainly derived from the power of the state, and is manifested through the deterrence of state power (Su, 2012: 268). Specifically, the establishment of relevant laws and regulations is the cornerstone of education supervision and guidance bodies in exercising authority. Education supervision and guidance bodies escort the development of education through law enforcement administrative actions.

In order to promote the legalization of education supervision and guidance and ensure that education supervision and guidance has laws and rules to follow, in April 1991, the State Education Commission issued *The Interim Regulations on Education Supervision and Guidance* (hereinafter referred to as *The Interim Regulations*). As the first regulatory document on the education supervision and guidance institution since the founding of the People's Republic of China, Article 1 of *The Interim Regulations* states: "The purpose of the education supervision and guidance institution is strengthening the administrative supervision of education work." By defining the essential attributes of education supervision and guidance, the understanding of supervision and guidance work at all levels of government, education administrative departments, and schools has been unified and improved. This shows that education supervision and guidance represents the government's exercise of state power and state supervision over education work.

This indicates that China's education supervision and guidance has administrative supervision power and has a certain administrative authority.

The Education Law of the People's Republic of China, passed in March 1995, clearly stipulates that the state implements an education supervision and guidance institution and an evaluation institution for schools and other educational institutions. Since then, the education supervision institution has become one of the basic legal national education institutions. The state has determined the legal status of education supervision and guidance in education administration in legal form, and strengthened the authority of education supervision and guidance. In October 2012, *The Education Supervision Regulations* (hereinafter referred to as *The Regulations*) were promulgated and implemented. *The Regulations* were China's first specialized education supervision and guidance regulations. This marked the basic formation of an education administration management institution that coordinates the decision-making, implementation and supervision of education in China, and also marked that the establishment of a modern education supervision institution with Chinese characteristics had reached a new height (Zhang, 2012). On the basis of summarizing and adhering to the successful experiences of previous education supervision and guidance practices in China, *The Regulations* took into account the new situation and requirements of current education, expanded the scope of education supervision and guidance, and explained the duties and implementation processes of education supervision and guidance. In 2014, *The Evaluation Methods for Provincial People's Governments in Carrying Out Education Duties* pointed out the evaluation of the provincial People's government's leadership, management, security, and promotion of the reform and development and stability of education in its administrative region, breaking the poor government supervision of the past caused by the layered structuring and guaranteeing the realization of supervision and reflecting the authoritative nature and seriousness of supervision and guidance.

II. The New Era Calls for a Deepening of Education Supervision and Guidance Reform

The report of the 19th National Congress of the Communist Party of China states: "Building a strong nation in education is a basic project in the great rejuvenation of the Chinese nation. Education must be given priority, education modernization must be accelerated, and education must be carried out in a way that satisfies the people." Presently, Chinese education has entered a new historical development period; various levels and types of education are undergoing vigorous development, education investment has continued to rise, and comprehensive education reform has continued to advance. To ensure the healthy, orderly, and steady development of education, professional education supervision and guidance is required to conduct inspections, supervision, evaluation, and guidance.

(1) The Workload for Education Supervision and Guidance Is Large

Since Reform and Opening Up, China's education has made remarkable achievements. All types of education at all levels across the country have had flourishing development. Fairness in education has been further promoted, enrollment opportunities have continued to expand, educational resource allocation has become more reasonable, and education quality has improved. The scale of preschool education has continued to grow, and the gross enrollment rate has continued to increase; the level of popularization and consolidation of compulsory education has further increased; the scale of high school education has further expanded, and the proportion structure has become more optimized; the scale of higher education has grown moderately, and the focus is now turning towards optimizing the structure and improving quality.

In the 1980s, education in China developed in restoration and restructuring; the quality of education was significantly improved, as were school running conditions. In particular, higher education was restored, its scale expanded, and structural adjustments achieved remarkable results. Since the 1990s, China's education sector has carried out a series of major reforms and innovations in adhering to the education policy of education heading towards modernization, the world, and the future. By the beginning of the 21st century, nine-year compulsory education was implemented in a planned and phased manner, and the "two basics" objective was successfully achieved; higher education has developed rapidly, and a multi-level, multi-form, and complete institution of academic subjects has initially formed, education investment has grown significantly, and school running conditions have improved. In addition, with the convening of the Third Plenary Session of the Eleventh Central Committee, the state has begun to allow social forces to run schools. Article 19 of the 1982 *Constitution* stipulates: "The state encourages collective economic organizations, state enterprises and institutions, and other sectors of society to establish educational institutions of various types in accordance with law" and for the first time legally recognized the status of private education. After entering the 21st century, with the enactment of *The Law to Promote Education by Private Schools*, the relevant management and support institutions of private schools were further improved, social forces were further encouraged to launch education, education supply-side reform was promoted, and the growing diverse education needs of the people were met, which had important and far-reaching significance (MOE, 2017b).

Since Reform and Opening Up, with the vigorous development of education at all levels, the scope of education supervision and guidance also gradually expanded. In 2016, there were 239,800 kindergartens and 229,800 schools at the compulsory education stage in the country, and the nine-year compulsory education consolidation rate reached 93.4%; there were 2,080 special education schools, an increase of 27 from the previous year; and 24,700 schools at the high school stage; the total number of people in all types of higher education in the country reached 36.99 million, and the gross enrollment rate of higher education reached 42.7%; there were 171,100 private schools of all levels and types, an increase of 8,253 over the previous year (MOE, 2017c). Through "supervision" and "guidance" of schools, the improvement of the quality of school education and teaching was promoted, the continuous development of teachers and students was promoted, and a reliable and scientific basis for government and education administration decision-making departments was provided (Wang, 2014). In recent years, as the scope of supervision and guidance work has expanded, the content of supervision and guidance has become more detailed. Based on the previous comprehensive supervision and guidance, various forms of special supervision and guidance have been carried out. While covering all levels of education, it also involves the micro-level of schools. For example, attention is paid to hot and difficult issues such as school building and repairs in rural schools, school bullying, and balanced development of compulsory education.

(2) National Major Education Reform Projects Call for Education Monitoring, Supervision, and Guidance

According to the strategic deployment of "prioritizing the development of education and building a country with strong human resources," China's education reform and development has been further promoted, especially after the release of *The National Medium-and-Long-Term Education Reform and Development Plan Outline (2010–2020)* (hereinafter referred to as *The Plan Outline*). In accordance with the spirit of *The Plan Outline*, "based on the principles of overall planning, step-by-step implementation, pilot advancement, and dynamic adjustment, some regions and schools will be selected for major reform pilots," China began promoting a new round of education reform.

In October 2010, the General Office of the State Council issued *The Notice on Launching a Pilot Program for the Reform of the National education institution* to fully launch pilot work for the reform of the national education institution. The basic content of national education institution reform pilots was divided into three categories, namely, special reform pilots, comprehensive reform pilots in key areas, and provincial government comprehensive education reform pilots. Special reform includes ten pilot tasks: There are three basic education tasks, which are to accelerate the development of preschool education, promote the balanced development of compulsory education, and explore ways to reduce the burden of schoolwork for primary and secondary school students. There are three higher education tasks, which are reforming the talent cultivation mode, reforming the school running mode for higher education institutions, and constructing a modern university institution; the other four are reforming the vocational education school running mode, improving the development environment for private education, improving the teacher management institution, and improving the education investment mechanism.

In order to ensure the smooth progress of education reform, *The Plan Outline* clearly proposes that by 2012, national fiscal education expenditure will reach the goal of 4% of GDP. How to ensure the implementation of funds for education reform projects requires strengthening education supervision and supervision and guidance. At the same time, China's education still faces some difficult new situations, new tasks, and new problems, such as the balanced development and construction of compulsory education, the building of teaching staff teams, the improvement of education quality and so on. An effective solution to these problems will greatly improve China's education development quality. However, these problems cannot be solved without the formulation and implementation of education reform. Therefore, effective monitoring, management, supervision, and guidance are important ways of ensuring that people, finances, and things find their proper place, and it is also an important means of monitoring the feasibility of education reform.

Article 63 of *The Education Law of the People's Republic of China* states that People's governments at all levels and their education administration departments should strengthen the supervision and management of education funds of schools and other educational institutions, and improve the efficiency of education investment, explaining the importance of education investment monitoring and supervision and guidance in legal form. At the same time, in order to further ensure that education funds can be used properly, in 2011, *The Opinions of the State Council on Further Increasing Financial Investment in Education* clearly stated that monitoring and analysis should be strengthened. All regions should strengthen monitoring, analysis, supervision, and inspection of various policies to implement the statutory increase in education investment; increase the proportion of financial education expenditure; broaden the sources of education finance funding; and discover and solve relevant problems in policy implementation in a timely fashion. The Ministry of Finance should work with relevant departments to formulate scientific and reasonable analysis and evaluation indicators, evaluate and analyze the state of financial investment in education in various provinces (autonomous regions, municipalities), report the analysis results to the State Council in a timely manner, and serve as an important basis for the central government in arranging transfer payments.

(3) The Complexity of the Education Institution and the Connotative Development of Education Calls for Professional Education Supervision, Guidance, and Evaluation

As an important part of social undertakings and an important issue of people's livelihoods, education has always received great and extensive attention from all walks of life. At present, China's education reform has entered the "deep water zone." The internal and external environment of education development is more complicated: the complexity of educational decision-making has increased, and the implementation of reform measures and innovation exploration has become more difficult (Zhong, 2013). It is required that education supervision and guidance work should serve the targets of supervision and guidance more, provide them with more professional guidance, help improve work, and promote the sustainable and healthy development of education.

Since the 1980s, in order to further improve the quality of and promote fairness in education, changes to education have been initiated worldwide. Michael Fullan applied complexity theory to the practice of changes in education. He believes that change is a journey, not a blueprint. Change is nonlinear, full of uncertainty, sometimes even contrary to common sense (Fullan, 2004: 33), and the education process is so complicated that it is difficult to control (Fullan, 2004: 27). At present, in China, education reform has entered a comprehensive reform stage. The urgent needs of the masses for high-quality education and the serious shortage of high-quality education resources has become the main contradictory problem in education right now; the connotative development of education is arduous, the construction period is long, and a strong contrast has been formed with the expectations of society; the number of stakeholders in education will increase, and the interest demands will present a diversified value orientation; the internal reform of the education institution will become more relevant, and institution reform will become an inevitable requirement; education and economic and social relations will become more closely linked, and internal and external coordinated reform has become a general trend (Zhong, 2013). Facing such a severe situation in education reform, scientific education supervision, guidance and evaluation is an important guarantee for building a socialist education institution with Chinese characteristics, which is of great significance to the development of education, deepening education reform, and improving the quality of education (Su, 2012: 147).

Education supervision, as an activity implemented by the government to control education, not only undertakes the functions of monitoring, inspection, assessment, and evaluation but also bears the responsibilities of supervision, guidance, advice, and service. Supervision, guidance and evaluation is a new macro management method that organically combines supervision, guidance and evaluation (Gao

& Huang, 1997: 117) and is the core of education supervision and guidance work. It is only by relying on and using the support of evaluation that can we further enhance the scientific nature and authority of education supervision and guidance. In view of the complexity of the current education institution, professional education supervision, guidance and evaluation are needed even more to find problems, detect gaps, and provide support and services in the process of education reform. This requires education supervisors to further strengthen their own professional service capabilities and become the foundational education experts in one aspect of education administration management, teaching business management, or subject teaching work, become promoters and guides for school professional development, and thereby promote education reforms involved in the "deepwater zone" of education reforms to achieve steady, rapid, and healthy development of education.

III. The Strategic Position of Education Supervision in the New Era

At present, education management is gradually changing to education governance, and the diversification of education governance subjects has changed the government's situation of "juggling management, running and evaluation." The reform of separation of management, running and evaluation, as a basic requirement for promoting the modernization of the education governance institution and governance ability, urges the government to change its functions and improve education management methods; make use of the role of schools as the main body and accelerate the construction of modern school institutions; make use of the role of evaluation by society and mobilize social participation to support supervision of education, that is, how to manage the government, how to run schools, and how society conducts evaluation as the three major tasks used to promote the modernization of the education governance institution and governance capacity (Yuan, 2014a). Education supervision and guidance is the main way for the government to evaluate education. Its uniqueness and irreplaceability highlight the strategic position of the education supervision and guidance institution in education activities. In this context, building a new evaluation institution that focuses on education supervision and guidance and is supplemented by third-party evaluation agencies is necessary in making use of the due role and value of the institutional framework of separation of management, school running and evaluation, and promoting the modernization of education governance in China.

(1) Strategic Position of the Education Supervision and Guidance Institution

Education supervision and guidance is an important way for the government to supervise, guide and evaluate education activities, and it is also the main basis for formulating education policies, guidelines, and regulations. At the same time, when it comes to developing school evaluation, guidance and supervision, answers need to be found from the feedback of the education supervision and guidance personnel to questions such as how well schools have performed planning and organization work, and what are the reasons for poor execution. In the UK, emphasis is placed on "improvement and development as the core of supervision and guidance" while emphasizing that "schools provide written self-assessment reports to supervision and guidance personnel, school self-evaluation provides a reliable basis for external supervision and guidance, and external supervision and guidance combined with school self-evaluation serves as an important mechanism for schools in achieving improvement and increasing their own ability to develop" (OFSTED, 2012). In 2015, the MOE issued *The Opinions on Deeply Advancing the Separation of Education, Management and Evaluation and Promoting the Transformation of Government Functions*, which explicitly proposed the establishment and improvement of an education evaluation institution with multiple participants including the government, schools, professional institutions, and social organizations. Based on this, a few regions have given the main work of supervision and evaluation away to third-party evaluation agencies. However, there are still many problems in the current social organization, institution cultivation, and admission qualifications. In contrast, education supervision and guidance is irreplaceable.

Objective, scientific, open, and fair evaluation is the prerequisite for enhancing the pertinence and effectiveness of education, and it can provide a reference for government decision-making and provide a basis for school improvement (Liu, 2015). Education supervision and guidance activities are administrative evaluation activities combining supervisory behavior with instructional behavior. Compared with third-party evaluation agencies, the education supervision and guidance institution has the following advantages: First, from the analysis of the function of education supervision and guidance, it includes a number of functions including supervision, evaluation, guidance, feedback, and coordination, whereas third-party organizations rely on administrative power and educational laws, and have more advantages in aspects such as authority and professionalism. Second, from the perspective of third-party evaluation agencies, current issues such as qualifications, admission, certification, and staffing still need to be improved, and at this stage, they cannot meet the needs of education reform and development in terms of quantity. Third, for third-party agencies, a series of problems including how the government's supervision and evaluation of education-related behaviors can be done subjectively and scientifically and detailed issues in cross-level and same-level supervision and guidance have presented challenges to the involvement of third-party organizations in public education. Finally, third-party evaluation agencies are based on the market mechanism and the functions of public services education are implemented in the form of a contract. They cannot replace the state and enjoy political coercive force. It is also impossible for them to effectively allocate most resources spontaneously in place of the market (Yu, 1999). Supervision and guidance in education is based on the administrative subject regulating the behavior of administrative objects according to the state's requirements for public utilities, and has certain legal guarantees.

(2) Establishing an Education Supervision, Guidance and Evaluation Institution Focusing on Education Supervision and Guidance and Participation of Multiple Parties

The reform of separation of management, school running, and evaluation is not simply empowering and delegating schools and social organizations, but a search for an effective education governance mechanism in the environment of the current market economy institution and a society with multiple stakeholders in reasonably decentralizing the rights of schools and society through the common management and cooperation of multiple subjects, reshaping the power-responsibility relationship among the government, schools, and society, and establishing a composite model of multiple-party participation in education, and pursuing and achieving "good education."

As far as "evaluation" is concerned, it is in fact a diverse evaluation institution combining government supervision, guidance and evaluation, school self-evaluation, and third-party evaluation. However, the "multi-center" in which education governance subjects participate is not "non-centered." Based on the current situation of there being various educational evaluation subjects, third-party evaluation agencies cannot be used as the center of "evaluating education." As an imported product, third-party evaluation agencies had a late start in China. Regardless of whether it is because the institution or mechanism is still incomplete and affected by the traditional administrative management model, the government habitually controls and supervises education activities through power and orders. This overly stringent control and regulatory path reveals its lack of "confidence" in third-party evaluation agencies.[1] Since the restoration and reconstruction of education supervision and guidance, the education supervision and guidance institution has been continuously improved and developed, and has gradually embarked on the track towards legalization, standardization and becoming more scientific. Therefore, in this context, weighing the advantages and disadvantages of the two, relying on a third-party evaluation agency as the center of the evaluation institution cannot achieve scientific and professionalized evaluation. The professionalism, standardization, and scientific nature of education supervision and guidance urges it to work with third-party evaluation institutions to bring the benefits of education evaluation into effect and build a new education evaluation institution that is mainly based on education supervision and guidance and supplemented by third-party evaluation institutions, jointly promoting the modernization of education governance in China (Figure 7.1).

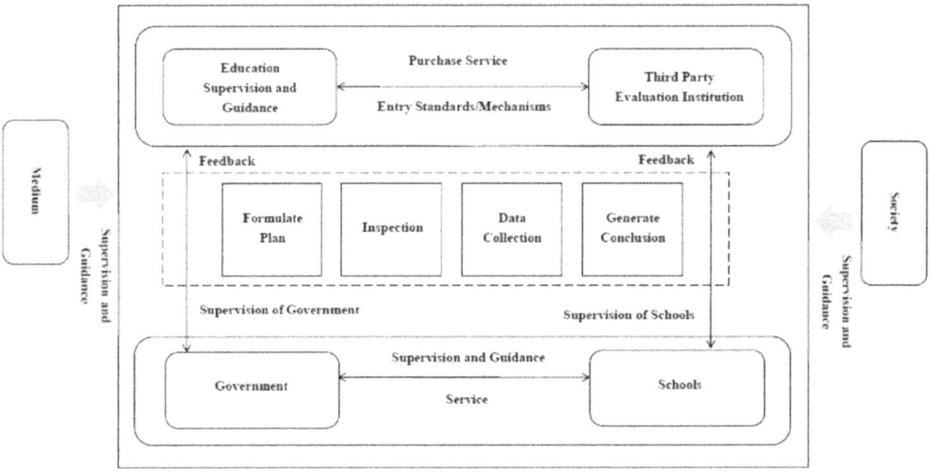

Figure 7.1 Education Supervision, Guidance and Evaluation Institution Based on the Separation of Education Management, School Running, and Evaluation

Admission criteria for third-party evaluation agencies are formulated by the government and public bidding is conducted. The winning third-party evaluation agency and education supervision and guidance agency should jointly inspect and collect relevant materials regarding the actual situations of schools and the government in education affairs according to the formulated supervision and guidance plan. Finally, according to the results of the evaluation, whole process guidance will be conducted for the situations that appear in government and in schools. During the process of promoting the reform of separation of education management, school running, and evaluation, the essence of "society evaluating education" is accepting evaluation by society of education quality and social monitoring of decision-making in education (Yuan, 2014b). Therefore, in this process, participation by society and the media allows the media to present the evaluation results to the public and facilitates public participation in education management.

The modernization of the education governance institution is a historical transcendence of the previous education management institution. The value it pursues lies in making the education governance institution more scientific, democratic, lawful, and making education governance better able to show the efficiency and fairness of education (Chen & Wan, 2016). This new type of evaluation institution makes up for the shortcomings of education supervision and guidance and third-party evaluation agencies at this stage. It breaks the previous situation of education supervision and guidance being the mainstay and school self-assessment being merely supplementary. It has created a new format for the education supervision and guidance institution and the work of third-party evaluation agencies. The new structure guarantees scientific, standardized, and objective results in education evaluation, and the democratization and socialization of participating subjects.

SECTION 3 REFORM OF THE EDUCATION SUPERVISION AND GUIDANCE INSTITUTION

The formulation of an education supervision and guidance institution, as an important part of the education administrative management institution, directly restricts the development of education supervision and guidance activities. In order to meet the needs of the comprehensive reform of China's education sector and give full play to the active role of education supervision and guidance, education supervision and guidance must correct its internal and external disadvantages, and gradually realize the independence of institutions, professionalization of personnel, integration of functions, and socialization of services to ensure and promote the healthy development of education.

I. Independence of Education Supervision and Guidance Institutions

The meaning behind the reform of the education supervision and guidance institution is the supervision and guidance institutions and norms, that is, the reform of the education supervision and guidance institution. At the core is the reform of the responsibility and authority institution of education institutions. However, at present, China's education supervision and guidance institutions are not completely independent, and their affiliations have seriously affected the development of supervision and guidance work.

Taking Shandong Province as an example, its supervision and guidance agency is called "The Shandong Provincial Government Supervision and Guidance Office." It is a supervision and guidance agency established in the name of the government. From the perspective of people, property, and institutional management mechanisms, the Shandong Provincial Government Supervision and Guidance Office is actually an institution in the provincial education agency. Parallel to other agencies under it, it is under the leadership and restriction of the education administration department. The same is true of education supervision and guidance institutions at the municipal and county levels. Under this administrative framework, education supervision and guidance offices need to coordinate with the education department in order to perform supervision of the government, and it is difficult for the education department to form an administrative binding force on township level governments. As a result, education supervision and guidance offices are on the edge of administration. It is difficult to imagine the difficulty and effectiveness of supervision of the government (Sun, 2013). At the same time, *The Education Supervision and Guidance Regulations*, as a programmatic document that guides the implementation of supervision and guidance work, fails to clarify the nature, organizational structure, and horizontal relationship with educational administration departments, the degree of authority, and even the different priorities of supervision and guidance institutions at all levels, causing the unreasonable centralization of education supervision and guidance departments, unclear affiliative relationships of supervision and guidance institutions, and unclear responsibilities and degrees of authority, making it so that internal relationships have always been difficult to straighten out (Yang, 2007).

From this it can be seen that the setup of institutions is one of the important factors hindering supervision and guidance. At present, there are three different types of education supervision and guidance institution set-ups in the world: First, the completely independent form, mainly represented by the UK. The Office for Standards in Education, Children's Services and Skills (Ofsted), as an education supervision and guidance institution, has an independent yet close relationship with the Education Administration Department—the Department for Education. On the one hand, Ofsted has the right to decide how to carry out its work, including the formulation and implementation of plans, the management and use of school supervision, etc.; the chair has the power to report directly to the Minister of State; and nobody has the right to modify the submitted reports (Shi, 2009). On the other hand, the Royal School Inspectorate needs to conduct supervision and guidance in accordance with the requirements of the Council for Science and Technology. Second is the relatively independent form, which is used by most countries. Taking the Netherlands as an example, its supervision and guidance department is located in the MOE, Culture and Science, and it does not supervise matters, but only coordinates its relationship with parliament. Subject-specific reports provided by supervisory bodies are adopted by the MOE and Parliament as needed in policy formulation. It plays advisory, commissioning, and negotiating roles in educational policy development, but does not participate (Jiang, 2002). Third, the dependency form. Countries such as the United States and Canada have not set up special education supervision and guidance institutions, but infiltrated the states through education policies, laws, and funding programs to perform support and guidance functions (Table 7.1).

Table 7.1 Forms of Education Supervision and Guidance Institution Setups

Setup	Example Country	Main Features
Complete Independence	United Kingdom	Ofsted independently conducts supervision and guidance work and is responsible to the Minister of Education and Parliament with no administrative interference.
Relative Independence	The Netherlands	Units under the MOE, Culture, Science and Technology have decision-making power over the supervision and guidance department, but do not interfere in their daily affairs.
Dependence	United States	The U.S. Federal Department of Education does not have a special supervision and guidance institution, but regulates national education by providing funds for special education programs.

* "Independent" means that the education supervision and guidance institutions are independent of education administration departments.
Source: Peng Hongbin (2012). International Comparison and Inspiration of the Independence of Education Supervision and Guidance Institutions. *Foreign Elementary and Secondary School Education*, (2), 1–6.

Through inspections on the establishment of education supervision and guidance institutions in other countries, it is not difficult to find that independent or relatively independent education supervision and guidance institutions are conducive to the organizational capacity building of education supervision and guidance, and improve the professionalism of supervision and guidance; also, they are helpful for education supervision and guidance institutions to exclude interference from other administration institutions and they function independently. In China's current practice of promoting the reform of separation of education management, school running and evaluation, the role of education supervision and guidance has become prominent and the drawbacks of supervision and guidance institutions relying on education administration departments have made the calls for supervision and guidance institutions to be set up independently more and more prominent. Combined with the actual situation in China, starting from the central level, education supervision and guidance institutions can be completely separated from the national administrative department and set up under the National People's Congress to enable it to carry out supervision and guidance independently. Provinces, municipalities, and counties at all levels should make rectifications with reference to the central institutions. As we all know, the National People's Congress, as China's supreme state power body, has adopted a variety of methods to form a concerted effort to supervise the implementation of the work of "one house, two yards." In this way, the government, schools, and education supervision and guidance personnel are on an equal footing. Education supervision and guidance personnel focus on the beneficiaries of education, rather than on the organizations and organizational relationships that provide services.

II. Professionalization of Education Supervision and Guidance Personnel

How effective education supervision and guidance work is depends to a large extent on the quality of the supervision and guidance team. Although education supervision and guidance personnel are not teachers who are directly engaged in education or teaching, nor are they responsible for school education management, their special professional nature requires that they must be familiar with the country's education policies and education laws and regulations, have rich education and teaching experience, and be well versed in the basic laws of education and teaching so that problems in supervision and guidance can be identified, guidance can then be given, and then the problems can be solved.

As an administrative officer who exercises the power of education supervision and guidance on behalf of the national education administrative department, from the perspective of the composition of education supervision and guidance institutions at all levels, in most cases, education supervision and guidance personnel of provinces, municipalities, and counties are established by appointment. Most of the staff are senior teachers, primary and secondary school principals, and soon-to-be-retired teachers. Although in some areas, full-time supervision and guidance personnel have been hired to improve education supervision and guidance teams, this selection is not an open selection for the community, but rather the appointment of qualified personnel within the education institution.

Judging from the current situation of China's supervision and guidance personnel, the structure of educational supervision and guidance personnel is unreasonable (Sun, 2004): Some are older and less enthusiastic about the work; individual supervisors lack professional supervision and guidance knowledge and ability; in individual counties and municipalities, education supervision and guidance institutions have even become "old-age institutions" for personnel within education administration, which is not conducive to the development and progress of local education. Judging from the work functions of supervision and guidance personnel, due to the lack of relevant legal guarantees, it is difficult for personnel to restrict the supervision and guidance of local schools and they do not have authority; the government's supervision, guidance and evaluation of education affairs does not have legal enforcement power, which has led to education supervision and guidance personnel being in a state of inadequate supervision over the government and with no power in guiding schools.

The National Medium-and-Long-Term Education Reform and Development Plan Outline (2010–2020) states that China will have basically achieved education modernization by 2020, and education supervision and guidance must fully play a guaranteeing role in achieving this macro goal. Supervision and guidance departments are required to pay attention to the professional ability and quality of school supervision teams. At the same time, their professional service ability must be strengthened for supervision of schools, to become education experts in education administration, teaching business management or subject teaching in the field of basic education, and become facilitators and mentors in the professional development of schools. To this end, the construction of professional education supervision and guidance teams is being accelerated, improving the supervision, inspection, evaluation, and guidance capabilities of school supervision, and there is an effort to build professional supervision and guidance teams with a sufficient number of personnel, a reasonable structure, strong sense of responsibility and superb achievements, mainly with full-time supervision of schools, combining full-time and part-time personnel.

III. Integration of Supervision and Guidance Functions

In 2014, the Office of the State Council's Education Supervision and Guidance Committee issued *The Opinions on Deepening Education Supervision and Guidance Reform and Changing Education Management Methods* (hereinafter referred to as *The Opinions*). According to *The Opinions*, the state should establish a government supervision mechanism that urges local governments to perform their educational responsibilities in accordance with the law, a school supervision institution that guides schools at all levels and of all types to standardize school running and improve the quality of education, and a scientific evaluation and monitoring institution to evaluate the quality of education and teaching, forming an education supervision and guidance institution with the three unified elements of government supervision, school supervision, and evaluation and monitoring.

Evaluation and monitoring were proposed in the new era of education reform, which was conducive to correcting policy implementation deviations, realizing scientific decision-making, helping to transform government functions, forming accountability mechanisms, and then promoting and ensuring the achievement of education goals. In past education supervision and guidance practice, more attention was paid to the supervision, inspection and evaluation of education activity, and the function of guidance was basically abandoned. In fact, inspection and evaluation were only carried out to find problems quickly. The most fundamental purpose of guidance is helping the supervised object find out the cause of the problem and the method of solving it. At the same time, supervision and guidance institutions rely on the promotion of administrative power. Supervision and guidance personnel are keen to use administrative power to supervise and evaluate units that are being supervised and guided, but they ignore the need to use their own professional knowledge to guide the development of schools.

In the new era of China's education development, along with the comprehensive roll-out of the reform of separation of management, school running and evaluation, the decentralization of school autonomy is a great challenge for school administrators. School administrators have to put forward complete and effective plans and regulations for the development of schools, which has added a little pressure compared to before. At the same time, after the reform, the work of principals was incorporated into the performance evaluation institution, and the school development plan was used as the basis for supervising the development and construction of schools. If, as in the past, the strength of the school is the only thing relied upon to propose rectification of loopholes in school running, on the one hand, it increases the pressure on school running, and on the other hand, whether the proposed rectification measures are appropriate or not remains to be investigated. In this context, first of all, education supervision and guidance should adhere to the integration of monitoring, evaluation and guidance. During the process of education supervision and guidance, attention should be paid to monitoring and evaluation. At the same time, from the perspective of administration and professionalism, attention should be paid to "supervision" and "guidance."

Second, the integration of supervision of the government and supervision of schools should be adhered to. The basic tasks of education supervision and guidance in China are supervision of the government and supervision of schools. Supervision of the government aims to establish a supervision and evaluation mechanism for local governments to fulfill their educational responsibilities, strictly implement the accountability institution, guide local governments to give priority to the development of education, and improve the ability and level of basic public education services, while supervision of schools is aimed at improving school supervision team management, implementing the school supervision responsibility institution, monitoring and guiding schools of all types and all levels to standardize school-running behaviors, and comprehensively improve the quality of education.

Since Reform and Opening Up, the task of education supervision and guidance focused for a long time on supervision of government. In fact, supervision of government and supervision of schools exist interdependently of one another, and problems on one side will affect the planning and development of the entire cause of education. First of all, to judge whether or not a government has effectively developed local education undertakings, apart from the allocation of financial resources, human resources and other resources, concrete improvement and implementation in aspects such as school running conditions and the allocation of teachers must be looked at. Second, whether school education has really been developed depends on government input and support. Finally, from the nature of the two objects of supervision and guidance, the government and its education administration departments are legal administrative organizations that exercise educational management power. Schools are specialized educational institutions authorized to carry out educational activities. Effective supervision and guidance of these organizations must be performed by a competent authority (Huang, 2011: 13).

Education supervision and guidance activities, with governments, education administration departments, and schools as the objects of supervision and guidance, in accordance with relevant national policies, laws and regulations, and in accordance with the principles and requirements of supervision and guidance, use scientific methods to carry out supervision, inspection, evaluation, and guidance, and report on education work situations to People's governments at the same level and at higher levels as well as their education administration departments. During the process of promoting the transformation of government functions, education supervision and guidance must adhere to the requirements of combining supervision and guidance, and combining supervision of schools and supervision of the government, to provide practical and effective guidance for school development, and provide practical first-hand materials for the development of local education, and continue to promote the government in improving education administration, promote schools improving in terms of school running, and encouraging teachers to improve teaching in order to promote the continuous and high-quality development of education (Huang, 2011: 4).

IV. Socialization of Supervision and Guidance Services

As an important way of promoting the education governance institution and the modernization of education, the essence of the separation of management, school running, and evaluation relies on the pluralism and socialization of governed subjects. Judging from the nature of education, education is a public enterprise, and all sectors of society and citizens have the right to participate in management. However, at present, education supervision and guidance in China is mainly government-led administration supervision activities supported by administrative authorities. In this context, the space for social organizations or institutions participating in educational activities is small, and at the same time their professionalism and authority are weak.

In order to ensure the professionalism of education supervision and guidance, and at the same time comply with the requirements for the separation of education management and school running from evaluation, it is necessary to vigorously support and improve the construction of education supervision and guidance institutions and provide professional supervision, guidance and evaluation services. *The Decision of the Central Committee of the Communist Party of China on Several Major Issues Concerning Comprehensively Deepening Reform* states: "Strengthen national education supervision and guidance and entrust social organizations to conduct education evaluation and monitoring." This provides a policy basis for third-party institutions participating in education supervision and guidance. At present, some places have issued relevant documents to regulate third-party institutions participating in supervision and guidance, and these have been valuable explorations. For example, in 2016, *The Interim Measures of the Beijing Municipal People's Government Education Supervision and Guidance Office on Entrusting Third-Party Institutions to Conduct Education Evaluation and Monitoring Work* clearly stipulated the assessment qualifications and entrusted management of third-party institutions. Encouraging and supporting third-party institutions to participate in education supervision and guidance is conducive to advancing the modernization of education governance capacity. According to the actual situation in China, this can be gradually realized from the following aspects: First, the work of education supervision, guidance and evaluation is entrusted to qualified local education and scientific research institutions, colleges and universities, and private nonprofit education evaluation institutions through tendering. On the one hand, this can ensure the quality of education evaluation; on the other hand, it can ease the pressure of supervision work. Second is supporting private education evaluation institutions and local education supervision and guidance organizations in guiding and cooperating to improve their internal organizational structures and operating mechanisms, promoting the professional and scientific development of private institutions.

The transformation of the government's education management mode makes the significance and value of education supervision, guidance and evaluation more prominent. "Evaluation" cannot be simply understood as "social evaluation," as it is in fact a multidimensional evaluation institution combining government supervision, guidance and evaluation, school self-evaluation, and third-party social organizations or institutions. However, entrusting supervision to a third-party institution does not weaken the dominant position of the government and the education supervision and guidance department in education evaluation. In a sense, it is a useful exploration in transforming government functions, enhancing macro-monitoring capabilities, and improving supervision, guidance and evaluation professionalism (Huang, 2011: 111). First of all, it is helpful for the supervision and guidance department to free itself from complicated supervision and guidance tasks and concentrate on doing work such as planning and policy improvement; second, it is helpful for overcoming the problem of over-administration in education supervision and guidance and improving the professionalized development of education supervision and guidance. Finally, it is conducive to driving the enthusiasm of third-party social institutions and social organizations to participate in education management, and improving the concept and awareness of society and the public in participating in public education activities.

SECTION 4 REFORM OF THE EDUCATION SUPERVISION AND GUIDANCE MECHANISM

In the process of continuously advancing the modernization of the education governance institution and the capacity of education governance, and promoting the reform of the separation of education management, school running and evaluation, the education supervision and guidance mechanism, that is, the education supervision and guidance institution, has realized innovations in organizational structure, leadership affiliation, and management authority. The changes in the institution will inevitably bring about changes in the internal mechanism. In this context, the education supervision, guidance and innovation monitoring mechanism, evaluation mechanism, responsibility mechanism, and accountability mechanism will basically keep up with the pace of institution reform and adapt to the many changes in the new era of education reform.

I. Supervision, Guidance and Monitoring Mechanism

At present, China's education development is moving towards a more balanced, higher quality, and fairer connotation-enhancing development path. Effective monitoring of educational activities is an important means of grasping the current status of education development, identifying and correcting problems in education development, and ensuring better education development (Xu, 2016).

In 2010, *The National Medium-and-Long-Term Education Reform and Development Plan Outline (2010–2020)* clearly stated that it is necessary to establish national basic standards and a monitoring institution for education quality. The Third Plenary Session of the 18th Central Committee of the Communist Party of China (CPC) included "strengthening national education supervision and guidance" and "developing education assessment and monitoring" into the overall deployment of "comprehensively deepening comprehensive reforms in the field of education." At the same time, *The Decision of the Central Committee of the Communist Party of China on Several Major Issues Concerning Comprehensively Deepening Reform* proposed to "entrust social organizations to carry out evaluation and monitoring of education." In 2014, the Education Supervision and Guidance Committee Office of the State Council issued *The Opinions on Deepening the Reform of Educational Supervision and Guidance, and Changing Educational Management*

Methods, emphasizing the need to establish a supervisory mechanism that urges local governments to perform their educational responsibilities in accordance with the law, and guide all types of schools at all levels to standardize schooling and improve education quality, and scientifically evaluates and monitors education and teaching quality, forming an education supervision and guidance institution that combines the three elements of supervision of government, supervision of schools, evaluation and monitoring. The promulgation of some documents has provided institutional guarantees for the promotion of scientific development of education and carrying out education in such a way that the people are satisfied.

Scientific monitoring is a means of finding problems and a prerequisite and basis for effective supervision of the government and schools. By conducting supervision, guidance and monitoring, one can obtain accurate data and information in a comprehensive and timely manner, make judgments on the overall status of education, predict future trends, and adjust the implementation of policies to truly achieve effective management of education. For example, the Sichuan Provincial People's Government clearly stated in *The Arrangements for Key Reforms of Government Work in 2014* that education supervision, guidance and monitoring should be strengthened, local legislation for education supervision and guidance should be initiated, monitoring, guidance and supervision reports should be issued regularly, and monitoring, supervision and guidance should be done on the implementation of education guarantees by local governments; social organizations should be introduced for assessment and monitoring. At the same time, documents such as *The Guiding Opinions of the Sichuan Provincial Department of Education on Deepening Comprehensive Reform in Education (2014–2020)* and *The Notice on Special Reform Plans for Equitable Allocation of Compulsory Education Resources to Promote Fairness in Education* all include supervision, guidance and monitoring as an important part of the education supervision and guidance institution. To this end, Sichuan Province has established provincial-level evaluation and monitoring institutions to improve the commissioned evaluation and monitoring mechanism to provide basis and support for improving education, teaching, management, and decision-making (Education Science Forum Editorial Department, 2015).

II. Supervision, Guidance and Evaluation Mechanism

Supervision, guidance and evaluation of education is an important function of government organizations. Not only does the evaluation subject differ from the evaluation carried out by social organizations, there are also very large differences in the nature of the evaluation function. Education evaluations conducted by social institutions operate in accordance with market mechanisms, while evaluations conducted by government organizations operate in accordance with laws and policies. In summary, education supervision, guidance and evaluation conducted by government organizations has four characteristics, namely: compulsory, supervisory, instructive, and professional (Su, 2016).

Supervision, guidance and evaluation of education is based on certain educational goals and educational regulations and policies. Scientific, rational, and effective evaluation index institutions are formulated, and a series of relevant educational methods and means are used to conduct analysis of the educational activities of the supervised and guided units and the results they have achieved to make scientific judgments so that their achievements and deficiencies can be summarized. This provides a basis for decision-making by relevant departments at higher levels, and for the supervised and guided unit to carry forward the results and deepen reform (Huang, 2011: 185). In 2016, the MOE issued *The Opinions on Promoting the Comprehensive Evaluation Reform of Primary and Secondary Education Quality*, clarifying the framework of comprehensive evaluation indicators of education quality including the five aspects of moral development level, academic development level, physical and mental development level, interest and specialty development and academic burden status, and 22 indicators, and incorporated them into the scope of school supervision, guidance and evaluation. In recent years, in accordance with the actual situation in their area, all districts and municipalities have innovated and created supervision, guidance and evaluation mechanisms, which has had great significance in guiding the direction of education, promoting education reform, strengthening scientific management, achieving overall optimization of education, and improving the quality of schooling.

Taking Dalian as an example, Zhongshan District actively explores the three-in-one education management mechanism of "government macro-control, school-funded school-running, scientific supervision, guidance and evaluation," and closely centers on the school-running form of "one school, one product, every school has its characteristics, and everyone has their own specialty" to take the reform of the supervision and guidance mechanism as the starting point in implementing the effective transformation of government education management functions, making education supervision and guidance work the "correction mechanism" for government management education, conducting "follow-up evaluation" of policies through annual supervision and guidance evaluation, and investigating from the three levels of implementation subjects, beneficiaries, and decision-makers to test the scientific nature and rationality of policies and specific standards.

Zhongshan District adheres to the combination of internal and external evaluations. In one aspect, it constructs a "T" horizontal and vertical index institution to promote the development of "standards and characteristics" in schools; in another aspect, it guides schools to independently establish evaluation mechanisms and improve the construction of the rating system. Zhongshan District incorporated school self-evaluation into the framework of supervision, guidance and evaluation, and urged schools to establish an independent evaluation mechanism to achieve scientific and independent management. In terms of supervision, guidance and evaluation, on the basis of improving the 2009 *Comprehensive Supervision, Guidance and Evaluation Index System for School Management in Primary and Secondary Schools in Zhongshan District*, Zhongshan District has proposed horizontal and government-regulated common standards and requirements for conventional project indicators and key project indicators, ensuring that schools run according to the law and develop in a standardized way. At the same time, the independent development project indicators are used as a vertical and independently developed standard by schools, aiming to explore the school's own potential and guarantee its characteristic development. These three indicators total fourteen items and eighty checkpoints.

Meanwhile, since 2016, Dalian has made use of the education supervision, guidance and evaluation application system to realize the diversity of evaluation subjects, which not only plays the main role of the subject of the supervision and evaluation unit but also ensures the authority of the supervision, guidance and evaluation subject, especially including the evaluation activities or personal evaluations of social organizations, which provides effective channels for the management and evaluation of parents, students, and society to participate in education. Multi-subject evaluations such as multilateral interaction in supervision, guidance and evaluation are implemented to make evaluation results more objective, accurate, and convincing.

The innovation of the evaluation mechanism in Zhongshan District emphasized the flexibility and openness of supervision and evaluation, on the one hand, and ensured the characteristic development of the school, on the other hand. Taking Dalian as an example, Zhongshan District actively explored the trinity education management mechanism of "government macro-control, school-funded education, scientific supervision and evaluation," and closely centered on the school-running form of "one school, one product, the school has its characteristics, and everyone has its specialties." Take the reform of supervision mechanisms as the starting point to implement the effective transformation of government education management functions, make education supervision work the "correction mechanism" for government management education, conduct "follow-up evaluation" of policies through annual supervision evaluation, and investigate from the three levels of implementation subjects, beneficiaries and decision-makers to test the scientific nature and rationality of policies and specific standards. Zhongshan District adheres to the combination of internal and external evaluations. On the one hand, it constructs a "T" horizontal and vertical index system to promote the development of "standard and characteristic" schools; on the other hand, it guides schools to independently establish evaluation mechanisms and improve the construction of the rating system.

Zhongshan District incorporated school self-evaluation into the framework of supervision and evaluation, and urged schools to establish an independent evaluation mechanism to achieve scientific and independent management. In terms of supervision and evaluation, on the basis of improving the 2009 Comprehensive Supervision and Evaluation Index System for School Management in Primary and Middle Schools in Zhongshan District, Zhongshan District has proposed horizontal and government-regulated common standards and requirements for conventional project indicators and key project indicators. It ensures that the school runs according to law and develops in a standardized way. At the same time, the independent development project indicators are used as a vertical and independently developed standard by the school, aiming to explore the school's own potential and guarantee the school's characteristic development. These three indicators total fourteen items and eighty checkpoints. At the same time, since 2016, Dalian has applied the education supervision and evaluation application system to realize the diversity of evaluation subjects, which not only plays the role of the subject of the supervision and evaluation unit but also ensures the authority of the supervision and evaluation subject, especially the social organization or personal evaluation is included in evaluation activities, which provides effective channels for the management and evaluation of parents, students, and society to participate in education. Multi-subject evaluations such as multilateral interaction in supervision and evaluation are implemented to make evaluation results more objective, accurate, and convincing (MOE, 2016a). The innovation of the evaluation mechanism in Zhongshan District emphasizes the flexibility and openness of supervision, guidance and evaluation, on the one hand, and has ensured the characteristic development of schools, on the other hand.

III. The School Supervision Responsibility Mechanism

As early as the early 19th century, some prominent scholars regarded school district supervision and guidance as the most influential role in the field of public education (Kovalsky, 2012: 25). Britain, France, the United States and other countries all attach importance to supervising schooling with school districts, and the degree of specialization in supervising schooling is very high. School supervision improves schools by assessing the feedback provided to schools assessing the quality of their education and anticipating the consequences of students dropping out of school based on inspection standards and procedures (Ehren et al., 2013). The implementation of school supervision responsibility zones and listed supervision and guidance, as implementation of institutional innovation of a responsibility mechanism of education supervision and guidance, is an important measure promoting the normalization and institutionalization of school supervision work and strengthening supervision and guidance of primary and secondary schools.

In order to implement school supervision responsibilities, government education supervision departments have divided areas with primary and secondary schools and kindergartens in the area into several school supervision responsibility areas, and assigned to each district committee the responsibility of regular supervision and guidance of schools in the responsibility area. Supervision of schools in the responsibility area, through irregular follow-up inspections and supervision and guidance of schools in the area, encourages schools to fully implement Party and state education regulations and policies, standardize school running behavior, and continuously improve the quality of education and teaching (Zhou, 2009). As an extension of the school supervision function, the supervisory responsibility area adheres to the concept of "every school is progressing" and pays attention to the improvement of the quality inside and outside the school, thereby further strengthening the function of education supervision and guidance.

Listed supervision and guidance refers to the establishment of responsible supervision for each school in the school supervision responsibility area, and the name, photo, contact information and supervision and guidance matters of the person responsible for supervision of the school is marked in a prominent position on the school gate to conduct regular supervision of the school. As a normal and flexible form, listing supervision and guidance effectively guarantees the healthy development of schools and the implementation of education policies. At the same time, as an important measure to change the government's management functions, the implementation of listed supervision and guidance is an effective way to strengthen a school's connection with society and carry out satisfactory education for the people. It is also an important method of encouraging connotative development in schools.

With the advancement of the education governance institution and the modernization of education, listed supervision and guidance in the supervision of schools has received more and more attention from various cities, and the content of this supervision and guidance has been constantly improved. After 2015, in addition to the previous provisions, the state has included the implementation of school labor education, the management of paid remedial courses, and the supervision of bullying management in schools into the scope of primary and secondary school responsibility supervision school supervision listing. In 2016, the Education Supervision and Guidance Committee Office considered whether or not to implement supervision and guidance listing as an important item in its special supervision, guidance and inspection work when opening schools in spring. In October of the same year, Liu Yandong further emphasized the necessity and importance of constructing normal supervision and guidance in schools at the 10th National Conference of Appointment of Supervisors for Education

Supervision, Guidance and Reform, and called for the establishment of a supervision responsibility listing institution for supervision and guidance in primary and secondary schools, allocating 300,000 primary and secondary schools nationwide with more than 100,000 responsible supervisors, and establishing a "conventional army" of supervisors active in the school (MOE, 2016b), which provides a reference path for the construction of a modern school management evaluation mechanism and the improvement of education quality.

IV. The Supervision and Guidance and Accountability Mechanism

At the beginning of the 20th century, with the development of the Industrial Revolution and the advent of the era of scientific management, the education accountability institution in the United States was further developed. Businesses and corporations became very focused on "personal measurability, standardization, and grading. Schools played a similar role during the process of transforming large numbers of heterogeneous immigrants into disciplined citizens" (Sacks, 1999: 23). Since the 1990s, the discourse in American education policy has been dominated by "accountability." In education supervision and guidance activities, accountability is a core measure ensuring the effectiveness of education supervision and guidance. It has a very important role in implementing the education supervision and guidance institution, promoting education according to law, and promoting education reform and innovation (Wang & Chen, 2016).

On March 18, 2008, Shanghai established the Education Supervision and Guidance Affairs Center, becoming the first entity in the country to undertake education supervision and guidance recommendations and education administrative penalties at the time. It promoted implementation by law enforcement, adhered to joint law enforcement and flexible law enforcement (MOE, 2012b), and set up the precursor to the supervision and guidance accountability institution. In recent years, the state has promulgated a number of policies, regulations, and methods to continuously strengthen the accountability of education supervision and guidance and provide institutional guarantees for the establishment and implementation of the education supervision, guidance and accountability mechanism. In 2012, *The Education Supervision and Guidance Regulations* explained the accountability of education supervision and guidance in the form of special chapters. In February 2014, the MOE issued *The Interim Measures for Special Supervision and Guidance of Major Educational Emergencies*, which clearly states: "The establishment of a sound mechanism for supervision, inspection, assessment, and accountability and conducting an enquiry into accountability and handling of relevant responsible persons." In 2015, The Education Supervision and Guidance Committee Office of the State Council released *The Interim Measures for the Issuance of Education Supervision and Guidance Reports* (hereinafter referred to as *The Interim Measures*). *The Interim*

Measures clearly states that education supervision and guidance reports serve as an important basis for the assessment, reward, punishment, and accountability of the supervised and guided unit and its main responsible persons. During the process of promoting the reform of separation of education management, school running and evaluation, various cities and regions have also used supervision and guidance evaluation as an important reference for accountability. As a pilot for the reform of the separation of evaluation, school running and education management in China, in order to strengthen the supervision and classification guidance of schools and educational institutions at all levels and within the administrative region in accordance with the law, promote the separation of management, school running and evaluation, and modernize the education governance institution, Shanghai issued *The Opinions of the Education Supervision and Guidance Office of the Shanghai Municipal People's Government on the Implementation of Education Supervision and Guidance of Schools of All Types and at All Levels in the City*, which clearly set the results of the implementation of educational supervision and guidance by schools of various levels and various types as an important basis for the assessment of relevant government departments' performances in implementing educational responsibilities and implementing accountability.

The establishment of the supervision and guidance accountability institution is not only about accountability. It is more important to determine the educational responsibilities of each subject through the construction of the accountability institution to provide management institutions and methods that ensure the balance of rights and responsibilities of education subjects or equal rights and obligations to guide, supervise, and inspire various educational subjects to change the method of education development, and ultimately achieve the purpose of improving the quality of education and promoting the all-round development of students (Jia et al., 2012). Whether it is the accountability of the education administration department at the macro level, or the detailed accountability of schools and teachers, in the context of the reform of separation of management, school running and evaluation, the separation of government power does not necessarily mean that schools can do as they please, educational activities of education administrative departments and schools move between freedom and regulation, and the strengthening of supervision, guidance and accountability is not only the monitoring of the performance of education activities by the government, education administration departments and schools but also the internal power of coordinating scientific development of education.

The education supervision and guidance institution is an important part of the education management institution. It plays a supervisory role in the implementation of education policies, has the role of accountability and evaluation of school running behavior and education quality, and also plays a certain guiding role in the direction of education development. Establishing a scientific education supervision and guidance institution has become one of the important ways to improve the quality of education in various countries (Wang, 2013).

A historical review of China's education supervision and guidance institution reveals that China has now established a four-level education supervision and guidance network at the central, provincial, municipal, and county levels, and an education supervision and guidance institution based on a framework of the three major institutions of government supervision, education supervision, and evaluation and monitoring. With the continuous changes in education reform and the environment, the status of education supervision and guidance in education management cannot be shaken. At the same time, as China enters a new period of historical development, comprehensive education reforms are continuously promoted, the reform of the educational supervision and guidance institution is improved, and it is particularly critical to building an education supervision, guidance and evaluation institution that focuses on supervision and guidance and has multiple participation. To this end, it is necessary to open up the inside and outside of education supervision and guidance and promote scientific, open, and efficient education supervision and guidance to ensure the healthy, orderly, and stable development of education.

NOTE

1 Jin, Shaorong & Xinzhi Liu. (2013). NGO Participation in Public Education Governance: Goals, Dilemmas, and Directions. *Research on Education Development*, (5), 49–54.

REFERENCES

Chen, D. (1995). Strengthening education supervision and guidance is a necessary part of reforming of basic education. *China Education Journal*, *3*, 45–48 (in Chinese).

Chen, J., & Wan, Z. (2016). Thoughts on the modernization of the education governance institution and governance ability. *Education Research*, *10*, 25–31 (in Chinese).

Ehren, M. C. M., Altricher, H., McNamara, G., & O'Hara, J. (2013). Impact of school inspections on teaching and learning-describing assumptions on causal mechanisms in seven European countries. *Educational Assessment, Evaluation and Accountability*, *25*, 3–43.

Fu, Y. (2008). Exploring a scientific approach to improving the quality of basic education – An interview with the project team of "Establishing an Academic Quality Analysis, Feedback and guidance institution for Primary and Secondary School Students". *Basic Education Curriculum*, *02*, 4–6 (in Chinese).

Fullan, M. (2004). *The power of change-perspective on educational reform.* Beijing: Education Science Press.

Gao, W., & Huang, C. (1997). *A concise course on education supervision and guidance.* Beijing: Beijing Science Press (in Chinese).

He, D. (2003). *Important education documents of the People's Republic of China (1998–2002).* San Ya: Hainan Press (in Chinese).
Huang, W. (Ed.). (2011). *Education supervision and guidance studies.* Beijing: Renmin University of China Press (in Chinese).
Jia, J., Gao, L., & Chu, H. (2012). Building a quality-based education accountability institution. *China Education Journal, 3*, 21–24+89 (in Chinese).
Jiang, M. (2002). The current basic education supervision and guidance institution in The Netherlands and lessons to be learned. *Global Education Outlook, 9*, 72–76 (in Chinese).
Jin, S., & Liu, X. (2013). NGO participation in public education governance: Goals, dilemmas, and directions. *Research on Education Development, 5*, 49–54 (in Chinese).
Kovalsky, J. T. (2012). *The school superintendent theory, practice, and cases* (2nd Ed.). Beijing: Renmin University of China Press (in Chinese).
Lee, J. Ding, et al. (2008). School Supervision and Education in China: the Shanghai perspective. Quality Assurance in Education.12(2):148-163.
Le, Y. (2015). The reform of the local government's education supervision and guidance organizations should move from dependence to independence. *China Education Journal, 2*, 17 (in Chinese).
Lee, J. C.-K., & Ding, D., et al. (2008). School supervision and education in China: The Shanghai perspective. *Quality Assurance in Education, 16*(2): 148–163 (in Chinese).
Liu, L. (2015). Thoughts on the separation of evaluation and management of basic education in China in the new situation. *China Education Journal, 3*, 1–6 (in Chinese).
Lu, Y. (2014). Professionalization of education supervision and guidance personnel and their institution guarantees. *Education Guidance, 4*, 49–52 (in Chinese).
Lu, Z. (2017). First Shanghai education supervision and guidance forum held campus bullying rectification plan released late this month. Retrieved from http://sh.eastday.com/m/20171116/u1ai11002696.html (in Chinese).
MOE. (2003). Overview of China's education supervision institution. Retrieved from http://old.moe.gov.cn/publicfiles/business/htmlfiles/moe/moe_163/200409/3084.html (in Chinese).
MOE. (2012a). Four measures for "Escorting" the education supervision regulations. Retrieved from http://www.gov.cn/jrzg/2012-10/23/content_2248983.htm (in Chinese).
MOE. (2012b). Shanghai establishes innovative education administrative law enforcement system for entity institutions – Rigid and flexible law enforcement, escort education development. Retrieved from http://old.moe.gov.cn//publicfiles/business/htmlfiles/moe/s5147/201203/132353.html (in Chinese).
MOE. (2013). *Opinions of MOE on promoting the comprehensive evaluation reform of primary and secondary school education quality.* Retrieved from http://old.moe.gov.cn//publicfiles/business / htmlfiles / moe / s7054 / 201306 / 153185.html (in Chinese).
MOE. (2014). Improving supervision and guidance institutions and strengthening team construction. Retrieved from http://www.moe.edu.cn/jyb_xwfb/s5989/s6635/s8537 / s8539 / 201412 / t20141219_182054.html (in Chinese).
MOE. (2016a). Dalian, Liaoning Province: Using information technology to promote the transformation of educational supervision. Retrieved from http://www.moe.edu.cn/s78/A11/s3077/s8391/201601/t20160106_227055.html (in Chinese).
MOE. (2016b). Circular of MOE on printing and distributing vice premier Liu Yandong's speech at the deepening of educational supervision and guidance reform and the tenth national school

supervision and appointment work conference. Retrieved from http://www.moe.edu.cn/srcsite/A11/s7057/201611/t20161122_289661. html (in Chinese).
MOE. (2017a). 2016 National education supervision and guidance work report. Retrieved from http://www.moe.gov.cn/jyb_xwfb/gzdt_gzdt/s5987 / 201704 / t20170405_301851.html (in Chinese).
MOE. (2017b). The significance of the revision of *The Private Education Promotion Law* and its relation to the promulgation of *The Opinions*. Retrieved from http://www.moe.edu.cn/jyb_xwfb/xw_fbh/moe_2069/xwfbh_2017n/xwfb_170118/170118_sfcl/201701/t20170118_295177.html (in Chinese).
MOE. (2017c). 2016 national statistical bulletin on education development. Retrieved from http://www.moe.edu.cn/jyb_sjzl/sjzl_fztjgb/201707/t20170710_309042.html (in Chinese).
OFSTED. (2012). The framework for school inspection from September 2012. Retrieved from http://www.ofsted.gov.uk/resources/framework-for-school-inspection-september-2012-0.
Sacks, P. (1999). *Standardized minds: The high price of America's testing culture and what we can do to change it*. Cambridge, MA: Perseus Books.
Shi, D. (2009). Comparative study of education supervision and guidance institutions in Britain and Germany and lessons to be learned. *Educational Measurement and Evaluation*, *6*, 54–60 (in Chinese).
Su, J. (Ed.). (2012). *Education supervision and guidance*. Beijing: Beijing Normal University Press (in Chinese).
Su, J. (2016). The construction of an education evaluation mechanism against the background of separation of management, school running and evaluation. *Beijing Education (Higher Education)*, *12*, 56–58 (in Chinese).
Sun, S. (2013). Analysis and suggestions on educational supervision and guidance and supervision of the government. *Education Measurement and Evaluation*, *1*, 28–32 (in Chinese).
Sun, Y. (2004). Problems in China's perspective supervision and guidance institution and suggestions for improvement. *Education Research*, *10*, 64–68 (in Chinese).
The Education Science Forum Editorial Department. (2015). Setting up education monitoring and evaluation, and further promote the separation of management, school running and evaluation – Interview with Liu Dong, head supervisor of state education monitoring, Sichuan Province People's government education supervision and guidance group. *Education Science Forum*, *4*, 13–15 (in Chinese).
The Office for Standards in Education. (2009). *Children's services and skills department report 2008–2009*. Norwish: The Stationey Office.
Tu, W. (Ed.). (2015). *A new theory on educational supervision*. Beijing: People's Education Press (in Chinese).
Wang, L. (2013). The institutional setting, functional scope and team building of the current education supervision and guidance institution in Britain. *Comparative Education Research*, *10*, 34–38 (in Chinese).
Wang, X. (2014). Research on the supervision, guidance and evaluation institution for the connotative development of primary and middle schools. Doctoral Dissertation of Liaoning Normal University (in Chinese).
Wang, Y., & Chen, E. (2016). A probe into the path towards a sound education supervision, guidance and accountability mechanism. *Educational Research*, *5*, 12–17 (in Chinese).
Xu, H. (2016). Inspection of basic education monitoring in China and policy suggestions. *Educational Measurement and Evaluation*, *3*, 12–18+33 (in Chinese).

Yang, R. (2007). Thinking about the construction of China's education supervision and guidance policy institution. *Educational Research*, *8*, 28–33 (in Chinese).
Yu, K. (1999). Theory of governance and good governance. *Marxism and Reality*, *5*, 35–39 (in Chinese).
Yuan, G. (2014a). Accelerating the modernization of the education governance institution and governance capacity. Retrieved from http://www.gov.cn/gzdt/2014-02/16/content_2605760.htm (in Chinese).
Yuan, G. (2014b). Deepening comprehensive reforms in education and accelerating the modernization of the educational governance institution and governance ability. *China Higher Education*, *5*, 4–11 (in Chinese).
Zhang, J. (2012). Innovative institution collectively achieves full educational coverage. *China Education Daily*, October 12 (in Chinese).
Zhong, B. (2013). Strengthening comprehensive reform and stabilizing the deep water zone of education reform. *Education Research*, *7*, 4 (in Chinese).
Zhou, D. (2009). Reviews and reflections on China's educational supervision and guidance institution over the past 60 years. *Educational Measurement and Evaluation*, *9*, 4–12 (in Chinese).

CHAPTER EIGHT

The Education Finance Institution

YAOZONG HU AND ZHIMIN LIU

Education finance is an important guarantee for national education governance, and it is also a guiding force for the continuous breakthrough and development of education reform. Since Reform and Opening Up, the reform of China's education finance institution has been synchronized with the reform of the socialist market economic institution. After forty years of development, from exploration in the early stages of Reform and Opening Up, diversified fundraising for education, and the establishment of a public education finance institution, the beginnings of a modern education finance institution gradually and eventually took shape. Looking back at the establishment of China's education finance institution in the forty years of Reform and Opening Up, we have tried to construct a path from the reform of the financial institution to the reform of the education finance institution, and then to the construction of the education institution and the development of education under the support of education finance. From the perspective of the construction of the education finance institution, the aim is to provide a glimpse into the development process of China's modernization of education.

SECTION 1 EXPLORATION OF THE EDUCATION FINANCE INSTITUTION IN THE EARLY PERIOD OF REFORM AND OPENING UP

After the founding of the People's Republic of China, in order to adapt to the basic economic institution of the planned economy institution, China formed a fiscal institution of unified revenue and expenditure.[1] After the focus of Party and state work shifted to economic construction in 1978, the financial sector began to explore the implementation of a hierarchical contracting fiscal institution. At this time, the education finance institution as an idea and understanding was not formally put forward, but the human capital theory and education proposed internationally after the Second World War was an investment concept that greatly impacted people's rigid understanding of education just being a consumer undertaking, in practice, a decentralized education finance institution that decentralized power to localities, society, and schools gradually took shape.

I. Hierarchical Contracting Financial Institution

In the field of finance, people referred to the financial institution in the early stages of Reform and Opening Up as the hierarchical contracting institution, which refers to the financial institution implemented before the implementation of the reform of the economic institution in China after the Third Plenary Session of the Eleventh Central Committee and the implementation of the tax-sharing fiscal institution in 1994. Although three major reforms and adjustments were made in 1980, 1985, and 1988, their common features were hierarchical contracting and self-balancing based on the division of revenues and expenditures, so it was commonly known as the hierarchical contracting institution, or "the divided meals" institution.

The hierarchical contracting institution was started on a trial basis at the beginning of Reform and Opening Up. From 1976 to 1979, the financial institution implemented a hierarchical contracted financial institution that linked revenue and expenditure and divided the total amount. Each year, the central government approved the revenue tasks and total expenditures of provinces, municipalities, and autonomous regions, and used the proportion of expenditure as income as the local share.[2] During implementation, over-collection could be distributed as income according to the share proportion. If the local total share was less than 30%, the over-collection portion could be divided by 30%. In areas where the total share was more than 70% and areas where subsidies are received, the over-collection part was divided by 70%. Short-term income would reduce expenditure accordingly and balance would be sought.

In February of 1980, the State Council issued *The Interim Provisions on the Implementation of The Financial Management Institution of "Dividing Revenue and Expenditure and Hierarchical Contracting,"* and began to implement a financial contracting institution that delegates power to local governments. This reform changed the centralized financial institution of "collective revenue and unified expenditure" that was used in the past, and established a decentralized institution of "separating food and cooking" between the central and local governments. The main purpose was to classify and divide income into three categories: divided fixed income, fixed ratio income, and adjusted income. Financial expenditure was mainly divided according to the affiliation between enterprises and institutions. In the range of revenue and expenditure, local governments that received more could spend more and those that received less strove to achieve balance (Zhong, 2012: 75–81). From 1985 to 1987, a transitional method of "gross share" was temporarily implemented. In addition to the central fiscal fixed income not participating in the sharing, the local fiscal fixed income and the central and local fiscal shared revenue were added together and linked to local fiscal expenditure, from which the proportion was determined and gross share was carried out. In 1988, the financial contracting institution was introduced throughout the country.

The hierarchical contract financial institution broke the past situation of "uniform revenue and expenditure, and disjointed revenue and expenditure," not only expanding local fiscal power but also combining local responsibilities, powers, and benefits so that localities had the motivation and ability to develop the local economy and various undertakings, vigorously mobilizing the enthusiasm of local financial management and education.

II. The Embryonic Form of the Decentralized Education Finance Institution

After the Third Plenary Session of the Eleventh Party Central Committee, with the change in the focus of socialist construction work of the Party and the country, education, as a fundamental issue affecting the overall situation of socialist construction and the historical fate of the country gradually received the attention of the entire Party and society. In April 1978, the National Education Work Conference was convened to restore teaching order and proposed that education should be adapted to the development of the national economy. In 1980, the Fifth Plenary Session of the Eleventh Central Committee of the Communist Party of China put forward the task of "determining an educational plan and educational institution suitable for the needs of national economic development." In September 1982, the 12th National Congress of the Communist Party of China officially identified education as a strategic focus of development, liberating education from being a long-term political tool. Education in China was fully restored thereafter and the scale of education grew rapidly (Yang, 2006: 64–67).

In the late 1970s and early 1980s, the education community and even the entire ideological community established the guiding status of Deng Xiaoping's educational theory. Deng Xiaoping's educational theory provided clear guidance for the transformation, reform, and development of China's Educational Finance Thought. First, Deng Xiaoping clearly pointed out that "Education is the foundation" from the height of socialist economic construction. After the Third Plenary Session of the 11th CPC Central Committee, Deng Xiaoping personally took hold of the basic work of education. Second, Deng Xiaoping put forward the educational thoughts of "to master science and technology we must master education" and "education work should be mastered in the same way as economic work." In 1977, Xiaoping Deng clearly pointed out that the fundamental task of socialism is developing productive forces, and science and technology are the primary productive forces. "The key to modernization is to be able to go up with science and technology. It is not possible to develop science and technology without mastering education" (Deng, 1983: 40). In May 1977, his famous speech on respecting knowledge and talent, to a large extent, established the development direction and basic value of education in the new era. Third, Deng Xiaoping established the strategic idea of prioritizing the development of education and attaching importance to increasing investment in education. Comrade Deng Xiaoping regarded education as a major cause for the entire Party and society. "Education is not just a matter for the education department. Party committees at all levels must take it seriously as a major cause. All walks of life must come to support education and put great efforts into education." In September 1982, the 12th National Congress of the Communist Party of China was held. This forward-looking conference was the first time in the Party's history that it had raised education to be one of its strategic priorities. This was a major turning point in the history of China's education development and an important reflection of Deng Xiaoping's thinking on education.

During this period, the introduction and construction of educational economics promoted an upsurge in theoretical research on educational economics and triggered discussions on the essence of educational investment. In April 1979, the central government convened a national conference on educational science, which formalized the study of educational economics. In June 1980, the Editorial Department of Educational Research held a symposium on education. The fourth issue of Educational Research in the same year published the views of economists including Yu Guangyuan, Song Tao of Renmin University of China, Xiao Zhuoji of Peking University, and Gu Mingyuan of Beijing Normal University on the shortage of education funding and the establishment of educational economics. The call of these experts paved the way for the establishment of educational economics in China. In August 1980, according to the instructions of the Party group of the Ministry of Education, the Central Institute of Educational Sciences held an educational economics research exchange meeting in Beijing, and published *The Proposal on the Establishment of a National Educational Economics Research Institute*. In August 1981, a preparatory group of the newly established National Educational Economics Research Institute arranged and held a workshop in Beijing, and for the first time systematically introduced the emergence, development, and basic content of Western and Soviet educational economics in China. Since then, a number of translations, treatises, and textbooks have been published. In September 1984, the China Society for Educational Economics was established in Huangshan. In 1985, the China Society for Educational Economics and Huazhong Normal University co-founded "Education and Economy" magazine. Educational economics was formally established in China, and it provided a theoretical basis for the reasonable determination of educational investment ratios and the rational allocation of educational resources.

The reform of the financial institution and the education institution determined the arrangement of the education finance institution. In 1980, after the State Council issued a document implementing the financial management institution of "dividing revenues and expenditures and hierarchical contracting," the education industry actively adjusted to the general situation and responded quickly. The Party Group of the Ministry of Education issued *The Recommendations on the Arrangement of Educational Funding after the Implementation of the New financial institution* (hereinafter referred to as *The Recommendations*) on March 10, 1980, and proposed that from 1980 onwards, funding for education would be financed by the financial departments of central and local governments. This new education funding management institution determined that the central government financial department would only cover the funds of higher education and secondary schools under the central ministries and commissions. Funding for colleges and universities, and primary and secondary schools under provincial and municipal governments would be the responsibility of provincial and municipal People's governments (Lin & Lü, 2011). *The Recommendations* required all localities to embody the spirit of the central government's emphasis on education and gradually increase education funding. Localities with better conditions were to arrange as much education funding as possible. Since staff funding for schools at all levels, especially primary and secondary schools, took up a larger proportion and public funds were relatively low, reducing public funding for education further would have made education even more difficult. Given this, schools had to run themselves in a frugal manner. Funds saved would not be recovered, and education departments at all levels were to make overall arrangements to fill the gaps and improve the conditions for running the school (Long, 2009).

In 1983, the Central Committee of the Communist Party of China and the State Council issued *The Notice on Strengthening and Reforming Rural School Education*, giving a series of instructions on strengthening and reforming rural school education. It pointed out that it was necessary to mobilize the enthusiasm of rural cooperative organizations, factories and mining enterprises, farmers to run schools and solve rural education funding problems through various channels by "walking on two legs" with the state running schools as the main body. Generally speaking, during this period, no government financial compulsory education investment institution was established in a true sense, which was reflected in the limits on management authority. At that time, compulsory education mainly administered by the state, centralized with a single financial management mode. At this stage, the development of rural compulsory education in China still faced problems such as poor schooling conditions, shortage of funds, low teacher salaries, and rising dropout rates in primary and secondary schools (Yang & Zhang, 2012). In line with this, the central government alone taking responsibility for educational finance for institutions of higher education was replaced by separate arrangements between the central and local governments, with hierarchical responsibilities, that is, schools run and managed by central government ministries and commissions should be funded by the Ministry of Finance; schools organized and managed by local governments should be funded by local financial departments. The central government no longer unified higher education finances, and a decentralized higher education finance institution began to take shape (Yang et al., 2010).

III. Analysis of the Decentralized Education Finance Institution

Education was the country's worst hit sector during the Cultural Revolution. Due to the influence of the extreme left ideology of "class struggle as the key link," the nature of education was repeatedly tortured politically, and schools also became "tools of the class struggle." After the Third Plenary Session of the 11th Central Committee, education was fully restored. The popularization of primary school education began and made great progress in accordance with the school policy of "walking on two legs." A number of key primary and secondary schools successively emerged. The structural reform of secondary education and the development of vocational and technical education continued to advance. Higher education was mainly focused on restoring the college entrance examination, straightening out aspects such as the higher education management institution, adjustment of subjects and the professional structure of higher education institutions, and construction of key universities. Graduate education was also restored during this period. The establishment of the Educational Economics Research Association and the establishment of educational economics in China demonstrated the enthusiasm of the people for focusing on education funding and the whole of society on running education. It also laid a foundation for the reasonable determination of educational investment ratios and the rational distribution of educational resources. The establishment of Xiaoping Deng's educational theory provided clear guidance for the transformation, reform, and development of China's thinking on educational finance. The reform of decentralization of educational finance adapted to the transition of the national economic institution from a traditional highly centralized planned economy to a socialist planned commodity economic institution. The ownership structure gradually diversified, and the allocation of resources shifted from planned allocation to a combination of planning with market regulation. Basic education finance gradually formed an institution of "hierarchical management centered around the township"; finance in higher education formed an intergovernmental fiscal decentralization institution, and a cost sharing and cost compensation mechanism was established at the same time. At this stage, education expenditure increased significantly on an absolute scale.

The reform of decentralization of education finance achieved remarkable results, but the scale of education investment is still at a low level: The allocation and use of funds are still significantly disconnected, the structure of education investment is not reasonable, and the contradiction between education demand and supply is still very acute. The power of localities to coordinate education funding has been greatly expanded from the past. However, the primary responsibility for financing education has been given to localities, which has increased burdens on them, and has also exacerbated regional inequities in education. At the same time, the long-term ideological inertia in China's fiscal thinking that regards education as consumption and safeguards the important industries of production, national defense, and agriculture still occupies a certain place in national decision-making. The long-term local ideological inertia of local governments where education is neglected still exists. Therefore, although there has been a considerable increase in investment in education, the problem of funding shortages has not been fundamentally resolved.

SECTION 2 ESTABLISHMENT OF A MULTICHANNEL FINANCING INSTITUTION FOR EDUCATION

From 1985 to 1997, the new fiscal and taxation institution, with the reform of the tax-sharing institution as an important symbol, transformed from exploration to reality, and the definition of the relationship between central and local powers and financial powers entered a new stage. The field of education finance, while continuously increasing government investment in education, has attracted various parties in society to jointly invest in education, forming a new pattern of raising education funds through multiple channels.

I. Raising Funding for Education through Multiple Channels

After the development of education in the early days of Reform and Opening Up, the scale of education in China has become increasingly large, and funding shortages remain the primary problem facing education reform and development. To solve this problem, it is necessary to mobilize the enthusiasm of governments at all levels, teachers, students and staff, and all aspects of society to participate in education. In 1985, *The Decision of the Central Committee of the Communist Party of China on the Reform of the Education Institution* was promulgated, clarifying that basic education management power belongs to the locality. In order to ensure the development of education at the local level, in addition to state funding, an appropriate proportion of local mobile financial resources should be used for education, and it was required that township fiscal revenue be used mainly for education. Local governments can collect additional educational fees, and encourage and guide state-owned enterprises, social groups, and individuals to run schools. On a voluntary basis, units, collectives, and individuals are encouraged to donate funds to fund education, forming the beginning of a multichannel education funding policy. Therefore, after 1985, there have been three main sources of funding for compulsory education: state funding for compulsory education, investment from society in compulsory education, and education costs borne by individuals (Li, 2008: 29).

In the mid-1980s, the Party Central Committee and the State Council issued four documents on fundraising for schools and rebuilding schools, including *The Notice of the State Council on Raising Funds for Running Rural Schools*, *The Interim Provisions on the Collection of Educational Surcharges by the State Council*, and *The Several Regulations on Strengthening General Education Funding Management*, which provided preliminary provisions on the principles and scope of education funding. In 1988, the State Council established a research group on education development and reform headed by Li Tieying, which conducted in-depth investigations and studies on the development direction and planning of Chinese education over the next ten years. In 1989, the Politburo of the Central Committee discussed and adopted *The Decision of the Central Committee of the Communist Party of China on Several Issues concerning the Development and Reform of Education*, which was drafted by the group. This document provided more systematic and improved rules for financing channels of education. This can be summarized as finance, tax, fees, industry, society, and foundations, that is, gradually establishing a new institution for raising funds for education through multiple channels, mainly through state financial appropriation and collecting taxes and fees that go towards education, supplemented by the collection of tuition and other miscellaneous fees from students in non-compulsory education, school income, social fund raising and establishment of education funds. In the same year in Shandong, the State Education Commission and the Ministry of Finance jointly held a national "on-site meeting for multichannel education fundraising and improving school conditions." Li Tieying summarized the successful implementation of graded school running, graded management, widened channels, multi-party fundraising, and improved schooling conditions and development of education over a number of years. He recommended the formulation of plans, policies, and regulations to raise education funds through multiple channels; improve the conditions for running schools; and raise the issue of solving the problem of insufficient education funds. In addition to increasing national strength, it is also necessary to reform to establish a new institution for financing education in line with China's national conditions, and to raise education funding through six channels: financing, taxation, fees, industry, society, and foundations. The above meetings and "The Multi-channel Education Financing and Improving Conditions for Running Schools Meeting" held in Henan laid the foundation for the final formation of a multichannel education financing policy institution.

Under the leadership of the State Council, the State Education Commission, in conjunction with the relevant central government departments, further improved various aspects of the institution of financing education through multiple channels and recommended that they be reflected and regulated in relevant documents and legal provisions. Subsequently, *The Outline of China's Education Reform and Development* issued by the Central Committee of the Communist Party of China and the State Council in 1993, *The Implementation Opinions of "The Outline of China's Education Reform and Development"* issued by the State Council in 1994 (hereinafter referred to as *The Implementation Opinions of "The Outline"*), *The Education Law* promulgated in 1995, and *The Action Plan for the Revitalization of Education for the 21st Century*, promulgated in 1998, have made clear and specific measures on the expenditure, growth, and management of the six source channels and have formed a relatively complete "multichannel education financing" policy institution (Xu, 2003). Among them, the 1994 *Implementation Opinions of "The Outline"* explicitly put forward "multichannel education financing": the state supported schools in developing school-run industries, and continues to implement tax reduction and exemption policies for school-run industries including various vocational schools; increased the policy-based low-interest loans for school-run industries year by year; establish an education bank and the use of financial means to expand the source of education funds; continued to encourage factories and mining enterprises, social forces, and people from all walks of life at home and abroad to donate funds to help schools and raise funds to carry out schooling in rural areas.

The improvement of the multichannel education financing policy institution and the establishment of the strategic priority of education development have effectively mobilized the enthusiasm of governments at all levels from central to local to run education and effectively make up for the lack of education funding. Governments at all levels have successively introduced a series of specific policies and measures. State financial education funding has increased year after year; urban and rural and local education surcharges have been levied, forming a relatively stable source of funding for basic education; the government has established the principle of "rely on the people to run schools" and adhered to the "walk on two legs" policy; promoted and encouraged enterprises, institutions, social groups, and other people from all walks of life to raise funds to run schools and donate funds to schools; carried out work-study programs and paid services in society; collected tuition and miscellaneous fees during non-compulsory education stages; in addition to certain amounts of special subsidy funds allocated by the government, economically underdeveloped areas have used foreign capital to support education, such as World Bank loans. Focused on solving the problem of insufficient funding in education, various levels and all types of education institutions in various fields have successively summed up a wealth of successful experience. Especially after China's education funding formed six main source channels, the total investment in education funding has increased rapidly (Xu, 2003).

II. The Establishment of Education Investment Theory and the 4% Target

In the early 1980s, the relationship between education and the economy began to receive great attention in China, and discussions on education investment issues appeared in the press. People gradually realized that education is of great significance to the development of the national economy, and education is the basis for realizing the modernization of the country. Therefore, there was an upsurge in discussions regarding increasing investment in education and developing the cause of education.

The input of resources for education was not included in the scope of (economic) investment for a long time. The main reason for this was that as an activity, institution, or department, education was not a material product, but a spiritual product. Education and the economy are different sectors of social activities. It is only when people observe and analyze society as a whole with economic properties that it becomes clear to them that education has significant economic effects. It is precisely because of these effects that discussions arose regarding the (economic) functional nature of education investment (Qiu, 1990). From the perspective of investment sources, this includes all expenditures on education by the state finance department, state-owned and collective institutions, families and individuals, of which, expenditure by the state finance department makes up the main part (Wang, 1987). The amount of national education investment and its proportion in the national economy in a certain period is ultimately determined by socioeconomic level. The level of social and economic development determines not only the demand for education investment, but also the possible amount of education investment. Therefore, in countries and periods with different levels of socioeconomic development, the proportion of education investment in the national economy is different. In January 1980, in his speech "The Present Situation and the Tasks Before Us," Xiaoping Deng stated: "The development of the economy and the development of science and culture are out of proportion, and the amount spent on education, science, culture and health is too small and is disproportionate."

In order to ensure a reasonable proportion of Chinese education funding as a part of national income, and thereby analyze the economic benefits of education investment, the state treated this issue as a key scientific research project in philosophy and social sciences during the Sixth Five-Year Plan period.[3] Professor Li Yining and Chen Liangkun from Peking University, Meng Mingyi from the Central Institute of Educational Sciences, and Wang Shanmai from Beijing Normal University were among some of the professors entrusted to chair the research work of the project, of which participants came from twenty-three units (Li, 1987).

According to the analysis of international comparative research, the research group made a basic judgment on the state of China's education investment, and believed that education expenditure in China at that time as a proportion of gross national product was slightly lower than the international average level based on countries with equivalent per capita GDP. Compared with the investment in education of developing countries with high populations, the level of investment in education in China was much lower (Li, 1987). In determining the reasonable boundary for education funding allocation, the sub-project headed by Chen Liangkun of Peking University considered starting from international comparisons, trying to find the regularity of government funding for education. The research team collected various data from more than one hundred countries from 1961 to 1980 from the yearbooks of UNESCO, the World Bank, and the International Monetary Fund, forming a unified evaluation and forecasting model on proportions of education funding. According to China's strategic goal of economic development at the end of the 20th century, which was quadrupling per capita GDP from its level in 1978, by the end of the 20th century, the target of China's per capita GDP was roughly 800–1000 US dollar. When 800 US dollars is substituted into the model, the result is 4.06%, that is, once per capita GDP reaches US $800, the average level of education expenditure in GDP corresponding to this level of economic development is 4.06%.

In order to test its applicability, Wang Shanmai of Beijing Normal University organized a group of researchers to set up the sub-project "Education Investment in the Soviet Union and Eastern European Countries and its Comparisons with China." Using calculations from the model, the result was that when per capita

GDP reached 1,000 US dollars at the end of the 20th century, a reasonable proportion of funding for education would be 3.79%, just around 4%. At this point, there was a consensus in research circles that "4%" was to be the target for public education investment by the end of the 20th century that was compatible with the economic level at that time (Liu, 2011).

III. The Practice of Increasing Investment in Education Funding

The 1985 *Decision of the Central Committee of the Communist Party of China on the Reform of the Education Institution* recognized the need to increase investment in the development of education, and determined that "in a certain period of time after now, the increase in education funding by the central and local governments should be higher than the increase in fiscal recurrent income. Also, education spending should be gradually increased based on the average number of students at school." The 1993 *Outline of China's Education Reform and Development* stated the need to "reform and improve the educational investment institution and increase education funding," stressing that "increasing investment in education is a fundamental measure for implementing the strategic position of education. Governments at all levels, all sectors of society and individuals must make the effort to increase investment in education and ensure the development of education as a priority. It is necessary to gradually establish an education funding institution with a variety of funding channels, mainly through the collection of national fiscal funds, supplemented by the collection of taxes for education, collection of tuition and other fees for students at non-compulsory education stages, income from school-run industries, social fundraising, and the establishment of an education fund. Through legislation, a stable source and growth of education funds is guaranteed." In addition to the *Principle* of 1985, it was required to effectively ensure that teachers' salaries and per capita public expenditures increase year after year. The "three growths" were specified, and it was proposed that by the end of the 20th century, the proportion of national fiscal education expenditures to GDP was to reach 4%. In 1998, *The Action Plan for Revitalizing Education for the 21st Century* was promulgated, emphasizing that "developing education should be thought of as building infrastructure, and as a basic investment, every effort should be made to increase education investment" to implement the "three growths."

In practice, the Party Central Committee and the State Council identified the development of education as one of the strategic priorities of the country's economic construction, and the absolute amount of investment in education has increased at a rapid rate. In 1997, total national fiscal expenditure on education reached 186.254 billion yuan, a 6.08-fold increase from 26.290 billion yuan in 1985, with an average annual increase of 18.28%. Education expenditure in the fiscal budget reached 135.773 billion yuan, a 5.04-fold increase from 22.489 billion yuan in 1985, a 12.03-fold increase from 121.191 billion yuan in 1976, with an average annual increase of 17.10% (Zhou, 1996). The total investment in national education expenditure reached 253.173 billion yuan, a 7.26-fold increase from 30.668 billion yuan in 1985.

IV. Analysis of Multichannel Education Financing Policies

The reform of the tax-sharing institution has smoothed out intergovernmental fiscal relations, maintained the central government finance department's strong dominance in central and local relations, and enabled the state's fiscal revenue to continue to grow with the prosperity of industrialization and enterprises. It is also an important prerequisite for the government's ability to increase fiscal education funding as a proportion of education investment. The formulation and implementation of a multichannel fundraising policy institution for education has largely eliminated the shortcomings and disadvantages of traditional single-source education funding, and has played a positive role in promoting the overall development of education and socioeconomics: mobilizing the enthusiasm of governments at all levels from central to local governments to carry out education, with governments at all levels successively introducing a series of specific policies and measures, national financial education funding has increased year after year; additional fees for urban and rural education have been levied, forming one of the more stable sources of funding for basic education; the government has established policies of "relying on the people to run schools," and adhered to "walking on two legs," promoting and encouraging fundraising mechanisms such as fundraising and donating to run schools from factories and mining enterprises, administrative institutions, social organizations, rural economic organizations, and people from all walks of life, forming six main channel sources and promoting a substantial increase in total education funding. The proposal of education investment theory and the 4% target emphasized the economic benefits of education investment and the reasonable proportion of education funds to national income, promoting a substantial increase in financial education investment, which has been of great significance to the development of education in China. The introduction of the higher education cost sharing institution has reduced the government's share of direct education costs for the higher education stage, and the proportion of burden for all parties, especially individuals, has increased significantly. This has promoted the rapid development of higher education and provided lessons for education at other stages.

The policy of raising funds through multiple channels has yielded significant results, but problems also remained. The main manifestations are as follows: First, insufficient investment in education, the role of the main channel of financial investment is weakening, and the proportion of public education expenditure is relatively low. Comparing 1995 to 1990, the proportion of national fiscal education expenditure in total education expenditure decreased from 85.3% to 75.2%, of which the proportion of education funding in the fiscal budget to total education expenditure decreased from 67.4% to 54.8%. Second, there is a large difference in the per capita investment of students in universities, primary and secondary schools, and education funding leans too far towards higher education. There is too much emphasis on "multichannel funding" at the compulsory education stage and the role of the government as the main channel has weakened, leading to the transfer of government responsibility and an increased burden on those being educated. Third, the sources of education funding are not reasonable. Guided by a multichannel policy, arbitrary charging is facilitated. Given the situation of being insufficiently funded, schools charge a variety of miscellaneous fees, overwhelming those being educated. In addition, in the later stages of the multichannel financing education policy, due to the uneven economic development in the eastern, central, and western regions[4], there are obvious differences in educational funding between regions, which has widened the regional gap in educational development.

SECTION 3 THE PUBLIC EDUCATION FINANCE INSTITUTION

Since 1998, the Chinese central government has proposed the construction of a public financial institution, emphasizing the public nature of fiscal functions. The construction of the public education finance institution began to be included in the policy agenda as a component of the public financial institution, and a basic education finance institution consisting of an education funding institution, an external proportional distribution institution, tuition and student subsidy institution, and a financial transfer payment institution was initially formed.

I. The Public Finance Institution

The concept of "public finance" was put forward for fiscal transformation in the course of economic and social transition. During the process of transforming the traditional institution into a socialist market economy institution, it was objectively necessary to form a basic guideline for the adjustment of fiscal functions and fiscal forms, that is, the guidance of public finance. In 1998, the central government made it clear that the goal of finance institution reform was to establish a public finance institution. The establishment and improvement of the public finance institution mainly includes reform of the fiscal revenue institution and reform of the fiscal expenditure institution. The reform of the fiscal revenue institution involves reform of rural taxes and fees, reform of the "two lines of revenue and expenditure" management, reform of the management institution for non-tax revenue collection, and standardization of the fiscal transfer payment institution. The reform of the fiscal expenditure institution involves measures such as departmental budget reform, reform of the centralized treasury collection and payment institution, and reform of the government procurement institution (Shen, 2005).

The most important internal orientation of the public finance institution is emphasizing the public nature of finance, therefore, public finance has the following four basic characteristics. First, meeting public needs should be considered to be the main goal and focus of fiscal allocation. Focusing on economic construction and the scientific concept of development requires both the state to seize the dominant public needs and emphasize meeting the public needs of society as the focus of the fiscal institution. Second, finance should take the provision of public goods and services that the market cannot effectively provide as the basic way to meet social public needs, that is, reasonably grasp the relationship between the government and the market, and the two should form a complementary division of labor to promote the full liberation of productivity, comprehensive optimization of resource allocation, and maximization of overall social benefits and overall welfare. Third, we must standardize public choices on the premise of equal civil rights and balances of political rights to serve as the decision-making and supervision mechanism for financial distribution. Efforts to achieve democratization, legalization, and constitutionalization ensure the scientific nature of decision-making, and maximization of the satisfaction of public needs. Fourth, in the management and operation of public finances, we must use open, transparent, complete, predetermined, and strictly enforced budgets with modern significance as the basic management institution. We must strive for a thorough and perfect financial management institution to prevent distortion of public power, standardize government behavior, implement public will, and pursue the maximization of public interest (Jia, 2011). Public finance is a form of finance that adapts to the requirements of the times and can be adapted to and matched with the requirements of the new socialist market economy institution and overall economic and social development requirements in the new era.

II. Composition of the Public Education Finance Institution

In terms of institution functions, the public education finance institution includes the education funding institution, the education budgeting institution, the public education fund allocation institution, the tuition and student subsidy institution, and the education finance transfer payment institution.

The education financing institution is an institution that provides funding for education through a combination of government tax and expenditure budget institution, education charging institution, and education donation institution. The government's funding for education comes mainly from general taxes, as well as specific taxes and budget deficits set for education. The collection of tuition and miscellaneous fees from the educated is the earliest and still widely used method of financing. Education donation is an auxiliary channel for education institutions to raise education funds. Education donations are closely related to economic development level, the taxation institution, social and cultural traditions, the education institution and so on. The core problem of the education financing institution is clarifying two relations. One is the cost sharing relationship between the government and the people being educated, and the other is the fund sharing relationship between government levels.

The public education funding allocation institution is also known as the education funding institution, which refers to the institution of allocating and distributing education funds to schools that provide education services under the condition that their budget is used for education expenditure. It includes the main body of the allocation or appropriation (the answer is who allocates or appropriates), and the mode of allocation or appropriation (the answer is the standard and model of appropriation). With regard to the former, there are two types of allocation of grants. One is government grants, and the majority of state education grant bodies are part of the government; the other is a third-party executive agency as a grant body. In response to the latter, there are currently two international funding models, one is direct funding to schools that provide educational services, called direct funding; the other is indirect funding, or "education vouchers." The government issues education vouchers to students, and after the students choose a school, the education vouchers are handed over to the selected school. The school uses the obtained education vouchers in exchange for financing from the government.

The funding model involves the content and basis of funding. According to the function of expenditures, education grants can be divided into funds for maintaining the normal operation of schools and funds used for school development. The former includes recurring funds for schools and capital expenditures. Recurrent funds are called education expenses in China, including personnel and public funds; the latter is called education infrastructure funds in China, and is mainly used for purchasing costs of teaching equipment above the government-defined limit and infrastructure costs for various buildings in the school. In terms of appropriation, recurrent funding is determined in accordance with the per-capita funding required by the national and provincial local governments for basic education standards at all levels and types. The funds for development are determined according to various projects and required costs established by the country's specific education development policy at a certain period of time. The former is based on fairness, and equalized appropriations are adopted on a per student basis. Most of the latter are efficiency-oriented, introduce market competition mechanisms, and allocate funds through bidding.

As for the tuition fee institution, tuition fees are an important part of the financial institution of public education, and they are also a part of the administrative fee institution of the financial institution. The basic foundation for the establishment of internationally accepted tuition fees is the cost of education per student and the level of income of residents. The education costs mentioned by the former should be the cost of training students in the school, not including the personal education costs paid by the students (or families), or the indirect education costs (or opportunity costs) of society and those being educated. However, there are two major difficulties in operating the basis for determining the educational cost of tuition fees: First, it is impossible for schools and the government to provide accurate and systematic cost information under the current institution; second, it is difficult to determine the proportion of educated people in education cost sharing. The latter refers to development needs based on the survival needs of educated residents. Residents' education expenditures, including tuition fees, are part of their total expenditures. The ability to pay tuition fees depends on the structure and level of household expenditures, and ultimately on their income level.

The student financial assistance institution is an institutional arrangement that provides financial support for students with financial difficulties in the family to improve their educational opportunities. It is composed of the key elements of financial assistance responsibility main bodies, financial assistance fund collection and burdens, allocation and management financial assistance funding, etc. The student aid institution was created mainly to promote education equity and improve education efficiency. The state has formulated a "reward, loan, assistance, supplement, reduction" and "green channel" institution to support students with financial difficulties and has established a three-level education student financial assistance institution.

The education finance transfer payment institution refers to the institution and regulation of education finance transfer payments between central and local governments or between different levels of government. It is part of a hierarchical intergovernmental financial transfer payment institution and is based on the asymmetry of responsibilities over educational affairs and financial resources between different levels of government, and the imbalance of financial resources between regions. Its significance lies in solving the problem of insufficient education funding and unbalanced regional development, and achieving balanced development of education. The necessity of the education finance transfer payment institution lies in: first, the vertical imbalance of education finance at different levels of government; second, the imbalance of horizontal education finance between governments in different regions; and third, correcting regional spillovers of educational benefits. The direct goal of the education finance transfer payment institution is balancing the education finance supply and the equalization of public education services. Intergovernmental financial transfer payments are divided into general transfer payments and special transfer payments. General transfer payments, also called unconditional transfer payments, are the subject of intergovernmental transfer payments. It does not require fund support from the local government it is transferred to, nor does it stipulate the use of transfer funds. Special transfer payments are also called conditional transfer payments. Conditions include requiring lower-level governments to provide funding packages, or specifying the purpose of transfer payments, or both. The education finance transfer payment institution is part of the special financial transfer payment institution, which mainly reflects the specific education policies and educational development goals of the central and upper-level local governments in a specific period. China's current education finance transfer payments can be divided into two categories: one is a special purpose transfer payment for a specific purpose, which covers all types of education at all levels, most of which are special allocations from central to local education; the other type is general transfer payments from the central government to local governments. They are used for education in a certain proportion, but the specific proportion is not stipulated and nor is the type or level of education.

III. The Increase in Financial Education Funds under the Guidance of "the Three Growths"

On February 26, 1993, the CPC Central Committee and the State Council issued and implemented *The Outline of China's Education Reform and Development* (hereinafter referred to as *The Outline*), and *The Education Law of the People's Republic of China* (hereinafter referred to as *The Education Law*) was implemented on September 1, 1995. These two statutory documents set clear requirements for education funding, which were summarized as "the three growths," that is, growth in education appropriations within the budget of the central and local governments being higher than the regular income growth of the same level of finance, per capita education fees for students in schools must gradually grow, and teachers' salaries and student per capita public funds must grow year after year.

Guided by *The Three Growths* policy tool, the government at all levels, with the objective of achieving the 4% goal, continued to promote the implementation and increase of financial education funding. In 1993, *The Outline* clearly stated that the state's financial expenditure on education as a proportion of gross national product should be gradually increased, reaching 4% by the end of the century. Regarding the proportion of education expenditures in the fiscal budget, in 1995, Article 54 of *The Education Law* stipulated: "State fiscal education expenditure as a proportion of gross national product should gradually increase with the development of the national economy and fiscal revenue. Education expenditure as a proportion of total fiscal expenditure of government at all levels should gradually increase with the development of the national economy."

In 2006, the Sixth Plenary Session of the 16th Central Committee of the Communist Party of China adopted *The Decision of the Central Committee of the Communist Party of China on Several Major Issues Regarding the Construction of a Harmonious Socialist Society* which reiterated: "Clarify the responsibilities of governments at all levels in providing public education services, ensure that the growth rate of financial education funding is significantly higher than the growth rate of recurrent fiscal revenue, and gradually increase education funding as a proportion of GDP to 4%." In Article 56 of *The National Medium-and-Long-Term Education Reform and Development Plan Outline (2010–2020)* (hereinafter referred to as *The Plan Outline*), it was once again stated: "Increase national fiscal education expenditure as a percentage of GDP so that it reaches 4% by 2012." *The Planning Outline* drafting group determined the following guidelines: "By 2020, national fiscal education expenditure as a proportion of GDP can reach 5%, and full-caliber education expenditures as a proportion of GDP can reach 7% to 7.2%." The 4% goal has become the most important educational policy goal with a high degree of political sensitivity, mobilizing support from governments at all levels and all sectors of society, and unifying the thinking of the entire Party and society.

IV. Analysis of the Public Education Finance Institution

The establishment of the public education finance institution meets the requirement of the state of establishing a public financial institution, and effectively promotes the government's desire to meet the people's public education needs. During this period, "the three growths" were implemented, the 4% target was achieved, and the growth rate of financial education funding continued to increase, even reaching a high of 30.43% in 2006, with an average annual growth rate of 18.13% from 1998 to 2012. The public education finance institution has a positive effect on the provision of education services, and has met public needs in the field of education. The establishment and implementation of the education financing institution, education budget institution, public education funding allocation institution, tuition and student subsidy institution, and education finance transfer payment institution have promoted the comprehensive development of education in China. The most obvious manifestation is that the comprehensive improvement of the level of rural compulsory education security and the move towards popularization of higher education.

The comprehensive popularization of rural compulsory education. In the mid-to-late 1990s, the central government initiated a series of large-scale financial transfer payment projects for rural compulsory education, including projects such as renovations of dilapidated buildings in rural primary and secondary schools, the construction of rural boarding junior high schools, and successively introduced a series of policies aimed at raising rural compulsory education fee guarantee levels. In 2001, the state proposed a "two exemptions and one supplement"[5] policy specifically for rural compulsory education investment. In December 2005, *The Notice of the State Council on Deepening Reform of the Rural Compulsory Education Fund Guarantee Mechanism* (i.e., *The New Mechanism*) was issued, requiring that "in accordance with the basic principles of 'clear responsibility at all levels, shared responsibility at the central and local levels, increased financial input, higher levels of support, and step-by-step organization and implementation', compulsory education in rural areas should be gradually introduced into the whole scope of public financial security, establishing central and local sub-projects, and a proportion-sharing mechanism for rural compulsory education funding." The major reform of the compulsory education finance investment institution has redefined the central government's compulsory education investment responsibilities.

Higher education has achieved popularization. The 1999 *Action Plan for Revitalization of Education for the 21st Century* (hereinafter referred to as *The Action Plan*) states: "In order to provide more high school graduates with access to higher education, the total number of students in higher education in 2000 will reach 6 million. The increase in the enrollment plan will be mainly used for local development of higher vocational education. The enrollment rate for higher education will increase from 9.1% in 1997 to about 11% in 2000." The introduction of *The Action Plan* was the prelude to higher education enrollment expansion. Enrollment expansion of colleges and universities has effectively promoted the leaping development of higher education in China, and the reform of higher education has made historic progress. The continuous expansion of the scale of enrollment in higher education has also brought financial pressure on the Chinese government in four aspects: the expansion of college and university enrollment, the rapid increase in the average cost of higher education, the tightening of public finances, and the cost of infrastructure construction and daily management in colleges and universities going higher and higher.

The Chinese government has carried out many useful reforms and explorations in improving the fiscal policy of higher education and establishing a multichannel financing mechanism for running schools. It has established a higher education fiscal policy institution that focuses on financial appropriations and raises funds through multiple channels in accordance with the law. It has also established a student aid institution that mainly consists of student loans and a combination of "award, loan, assistance, supplement and reduction." The reform of the financial institution of higher education has provided a basic guarantee for the expansion of higher education in China.

SECTION 4: THE FUTURE-ORIENTED MODERN EDUCATION FINANCE INSTITUTION

In November 2013, *The Decision of the Central Committee of the Communist Party of China on Several Important Issues Concerning Comprehensively Deepening Reform* issued by the Third Plenary Session of the 18th CPC Central Committee comprehensively and systematically analyzed the basic objectives, basic content, and course of action of the new round of fiscal and taxation reform from the perspective of national governance, and clearly proposed the construction of a modern financial institution. In order to adapt to the new situation and tasks of the development of education, it further states that it is necessary to build a modern education finance institution for the future, implement a full-caliber education budget institution, combine a sound education investment mechanism with the promotion of education reform, and strive to build the field of education investment into a demonstration zone of national fiscal reform.

I. Full-Caliber Education Budget Institution

On June 1, 2010, the Ministry of Finance issued *The Notice on Incorporating Revenues Managed by Extra-budgetary Funds into Budget Management*, stating that from January 1, 2011, revenues managed by extra-budgetary funds (excluding education charges) will be all included in budget management. After 2011, China initially established a full-caliber budget management institution consisting of public financial budgets, government fund budgets, social security budgets, and state-owned capital operating budgets.

Education budgeting, as the government's education revenue and expenditure plan, should fully reflect the government's educational responsibilities under the modern financial institution framework. Therefore, a full-caliber education budget institution should be established. In terms of budgeting, first of all, the three statutory requirements for the increase of educational funds should be met. Second, the transparent, scientific, and reasonable budgeting should be guaranteed to meet the development of educational undertakings under the premise of financial resources. Funds for compulsory education, especially rural compulsory education, should be fully borne by the government, and most of the funds for higher education and vocational education should be borne by the government; as the basis for the reasonable preparation of education budgets, government departments should evaluate the use of education funds. Since there is no inherent pressure on education institutions to minimize costs, the efficiency of the use of funds in public schools should always be questioned by society, parents of students, and management departments. Education budget performance evaluation is an important means for ensuring the efficient use of education funds in the context of tight educational funding. The establishment of a full-caliber education budget institution requires macro-level institutional and legal construction, institutional restructuring, and micro-level basic work improvements and process optimization.

Institutional and legal amendments. In accordance with the requirements of public finances, *The Budget Law* and *The Regulations for the Implementation of the Budget Law* should be amended to add to and clearly define the concept, content, form, and preparation methods of departmental budgets; budget revenue and expenditure content should be clearly defined in accordance with public finance standards; the budget preparation time should be adjusted and extended; in *The Budget Law* there should be a clear reflection of the separate operating mechanism of budget preparation, implementation and supervision; budget binding should be hardened, and budget adjustment should be strictly controlled. Legislation guarantees the seriousness and authority of public education investment. There must be laws that should be followed, enacted seriously and investigated when broken when it comes to the financing, distribution, and use of education funds, the establishment of educational programs, the determination of spending standards, and the allocation of public education resources between regions and schools. To do this requires the direct leadership of the People's congress or its special committee. The distinction between intra- and extra-budgetary funding should be eliminated. The department budget including all funds and regulating various charges, such as "the three limits" regulation of Beijing's school selection should be ensured. Intra-budgetary funds and extra-budgetary funds are also taken from the people, but the channels and methods are different. As long as a mechanism for the fair distribution of financial funds is established to ensure financial guarantees, in the long run, it is entirely possible to cancel extra-budgetary funds so that all funds can be included in the scope of budget management. The procedures for setting public school fees should be standardized. Tuition fees are public service fees and should be demonstrated through price hearings. It is the responsibility of the pricing department to announce the implementation to the public.

Reform the education finance accounting institution. Reform the education accounting institution in China by drawing on the accounting standards of Western nonprofit organizations to provide more information to the public; reporting on the accrual basis is conducive to the realization of financial reporting goals and fully reflects the entire school's economic resources.

Institutional restructuring. Establish specialized agencies responsible for education budgeting or funding. Most developed countries have specialized "intermediary" budgeting or appropriation agencies, while China's budgeting and appropriation power is concentrated in the finance and education departments, and the distribution of fiscal funds has no way of being transparent. If an education appropriation committee or an independent third-party agency is set up in the People's Congress, it will be able to adjust the budgeting relationship between the government and schools. With the joint participation of society (the People's congress deputies) and the school, the preparation of the education budget will better consider the actual funding needs of the school and the possibility of government resource supply, which is conducive to the government's implementation of macroeconomic regulation and control, as well as the school's self-hosted school running.

Clearly structure the budget supervision institution. Clearly divide the responsibilities and powers of the internal supervision of audit departments, People's congress organizations, and financial departments. Where possible, the National People's Congress and its Standing Committee's own auditing agency shall be established.

Budget preparation. Adjust the budget preparation time and implement the standard cycle budget; after basic work is done, the idea of performance budgeting can be introduced into budget preparation. Government outputs are cost-based for performance purposes, disaggregated by functional use and with focus on the final product. The plans can measured and evaluated performance from the cost and purpose of the final product, and projects are selected to be included in the budget. The budget should be transformed from an input-type budget to an output-focused budget, and an index institution that conforms to the law of educational development and reflects the efficiency of the use of fiscal funds should be designed as soon as possible.

II. Investment in Financial Education Funds in the Post 4% Era

After the 4% target was achieved, different scholars put forward different opinions on whether to continue to determine fiscal education expenditure as a proportion of GDP, but the ultimate goal was to ensure that government investment in education continued to increase. The 4% target was set by China in a special historical context. China's financial education funding input should establish a long-term mechanism for financial education funding input from legislative, administrative, fiscal and other aspects, and build a diversified education funding guarantee institution including capital markets, education donations, value-added school property preservation, and private capital schooling and establish an independent education funding review and supervision mechanism. With regard to the use of financial education funds, China should establish a relatively independent education funding mechanism, establish an "accountable use and supervision institution" for education funds, and change the thinking of using funds in order to effectively protect and use education funds and make full use of the benefits of education funds (Bao, 2012).

From the perspective of the total investment in education expenditure, the proportion of national financial education expenditure to GDP has exceeded 4% for five consecutive years. In 2012, the total national education expenditure was 2.87 trillion yuan, of which fiscal education expenditure exceeded 2 trillion yuan for the first time and this exceeded the figure of 4% as a proportion of GDP for the first time. Total investment in education in 2016 was 3.89 trillion yuan, of which fiscal education funding reached 3.14 trillion yuan. In the five years from 2012 to 2016, the cumulative fiscal investment in education across the country was 13.5 trillion yuan, exceeding all the total investment from 1952 to 2011. From the perspective of the use of fiscal education expenditure, there are three "more than halves," fully embodying the principles of "maintaining basics, keeping the bottom line, making up for shortcomings, promoting fairness, and improving quality." First, from the perspective of the distribution of education at all levels, more than half was used for compulsory education. In 2016, compulsory education accounted for 52.85% with the highest proportion. Preschool education grew fastest among all types of education at all levels, with a 77.3% increase in five years. Second, from the perspective of regional distribution, more than half was used in the central and western regions. In 2016, fiscal education expenditure in central and western regions reached 1.71 trillion yuan, accounting for 59% of the national total. In the past five years, the growth rate of fiscal education funding in central and western regions has been significantly higher than that in eastern regions, and fiscal education finance funding has further tilted towards the central and western regions. Third, from the perspective of expenditure, more than half was used for teacher salaries and student aid. In 2016, teacher salaries and student aid accounted for 61%. In the past five years, teacher salaries and student aid expenditures have increased significantly, and the proportion of expenditures on school operations, building construction, and equipment purchases has declined. Education expenditures are beginning to show a shift from focusing on "things" to focusing on "people." Judging from the work of student funding, "four continuous growths" can be seen, which fully reflects continuous improvement in the level of guarantees for fair education. First, the number of aided students continues to grow. The state has supported a total of 425 million students (children) of various types, and the number of students supported annually increased from 84.14 million in 2012 to 91.26 million in 2016, with an increase of 7.12 million. Second, the amount of funding continued to grow. The country's cumulative funding for the year was 698.2 billion yuan, and annual funding increased from 112.6 billion yuan in 2012 to 168.9 billion yuan in 2016, with an increase of 56.3 billion yuan. Third, financial investment continued to grow. The financial investment in student funding reached 478.1 billion yuan, accounting for 68.5% of the total funding. Annual financial investment increased from 82.5 billion yuan in 2012 to 110.9 billion yuan in 2016, with an increase of 28.4 billion yuan. Fourth, investment in schools and society has continued to grow. State student loans, school capital investment, donations from enterprises, institutions, social organizations, and individuals contributed 220.1 billion yuan, accounting for 31.5% of the total funding, and annual capital investment has almost doubled (MOE, 2017).

III. The Combination of Improving the Education Investment Mechanism and Promoting Education Reform

The construction of a modern education finance institution should focus on the reform and innovation of the development of education, and focus on cultivating young people with morals and the reform and innovation of all levels and types of education, and combining the improvement of the educational investment mechanism with promoting the reform and development of education.

Education investment should serve the country's major strategic needs. Education is the key to promoting the economy and protecting the environment. It is also the key to maintaining and improving the country's political progress and economic competitiveness. China is in the historical stage of transition from an upper-middle-income country to a high-income country. For major strategic plans deployed by the central government since the 18th CPC National Congress, such as "the Belt and Road" initiative, Beijing-Tianjin-Hebei integration, the construction of the Xiong'an New District, and the Yangtze River Economic belt, and the construction of the Guangdong-Hong Kong-Macao Greater Bay Area, education is urgently needed to provide high-quality human capital. In the direction of education investment, relevant, forward-looking themes, school layouts, teaching staffing, professional structure, and even newly added education projects should be designed, followed by close implementation of these characteristics in the new period and new stage.

Investment in education should focus on guiding the solution to difficult and hot issues in education. Chinese society is experiencing huge historical changes. People in economically developed regions expect high-quality education, and the demand for school choices in large cities continues to be high. The two-child policy has been implemented, and in the future, the number of people receiving education will increase by two to three million each year. The distribution and structural changes in the population receiving education brought about by the quickened urbanization process; the disparities in the conditions of educational development brought about by unbalanced and uncoordinated economic development, all pose challenges to investment in education. Fiscal education investment should be focused on special regions, special populations, weak links, and key areas. This is in response to the attention of education investment focusing on problems and hot issues in education, and conveys the country's determination and attitude towards solving these problems.

Increase the proportion of human capital investment in education. Raising the salary of teachers' human capital has been a common choice for major countries in the world for shaking off economic downturns and improving the quality of education since the financial crisis. In order to further ensure that the average salary of primary and secondary school teachers is not lower than or higher than the average salary of local civil servants, a performance-based salary policy for teachers has been implemented since 2009. This made up for the differences in the wage levels of teachers and civil servants in the same county created by self-created subsidies at all levels after the establishment of the subsidies institution in 1993. However, in recent years, many local civil servants have added housing subsidies, official car subsidies, annual target assessment awards, and annual leave fees in addition to the sunshine salary. This has created a new gap between the wages of teachers and civil servants and is a focus point for increasing investment in education in the future. Since the 18th CPC National Congress, the central government has issued a series of policies on implementing subsidies for hard and remote areas, subsidies for work in towns and townships, as well as concentrated rural subsistence allowances for rural teachers in hardship areas and remote areas, becoming a new channel opened by the central government for basic education teachers' salaries. From 2012 to 2016, the central government invested a total of 6.023 billion yuan to implement local financial support for teachers' salaries in weak areas.

Promote fairness in education finance and increase investment in social education. It is necessary to establish an institution of diversified student funding that fully covers scholarships, assistance, loans, credits, subsidies, and benefits, and highlight the basic value orientation of public finances that adheres to fairness. While establishing comprehensive student funding, future education investment must increase the proportion of social education investment. At present, the total amount of education investment in China is still low. In 2013, China's per capita education expenditure was 360 dollars, and total education investment accounted for 5.3% of GDP. In 2009, the United States' education expenditure per capita was US $3,300, accounting for 7.3% of GDP. The per capita education expenditure of the OECD countries in 2009 was US $2,200, and the total investment in education as a proportion of GDP was 6.3%. Since 2005, China's fiscal education expenditure has maintained a rapid average annual growth rate of 17.4%, while the growth in the average annual rate of non-fiscal education expenditure has dropped to 2.6%. It is necessary to reverse this situation of "single-legged" growth in fiscal education expenditure within education expenditure and expand the scale of private and social investment in education.

IV. Build Education Investment into a Demonstration Zone for National Fiscal Reform

Fairness, efficiency, and adequacy are the three criteria for government financial education investment. Needless to say, while China's education funding has been generally in short, problems such as inefficient use, extensive management, and excessive non-institutionalized special transfers in the distribution process still exist. *The Opinions*, while focusing on fairness in education finance, viewed faithfully observing efficiency as a natural choice. Emphasizing the strengthening of fund supervision, ensuring the standardized and safe use, and improving the efficiency of fund use. These policy innovations reflected the three-tiered significance of the efficiency of the allocation of financial education resources: making up for failures in the education market and correcting externalities; protecting vulnerable groups and maintaining a level playing field; and achieving reasonable allocation of resources in accordance with the goals of low input and high output.

As an institutional arrangement through which the state draws, spends, and manages public resources through political power, finance has both the economic attributes of improving resource allocation efficiency and adjusting economic interest relations, and the political attributes of national development goals and decision-making behaviors. Education finance is a key area where national fiscal expenditure accounts for a relatively high proportion. The rational division of financial power and expenditure responsibilities in the field of education, the establishment of a full-caliber budget institution, the improvement of the financial transfer payment institution, and the reduction of the proportion of special transfer payments have been the key elements of the reform of the national fiscal and taxation institution in recent years. Adjustments in power between central and local governments and schools and between different departments have been tough battles where one adjustment in one area affects everything else. Policy makers, fund managers, and reform participants in the field of education should make good use of all funds at every stage of education investment and every part of education work, and play an exemplary role in the construction of the country's modern financial institution. Continuously improving the education investment mechanism, especially the fiscal education funding input mechanism, will certainly provide strong resource support for achieving the main goals of the reform of the education institution and mechanism, and for building modern education with Chinese characteristics and world-class standards.

NOTES

1 Unified revenue and expenditure: Unified revenue and expenditure was the revenue and expenditure management method under the highly centralized management institution in the early

days of the founding of the People's Republic of China, and contained two implications. (1) In terms of the financial relationship between the central and local governments, the local budget revenue was handed over to the central government, and this was to be approved by the central government according to the plan. Local revenue and expenditure was not linked. (2) In terms of the relationship between the state and enterprises, all or most of the profits realized by enterprises in that year were turned over to the state. The capital investment, additional liquidity, and four expenses required by enterprises to expand reproduction were basically financed by the state.

2 China's administrative divisions have five administrative levels: central (national); provincial (autonomous region, municipality); prefecture-level city (region, autonomous prefecture, city); county (city); and township (town). Local government refers to the four levels of administrative agencies apart from the central government.

3 "The Sixth Five-Year Plan" period refers to China's implementation of the Sixth Five-Year Plan from 1981 to 1985. During this time, China gradually implemented and improved the economic contracting responsibility institution, and township enterprises achieved rapid development.

4 Eastern, central, and western Regions: In order to scientifically reflect the socioeconomic development of different regions of China, and to provide the basis for the Party Central Committee and the State Council to formulate regional development policies, China's economic regionalization is divided into four regions: east, central, west, and northeast.

5 "Two exemptions and one supplement" refers to a subsidy policy implemented by the Chinese government for students from poor families in the rural compulsory education phase. The main content is the exemption of miscellaneous fees, book costs, and stepwise subsidies in the living expenses of boarders.

REFERENCES

Bao, C. (2012). The guarantee and use of China's educational funds in the post-4% era. *China Education Journal*, *09*, 9–12 (in Chinese).

Deng, X. (1983). *Selected works of Deng Xiaoping* (Vol. II). Beijing: People's Publishing House (in Chinese).

Jia, K. (2011). China's public financial institution reform in the twelfth five-year plan period. *Financial Research*, *07*, 2–13 (in Chinese).

Li, X. (2008). *Compulsory education financial institution reform in the changing financial institution of China*. Beijing: Peking University Press (in Chinese).

Li, Y. (1987). Research report on a reasonable proportion of education investment in national income and an analysis of the economic benefits of education investment. *China Higher Education Research*, *Z1*, 23–74 (in Chinese).

Lin, L., & Lü, G. (2011). Reform and reflection on the educational finance institution since the establishment of New China. *Contemporary Education Forum*, *08*, 10–12 (in Chinese).

Liu, Y. (2011). Research-based education policy formulation process: Policy analysis of education funding 4% of GDP. *Peking University Education Review*, *9*(02), 132–142+191–192 (in Chinese).

Long, Z. (2009). Changes in China's educational finance institution. *Theory and Practice of Contemporary Education*, *1*(04), 7–9 (in Chinese).

MOE (The Ministry of Education of PRC). (2017). Introducing China's educational reform and development since the eighteenth national congress of the CPC from data. Retrieved from http://www.moe.gov.cn/jyb_xwfb/xw_fbh/moe_2069/xwfbh_2017n/xwfb_20170928/201709/t20170928_315538.html (in Chinese).

Qiu, Y. (1990). Analyzing the function of education investment. *Research in Educational Development, 04*, 65–70+57 (in Chinese).

Shen, B. (2005). Education investment issues involved in the reform of the public financial institution. *Education and Modernization, 01*, 60–65 (in Chinese).

Wang, S. (1987). A historical analysis of the proportion of education investment in China. *Journal of Beijing Normal University (Social Science Edition), 05*, 66–75 (in Chinese).

Xu, Z. (2003). Analysis of the multi-channel education financing policy. *Journal of Suzhou University of Science and Technology (Social Science Edition), 01*, 133–137 (in Chinese).

Yang, H. (2006). *Outline of the history of educational finance development in contemporary China*. Beijing: People's Publishing House (in Chinese).

Yang, H., & Zhang, C. (2012). The financial institution of rural compulsory education in China since reform and opening up: Evolution, features and policy suggestions. *Journal of Hebei University (Philosophy and Social Science Edition), 37*(04), 27–33 (in Chinese).

Yang, H., et al. (2010). Evolution, characteristics and development strategies of China's higher education finance institution since reform and opening up. *Journal of Hebei University (Philosophy and Social Science Edition), 35*(03), 76–82 (in Chinese).

Zhong, X. (2012). *Local finance studies* (3rd Ed.). Beijing: Renmin University of China Press (in Chinese).

Zhou, M. (1996). The characteristics of China's education investment and the problems it faces. *Education Science, 02*, 9–14+34 (in Chinese).

CHAPTER NINE

The Institutions of Opening Education to the Outside World

JING CHEN

Since the founding of the People's Republic of China, China's internationally open education system has changed several times, advancing in twists and turns. Early on, international openness of education in China focused on learning the Soviet model. In the teaching and curriculum institution, most of the experiences of the Soviet Union were used, and a large number of Soviet experts were introduced to carry out subject institution reform and research with universities. Since the 1960s, China's education exchanges with the outside world stagnated, and only exchanges with very few socialist countries were retained. Reform and Opening Up in 1978 completely revitalized the internationally open institution of Chinese education, not only restoring this cause but also reversing the purpose, scope, content, and form of opening up. Since Reform and Opening Up began, China has gradually formed an institution of education that is open to the outside world that includes a study abroad institution, an introduction institution, an open curriculum institution, and a foreign-related schooling institution. With the development of the knowledge economy and the advancement of globalization, knowledge has increasingly become an important factor in world trade and economic competitiveness. China's connection with global education is also getting closer, and related institutions are constantly developing (Coulby & Zambeta, 2005: 47). This chapter mainly looks at the construction path of China's institution of education open to foreign countries in the forty years of Reform and Opening Up, actively participates in the process of institution construction in global education governance, and then presents the development context of China's education opening up to the outside world from "introduction" to "going out" in a comprehensive manner.

SECTION 1 HISTORICAL RETROSPECT OF AN EDUCATION INSTITUTION OPEN TO FOREIGN COUNTRIES

There are three important points in time in the forty years of opening up to foreign countries in education: China's education reopening to the outside world in 1978, joining the World Trade Organization in 2002, and the promulgation of *The Several Opinions on Properly Opening Up to Foreign Countries in the New Period of Education*, and *Advancing the Construction of "The Belt and Road" Education Action*.

The opening of education to the outside world in 1978 started with the relatively backward level of education development in China and a relatively closed development environment. First, starting in 1978, the study abroad institution took the lead in making a recovery, which began the prelude to the opening up to the outside world of China's education. Second, in terms of studying in China, China began to establish an enrollment institution, training institution, student management institution, and scholarship institution for studying in China in the 1980s. Third, in terms of attracting intelligence, China gradually broke through ideological imprisonment at the beginning of Reform and Opening Up, and began to explore relevant institution cautiously. In the 1990s, *The Notice on Overseas institution and Individuals' Cooperation in Running Schools in China* opened up an institutional environment for Sino-foreign cooperation in running schools and promoted the development of cooperation in running schools.

Joining the World Trade Organization (WTO) in 2002 was a new stage for the opening up of education in China. With regard to public study abroad, China has expanded the size of the number of students it sends abroad and has paid more attention to the benefits of studying abroad. It has proposed the "three first-class" selection goals. *The Study Abroad China Plan* of 2010 sets out the development goals of "making China the largest destination country for studying abroad in Asia by 2020," as well as the development strategy of building an international brand of Chinese education. In terms of attracting talents, China has adjusted the structure of talent introduction, expanded the scale of introduction, raised the level of introduction, paid more attention to the efficiency and effectiveness of attracting talents, and entered a new stage of legalization and refinement in institutional construction. Entry into the WTO not only posed new challenges to the scope, content, and form of educational exchanges but also placed higher demands on the cultivation and utilization of talents. To this end, China has established an open curriculum institution, continued to advance the construction of credit conversion and academic degree certification institution, and begun to explore related evaluation institution.

Since joining the WTO, China has successively promulgated *The Regulations on Sino-foreign Cooperation in Running Schools*, *Implementation Measures on Regulations on Sino-Foreign Cooperation in Running Schools* and other documents, which have improved the construction of cooperative school-running institutions and promoted the standardized development of related undertakings. With the deepening development of Reform and Opening Up, the internationalization of Chinese education has begun to transform from a learning-oriented development mode to an export-oriented development mode. Running schools overseas has become a major strategy for China in "going global." During this period, China has built and strengthened overseas school running models such as Confucius Institutes and Network Confucius Institutes, and gradually established and improved overseas school running institutions. In view of the Chinese government's selective commitment to opening up to the world in primary education, secondary education, higher education, adult education, and other education services in the WTO accession agreement, China has made strategic adjustments to the education service trade institution in a timely manner. On the one hand, China's education institution actively and steadily promotes the development of trade in education services on the basis of adhering to the public welfare nature of education; on the other hand, China vigorously rectifies the negative chaos in the education market through institutional norms and promotes the standardization and legalization of service trade development.

In 2016, China's education began a new starting point. The General Office of the Central Committee of the Communist Party of China and the General Office of the State Council issued *The Several Opinions on Properly Carrying Out the Opening-up of Education in the New Era*, and put forward the strong voice of the era of "strengthening Chinese education." Facing the complicated international situation and the various uncertainties of the global structure, China is playing an increasingly important role in the globalized world economic system. In this context, China has gradually assumed the role of a great power in global education governance, and has expanded its "going global" strategy to education. Telling Chinese stories and spreading Chinese voices has become an important part of the opening up of education. According to *The Several Opinions on Properly Carrying Out the Opening-up of Education in the New Era*, *The Promotion of 'The Belt and Road' Education Initiative* issued by the Ministry of Education put forward the vision of building a "Belt and Road" education community and related supporting measures. In January 2017, "active participation in global education governance" in *The Thirteenth Five-Year Plan's Development of the National Education Cause* became a significant new highlight in the development of China's opening up institution. In addition, the propositions on deepening multilateral education cooperation, in-depth participation in the formulation of international education rules, and the development of international aid for education will further highlight the major role that Chinese education plays in promoting the transformation of global governance with China as a major power.

SECTION 2 THE STUDY ABROAD INSTITUTION

China's study abroad institution is divided into two categories: Chinese students studying abroad and students from abroad studying in China. Since the beginning of Reform and Opening Up, China has restarted the institution of sending students abroad for study. After nearly forty years of development, China's study abroad institution has made achievements in many aspects: the public study institution has been adjusted multiple times to improve efficiency; the self-funded study institution has gradually moved from restriction to liberalization; and the study abroad management institution has been further improved, moving towards "full chain" and specialized development. With regard to foreign students coming to study in China, China has promoted the expansion of the admissions institution through the establishment of a degree institution; gradually improved its training institution through systematic and integrated construction; formed institution design of ministries and committees, and university supervisors in the management of foreign students coming to China; quantities, forms, and sources have been greatly improved and expanded, and more emphasis has been placed on promoting benefits through evaluation.

I. Restarting the Study Abroad institution

In 1978, *The Report on Increasing the Number of Selected Overseas Students* opened the first wave of those going to study abroad after Reform and Opening Up began, and also opened the prelude to building an institution of studying abroad. Since then, the public institution for sending students abroad has gradually completed the transition from quantitative expansion to structural optimization; the self-funded study abroad institution wavered between easing and tightening for a long period of time, and then opened up. The study abroad management institution was then established and gradually developed into a "full chain" and specialized management structure.

(1) Studying Abroad on Government Scholarships: From Increasing Numbers to Increasing Efficiency

After the founding of the People's Republic of China, the destinations of Chinese students selected and assigned to go and study abroad were mainly socialist countries headed by the Soviet Union (Zhang & Yu, 2013: 505). During the Cultural Revolution, studying abroad was interrupted (Zhang & Yu, 2013: 607). For a period of time after the end of the Cultural Revolution, despite the recovery of various cultural and educational undertakings in China, studying abroad remained in a delicate stage of wavering and progress was slow (Zhang & Yu, 2013: 607). At the beginning of Reform and Opening Up, the country was faced with a situation of waiting for all that which was left undone to be restarted. Talented people were urgently needed for the country's economic and social construction. On June 23, 1978, Xiaoping Deng delivered an important speech on *increasing the number of dispatched students* (MOE and Central Literature Research Office of CPC, 2002: 148). In the same year, the Ministry of Education implemented the spirit of Xiaoping Deng's important directives and submitted "The Report on Increasing the Number of Students Selected to Go Abroad" to the Central Committee on July 11. Based on this, China sent about fifty public visiting scholars to the United States on December 26 of that year, which opened the reconstruction of China's institution of publicly sending students abroad. During this period, China's general policy of studying abroad was based around "opening channels and striving to send more students abroad" (Chen, 2004), setting the main goal of the study abroad institution as increasing the number of overseas students. In July 1981, the State Council proposed that "the governments of provinces, municipalities, and autonomous regions and qualifying units can make external contacts by themselves to open up channels and speed up the process of sending students abroad," and opened the door for public students to be sent by units for the first time (Chen, 2004). This measure has, to a certain extent, transferred the power of the state selecting and sending students abroad for study to lower levels, expanded the level of the institution of the state sending students abroad to study, and broadened the coverage of the study abroad institution.

After several years of sending students abroad, students sent abroad by the state achieved the goal of "opening channels and striving to send more students abroad" in terms of numbers. In 1986, the state made new adjustments to the study abroad institution. In the same year, *The Notice of the CPC Central Committee and the State Council on Several Issues Regarding Improving and Strengthening the Work of Students Studying Abroad* (hereinafter referred to as *The Notice*) adjusted the study abroad policy to "dispatch as required, guarantee quality, consistency of study with use," and proposed to shift from enriching "quantity" to "guaranteeing quality." Accordingly, the study abroad institution during this period shifted from public students sent by the state from graduate students to a focus on sending fellows and visiting scholars, and has actively explored paths for Sino-foreign cooperation in scientific research and doctoral training. In order to ensure the quality of overseas students, during this period China began to appropriately adjust the subject ratio of students sent overseas by the state, with a clear focus on studying applied subjects. At the same time, *The Notice* focuses on the comprehensive construction of the study abroad institution; proposes the establishment of a supporting institution; and explores a scholarship institution, loan institution, and the institution for signing agreements between state-sent overseas students and the units sending them. According to *The Notice*, in the same year, China issued the first comprehensive, systematic, and publicly published working paper for studying abroad, namely, the State Education Commission's *Interim Provisions on the Work of Students Studying Abroad* (hereinafter referred to as *The Provisions*) (The State Council of PRC, 1986; The State Education Commission of PRC, 1987)[1]. *The Provisions* were published in full in The People's Daily on June 11, 1987, becoming China's first publicly published regulatory document on education policies for studying abroad. Guided by the policy of "sending students abroad according to demand, ensuring quality, and keeping learning and usefulness consistent," *The Provisions* set the institution requirements for the conditions, selection, agreement, preparation for going abroad and studying, as well as financial treatment for overseas personnel. As a document with a regulatory nature, *The Provisions* cover a wide range of content regarding overseas study, and are still an important institutional basis for guiding China's study abroad activities.

Since the 1990s, "enhancing efficiency" has become the theme of China's study abroad institution. China has made several adjustments to the policy of the state sending students abroad to study, mainly focusing on personnel selection conditions, procedures, management institution, and funds. The institutional framework for the state sending students abroad to study has become more complete and stable. Against the context of the knowledge economy, the high-tech industry has become a new economic growth point. Studying abroad also focuses on cultivating knowledge and technological innovation talents to support the adjustment of the national industrial structure. In December 2002, responding to the need to cultivate high-level talents, the Ministry of Education formulated the work ideology of "expanding scale, improving levels, ensuring focus, and increasing efficiency" in accordance with "The Outline of National Economic Construction and Social Development" for the state sending students abroad to study. Several major adjustments were made to the state study abroad program that year: First, seven major areas were identified for support: communications and information technology, agricultural high technology, life science and population health, materials science and new materials, energy and the environment, engineering sciences, applied social sciences, and WTO-related subjects; second, adjustments were made to the types of overseas students, the establishment of "senior research scholars," and greatly increased funding for such scholars; third, traditional "general visiting scholars" and "senior visiting scholars" merged into "visiting scholars," and the funding period was adjusted to 6–24 months. Fourth, foreign language training and examinations were set up for those who had not yet taken the foreign language proficiency test but had received key recommendations from their units (The Secretariat of the Management Committee of the National Study Abroad Foundation, 2003). This measure made institutional adjustments to the structure types, dispatch conditions, and selection procedures of Chinese students studying abroad, closely focused on the needs of the country's economic and social development, and gradually refined the relevant institutions. The relationship between studying abroad and national competitiveness has become increasingly prominent. In 2005, the United States released the report "Global Competitiveness & National Needs: One Million Students Studying Abroad" (also known as The Lincoln Study Abroad Program), which proposed a substantial increase in the number of students sent overseas. In 2005, the Ministry of Education proposed a "three first-class" selection method, that is, selecting first-class domestic students, sending them to (overseas) first-class universities and subject majors, and following first-class mentors. In 2007, "The State Constructed High-level Postgraduate Study Abroad Program" was established, which further raised the standard of Chinese programs for studying abroad and emphasized the benefits of studying abroad.

(2) The Self-Funded Study Abroad Institution: From Restricted to Open

Unlike the gradual development of the state-sponsored study abroad institution, at the beginning of Reform and Opening Up, the self-funded study abroad institution wavered between "loosening and tightening" for a considerable period of time (Miao, 2008). In January 1981, the State Council approved the Ministry of Education and seven other departments' *Instructions for Self-Funded Studying Abroad*, and explicitly stated that self-funded studying abroad is an important channel for cultivating talented people in the country, and that self-financed students are a part of Chinese students studying abroad. Since then, in 1982 and 1984, the State Council issued *The Decisions on Several Issues Concerning Self-Funded Studying Abroad* and *The Interim Provisions on Self-Funded Studying Abroad*. Although various restrictions were imposed on citizens studying abroad at their own expense, restrictions were looser in general than in previous historical periods. In 1986, *The Several Provisional Regulations on the Work of Overseas Studying Personnel* issued by the State Education Commission separately listed the section of "Self-funded Studying Abroad" and set up eleven regulations, which basically absorbed the main policy content of all previous documents and laid the groundwork for the institutional framework of the self-financed overseas study for the long-term future. In January 1990, the State Education Commission issued *The Supplementary Provisions on Self-Funded Studying Abroad for Students with University Degrees and Above*, and once again tightened the policy on self-funded studying abroad (Miao, 2008).

On October 12, 1992, the Fourteenth National Congress of the Communist Party of China proposed: "We warmly welcome students studying overseas to care for, support and participate in the modernization of the motherland in various forms. We welcome them back to participate in socialist construction regardless of their past political attitudes, making proper arrangements, and implementing a policy of freedom of access and convenience" (Jiang, 1992). In 1993, *The Outline of China's Education Reform and Development* formulated a macro plan for the further expansion of education to the outside world according to the spirit of the above speech. In November of the same year, at the Third Plenary Session of the 14th Plenum of the CPC, *The Decisions on Several Issues Regarding the Establishment of a Socialist Market Economy system*, the abovementioned "Supporting Studying Abroad, Encouraging People to Return to China, and Freedom to Come and Go" established and affirmed working guidelines for studying abroad in the form of a central government document for the first time. This new institution spirit meets the needs of establishing and developing a socialist market economy under the new situation of Reform and Opening Up, and reflects the government's desire to respect citizens' studying abroad. In July 1993, the State Education Commission issued *The Notice on Issues Related to Self-Funded Study Abroad*, removing the restriction of students not being allowed to study abroad at their own expense during the service period, and lifted the restriction of the policy institution on the majority of young Chinese people from applying to study abroad at their own expense (Miao, 2008).

After joining the WTO, in order to implement the relevant commitments made on trade in services, the state decided to simplify the examination and approval procedures for those with a college degree or above to study abroad at their own expense. In February 2003, the Ministry of Education issued *The Notice on Simplifying the Examination and Approval Procedures for Self-Funded Studying Abroad for Persons with College Degrees or Above*, which simplified the procedures for self-funded study abroad and reduced unnecessary burdens on the institution. With the gradual reduction of the various thresholds for self-funded study abroad, and the gradual transition of management methods from restriction to service guidance (Zhang & Yu, 2013: 614), the Chinese government has also encouraged outstanding self-funded students by increasing financial support. In 2003, the Management Committee of the National Study Abroad Fund established the "National Outstanding Scholarship for Self-Funded Students Studying Abroad," which "opened the way for the establishment of government scholarships for self-funded students studying abroad, and further greatly supported and encouraged self-funded studies abroad" (Zhang & Yu, 2013: 742).

(3) Management Institution of Studying Abroad: "Full Chain" and Specialized Development

The distribution of the management rights for studying abroad has gone through a process of adjustment from decentralization to centralization, and is now moving towards "full chain" development. In 1986, the State Education Commission's *Several Interim Provisions on the Work of Students Studying Abroad* proposed that in accordance with the principle of simplified administration and decentralization, the number of students sent abroad by the state to study should be allocated to employers in addition to the part under the unified control of the state. On a trial basis, the method of using the funds of overseas students will be gradually implemented, which is controlled by the dispatching units. Starting from this year, China gradually adopted a selection method based on a combination of examinations, assessments and recommendations. In 1989, the State Education Commission again issued a policy to recover the publicly allocated indicators originally assigned to grassroots organizations back to the central government. Except for individual units, all central departments, provinces, autonomous regions, and municipalities should recommend candidates in accordance with unified regulations, then State Education Commission experts conduct an appraisal of the recommended candidate. Finally, the State Education Commission reviews and decides on the admission list based on the results of the expert review, forming a model with "quota limit declaration, expert review, and selection of best candidates" (Zhang & Yu, 2013: 612). This adjustment of management authority not only played the role of centralizing authority but also showed a trend of "chain-like" development. In 2007, the Ministry of Education and the Ministry of Finance jointly issued *The Administration Provisions for Postgraduates Sent by the State to Study Abroad (Trial)* (hereinafter referred to as *The Provisions*), marking that China's study abroad administration institution had entered a period of comprehensive improvement. According to *The Provisions*, the selection of public postgraduates is still conducted in accordance with the method of "individual application, unit recommendation, expert review, and admission on merit." The state implements the management method of "signing the contract and sending students abroad, and compensation for breach of contract." *The Provisions* clearly define the responsibilities of the selection, dispatch and management departments of public graduate students, the selection and dispatch methods, the management and contact methods abroad, the return and service methods, the breach of contract recovery methods, and the evaluation methods.

The specialization of management institution is another important part of the Chinese study abroad management institution. In 1981, in order to meet the development work needs of studying abroad, with the approval of the State Council, the Ministry of Education's Beijing Overseas Training Department was established on the basis of the former Ministry of Higher Education's Overseas

Student Training Office. With the development of the cause of studying abroad, some problems have also emerged in the management work for studying abroad, such as the fact that some state-sponsored overseas students never return to China, resulting in brain drain and loss of the benefits of studying abroad. To address these shortcomings, the state began to develop new management mechanisms for studying abroad to promote the development of this work. On March 31, 1989, following the instructions given by Comrade Xiaoping Deng at the enlarged meeting of the Standing Committee of the Politburo of the Central Political Bureau of Beidaihe in 1987, "establishing a service agency by the State Education Commission to engage in study abroad services," China established the Chinese (Ministry of Education) Service Center for Scholarly Exchange (CSCSE) on the basis of the training department. In 1996, drawing on international practices, China established the National Overseas Student Fund Management Committee (referred to as the Overseas Student Fund Committee), which is specifically responsible for work relating to Chinese students studying abroad and foreign students studying in China. Its establishment marked a major adjustment in the management institution for studying abroad in China. Since then, China has implemented the "personal application, expert review, equal competition, merit admission, contract assignment, and compensation for breach of contract," replacing the tiered distribution quota plan method of the past. Over the past forty years of Reform and Opening Up, in order to improve the study abroad work institution, the Ministry of Education has also set up fifty-eight education offices or education groups in embassies and consulates in thirty-nine countries, and established more than 2,000 overseas Chinese organizations and more than 300 professional academic groups of Chinese students studying abroad. At the same time, in addition to the establishment of the National Study Abroad Fund Management Committee, the China Study Abroad Service Center, and the Ministry of Education's Study Abroad Training Department, the National Study Abroad Work Research Association and other institutions have been established, and nearly 400 intermediary institutions for studying abroad have been approved. Together, they form the organizational structure and institutional network of Chinese study abroad management.

II. Promoting the Study Abroad Institution in China

The establishment of the Chinese degree institution in the 1980s laid a good institutional foundation for the development of the cause of foreign students coming to China to study. In 2010, China issued and implemented *The Program for Foreign Students Coming to China*, which put forward the development goal of "making China the largest study destination country in Asia by 2020" and the development strategy of building an international brand of Chinese education.

From then on, institution construction became the core of the construction of foreign students coming to China to study, and China began to promote the reform of the management institution, investment institution, school running institution, and internal management institution of education for studying in China. *The Belt and Road Education Action Plan* established the "Silk Road" Chinese government scholarship, implements the "Silk Road" study abroad promotion plan, and promotes "study in China" brand building, indicating that the construction of China's study abroad institution has entered a higher level of development.

(1) Expansion of the Student Admissions Institution

In January 1979, the Ministry of Education, the Ministry of Foreign Affairs, the Ministry of Culture, and the Ministry of Public Security jointly held the Second National Work Conference for International Students in China, which proposed to mobilize the enthusiasm of foreign students to study and facilitate their employment and functions after graduation and return to their home countries to establish degree institutions and issue degree certificates to international students. In 1980, the Standing Committee of the National People's Congress reviewed and passed *The Regulations on Higher Education Degrees of the People's Republic of China*. In 1981, the State Council approved and issued *The Interim Implementation Measures of the People's Republic of China Degree Regulations*. From that point on, China had officially established a degree institution. In the early 1980s, there were already a small number of foreign students in China, and the openness of the admissions institution at this time was relatively limited. In terms of education level categories, China expanded the level of enrollment to technical secondary school students, junior college students, undergraduate students, graduate students, and advanced students (The State Council of PRC, 1985) and then adjusted it to undergraduate students, graduate students, doctoral students, general advanced students, and advanced students in 1986 (The National Education Commission of PRC, 1986). The accepted international students were limited to those majors that are open to China, that is, liberal arts, science, engineering, agriculture, medicine, art, and sports (The National Education Commission of PRC, 1986). In 1985, the State Council approved the *Measures for the Administration of Foreign Students* (hereinafter referred to as *The Measures*), and proposed the enrollment policy of "adhering to standards, selecting the best candidates, creating conditions, and gradually increasing." At that time, due to various reasons, China did not fully open the institution for recruiting foreign students to China, including the introduction of foreign institutions.

The enrollment categories designed in the 1980s have basically continued to this day. In 2017, "The Administrative Measures for School Recruitment and Cultivation of International Students" divides international students into two categories: degree education and non-degree education. Specifically, those receiving academic education are junior college students, undergraduates, graduate students, and doctoral students; those receiving non-degree education are preparatory students, advanced students, and research scholars. In accordance with *The Regulations Relating to Foreign Students Studying in China* in 1986, entrance examinations were entrusted to the Chinese embassy (consulate) to preside over. *Regulations Relating to Foreign Students Studying in China* also stipulates the age, admission requirements, length of study, and application methods for enrolling the five categories of students.

The Interim Provisions of the National Education Commission on Recruiting and Cultivating Foreign Graduate Students Studying Abroad in China issued in 1988 proposes that recruitment of foreign graduate students studying in China must adhere to standards and guarantee quality; it must also take into account the actual conditions of the countries sending the students and foreign students, and "relaxing requirements" as appropriate. This has relaxed the conditions for foreigners studying in China to a certain extent. As a result, there has been a systematic breakthrough in the admissions examination for foreign students studying in China, and classification rules have been made for international students with different academic backgrounds and different degrees. The enrollment forms are expanded into two categories: examination admission and exemption admission, which include three forms: unified domestic examinations, exams with questions set individually by schools, and recommended methods for exemption from school examinations. Relatively complete classification rules have been set for the entry requirements and qualifications for applying for master's and doctoral degrees in China. This enrollment institution framework was in use until 2000, and greatly promoted study in China for more than ten years.

On January 31, 2000, the Ministry of Education, the Ministry of Foreign Affairs, and the Ministry of Public Security jointly signed *The Regulations on the Administration of Accepting Foreign Students in Colleges and Universities* (hereinafter referred to as *The Regulations*), and adjusted its relevant work policy to "deepening reform, strengthening management, ensuring quality and developing in an active and stable manner." The biggest breakthrough of *The Regulations* was delegating the power of enrolling foreign students to universities, who formulate foreign student enrollment rules, publish admissions regulations, conduct admission qualification examinations, examinations or assessments for those who apply to study in China, and independently determine the admission of foreign students. At this point, the Ministry of Education's overall admissions institution for college students studying in China has been perfected and colleges and universities have learned to use their power in enrolling students.

The 2010 *Study Abroad in China Program* began the period of deepening the development of China's study abroad in China institution. During this period, China proposed the work principle of "enlarging scale, optimizing structure, standardizing management, and ensuring quality," reforming the admissions methods for overseas students in China, and adopting flexible international admissions methods combining auditing, inspection, and examination. On the basis of improving the preparatory education institution, the study standards for foreign undergraduate majors coming to study in China were gradually established. The electronic registration institution for the student statuses of freshmen and academic qualifications were strictly implemented, and the admissions institution was gradually brought up to international standards. In order to set the entry threshold for studying abroad in China, the construction of a quality certification institution for studying abroad in China was initiated (MOE, 2015), becoming the direction of construction for China in improving its admission institution for foreign students studying in China.

(2) Institution Construction and Integrated Development of the Training Institution

In October 1985, *The Administrative Measures for Foreign Students* (hereinafter referred to as *The Measures*) approved by the State Council was an earlier document for systematically constructing a training institution for foreign students in China. *The Measures* stipulate the language learning of foreign students in China, and establishes a Chinese language learning institution for foreign students. It also preliminarily designs the Chinese language learning, public courses and teaching materials, books, archives, materials and other training institutions. In January of the following year, *The Regulations Relating to Foreign Students Studying in China* (hereinafter referred to as *The Regulations*) for the first time comprehensively stipulated the training institution for those coming to China to study. Based on the basic framework of Chinese language learning as stipulated in *The Measures*, *The Regulations* further required undergraduates and advanced students of science, engineering, and other majors to study basic Chinese for one year. In terms of the academic institution, *The Regulations* set up preparatory studies. *The Regulations* provided a more in-depth classification of Chinese learning for foreign students coming to China. For the first time, the contents of professional study, performance assessment and upgrading and repetition institution, as well as graduation, course completion, and professional certificate institutions were standardized.

In the late 1980s, the situation of early students coming to China to enter the postgraduate study stage appeared. As a result, the Chinese language learning institution underwent adjustment. In 1988, *The Provisional Regulations of the National Education Commission on Recruiting and Cultivating Foreign Postgraduates Coming to China to Study* (hereinafter referred to as *The Provisional Regulations*) required that foreign postgraduates studying in China who have graduated with undergraduate degrees from Chinese universities or foreign graduate students coming to China majoring in Chinese language and literature and history will be taught or instructed in Chinese after enrollment, and their essays will be written and defended in Chinese. For foreign graduate students without undergraduate degrees from a Chinese university or who are studying non-Chinese majors in language, literature, and history, qualified institutions and subjects and majors can be taught or guided in a foreign language, and their papers can be written and defended in that language. At the same time, the improvement and development of China's degree institution has also affected the training institution for students coming to China to study. *The Provisional Regulations* for the first time provide regulations on the length of study for postgraduate degrees, of which the postgraduate program lasts for two to three years; the doctoral program normally lasts for three years. So far, the training institution for foreign students in China has made great progress in the areas of Chinese language learning, curriculum setting, and years of study.

Under the basic framework established in the 1980s, the training of overseas students in China since the beginning of the new century has gradually become more integrated with domestic students. In 2000, *The Regulations on the Administration of Accepting Foreign Students in Higher Education Institutions* pointed out that the organization of teaching internships and social practice for foreign students in higher education institutions should be carried out with Chinese students in the school according to the teaching plan; in 2017, *The Administrative Measures for Schools' Recruitment and Training of International Students* required colleges and universities to incorporate the teaching plan of international students into the school's overall teaching plan.

With the development of science and technology and the deepening of education's opening to the outside world, China's training model for foreign students began to change. In order to effectively respond to new developments, in 2010, in accordance with the deployment of the *Study Abroad in China* plan, China conducted a pilot program of a flexible academic institution for academic education, researching and developing various forms of bringing studying abroad in China to outside the country, such as a study in China online education and remote training. In terms of curriculum construction, there will be a focus on creating branded degree majors, optimizing the professional structure, and building a professional curriculum institution that is more attractive to students coming to study in China. Colleges and universities will be supported in their efforts to build degree majors in Chinese-language teaching, a certain number of degree courses in English will be offered, and there will be a focus on supporting degree courses with Chinese characteristics and international comparative advantages, increasing their international influence.

(3) Decentralization of the Student Management Institution

The focus of construction of the management institution for foreign students in China has undergone the process of transferring from ministries and commissions to higher education institutions, and has formed a situation in which the Ministry of Education carries out coordination and colleges and universities carry out supervision.

Ideological and political management is an important management institution for studying in China. In 1985, *The Measures for the Administration of Foreign Students* (hereinafter referred to as *The Measures*) approved by the State Council proposed that in the management of ideological and political work and political activities, foreign students should be enrolled in education and introduced to China's relevant laws and regulations. In addition, *The Measures* more systematically regulates the management of student status, life and social management of foreign students in China. Specifically, the regulations for the management of student status and rewards for international students are stipulated. According to *The Measures*, the school discipline of foreign students who have made mistakes is divided into warnings, serious warnings, demerits, staying in school on probation, ordering withdrawal and expulsion. The management of international students' performance assessment, promotion and retention (downgrading), suspension and withdrawal should be the same as that of Chinese students in principle.

In terms of life management and social management, *The Measures* clearly stipulate that the material lives of foreign students should be properly taken care of, but different from entertaining foreign guests and experts. In order to strengthen the management of an international student hukou and dormitory, necessary rules and regulations need to be established. At the level of organization and leadership, *The Measures* clearly state that the work of international students is managed by the National Education Commission, and the management responsibilities of the Ministry of Foreign Affairs, the Ministry of Culture, the Ministry of Public Security, relevant departments of the State Council and embassies and consulates abroad, all People's governments of relevant provinces, autonomous regions, and municipalities, relevant ministries and commissions, institutions, and localities and units have been specified in detail. Subsequently, *The Regulations on Foreign Students Studying in China* further clarified the on-campus management institution for foreign students coming to China, formulated measures for attendance, suspension, discontinued schooling, and disciplinary measures, as well as the fee standards for self-funded international students. At this point, China has initially established a management institution for foreign students in China.

With the sharp increase in the number of students coming to China to study and the development of the reform of the national administration institution, in 2000, *The Regulations on the Administration of Accepting Foreign Students in Higher*

Education Institutions carried out in-depth reforms of the management institution for foreign students established in the 1980s. At the level of leading institutions, the Ministry of Education entrusted the National Study Abroad Fund Management Committee to be responsible for enrollment and specific management of international students. On the basis of the previous management institution, management authority has been transferred downwards, and a large number of management powers has been transferred to colleges and universities. Starting from this period, colleges and universities have been specifically responsible for the admission, education, teaching, and daily management of foreign students. Due to the increase in the management power of universities, universities have adjusted the management institution for foreign students, and begun to set up school-level leaders to handle the work of foreign students at the university, established a management institution for foreign students in accordance with relevant regulations, and set up a centralized management organization or management personnel for the affairs of foreign students.

Regarding the management of diplomas, in 2001, *The Notice of the Ministry of Education on Reforming the Measures for the Administration of Diploma Certificates for Foreign Students* began to delegate the authority to print and issue undergraduate and college diplomas for foreign students in colleges and universities. Since 2011, the authority to print and distribute postgraduate diplomas for foreign students has also been delegated to the provincial (regional, municipal) education bureaus (education committees) and the Xinjiang Production and Construction Corps Education Bureau or universities (MOE, 2011).

With the increase in the number of foreign students in China, the new situation has brought even more and even higher requirements for the management of universities. In 2017, the Ministry of Education issued *The Administrative Measures for the Recruitment and Cultivation of International Students in Schools* (hereinafter referred to as *The Measures*) to vigorously build a management institution for international students in colleges and universities. Based on *The Study in China Plan* for the training institution for management staff of those coming to China to study, *The Measures* further requires universities to clarify the management organization for international students, and to be responsible for the coordination of the recruitment, teaching, daily management and service of international students, as well as other post-graduation work such as contacting alumni. In addition, *The Measures* requires universities to set up positions for international student counselors, understand the learning and living needs of international students, and properly carry out information, consulting, cultural and sports activities, and other work in a timely manner.

The establishment of the counselor institution reflects the change in the management philosophy of "the assimilation of management and service of foreign students studying in China with Chinese students." At the same time,

The Measures innovatively created a number of management institutions: First, higher education institutions are required to begin implementing an insurance institution for all international students. Second, colleges and universities should disclose to international students the basic information of the school, education and teaching situation, general regulations on enrollment, as well as international student management and service institutions. Third, colleges and universities are required to establish and publicly announce a management institution for the use of service facilities. Fourth, the supervision and management institution of relevant management work is to be regulated, with the proposal that the education administration department of the State Council establish and improve a quality supervision institution for the cultivation of international students. The administrative departments of education of provinces, autonomous regions, and municipalities shall supervise the training of international students in their respective administrative regions. The administrative departments of education, public security, foreign affairs, etc., of the State Council responsible for the management of international students shall use modern information technology to establish an international student information management institution and promote the information sharing work mechanism.

(4) Increase in the Effectiveness of the Scholarship Institution

US scholarship institutions for foreign students in the United States are experiences China can learn from. The Fulbright Project is a good example. Since its establishment, the project has developed into the world's largest educational scholar exchange program. With its strong bonus support, it has successfully attracted more than 370,000 foreigners into the United States, covering 160 countries and regions around the world. In 1986, *The Regulations Relating to Foreign Students Studying in China* listed and explained the government scholarships of the People's Republic of China. The State Education Commission of the PRC provides the scholarships for international students studying in China in accordance with bilateral government exchange agreements. In terms of content, bonuses include: monthly cash payments to foreign students, funds allocated to schools for student tuition, teaching materials, laboratory fees, medical costs, equipment costs, accommodation costs, activity costs, etc., and travel subsidies for holidays organized for the school organization. The Ministry of Education entrusted the State Study Fund Management Committee to take charge of enrollment and management of Chinese government scholarship students. At present, there are 279 Chinese universities undertaking the task of cultivating Chinese government scholarship students. Subjects include science, engineering, agriculture, medicine, economics, law, management, education, history, literature, philosophy, and art.

In order to improve the effectiveness of scholarships, in March 1997, the General Office of the State Education Commission issued *The Interim Measures for the Annual Review of Scholarships for Foreign Students* and began trials of the annual review institution for scholarships for foreign students. This institution is used to motivate scholarship students to study hard, and quickly eliminate students who do not work hard, have poor grades, and ignore school discipline. After three years of trials, the Ministry of Education officially implemented the annual review institution for Chinese government scholarships in 2000 and entrusted the China Scholarship Council to organize and implement the annual review.

In 2000, *The Regulations on the Administration of Accepting Foreign Students into Colleges and Universities* made new developments to the Chinese government scholarship evaluation institution, and passed the annual evaluation qualifications on to universities. In addition, the regulations broadened the sources of scholarships, allowing local governments， colleges, and universities to set up scholarships for foreign students individually or jointly, as needed. Chinese and foreign enterprises, institutions, social groups, and other social organizations and individuals may, with the consent of higher education institutions and provincial education authorities, establish scholarships for foreign students, but no unreasonable conditions shall be attached. A diverse scholarship institution will be established from this.

In the 21st century, the Chinese government has continuously increased its financial investment in studying in China. In 2010, *The Study in China Plan* proposed to ensure the steady increase in the scale of Chinese government scholarships, and to gradually implement reforms in the monetization of scholarship content. Local governments, schools, enterprises and institutions, and other social organizations and natural persons are encouraged to set up scholarships of various types for studying in China, and build a government-led, socially engaged, scholarship institution that is diverse in providers and in forms of scholarship. In 2015, *The Notice of the Ministry of Finance and the Ministry of Education on Improving the Chinese Government Scholarship Funding institution and Raising Funding Standards* (hereinafter referred to as *The Notice*) proposed that the Chinese government scholarship funding institution should be further improved, and the content of scholarship funding should be defined in the five categories of tuition fees, accommodation expenses, living expenses, comprehensive medical insurance expenses, and international travel expenses, and made the decision to raise funding standards.

SECTION 3 THE TALENT ATTRACTION INSTITUTION

According to the source the talent desired, the talent attraction institution is divided into two main parts: the service institution for those studying abroad returning to China and the service institution for students coming to China.

The service institution for those studying abroad returning to China refers to the institution of services related to attracting and arranging the return service of Chinese students studying abroad, which directly responds to the purpose of building a study abroad institution in China. After the founding of the People's Republic of China, the policies governing the return of overseas students can be roughly divided into two categories: one is the "freedom of movement" for former students studying abroad and the other is the "return to China strictly on time, posting must be obeyed" policy (Miao, 2008). In general, China's study abroad policy of "supporting studying abroad, encouraging return, and freedom to come and go" unifies the core points of study abroad work on encouraging return to China, smoothing out the relationship between study abroad work and repaying the motherland by serving it after graduation.

After Reform and Opening Up, with the great changes in the international and domestic situations, China adjusted and improved the service institution for those studying abroad to return to China, and a transformation occurred from "returning to the country to serve" to "serving the country," making the forms of those who have studied abroad serving the country more flexible and varied. The serving in China institution refers to the institution of introducing foreign talents to serve in China. Since Reform and Opening Up, China has broken through ideological obstacles in the construction of the foreign talent introduction institution. The institution has gone through the preparatory period, establishment period, and perfection period, and established relevant policy subjects, introduction mechanisms, reward mechanisms, guarantee mechanisms, etc., deepening its work towards legalization and refinement.

I. The Returning to China to Serve Institution: From Compulsory to Encouraging

At the beginning of Reform and Opening Up, how to attract overseas students to return to China to serve when material conditions were relatively backwards was a difficult problem. In July 1983, the Ministry of Labor and Personnel and the Ministry of Education jointly issued *The Report on the Issue of Distribution of Graduating International Students* for the year. Its specific principles were as follows: "State assigned international students will all be allocated work by the state; the work units' state assigned study abroad students will return to their original units where work will be arranged for them; self-funded study abroad students enjoy the same treatment after returning to the country, and the personnel department of each province, autonomous region, and municipality makes proper arrangements for their employment based on their abilities" (Zhang & Yu, 2013: 619). Compared with the planned economy period, this arrangement for returning to work was not changed or loosened much (Zhang & Yu, 2013: 619).

Later, specific measures were taken such as signing "The Study Abroad Agreement" with the sending unit before leaving the country, delisting those who did not return after the due date, or fining those who returned late (Zhang & Yu, 2013: 632). However, official statistics show that China sent about 150,000 students of various types abroad from 1978 to the end of 1991, and only about 50,000 returned in that period, meaning only a third returned to China after their studies (Zhang & Yu, 2013: 620). This shows that the forcing return to China to serve regulation may not have been the most effective institution design. Facing the issue of the use of returning talents, in May 1984, when Xiaoping Deng met with the Chinese American scholar Zhengdao Li, he said, "Thousands and thousands of people coming back is a big problem. We don't know how to utilize them" (MOE and Central Literature Research Office of CPC, 2002: 165). Zhengdao Li suggested establishing a post-doctoral research mobile station in China to attract Chinese students studying abroad to return and work in China. Xiaoping Deng affirmed this and stated that "it is necessary to establish hundreds of mobile stations and have it become an institution" (MOE and Central Literature Research Office of CPC, 2002: 165). In the same year, the Central Government introduced the Office of the Overseas Intellectual Leadership Group, the State Education Commission, and the State Science and Technology Commission to jointly submit the State Council's *Instructions on Striving for Doctoral Graduates who have Studied Abroad to Soon Return to China to Work* where some specific methods were proposed to consider the characteristics of returning overseas students and providing necessary support and care in research funding.

On January 25, 1992, Xiaoping Deng stated: "I hope all those who study abroad will return. No matter what their past political attitudes may have been, they can return and proper arrangements will be made for their return" (Zhang & Jiang, 1999: 3). This speech demonstrated the friendly attitude of Chinese leaders towards overseas students and leaders' ardent hopes for their return to the country to serve. In the same year, the General Office of the State Council issued *The Notice on Issues Relating to Overseas Students* (hereinafter referred to as *The Notice*), which clarified the purpose of welcoming overseas students back to work in China, and opened the door for the overseas students returning to China to serve.

The attitude of the central government set the tone for starting the service of returning home. The country has successively adopted many institutional measures to attract overseas students back to China to work. In terms of institution setup, the Ministry of Education set up the China (Ministry of Education) Study Abroad Service Center in 1989, which is mainly responsible for serving those returning to China.

In addition to setting up specialized institutions, setting up high-level projects is a major measure for China in attracting overseas students to return to China to serve and leverage their strengths. Since the 1990s, China has launched a number of projects, such as the establishment of a research fund for returning overseas students in 1990, the "Cross Century Talent Program" in 1993, and the "Chunhui Program" in 1996. These projects have provided convenient conditions for overseas students to return home and serve as a powerful platform for incubating high-level personnel in the country. Specifically, in order to alleviate the dilemma of the aging talents of Chinese science research teams in the early 1990s, and to attract a large number of young and middle-aged academic elites at home and abroad to participate in the construction of key disciplines in Chinese colleges and universities, China began to set up the "National Science Fund for Outstanding Youth," the Chinese Academy of Sciences' "Hundred Talents Program" in 1994, and "The Yangtze River Scholars Award Program," which was launched in 1998. Against this new historical background, on December 23, 2008, the General Office of the Central Committee of the Communist Party of China forwarded *The Opinions of the Central Talent Work Coordination Group on the Implementation of the Overseas High-level Talents Introduction Plan*, which centered around the strategic goals of national development and focused on introductory work for high-level overseas talents. This work is also known as the "Thousand Talents Program." The Talent Work Bureau of the Central Organization Department set up a special office for the introduction of overseas high-level talents to serve as a daily work unit of the working group that is responsible for the implementation of the "Thousand Talents Program." These projects that encourage overseas talents to return home have attracted a large number of high-level overseas talents, cultivated a group of leading academic leaders, and cultivated a number of important scientific research results.

Diversified service methods are a major institutional innovation for China to make good use of returning overseas students. In 2001, the Ministry of Education, the Ministry of Personnel, the Ministry of Science and Technology, the Ministry of Public Security, and the Ministry of Finance jointly issued *The Several Opinions on Encouraging Overseas Students to Serve the Country in Various Forms*, which stipulates that overseas students can serve the development of the motherland in various appropriate ways including part-time work, cooperative research commissioned research, starting a business, training talents, and engaging in intermediary services. This is the first comprehensive and systematic guidance document the country has issued to encourage overseas students to serve the country. It comprehensively summarizes the forms of overseas students serving the country and the security policies provided by the country. From compulsory return to encouraging return, this is the first time that China has attracted and used overseas students to emancipate their minds. From "return to the country to serve" to "serving the country" has once again broadened the thinking in terms of talent use, marking the entry of this work into a new stage of wider space and territory (Miao, 2008).

Against the background of increasing presence of information technology, integrating data and unblocking information has become another measure for China to implement return services. In 2007, *The Several Opinions of the Ministry of Education on Further Strengthening the Work of Introducing Excellent Overseas Talents* marked that the service institution for returning overseas students had entered a new stage. China has begun to explore the compilation of a list of outstanding overseas talents, and established and improved an information database of outstanding overseas talents. The Ministry of Education has established an institution for forecasting the demand for overseas study talents and publishing demand information, increasing the flow and transparency of relevant information. China set out to build a two-way platform for overseas talents studying abroad, such as online communication and negotiation, to provide services and entrepreneurship for overseas talents returning home, and to promote the connection between domestic employers and outstanding overseas students who intend to return to China.

In order to improve the quality of employment and standardize the employment mechanism, the General Office of the Ministry of Education issued *The Several Opinions on Further Strengthening and Standardizing the Introduction of Talents in Colleges and Universities* in 2013, and proposed to strictly regulate part-time and part-pay behaviors. In accordance with the principle of "priority of the job, classified management, emphasis of focus, and gradually standardizing," the standardized management and supervision and inspection of part-time work and part-time salaries of full-time talents was strengthened.

II. Service Institution in China: From Restricted to Open

In the early days of Reform and Opening Up, China went through a period of "crossing the river by feeling the stones (learning through trial and error)" in using foreign intelligence and hiring foreign experts. Facing the domestic situation where everything that was undone was being reinstated, China hired overseas experts mainly to introduce, digest, and assimilate advanced and practical technologies, skills, and methods, focusing on the introduction of scientific and technological talents. From 1978 to 1983, China's policies in this regard reflected the basic style of "striving for security and prudence." The policy texts of this period mostly emphasized "friendliness" in politics, proposed a policy of introducing foreign experts "not published in newspapers and periodicals," focused on obtaining foreign expert information through personal relations channels such as old relatives and friends, and conducting introduction work (Li & Liu, 2013). In these circumstances, the introductory work of various departments of the central government also had their own phenomena, where a systematic policy synergy had not yet been formed. Therefore, the early introduction work can be regarded as the preparatory period of the institution. From the central government to the local government and the unit, a perfect introduction policy had not yet been formed.

In 1983, Xiaoping Deng gave a speech on "Using Foreign Intelligence and Expanding Opening to the Outside World," proposing: "To use foreign intelligence, invite some foreigners to participate in our key construction and all aspects of construction." Xiaoping Deng's speech clarified his thinking orientation and opened a new situation for China introducing foreign experts since 1978. That year, the Central Committee of the Communist Party of China and the State Council issued *The Decision on the Introduction of Foreign Intelligence to Facilitate the Construction of the Four Modernizations*; on September 26 of the same year, the State Council issued "The Interim Provisions on the Introduction of Foreign Talents," marking the beginning of China's promotion of institutional construction for introducing foreign experts from top to bottom.

In 1996, the Ministry of Labor, the Ministry of Public Security, the Ministry of Foreign Affairs, and the Ministry of Foreign Trade and Economic Cooperation jointly issued *The Regulations on the Administration of Employment of Foreigners in China*, making foreigners, including foreign experts, have employment regulations to rely on when working in China. From the perspective of the institution, a series of policies clarified many mechanisms for introducing foreign experts, bringing this work into a period of institution establishment. First, the channels and forms of introducing foreign talents were expanded, "including official, semi-official, private, and various international organizations" (The Ministry of Labor of PRC, 1996; The Ministry of Human Resources and Social Security of PRC, 2017). Second, the subject of policy responsibility, with the State Administration of Foreign Experts Affairs as the core, gradually became clear. In management organization, with the State Administration of Foreign Experts Affairs as the core, the coordination of labor, diplomacy, public security, and various other departments was horizontally led, with vertical communication and guidance and mobilization of relevant departments of local governments at all levels, forming a crisscross, cooperative management network. The State Administration of Foreign Experts Affairs, as a specialized agency serving the institution of attracting talent, has undertaken six major responsibilities since its establishment, including policy and implementation management. The establishment of a specialized agency not only reflected the central government's emphasis on the introduction of intelligence but also completed the specialization of responsible subjects in the design of the institution and promoted the improvement of the management institution.

In terms of the operating mechanism, during this period, China designed the institution of qualifications and review procedures, introduction procedures, and confidentiality regulations for foreign experts, and began to implement the foreign expert certification institution. In terms of the reward mechanism, the Chinese government not only attaches importance to external conditions, such as the working conditions of experts coming to China, but also established the "Friendship Award" in 1991, which has become the highest honor that the Chinese government can bestow on foreign experts.

In 2003, after the first National Talent Work Conference was held and *The Decision of the CPC Central Committee and the State Council on Further Strengthening Talent Work* was issued, China's policy on the introduction of talents began a transformation from "self-cultivation as the foundation, supplemented by the introduction of talents" towards having an equal emphasis on cultivating and introducing talents (Liang, 2008). In order to increase efforts to attract overseas students and overseas high-level talents, the central government set up a talent work coordination group in 2003, and the central organization department set up a talent work bureau. The main body of the policy to introduce foreign experts was changed from the former national foreign expert bureau to the central government organization department, taking the lead and raising the specifications of the talent management organization.

After joining the WTO, China's demand for talent changed. To cope with new development needs, China adjusted its talent introduction policy towards "mainly relying on China's own talent, introducing as needed, highlighting key points, and emphasizing practical results," paying more attention to the domestic benefits of talent introduction. The top priority of talent introduction is focusing on promoting the sound and rapid development of the national economy, and vigorously introducing high-level overseas talents and the scarce talents needed by China's economic and social development (Liang, 2008). In December 2008, the United Nations Development and Reform Commission of the Central Organization Department, the Ministry of Education, and other departments issued *The Several Provisions on Providing Suitable Working Conditions for High-level Overseas Talents*, paying more attention to the level and efficiency of introducing talent. In terms of talent goals, there has begun to be a focus on the field of highly sophisticated foreign talent. Policy goals of pursuing quantity in the past have been changed, the structure of the introduction of personnel has been vigorously adjusted, importance has been attached to the introduction of teams, and importance has continued to be attached to talents in natural sciences, the engineering industry and technology, as well as fields where China lacks professionals such as finance and trade, economic management, social management, and international legal affairs. In order to effectively improve the utilization efficiency of experts, the State Administration of Foreign Experts Affairs issued *The Classified Guidance on Introducing Foreign Intelligence to Serve National Economic and Social Development* in 2011, established and improved the implementation mechanism for the introduction of classified guidance for foreign experts, and adopted different policies and approaches for introducing experts in different fields, advancing the targeted and refined development of relevant institutions and work.

In order to attract more high-level foreign experts to participate in China's modernization, in 2011, China implemented the "Thousand Talents Plan" high-level foreign expert project (referred to as the "Thousand Talents Plan for Foreign Experts," specifically non-Chinese foreign experts), hoping to use it for ten years. Around that time, 500–1000 high-level foreign experts were introduced, and 50–100 were introduced each year (The Organization Department of the Central Committee of CPC, et al., 2011). The "Thousand Talents Program for Foreign Experts" is by far the highest-level project in China for introducing foreign experts, and it is also the project with the largest scale of introductions and the most rewards. Under the unified deployment of the Central Talent Work Coordination Group, the high-level intelligence introduction work has formed a policy synergy and found important footholds in the design and implementation of the institution. At the same time, *The Measures for Foreigners to Enjoy Relevant Treatment in Permanent Residence in China*, jointly issued by twenty-five departments including the Organization Department of the CPC Central Committee, the Ministry of Human Resources and Social Security, and the Ministry of Public Security, as well as *The Opinions on Strengthening the Management of Foreigners' Permanent Residence Services*, issued by the General Office of the CPC Central Committee and the General Office of the State Council, have created a good legal environment for vigorously attracting overseas talents to come to China for innovation and entrepreneurship.

SECTION 4 FOREIGN-RELATED SCHOOLING INSTITUTION

The opening up of school running has enabled China's foreign-related schooling to achieve multilevel and wide-ranging educational exchanges and cooperation. Against the background of deeply integrating into the trend of world education, China timely proposed to train a large number of international talents with an international perspective, knowledge of international rules, and the ability to participate in international affairs and international competition *The National Medium-and-Long-Term Education Reform and Development Plan Outline (2010–2020)*. The training of international talents places higher requirements on language courses and presents new challenges to the talent training institution, which has led to the creation of an open curriculum institution. The foreign-related schooling institution has gotten a foothold in China, faces the world, coordinates domestic and international situations, and fully implements the two grand strategies of "bringing in" and "going out." In the open schooling institution, cooperative schooling is China's new practice of absorbing foreign high-quality education resources. Institutional construction has promoted the standardization of development of this work. Running schools overseas is a new measure for China to run schools internationally. It is also a major measure for making full use of national education radiating power and enhancing international influence. The establishment of the overseas education institution has laid the foundation for the development of Confucius Institutes and other overseas education units, and has become an important support point for promoting and standardizing overseas education.

I. The Establishment of an Open Curriculum Institution

In order to cultivate all kinds of specialized talents that are suitable for economic globalization, China set out to establish an open curriculum institution for all stages of education. In the field of basic education and vocational education, in accordance with the deployment of *The National Medium-and-Long-Term Education Reform and Development Plan Outlinc (2010–2020)*, while strengthening foreign exchange and cooperation in primary and secondary schools and vocational schools, China has gradually strengthened international comprehension education, promoted cross-cultural communication, and enhanced students' recognition and understanding of different countries and cultures. Relevant policies have been formulated around the development of internationalized courses in all places according to the local conditions. The main actions taken include: focusing on strengthening the construction of internationalized courses with advantages and distinctive subjects; introducing high-quality cooperative school-running projects; attaching importance to the development of internationalized curriculum talent teams, and gradually forming relevant talent introduction, management, and evaluation institutions; integration of international courses, and promotion of the development of international courses by way of increasing the development of online courses; thereby gradually increasing the proportion of bilingual or foreign language teaching.

In the field of higher education, some subjects with international characteristics and international tendencies, such as international trade and international finance, continue to be highlighted, mainly in the construction of bilingual courses. In the early 1990s, in order to vigorously promote international language work, China adjusted relevant institutions and formed operating institutions for the relevant institutions. From 1991 to 1992, the two textbook editing and reviewing committees of the original foreign language subjects were restructured into the foreign language teaching instruction committee of colleges and universities and the university foreign language teaching instruction committee respectively. In 1993, the General Office of the State Education Commission promulgated *The Regulations on the Work of the Guiding Committee on Foreign Language Teaching in Colleges and Universities* (The National Education Commission of PRC,

1993), establishing the institution's work institution and further improving the foreign language curriculum institution. Since China's accession to the WTO, the country's demand for international talents has become more pressing, and the construction of language courses has been accelerated. Bilingual teaching is an important breakthrough point in the internationalization of Chinese university courses. In terms of bilingual teaching, China not only pays attention to improving the foreign language teaching level of teachers and students' ability to apply foreign languages but also strives to strengthen the construction of bilingual courses and teaching materials. In bilingual teaching, the use of foreign language teaching materials or teaching in foreign languages is encouraged.

The need for language teaching extends from specialized language courses to public courses and other specialized courses. In 2010, *The Several Opinions on Strengthening the Undergraduate Teaching Work of Higher Education Institutions and Improving Teaching Quality* further required that undergraduate education create conditions for using English and other foreign languages for public and specialized courses. Especially for majors in high-tech fields such as biotechnology and information technology, as well as majors in finance and law that are needed after China's entry into the WTO, it is necessary to take a step forward and strive for foreign language courses to reach 5–10% of all courses in three years. For schools and majors that do not have the conditions to directly teach in a foreign language for the time being, a strategy of "implementing foreign language textbooks and teaching in Chinese in some courses, step by step" has been formulated. For the rapid development of information science and life sciences, internationally applicable and comparable disciplines and majors can directly introduce advanced original textbooks that reflect the forefront of the subject's development (MOE, 2001). This opinion further opened up China's higher education curriculum institution and provided institutional conditions for the internationalization of the higher education curriculum.

II. The Expansion and Standardized Development of Cooperative School Running

Sino-foreign cooperation in school running is a new phenomenon in the field of education after China's Reform and Opening Up, and is gradually becoming a new form of foreign exchange and cooperation in Chinese education. In September 1986, with the approval of the State Council, China established the first Sino-foreign cooperatively run school—Nanjing University-Hopkins University Sino-American Cultural Research Center. The Sino-US Cultural Research Center has become a successful example of cooperation between China and the United States in the field of education and academics. It has been valued and praised by leaders of China and the United States, and has been hailed as a place for "studying abroad without going abroad."

After China's entry into the WTO, Sino-foreign cooperation in school-running has accelerated. According to the relevant provisions of the WTO, China has made fundamental changes to *The Interim Provisions on Chinese-Foreign Cooperation in School-Running*. In March 2003, the State Council issued *The Regulations of the People's Republic of China on Chinese-Foreign Cooperation in School-Running*, characterizing Chinese-foreign cooperation in running schools as public welfare undertakings. In June 2004, the Ministry of Education promulgated *The Implementation Measures for the Regulations of the People's Republic of China on Sino-foreign Cooperative Education*. At the same time, the Ministry of Education also formulated a number of regulatory documents to set up an institutional framework for cooperative education (The State Council of PRC, 2013).[2] During this period, the state implemented the policy of "opening up, standardizing schooling, managing according to law, and promoting development" for Chinese-foreign cooperatively run schools, encouraged Chinese-foreign cooperatively run schools to introduce high-quality educational resources from abroad, encouraged Sino-foreign cooperation in running schools in the field of higher education and vocational education, and encouraged Chinese higher education institutions to run schools in cooperation with well-known foreign higher education institutions. The above regulations provide for the establishment, organization and management, education and teaching, assets and finance, change and termination of Chinese-foreign cooperatively run schools, as well as their relevant legal responsibilities, and have become the institutional basis for running cooperative schools.

Under the guidance of the regulations, China issued *The Administrative Measures for the Management of Schools for Sino-foreign Cooperative Vocational Skills Training*[3] (The Ministry of Labor of PRC and The Ministry of Social Security of PRC, 2006), which further improved the Sino-foreign cooperative school-running institution in the field of vocational education. In 2006, *The Opinions of the Ministry of Education on Several Issues Concerning Current Sino-foreign Cooperation in Running Schools* further proposed to strengthen the management of Sino-foreign cooperation in running schools using the "dual-campus" schooling model. The establishment and improvement of the abovementioned institution not only complies with the requirements of China's entry into the WTO for the administration of education by law in China but also meets the urgent hope of Chinese education going abroad; it is not only helpful for school running bodies at home and abroad managing schools themselves but also for the Chinese government to conduct supervision and management according to law.

In 2005, the Ministry of Education officially approved the establishment of the University of Nottingham Ningbo, which opened a new chapter in the vigorous development of international education cooperation in China. In May 2006, Xi'an Jiaotong-Liverpool University (XJTLU), co-founded by Xi'an Jiaotong University and the University of Liverpool, was located in Suzhou, with 80% foreign teachers. On August 15, 2012, New York University Shanghai was officially established and became a globally first-class Sino-US cooperative university with independent legal personality established by a world-class university in cooperation with China's "985" key universities.

With the in-depth development of cooperative school running, China has paid more attention to the improvement of school running efficiency. To this end, it has started to build an evaluation institution for Sino-foreign cooperative school running. In 2009, the Ministry of Education promulgated *The Sino-Foreign Cooperative School Running Evaluation Program (Trial)* and began to explore the evaluation index institution for Chinese-foreign cooperative education. With the increasing number of foreign-related schools, some prominent problems in foreign-related schools have gradually been exposed. To this end, the Ministry of Education successively issued *The Notice of the Ministry of Education on Further Regulating the Order of Chinese-Foreign Cooperation in Running Schools* and *The Notice of the Ministry of Education on Strengthening the Management of Standardization of Foreign-Related Schools* to advance the "two platforms" (establishing an information platform for the supervision of Sino-foreign cooperative school running and the certification work platform for Sino-foreign cooperatively run schools) and the "two mechanisms" (establishing a quality evaluation mechanism and a law enforcement and punishment mechanism for Sino-foreign cooperative school running), requiring that "education administrative departments in various places and universities carry out special clean-up and rectification of foreign-related schools in accordance with relevant national laws and regulations." The special clean-up of Chinese-foreign cooperatively run schools has emphasized the implementation and supervision of the institution, indicating that China's Sino-foreign cooperatively run schools have progressed from quantitative development to quality improvement.

III. The Booming Development of Overseas School Running

Overseas school running is the manifestation of the transformation of Chinese education internationalization from a learning-oriented development mode to an export-oriented development mode. China has successively issued documents such as *The Interim Administrative Measures for Overseas School Running of Higher Education Institutions*, and *The Notice of the Ministry of Education on Strengthening the Standardized Management of Foreign-related Schools* and other documents, focusing on overseas school running as the focus of the "going global" strategy, establishing and strengthening examples of overseas school running such as

Confucius Institutes and online Confucius Institutes, gradually establishing and improving overseas school running institutions.

In December 2002, the Ministry of Education implemented *The Interim Administrative Measures for Overseas School Running of Higher Education Institutions* (hereinafter referred to as *The Measures*), marking the establishment of China's overseas school running institution. According to the spirit of *The Measures*, the jurisdiction institution for overseas education is divided into different authorities and takes different paths according to the difference between academic education and nonacademic education. *The Measures* established the application institution and supervision institution for overseas school running, and played a significant role in standardizing and promoting overseas school running. Much of the content is still applicable in *The Notice of the Ministry of Education on Strengthening the Standardized Management of Foreign-Related Schools*, issued in 2012.

With the development of China's economy and the growth in China's international exchanges, the demand for Chinese language learning in countries around the world has increased dramatically. Since 2004, China has begun to explore the establishment of "Confucius Institutes," whose purpose is teaching Chinese and spreading Chinese culture overseas. The establishment and issuance of *The Confucius Institute Constitution* (hereinafter referred to as *The Constitution*) is a sign of the institutionalization of its operation. *The Constitution* clearly stipulates that as a nonprofit educational institution, the purpose of Confucius Institutes is improving the understanding of Chinese language and culture among the people of the world, developing friendly relations between China and foreign countries, promoting the development of a multicultural world, and contributing to building a harmonious world. According to the characteristics and needs of various countries (and regions), the set ups of Confucius Institutes can be flexible and diverse, but Mandarin teaching and standardized Chinese characters are used in Chinese teaching. Under the guidance of the institution, by December 31, 2016, 512 Confucius Institutes and 1,073 Confucius Classrooms had been established in 140 countries (and regions) worldwide. The achievements in overseas school running, represented by Confucius Institutes, have developed into an important brand for international Chinese education and promotion, and a cooperative platform for friendly exchanges between Chinese and foreign education and culture.

SECTION 5 GLOBAL EDUCATION GOVERNANCE

The concept of "global governance" was first proposed in the German system by the Chairman of the International Development Commission Willy Brandt in 1990 (Pang, 2006), but countries around the world have different understandings of this concept and its implementation path. In this regard, China proposed a smart solution of "consultation, construction and sharing." In the field of education, the report "The G8 and Education Governance" prepared by the Canadian scholar John Corton and others for the G8 summit in St. Petersburg in 2006 may be the first time that international political science has formally proposed the concept of "global education governance." *The Thirteenth Five-Year Plan for the Development of National Education* sets out the goal of "active participation in global education governance" and draws up the relevant blueprints.

I. Trade in Educational Services

Soon after Reform and Opening Up, the opening up and development of the study abroad institution gave birth to the education service trade market. In order to regulate this emerging market, China introduced a number of policies in the 1980s and 1990s: *The Reply on Institutions (Groups) and Individuals Enrolling Privately-funded International Students at Their Own Expense* in 1987, *The Notice Regarding Domestic and Foreign Organizations and Individuals Not Being Allowed to Recruit Self-Funded Overseas Students in China Without Authorization* in 1987, *The Opinions on the Establishment of Consulting Institutions for Studying Abroad* in 1988, *The Notice on Not Allowing the Issuing of Passports for Self-Funded Overseas Students Recruited by Private Organizations* in 1993, and so on in order to ensure the benefits of students who apply to study abroad at their own expense, and meanwhile, for not being familiar with the nature, status, and role of the new *intermediary organizations for studying abroad*, domestic authorities have adopted a more cautious approach (Miao, 2008). It was not until August 1999 when "The Administrative Regulations on Intermediary Services for Self-funded Studying Abroad" and its implementation rules were formally established that a standardized intermediary service institution was established, and the qualifications and admission standards of intermediary institutions were clearly defined, laying the institutional foundation for the orderly development and standardized management of the intermediary market for studying abroad at one's own expense.

After joining the WTO, in addition to nine-year compulsory education (including primary education and junior high school education) and special education services (such as the military, police, political, and party school education, etc.), the Chinese government made a commitment to opening to the outside world for primary education, secondary education, higher education, adult education, and other education services. These agreements directly promoted the strategic adjustment of China's education service trade institution.

Regarding the nature of trade in education services, in 2006, *The Opinions of the Ministry of Education on Several Issues in the Current Sino-foreign Cooperation in Running Schools* made it clear that education services are not trade in goods, nor are they general trade in services. It is necessary to adhere to the principle of public welfare of Sino-foreign cooperative education. In 2011, *The Outline of the Twelfth Five-Year Plan for the Development of Trade in Services* listed education services as one of the trade in services and established six major development goals: the introduction of high-quality educational resources, the acceleration of the ability building of domestic educational institutions, the vigorous development of studies in education in China, speeding up the international promotion of Chinese language, promoting the healthy development of overseas school running, and steadily opening up the international market for education services.

Under the abovementioned institutional framework, China's education service trade has increased significantly. Currently, study abroad services account for the largest share of China's education service trade. On the one hand, the Chinese education institution actively and steadily promotes the development of trade in education services on the basis of adhering to the public welfare nature of education; on the other hand, the vigorous development of the education market has also brought about some chaos and urgently needs institution regulation. For this reason, in 2002, the Ministry of Education, the Ministry of Public Security, and the State Administration for Industry and Commerce jointly issued *The Notice on Further Regulating the Order of Self-financed Study Abroad Intermediary Activities* and proposed to strictly review the qualifications of overseas institutions. The education administration departments in various places instructed study abroad agencies to improve internal management, and establish sound rules and regulations; establishing a monitoring mechanism for intermediary activities of self-financed studying abroad. Since then, China has adjusted the department responsible for examining and approving the qualifications for self-financed overseas study intermediary service agencies from the Ministry of Education to the education administrative department of the provincial People's government (MOE, 2013). In April 2014, the Ministry of Education and the State Administration for Industry and Commerce jointly formulated *The Model Text of the Entrustment Contract for Intermediary Service for Self-Funded Studying Abroad*, which promoted the standardization and transparency of this service.

II. Multilateral Education Cooperation

Deepening multilateral education cooperation and deepening participation in the formulation of international education rules are important measures for China to actively participate in global education governance, with a focus on promoting international high-level interaction mechanisms and talent cultivation mechanisms for international organizations. According to the deployment of the *Thirteenth Five-Year Plan* for the development of national education, international high-level interaction mechanisms include promoting the establishment of regular high-level consultation mechanisms with UNESCO, improving the mechanisms of multilateral education ministers such as the Shanghai Cooperation Organization and APEC, and improving the BRICS education cooperation mechanism to expand educational cooperation space on platforms such as APEC. The talent cultivation mechanism of international organizations is mainly there to improve the talent cultivation mechanism of international organizations, and systematically train and recommend outstanding talents to serve in international organizations. The purpose of these measures is helping China participate in the development of international education rules. In the institution deployment, mutual recognition of credits is the focus of promoting student exchanges and in-depth participation in relevant multilateral education actions. It is also an

Table 9.1 Countries (and Regions) for Which China Mutually Recognizes Degrees, Academic Qualifications, and Diplomas (as of 2011)

Year	Agreement Signing Country (Region)
1983	Armenia, Azerbaijan, Australia, China, North Korea, Vatican City, India, Indonesia, Kazakhstan, Kyrgyzstan, Laos, Maldives, Mongolia, Nepal, Philippines, South Korea, Russia, Sri Lanka, Tajikistan, Turkey, Turkmenistan
1988	Sri Lanka
1990	Bulgaria
1991	Algeria, Peru
1992	Mauritius
1993	Uzbekistan
1994	Cameroon
1995	Romania, Russia
1997	Egypt, Hungary
1998	Ukraine, Mongolia
2000	Belarus
2002	Kyrgyzstan, Germany
2003	United Kingdom, France, Australia, New Zealand
2004	Hong Kong (China), Austria
2005	The Netherlands, Canada (Ontario), Canada (Quebec), Portugal, Italy
2006	Ireland, Mexico, Kazakhstan, Sweden, Canada (Prince Edward Island), Canada (British Columbia), Canada (Saskatchewan), Canada (New Brunswick)
2007	Denmark, Spain, Thailand, Canada (Alberta), Canada (Manitoba), Canada (Nova Scotia), France
2008	New Zealand, Cuba, South Korea
2009	Vietnam, Philippines
2010	Mexico, Latvia
2011	Malaysia

important example of China's in-depth participation in the formulation of international education regulations.

Credit conversion, academic qualification, and degree certification conversion are the inevitable requirements for promoting personnel exchanges and building an internationalized talent cultivation institution. China signed UNESCO's *Asia-Pacific Regional Convention on the Recognition of Qualifications in Higher Education 2011* in 1983, and established bilateral agreements with Armenia, South Korea, Russia, and other countries to mutually recognize protocol for degrees, qualifications, and diplomas. After entering the WTO, the new situation required for China to formulate a policy of mutual recognition of credits, actively encouraging college students to take credits and exchanges in elective courses at foreign universities, and broaden their international horizons (MOE, 2007). Table 9.1 shows the countries (and regions) that had signed bilateral agreements with China on mutual recognition of degrees, academic qualifications, and diplomas by 2011. On this basis, by April 2017, China had signed mutual recognition agreements on academic degrees with forty-six countries and regions.

In 2009, China promulgated *The Procedures and Standards for the Evaluation of Overseas Educational Degrees (Trial)*, indicating that China has issued a plan for itself relating to global education governance issues. *The National Medium-and-Long-Term Education Reform and Development Plan Outline (2010–2020)* proposed to expand mutual recognition of academic degrees and qualifications between governments. Supporting the exchange of teachers, student exchanges, mutual recognition of academic credits, and mutual award of degrees between Chinese and foreign universities have always been an important part of China's opening up of education. In order to cooperate with the "Belt and Road" construction, China has also proposed to promote the connection of the academic degree certification standards along the "Belt and Road" to achieve the mutual recognition of bilateral multilateral academic degrees in the region. Following China's rising international status and the adjustment of education's opening-up policy, China's role in the regional and global education arena is changing. In 2016, China adopted the *"Belt and Road" education action plan* to let the world hear its voice, calling on all countries to improve the education quality assurance institution and certification mechanism, accelerate the development of each country's national qualification framework, and jointly build a regional vocational education qualification framework. This will help the existing education methods in the territories of the contracting states to be used as effectively as possible to produce mutual benefit, to ensure that teachers, students, researchers, and professionals can conduct a wider range of mobility and reduce the difficulties encountered by personnel trained abroad after returning to the country, providing institutional support for advancing understanding between people, providing support for talents, and achieving common development.

III. International Education Assistance

Carrying out international assistance is an important manifestation of China's fulfillment of its responsibility as a great power, and it is also a major measure for China to actively promote global education governance in the new era. According to the April 2011 White Paper of *China's Foreign Aid* by the Information Office of the State Council, after Reform and Opening Up, China adjusted the size, layout, structure, and areas of foreign aid, further strengthened aid to the least developed countries, and began adopting "various forms of technical and management cooperation such as escrow operation, lease operation and joint venture operation," paying more attention to the economic benefits and long-term effects of foreign aid projects, and providing more flexible aid methods. This work has formed a more efficient project management model, diversified aid funding sources and methods, and a rich aid content institution.

Among the many assistance programs, China's education assistance content mainly includes: building schools, providing teaching equipment and materials, sending teachers, training teachers and interns from developing countries in China, and providing government scholarships for foreign students from developing countries. Since the 1950s, China has begun to sponsor students from other developing countries to study in China, and has helped Asian and African countries build general and technical colleges and provide teaching instruments and laboratory equipment. In the 1960s, China began sending foreign aid teachers to developing countries.

From the 1970s to the 1980s, China, in response to the requirements of the recipient governments, accepted foreign students to build projects including the Tanzania-Zambia Railway, the Mauritania Friendship Port, coal mines in Tanzania, and textile mills in Guyana, and specially trained senior and middle technical and management talents. In recent years, China has become increasingly active in high-level dialogues on international aid for education. In 2000, the China-Africa Cooperation Forum was established, becoming an important platform for China and friendly African countries to conduct collective dialogue and an effective mechanism for pragmatic cooperation in the new circumstances. Through this stage of reform, the development of China's foreign aid has been further broadened, and the effects have become more significant. In addition to negotiating aid projects through traditional bilateral channels, China has also strengthened collective consultations with recipient countries at the international and regional levels. The Chinese government has announced a number of targeted foreign aid policy measures at meetings on regional cooperation mechanisms including high-level United Nations meetings on financing for development and the United Nations Millennium Development Goals, as well as the China-Africa Cooperation Forum, Shanghai Cooperation Organization, China-ASEAN Leaders' Meetings, China-Caribbean Economic and Trade Cooperation Forums, China-Pacific Island Countries Economic Development Cooperation Forums, the China-Portuguese-speaking Countries Economic and Trade Cooperation Forum and so on to strengthen assistance in agriculture, infrastructure, education, healthcare, human resources development cooperation, and clean energy.

According to statistics, by the end of 2009, China had helped developing countries build more than 130 schools. A total of 70,627 international students from 119 developing countries have received financial aid to come to China to carry out various professional studies. Among them, scholarships were provided to 11,185 international students in 2009 alone. A total of nearly 10,000 foreign aid teachers were dispatched. In terms of staff training, taking 2010–2012 as an example, China held more than thirty training courses for senior managers in institutions of higher learning, higher education management training courses, vocational education management training courses, training courses for primary and middle school principals and teachers, and modern distance education seminars to train more than a thousand educational officials, principals, and teaching staff in developing countries. During the same period, China provided assistance to 121 countries, including 30 countries in Asia, 51 countries in Africa, 9 countries in Oceania, 19 countries in Latin America and the Caribbean, and 12 countries in Europe. In addition, China has provided assistance to regional organizations such as the African Union.

In 2016, *The Promotion of the "Belt and Road" Education Initiative* proposed that education assistance should play an important role in the "Belt and Road" education joint action, gradually increasing education assistance, focusing on investing in people, assisting people, and benefiting people. Specifically, it is necessary to make full use of the important role of education assistance in "South-South Cooperation" and increase support for countries along the route, especially the least developed countries. On this basis, *The Thirteenth Five-Year Plan for National Education Development* further carried out in-depth and detailed planning for international education assistance, and planned to actively provide integrated assistance with high-quality teaching equipment, general teaching programs, and supporting teacher training. In conjunction with China's foreign aid projects, teachers and young students are encouraged to go to developing countries to participate in project construction and provide volunteer services. China's assistance in education has promoted the development of education in the recipient countries; helped the recipient countries to cultivate a large number of talents in education, management, science and technology; and provided intellectual support for the economic and social development of the recipient countries. At the same time, the development of education assistance institutions and mechanisms has also promoted the establishment and improvement of China's related institutions, which has played a further role in boosting China's position in global education governance.

NOTES

1 In 1987, The Several Interim Provisions Regarding the Work of Students Studying Abroad formulated five detailed provisions: The Detailed Administrative Rules for the Status of Students Sent Abroad to Study by the State, The Detailed Administrative Rules for Students Sent Abroad to Study by the State Applying for Extension of the Overseas Study Period, The Detailed Administrative Rules on the Number of Years Allowed Studying Abroad and Domestic Wages (or Subsistence Allowance) During the Period of Studying Abroad and the Calculation of Working Age During the Doctoral Degrees of Research Students Sent Abroad by the State, The Detailed Administrative Rules for Engaging in Postdoctoral Research or Internships Abroad, and The Detailed Administrative Rules for the Work and Funds of Students Chosen to Study Abroad by Work Units for the State.

2 In 2013, the Ministry of Education revised the original regulations and promulgated the new *Regulations on Chinese-Foreign Cooperation in Running Schools in the People's Republic of China*.

3 In 2015, the new *Administrative Measures for Running Schools for Sino-foreign Cooperative Vocational Skills Training* was revised and promulgated.

REFERENCES

Chen, X. (2004). Evolution and effectiveness of the education policy for overseas scholars in Mainland China since reform and opening up. *Fudan Education Forum*, *02*, 12–16 (in Chinese).

Coulby, D., & Zambeta, E. (2005). Introduction: Trends in globalization. In D. Coulby & E. Zambeta (Eds.), *Globalization and nationalism in education* ... Oxon: Routledge Falmer.

Jiang, Z. (1992). Accelerating the pace of reform, opening up, and modernization to seize greater victories in the cause of socialism with Chinese characteristics – Report from the fourteenth national congress of the communist party of China. October 12 (in Chinese).

Li, C., & Liu, X. (2013). Analysis of China's policy of introducing foreign experts since reform and opening up. *First Resource*, *02*, 11–18 (in Chinese).

Liang, B. (2008). Introduction of overseas talents and intelligence work in the new situation – Interview with Ji Yunshi, Member of the standing committee of the national committee of the Chinese People's political consultative conference and director of the state administration of foreign experts affairs. *International Talent Exchange*, *06*, 8–11 (in Chinese).

Miao, D. (2008). The formation, reform and development of the study abroad policy in New China. Academic Seminar on Chinese Study Abroad Culture (in Chinese).

MOE. (2001). *The notice of the ministry of education on the printing and distribution of "The Several Opinions on Strengthening the Undergraduate Teaching Work of Higher Education Institutions to Improve Teaching Quality"* (MOE [2001] No. 4). Retrieved from http://www.moe.gov.cn/s78/A08/gjs_left/s5664/moe_1623/201001/t20100129_88633.html (in Chinese).

MOE. (2007). *The several opinions of the ministry of education on further deepening the reform of undergraduate teaching and comprehensively improving teaching quality* (MOE [2007] No. 2) Retrieved from http://www.moe.gov.cn/srcsite/A08/s7056/200702/t20070217_79865.html (in Chinese).

MOE. (2011). *Notice of the ministry of education on further improving the management of foreign students academic certificates and electronic registration* (Foreign Teaching Department [2011] No. 3). Retrieved from http://www.moe.gov.cn/srcsite/A20/moe_850/201104/t20110427_119907.html (in Chinese).

MOE. (2013). *The notice of the ministry of education on issues relating to the devolution of the approval power of intermediary service institutions for self-funded studying abroad* (Jiao Wai Zong [2013] No. 50). Retrieved from http://www.moe.gov.cn/srcsite/A20/moe_862/201504/t20150403_189393.html (in Chinese).

MOE. (2015). *Notice of the ministry of education on printing and distributing the "Key Points of Work of the Ministry of Education in 2015"* (Education Law [2015] No. 3). Retrieved from http://www.moe.gov.cn/srcsite/A02/s7049/201502/t20150212_189347.html (in Chinese).

MOE (The Ministry of Education of PRC) & Central Literature Research Office of CPC (Eds.). (2002). *Zedong Mao, Xiaoping Deng, and Zemin Jiang on education*. Beijing: Central Document Publishing House, People's Education Publishing House, Beijing Normal University Press (in Chinese).

Pang, Z. (2006). Research on China's global governance. *Modern International Relations*, *03*, 60–62 (in Chinese).

The Ministry of Human Resources and Social Security of PRC. (2017). *The decision of the ministry of human resources and social security on amending "The Regulations on the Administration of Employment of Foreigners in China"* (Order of the Ministry of Human Resources and Social Security No. 32). Retrieved from http://www.gov.cn/gongbao/content/2017/content_5227814.htm (in Chinese).

The Ministry of Labor of PRC. (1996). *The notice of the ministry of labor, the ministry of public security, the ministry of foreign affairs and the ministry of foreign trade and economic cooperation on the issuance of "The Regulations on the Administration of Employment of Foreigners in China"* (Ministry of Labor [1996] No. 29). Retrieved from http://www.mohrss.gov.cn/SYrlzyhshbzb/zcfg/flfg/gz/201704/t20170413_269433.html (in Chinese).

The Ministry of Labor of PRC & The Ministry of Social Security of PRC. (2006). *The administrative measures for the management of Chinese-foreign cooperative vocational skills training schools* (Order of the Ministry of Labor and Social Security No. 27). Retrieved from http://www.gov.cn/ziliao/flfg/2006-08/21/content_366557.htm (in Chinese).

The National Education Commission of PRC. (1986). *Relevant regulations for foreign students studying in China* (January 1, 1986) (in Chinese).

The National Education Commission of PRC. (1993). *The notice of the general office of the state education commission on the printing and distribution of "The Regulations on the Work of the Guiding Committee of Foreign Language Teaching in Higher Education Institutions"*. (Ministry of Education and Social Sciences [1993] No. 3) (in Chinese).

The Organization Department of the Central Committee of CPC, The Ministry of Human Resources, Social Security & The State Administration of Foreign Experts Affairs. (2011). *Notice of the organization department of the central committee of the communist party of China, the ministry of human resources and social security, and the state administration of foreign experts affairs on printing and distributing "The Detailed Work Rules of 'The Thousand Talents Program' High-level Foreign Expert Project"* (Organization Department Notice [2011] No. 45) (in Chinese).

The Secretariat of the Management Committee of the National Study Abroad Foundation. (2003). The 2003 National Public Study Abroad Selection Guide, Annex, and Project Guide. Retrieved from http://old.moe.gov.cn/publicfiles/business/htmlfiles/moe/B16_xxgk/200301/xxgk_62531.html (in Chinese).

The State Council of PRC. (1985). *"Administrative measures for foreign students in China" Approved by the State Council* (State Council [1985] No. 121) (in Chinese).

The State Council of PRC. (1986). *Notice of the state education commission forwarded by the state council on "The Several Interim Provisions Regarding the Work of Students Studying Abroad"* (State Council [1986] No. 107) (in Chinese).

The State Council of PRC. (2013). *Regulations on Chinese-Foreign cooperation in running schools in the People's Republic of China* (Order of the State Council No. 638). Retrieved from http://www.gov.cn/gongbao/content/2013/content_2462993.htm (in Chinese).

The State Education Commission of PRC. (1987). *The notice of the state education commission on promulgating several detailed administrative rules regarding the work of students send abroad to study by the state* ([87] Jiao Wai Zong Zi No. 679) (in Chinese).

Zhang, K., & Yu, Z. (Eds.). (2013). *The history of Chinese people studying abroad* (Vol. 2). Beijing: Social Science Literature Press (in Chinese).

Zhang, S., & Jiang, B. (1999). *20 years of studying abroad.* Beijing: Higher Education Press (in Chinese).

Afterword

GUORUI FAN

Forty years of reform and opening up have not only been forty years of China's great economic and social transformation, reform, and development, but also forty years of transformation, reform, and development of China's education. Over the past forty years, China has made tremendous achievements in education reform and development. Education in all fields, aspects, and levels has achieved leapfrog development. Against the background of the construction of socialism with Chinese characteristics in the new era, education has ushered in new opportunities and new challenges. We need to construct a new structure of educational reform and development from a new perspective and with new mechanisms.

Combining major reforms, major turning points, and major breakthroughs in the field of education since China's reform and opening up, and analyzing the background, conditions, policies, and measures of the reforms will help to clarify the development path of institutional reforms and construction, and help to review current educational practices. Standing at a new starting point for the development of education in the new era, we need to look back at what challenging explorations have been made, what obstacles and restrictions have been broken through, and what lessons and implications have been gained. At the beginning of China's reform and opening up, facing a situation of social development that was awaiting rebirth, Deng Xiaoping made great efforts to turn the tide, using the field of education as a threshold, and resuming the College Entrance Examination as a major symbol, and thus started a new journey of education reform and opening up. The significance of carrying out the reform of the education system has gone far beyond education itself, and has become a major event shaping social development over the past forty years.

This book is a review and reflection on the changes of the education institutions in China's forty years of reform and opening up. The reason for the main focus of the analysis on institutional changes is, on the one hand, the major strategic directions, strategic ideas, and strategic initiatives of these forty years are clearly reflected in the institutional texts; on the other hand, making the institutions the objects of analysis can fully reflect the basic direction, main content and basic strategies of education reforms over the past forty years. To this end, schools are taken as the starting point and themes as the main line, respectively, presenting the reforms of the school system and the educational management system at the macro level; the reforms of the school leadership and management institutions, of curricula and teaching materials institutions, of the teacher institutions, the education evaluation institutions at the micro level, of the examination and admission institutions, of the employment institutions , of the education supervision and guidance institutions, of the education financial institutions, and of the education opening up institutions all provide important support for school education. Through the analysis of the above three dimensions of the institutions, the ins and outs of the changes in the institutions have been roughly outlined, so as to reflect the strategic picture of the entire reform and development of education. Of course, it is difficult, or actually impossible, to make a very comprehensive analysis of all the institutions in the field of education. Throughout the past forty years of the education institutions and education reform process, we find that this has been a process of constant standardization and legalization after stepping out of the chaos of the Cultural Revolution. It has been a process from the promotion of reforms of scattered dots of the system with education policies and regulations to the regulation of education order with education laws and the promotion of the construction of education institutions.. It has been a process of empowering by the rule of law, advancing consultation and co-governance, and energizing a variety of educational stakeholders. It has been a process from regulation to empowerment.

This book is the fruit of collective contributions, and has gone through a process from discussion to drafting, rediscussion, modification, and polishing. The selection and determination of the theme of each chapter, the choice of historical materials, and the formation of arguments were all determined after multiple rounds of discussions. During the writing process, we also constantly communicated with authors of other relevant works in this series. We have always been to the same rhythm and we have strived to show the core content of each theme in a neat and orderly manner. The contributors of the book are young and middle-aged scholars from the Department of Education, the Department of

Education Management, the Institute of Basic Education Reform and Development, and the Institute of Education Governance of East China Normal University. The contributors for each chapter are as follows: Guorui Fan, Introduction and Chapter 1; Yemei Wei, Chapter 2; Lingchen Wen, Chapter 3; Mingfeng Du, Chapter 4; Minghao Liu, Chapter 5; Yong Sun, Chapter 6; Wenjie Yang, Chapter 7; Yaozong Hu and Zhimin Liu, Chapter 8; and Jing Chen, Chapter 9.

Reflecting on the historical development of education promotes the healthy and sustainable development of education. At present, China is entering a new era of socialism with Chinese characteristics. In such a new era, education has a fundamental, leading, and far-reaching role in social development. As pointed out in the report of the 19th National Congress of the Communist Party of China, "becoming a strong country in terms of education is a basic project of the great rejuvenation of the Chinese nation. Education must be prioritized, the modernization of education must be accelerated, and education must be offered in a way that satisfies the people." In future social development, society will be more open, more democratic, and more prosperous. Accordingly, in the construction of the education institutions and the development of education, a people-centered educational philosophy will be embraced, and new methods and approaches will be adopted including the Internet, big data, artificial intelligence, and other new technologies. By advancing the construction of education legislations and institutions, speeding up the process of modernizing the education governance system and governance capacities, and granting schools and social organizations more autonomy, a more open and democratic education system shall be built, which meets the needs of the public for personalized, diversified, and high-quality education, forming a healthy education ecology of "ensuring access to childcare and education."

Guorui Fan
East China Normal University

Contributors

Jing Chen received PhD in educational theory at East China Normal University. She is now the lecturer at Shanghai Normal University and visiting scholar at University of Wisconsin-Madison. Her areas of research are educational policy and educational governance with special attention towards the reform of school governance in China.

Mingfeng Du received PhD in educational theory at East China Normal University. He is now the research assistant of Institute of Schooling Reform and Development, Department of Education, East China Normal University. Du's main areas of research interest include theory of education, educational policy, school governance, and students' development. Du has published ten more journal articles and six more book chapters in the area above.

Guorui Fan is Professor of education theory and policies at Faculty of Education and Dean of the Institute of Education Governance (IEG), East China Normal University. He is also the Changjiang (Yangtze River) Scholar Distinguished Professor (Ministry of Education, PRC), the Expert on Special Allowances of the Government of the State Council. He served as the Dean of School of Education Sciences and the Executive Deputy Dean of Faculty of Education at ECNU. Now he is the Chair of Humanities and Social Sciences Research Committee at ECNU and the part-time Vice-President of Shanghai Education Society. His main research fields are education philosophy, education policy, school reform, and development.

Yaozong HU is Professor, doctoral supervisor, and the director of the Department of Education Management and the Research Center of the Economics of Education at East China Normal University. He also works as a member of the Division of Education Development and the Division of the Economics of Education at the Chinese Society of Education. He also serves as a researcher at the National Institute of Education Policy Research and a research fellow at the Shanghai Municipal Institute of Lifelong Education. His main research areas are educational finance, education policy, and performance management at schools.

Minghao Liu received the master degree of education in the Department of Education of East China Normal University. His main research fields are school development and reform, educational evaluation, teacher professional development, and so on. His master thesis mainly studies the professional well-being of rural teachers. Currently working in Beijing Offcn Education and Technology Company, he is mainly engaged in teacher certification and teacher recruitment examination training.

Zhimin Liu received the master degree of education in the Department of Education of East China Normal University. His main research fields are Educational Finance and Education Policy, especially on Chinese Educational Policy Evaluation and Chinese Educational Policy Development.

Yong Sun received PhD from East China Normal University. His research interests include the history, policy, and practice of Chinese educational reform. He is engaged in some educational policy making project of Shanghai, and his articles have been issued in many journals.

Yemei Wei received PhD from East China Normal University. Now she is a lecturer in the Faculty of Teacher Education in Nanjing Xiaozhuang University. Her main research interest is school governance, and she is committed to the teachers' participation in school and the improvement of school governance effectiveness. She uses mixed research method in her research.

Lingchen Wen is a PhD candidate in Faculty of Education and Institute of Education Governance (IEG) at East China Normal University. He has been a visiting scholar to University of Illinois at Urbana-Champaign. His research interests are Education Policy, Theory of Curriculum, and Philosophy of Education. His doctoral research is related to knowledge, curriculum reform from the views of epistemology, and sociology of knowledge.

Wenjie Yang received PhD in educational theory at East China Normal University. She is now a postdoctoral researcher of the National Institute of Educational Policy Research at East China Normal University and has been a visiting scholar to Ohio State University. Her main research interest focuses on educational theory, educational policy studies, school reform and development, and PISA-related fields.

www.ingramcontent.com/pod-product-compliance
Ingram Content Group UK Ltd.
Pitfield, Milton Keynes, MK11 3LW, UK
UKHW020222290926
15470UKWH00001B/326

9 781433 169083